KU-084-909

Also by this author

PORTRAIT OF THE BLUES

DENIM

Paul Trynka is a music journalist and the former editor of MOJO. He lives in South London.

'Paul Trynka gets under Iggy Pop's skin to reveal the real Jim Osterberg. *Open Up and Bleed* is a hugely impressive feat of research and insights, packed full of yarns that'll make your hair stand on end' Barney Hoskyns, author of *Hotel California*

'Compelling. Trynka paints an artful portrait of a rock star who is "decadent right through to his sweet, Midwestern heart"'
Observer

'Trynka captures the essential duality of a man as well-versed in Greek art as he is in panhandling for heroin on Sunset Boulevard . . . entertaining and insightful'
Q

'Trynka thrillingly depicts Iggy's battle between his ambitious ego and his reckless id'
Entertainment Weekly

'Paul Trynka's painstaking account of the life of rock 'n' roll's most iconic front man is the definitive dog's bollocks. Devotees of graphically-relayed excess won't be disappointed – but neither will those who want to know about the heart that beats beneath the bleeding chest and the brain behind the broken teeth'
Record Collector

IGGY POP

OPEN UP AND BLEED

PAUL TRYNKA

SPHERE

First published in Great Britain in 2007 by Sphere
This paperback edition published in 2008 by Sphere

Copyright © Paul Trynka 2007

The moral right of the author has been asserted.

All rights reserved.
No part of this publication may be reproduced, stored
in a retrieval system, or transmitted, in any form or by any means,
without the prior permission in writing of the publisher, nor be
otherwise circulated in any form of binding or cover other than
that in which it is published and without a similar condition
including this condition being imposed
on the subsequent purchaser.

A CIP catalogue record for this book
is available from the British Library.

ISBN 978-0-7515-3810-6

Typeset in Palatino by M Rules
Printed and bound in Great Britain by
Clays Ltd, St Ives plc

Sphere
An imprint of
Little, Brown Book Group
100 Victoria Embankment
London EC4Y 0DY

An Hachette Livre UK Company
www.hachettelivre.co.uk

www.littlebrown.co.uk

To Lucy and Curtis,
my Chinese rugs.

MORAY COUNCIL LIBRARIES & INFO.SERVICES	
20 24 76 48	
Askews	
B IGG	

CONTENTS

I Never Thought It Would Come To This

This wasn't magnificent, but it was definitely war. Scott Asheton hunched low behind his ride cymbal, which offered a little protection from the incoming hail. From his position at the back of the stage he could see the projectiles clearly once they flashed out of the lights – whisky bottles, Stroh's bottles, heavy black champagne bottles, glasses, coins and lit cigarettes – and Scott's vantage point and keen eyesight meant he could also spot the occasional bags of weed as they hit the stage, and point them out to his guardian John Cole, who'd throw the drugs inside Scott's bass drum for safe-keeping. He looked over at Iggy, his singer and one-time drug buddy, increasingly irritated as he realised that each time the singer whipped the crowd into a new surge of fury, he would come and stand over by the drum kit, attracting more missiles in Scott's direction. But he didn't blame Iggy. The singer was only a little more messed up than he was.

Each member of the Stooges was in his own private world as they battled through their doomed set on the freezing-cold night of 9 February 1974 at the Michigan Palace, the decayed, depressing 1920s movie hall in downtown Detroit. Pianist Scott Thurston was a recent arrival, but he'd grown to respect his bandmates for their dumb heroism and what he thought of as their forlorn hillbilly hope, a hope he'd come to share: that maybe they could spruce up their act and grab victory from 'whatever was happening'. But this was . . . degraded, he decided. As he watched Iggy surge into the crowd to provoke them once again, he felt admiration tinged with pity. The guy was driven. Driven to everything except success.

James Williamson, the hotshot tough guy guitarist who'd seen the Stooges as his meal ticket to fame, the sensitive thug derided by most of the Stooges and their tiny camp of followers as 'the Skull', concentrated on keeping his guitar in tune and cranking out his magnificent, dangerous guitar riffs, and looked over at Iggy with something closer to contempt. Wearing a bizarre sci fi outfit crafted by Hollywood designer Bill Whitten, James looked striking from the back of the hall, but up close you could see his costume was dirty and frayed. Even a month or so ago, James had been driving the band forward, compelled to write and rehearse new material even when there was no prospect of a record company ever releasing it. But now he too was starting to despair. His singer was a failure, and he was a failure too. The Stooges had fucked their way through some damn good orgies, but his own burning drive for success was fizzling out. Once, he'd enjoyed the psychodrama, but now it was unbearable. Iggy had sold James out, and now he couldn't even keep his own act together. Nonetheless, James felt a twinge of sympathy, knowing what his one-time friend had been through.

Ron Asheton felt drained. He'd survived the most painful humiliations, sacked as the Stooges' guitarist, demoted to playing bass, estranged from his brother and his singer, clinging to the hope that the band he'd co-created could fulfil their destiny and become the American Stones. But, free of the drugs that had numbed most of his bandmates, he knew, with inescapable clarity, that this tour was beating a dead horse – a dead horse that was turning to dust. Until now, he'd survived on gallows humour, entertaining all those around him with his deadpan observations on the desperate state of his singer and his band. He'd porked some girls, had some good times, but now the good times had gone.

Then there was Iggy. Indestructible Iggy, who hoovered up whatever drugs were placed in front of his nose, who'd been thrown unconscious onto the stage by his tour manager several times over the preceding months, who'd been knocked flat by bikers a couple of days ago but invited them back to the Michigan Palace for more. Who now seemed so physically and mentally damaged, by himself and those around him, that at times both his life force and his luminous beauty looked to be draining away. By now, at least one of his closest confidantes had concluded that he'd suffered some kind of breakdown that had left his nervous system permanently damaged. His face was puffy, and there were lines etched round the hypnotic blue eyes that had charmed so many of America's desirable chicks. Tonight he'd chosen to enrage the biker audience, who were convinced he was a fag, by wearing some kind of black leotard, augmented with a shawl fashioned into a see-through skirt. Despite the ludicrous outfit, he was telling them, or maybe because of it, their girlfriends still wanted to fuck him. And just in case the message wasn't explicit enough, he enunciated lasciviously the title of the next song, 'Cock In My Pocket'. Even now, as he danced around the stage, lithe, balletic, there was a shamanic power that electrified the crowd, half of them besotted, half of them contemptuous, or perhaps simply numbed by the Quaaludes that had become the drug *du jour* at the Palace. Relentlessly, James Williamson's thuggish, psychotic guitar kept propelling Iggy forward as he threw himself into songs like 'Gimme Danger' or 'I Got Nothing', songs he'd written about feeling doomed, songs he was compelled to keep writing even when no record company was interested in releasing them. Now everyone in the audience, friend or foe, seemed to know he was doomed too. As he quipped, 'I don't care if you throw all the ice in the world, I'm making ten thousand, baby, so screw you,' everyone present knew this was empty bravado. And if Iggy Pop didn't know it, Jim Osterberg, the man who'd created this out-of-control alter ego, did.

Earlier that evening, during his short conversation with Jim, Michael Tipton, who was planning to tape that night's performance on an open-reel recorder, had realised that this would be the last Stooges show – an occasion for Iggy to play around, to mock the audience and his own desperate state. Many fans and foes alike turned up at Stooges shows eager to see what ludicrous outfit Iggy would wear that evening, to enjoy the banter and occasional hostilities between band and audience, but this evening's was a more pointless circus than any of them had witnessed before. 'I *am* the greatest!' Iggy screamed at the audience in the show's dying moments as a hail of eggs flew on the stage, one of them hitting him in the face. As eggs soared over in Iggy's direction, Ron kept a lookout for lit cigarettes, worried they'd set fire to his hair. When a heavy coin shot out of the lights and clipped him painfully on his scalp, Ron put his hand up to where it hurt, and saw blood on his fingers.

For everyone around the Stooges, there was a sense the circus couldn't continue for much longer. Natalie Schlossman, their one-time fan club organiser, had looked after the band for nearly four years, nursemaiding Iggy when he was out of control, often tucking him up in bed and taking away his clothes in the forlorn hope he wouldn't trawl the hotel corridors in search of drugs. By now, Natalie had walked in on the band in every possible sexual combination – James in a blood-soaked bathroom with two girls, Iggy in a bedroom with three girls, Scottie Thurston and Ron in a hotel room with one girl, twenty different people in an orgy in Iggy's room – but she regarded their activities with a benign, maternal concern, cooking for them and washing their increasingly scummy costumes. Whatever pathetic state she'd found Iggy in, Natalie knew that on stage he'd reach inside himself to tap into something pure and honest. But now she found herself disturbed by the malevolent miasma around the band, for which she mostly blamed James Williamson. If it were over soon, it would be a blessing for everyone involved.

Walking over to Tipton, Iggy asked whether they should play 'Louie Louie'. James Williamson glowered at the prospect of the hackneyed garage classic, but he cranked up the song's brutally simplistic three-chord riff, and the band lurched after him. As Iggy yelped, and shouted, 'I never thought it would come to this,' the Stooges' moronic inferno rose in intensity, and Iggy gave the audience a 'fuck you' smirk before launching into an obscene version of the lyrics that had enlivened his own star turn as Jim Osterberg, the singing drummer, nearly ten years before. Now the song that had marked the beginning of his career seemed appropriate with which to mark its end. Back in 1965, 15-year-old society debutantes had innocently thrown his favourite sweets onto the stage during an idyllic summer sojourn when he'd hung out with Michigan's wealthiest and most cultured industrial barons. Now it seemed his audience's cultural ambitions amounted to watching messy car crashes. A dumb Detroit anthem with schoolboy pottymouth lyrics, hopelessly mangled from Richard Berry's original song, 'Louie Louie' was pitched right down at their intellectual level. 'She got a rag on, I move above,' he sang, his voice raw but each word enunciated clearly, and the singer leered at the audience to make sure they recognised the reference to menstruation, 'it won't be long before I take it off . . . I feel a rose down in her hair, her ass is black and her tits are bare'.

This time around, as James Williamson ripped into a vicious, trebly guitar solo, Iggy restrained himself from leaping into the audience. There were only a few minutes to go. James's blizzard of notes transformed themselves into a pumped-up, bug-eyed, steroid version of the song's hoodlum riff before the guitarist eased himself back down to comparatively restrained broken chords and Iggy gently crooned the last verse. Then suddenly it was all over, Scottie ringing out a roll on his snare drum as Iggy proclaimed, 'Well, you missed again, so better luck next time,' and disappeared into the wings. But there would be no next time.

This sorry, funny, pitiful gig wasn't an especially low point in the Stooges' doomed recent history. They'd endured bigger humiliations, retreating from the stage shamed and beaten. This time, they'd even got to finish the set. But their singer's fighting spirit had finally been knocked out of him. All through, he'd stayed true to the music he was convinced would transform the world, and it was all turning to shit. The following morning he telephoned his fellow Stooges to say he could take no more.

If he'd only known what lay ahead, maybe he'd have clung onto his fellow Stooges for company, for the truth was he had not hit bottom yet. There was an infinitely bigger distance to fall, a descent into a Hollywood underworld whose inhabitants would close in on him like vultures eager for their share of carrion, persuading him to repeat the ritual sacrifice and self-harm, or adopting him as a debauched trophy boyfriend before they publicly mocked his pathetic state. And the singer finally seemed to abandon his burning ambition, telling the few people who would listen that there was a hex on him, and on the Stooges. And that there was no way out.

After that would come a confused, half-awake existence, confinement in a mental institution, and shelter in an abandoned garage shared with a Hollywood rent boy. And then jail. This was the oblivion so many people considered his rightful destiny. Where several of his friends ended their confused, desperate lives with heroin overdoses, or simple alcohol abuse, Iggy's fate seemed to be that of some accursed totem, a laughing stock, an object lesson in abject failure.

Yet, even as the doomed singer dropped below anyone's radar, word of the Stooges' dumb, heroic demise was starting to spread. For some, that last stand was a modern-day rerendering of Western mythology, the unflinching, dusty heroism of five gunslingers going to their doom in certain knowledge of their fate. For others, the parallels were almost biblical, for soon an English writer, Iggy's very own John the Baptist, would be on a plane from Los Angeles to Paris carrying a tape of the Michigan Palace show, a religious relic that would soon pass from believer to believer. As each young music fan examined the sleeve of *Metallic KO*, an album based on Michael Tipton's recordings, with its silver and black photo of Iggy laid out like Jesus in a homoerotic Deposition, they concluded that this music constituted a vital message. This music was the long-awaited antidote to a bland world of overblown progressive pomp, of complacent country-rock cosiness, of manufactured music controlled by faceless producers and session men. Iggy's Stooges, in contrast, were the real thing: heroic, doomed, and too dumb to realise it. Their frontman became a symbol: of animalism, boredom, energy and lethargy – and of a devotion to his music that very nearly cost him his life, and perhaps still could.

And then the young fans who listened to this album embarked on quests of their own. Brian James, a guitarist in a band called Bastard, set out to 'find my own Iggy', a quest that would lead to the formation of two crucial groups called the London SS – from whose ashes would spring the Clash and Generation X – and the Damned, who would later release the call to action of a new movement that would become known as punk. Ian Curtis, an aspiring singer from Manchester, would buy the record too, playing it to his friends in Warsaw, later renamed Joy Division. Joy Division's bassist, Peter Hook, was one of many who enthused that *Metallic KO* was 'a real gig, a real live record', the only live album that reflected how it felt at his own fast-rising band's chaotic shows, where everything balanced 'on a knife edge'. Other English kids like John Lydon and Glen Matlock were listening too, and would adopt the Stooges' songs for their own band, the Sex Pistols. Another evening, during one of his first visits to New York, Joe Strummer would play the album over and over as he spent the night with a new lover, immersing himself in its volume and intensity. Even decades later, kids like Anthony Kiedis or Jack White listened to the Stooges and resolved to follow their musical blueprint. Not every single person who listened to *Metallic KO*, or its predecessors, formed a band. But enough of them did to ensure that, within a few years, the invincible singer was on the rise again, revered by a new audience. It was another incredible twist in a life and career that would always subvert expectations, both in its highs and in its lows.

*

By 1976, Iggy Pop had regained his aura of invincibility, and emerged from limbo to greet a new, expectant generation of fans. But as these fans met the self-acclaimed 'World's Forgotten Boy', shocked that Iggy Pop had survived intact, there was another surprise in store for them. Don Was, famed producer for the Rolling Stones, Bob Dylan and others, who had seen the Stooges in his youth and helped engineer Iggy's career revival in the 1990s, puts it as well as anybody.

'Meeting the guy, I could not believe what he was like. I guess it didn't contradict anything else I believed about him. I was just shocked that a guy who was willing to cut himself up with broken glass was also so articulate. It didn't mean that he was too smart to have done those things, that all those stories weren't true. But it was a total shock.'

Don's surprise was explicable, for he was not just meeting Iggy Pop. He was also meeting Jim Osterberg: the ambitious, charming, charismatic boy from Ann Arbor who had created this legendary rock 'n' roll animal. Most of those who have been caught in the laser-beam intensity of a one-on-one meeting with this man speak of the same feeling. Jim's voice is warm, intelligent, reminiscent of that of Jimmy Stewart, as is his effortless charm: he seems the perfect American icon, warm, alive, acute and playful. Impressively lithe, he inhabits his body gracefully, like a cat. The conversation ranges from Bertolt Brecht to Greek mythology, the avant garde to t'ai chi, the difference between the Apollonian and the Dionysian ideal. He fixes his clear blue eyes upon you, staring into your own eyes in almost disconcertingly rapt attention, but occasionally looks away in a coy, boyish kind of way, or breaks into a broad, seductive smile when he gets to the end of a harrowing anecdote. His voice is rich and elegant; he listens intently to questions, laughing at the ridiculous nature of his own life, wittily describing the many ludicrous predicaments in which he's placed himself, caricaturing the self-destructive voices he'd hear in his head. For someone celebrated as perhaps the most committed, forceful performer ever to take a stage, he is shockingly and consistently self-deprecating. But never, even for one moment, does he suggest that his commitment to his music is anything but unyielding and absolute.

As you walk away from an encounter with Jim Osterberg, your head will probably be spinning, quite possibly with love and adoration, almost certainly with profound respect and a feeling of empathy. Fellow rock stars, casual members of the public, lords and media magnates, countless thousands of people will talk of their encounter with this driven, talented, indomitable creature, a man who has plumbed the depths of depravity, yet emerged with an indisputable nobility. Each of them will share an admiration and appreciation of the contradictions and ironies of his incredible life. Even so, they are unlikely to fully comprehend both the heights and the depths of his experience, for the extremes are simply beyond the realms of most people's understanding.

Many musicians have doubtless suffered similar mockery and violence, countless others have demonstrated a similar capacity for self-harm and drug abuse, and more than a few have been taken up as heroes, decades later, by new legions of disciples. Yet no other figure seems to speak, like Iggy Pop, to generation after generation of musicians at such an intimate, personal level, nor inspire wave after wave of music that pervades the mainstream. Just as the Damned's Brian James treasured his own copy of the Stooges' *Fun House* in the early 1970s, so would Nirvana's Kurt Cobain play the same band's *Raw Power* over and over, nearly two decades later, confiding to his journal that it was his favourite album of all time, even writing a song for his hero. Later still, in a new century, Iggy would finally appear at festivals alongside other celebrated fans, like the White Stripes or the Red Hot Chili Peppers, skipping, spinning and screaming before tens of thousands of 23-year-olds. Meanwhile, the musicians who topped the bill over him all those years ago, who threw lightbulbs at him or publicly dismissed him as a loser, play to shrinking crowds of ageing fans.

Every aspect of Iggy Pop that attracted outrage or incomprehension in the past – his appearance, his breaking down of the barriers between performer and audience, the eloquent simplicity of his music or the truculent anomie of his lyrics – has become an integral element of today's rock and alternative music. This is a turnaround that seems almost without historical parallel, yet it cannot be considered a simple fairytale ending. Not when one considers the physical and mental depredations, the disasters and the rejections, that went on for decade after decade, even when by all accounts Iggy Pop was happily rehabilitated and reconciled with his creator, Jim Osterberg.

The legend and the music of Iggy Pop is today celebrated. Yet behind it there are endless confused stories and mysteries. How could one musician be so revered, yet so reviled? And how could one man be so clever, and so stupid?

CHAPTER 1

Most Likely To

It was a beautiful drive up to Silver Lake, a resort just east of Lake Michigan where high school kids lucky enough to own their own automobiles would hang out on the beach for the summer. It was 1965, and Jim Osterberg had just joined the car-owning set, but as was his habit he had flouted the conventional entry requirements of parental approval, driving licence – even driving lessons. Lynn Klavitter, his steady date throughout twelfth grade, was impressed that Jim had saved up enough cash to afford the '57 Chevy station wagon, but wasn't so impressed by his driving on the 200-mile trip to the resort. Yet the more she asked him to slow down, calmly, avoiding confrontation, the more her kind-hearted, funny, but increasingly headstrong boyfriend floored the accelerator, insisting he was in control.

On the final stretch of Highway 31 up to Silver Lake, Lynn started to lose her temper as Jim coaxed the reluctant old red and white Chevy up to ninety miles an hour. Suddenly they were shouting at each other, and just as suddenly the wagon's back end started fishtailing, then swerving out of control. As the novice driver tried to correct the swerve, the car veered off the road; it flipped over once, then twice, then a third time, ploughing down two trees on the grass verge, crashing upside-down through bushes as wood splinters and dust filled the car.

As the Chevy groaned to a halt on its roof, its teenage passengers scrambled out of the open windows and looked at each other. The car was a total wreck, but apart from scratches from tree bark, and Jim's bruises from the steering wheel, they were both, unbelievably, unharmed. All was quiet. Calmly, Jim picked up the number plate that had been ripped from the Chevy, linked hands with Lynn and they walked off up the hill and all the way to the resort, where they would both lie on the beach in the sun.

It was maybe a couple of days later that Osterberg told his closest friend, Jim McLaughlin, how lucky he was to be alive. 'Here we go, another of Osterberg's tall tales,' thought McLaughlin, and promptly forgot about it. A few years later, Iggy Stooge mentioned to a journalist how he was special, that he'd survived what should have been a fatal accident and he was destined to make his mark. Even though the notion of an indestructible rock star seemed faintly ludicrous, like many of his inflated claims it made good copy.

These were optimistic, booming, postwar years in America, when anything seemed possible. It was a time and a place when a smart kid, brought up in an environment seething with intellectuals and scientific savants, driven by intelligent, hard-working, ambitious parents, could seemingly do anything he wanted. He could make friends with some of the most powerful figures in the industrial world, and witness first-hand an intimate arts scene peopled with characters who would later become superstars. With this environment, the right kind of kid – one with drive, a fierce intelligence and the right kind of charm – could become President of the United States. And this was the future that classmates and teachers in Ann Arbor predicted for Jim Osterberg, the witty, well-dressed classroom politician, a kid with an enviable knack of making connections with the rich and powerful.

Coachville Gardens trailer park sits in green surroundings on Carpenter Road, just outside the city of Ann Arbor, officially in the town of Ypsilanti, Michigan. Although it's gained the inevitable gaggle of sprawling out-of-town stores, Ypsilanti is still mostly a lush, quiet place where nothing much happens. There are plenty of isolated wooden houses where you can live undisturbed, watching out for cranes and squirrels in the summer, and taking your dogs for long, reflective walks through the crisp virginal snow in the winter. It's a beautiful setting, although, like many small country towns, there's occasionally a feeling of claustrophobia, and it's easy to bump into slightly odd characters who watch jerry-rigged cable TV late into the night, haunt internet chat rooms or get loaded on Class A drugs to numb their boredom.

Although these days Ypsilanti rather grandly terms itself a city, in reality it's overshadowed by its much bigger neighbour, Ann Arbor, which since 1837 has been defined by the presence of the University of Michigan. The university was celebrated for its diverse curriculum and liberal ethos and, together with the presence of General Motors and Ford in nearby Detroit, it would attract a constant influx of new residents to the city and stimulate thriving local industries in engineering, pharmaceuticals and electronics.

It was the influence of the university that ensured Ann Arbor was a classy town. People who lived there drank espresso, formed arts groups and took dancing lessons. In contrast, people from Ypsilanti were often regarded as Midwestern hillbillies. The two towns weren't totally uneasy bedfellows: plenty of academics might dispense intellectual wisdom at the university and then return home to a sprawling isolated farmhouse in Ypsi's beautiful countryside, but the divide was perceptible for anyone who crossed the city limits: the gap between people whose salary was generated by their intellects, and those whose weekly paycheck was earned with the rude labour of their hands on a farm or in a factory; between people of culture and rural rubes. It was on that divide that Jim Osterberg and Iggy Pop grew up.

As a rock star, Iggy Pop would often refer to his upbringing in a trailer park, the definitive blue-collar home. But as a schoolboy, Jim Osterberg was regarded as the middle-class boy most likely to succeed. Other kids admired, and some of them envied, his elegant dress, his parents' house in Ann Arbor Hills – an elegant enclave peopled by academics, architects and the nation's most significant captains of industry – and a confidence that seemed unshakeable.

In the late 1940s, Ann Arbor, along with most of Michigan, was undergoing an economic boom. Money still flowed in from military contracts, while industrial giants including Ford and General Motors were readying themselves for a huge expansion in demand as a million ex-servicemen prepared to spend their government home loans. In the east of the state, all the way over to Detroit and its huge River Rouge Ford plant, new factory buildings sprouted in once green and peaceful locations with resonant Native American names. Multi-storey buildings shot up on the Michigan University campus, and although housing was being developed all round the city, there was still a severe shortage. In 1948, a small group of businessmen headed by Perry Brown, who managed a machine shop in the city, and the Gingras brothers – Irv, Leo and George – developed a small trailer park on Carpenter Road, which they named Coachville Gardens, aiming to attract workers at the Ford factory and the local telephone company. Among the first people to move in, in the fall of 1949, were James Newell Osterberg, his wife Louella and infant son James Newell Junior, who had been born, prematurely, in Muskegon's Osteopathic Hospital on 21 April 1947. The unconventionally small family would become well known around Coachville Gardens: 'It was a small trailer with a very large mother and a very skinny tall father,' says Brad Jones, who lived nearby, 'like something you'd see in a cult movie. The trailer was very small, and the dad was an Ichabod Crane kinda guy, real tall and thin, and mom was just a square body. But you know what? They connected alright. Somehow it worked.'

Jim Osterberg's earliest memory is of being in Louella's lap, playing a game where 'she'd recite a kind of a chant, in Danish, then on the last word almost drop me to the floor and pick me back up. And I wanted to do it again and again.' Jim Junior grew up in the presence of his mother's warm, nurturing love, and his father's baseball accoutrements ('He had played some semi-pro baseball; he had an enormous bat, and the mitt, and everything that goes with it').

James Newell Osterberg Senior, the dominating influence in the life of the son who carried his name, was born on 28 March 1921; he was of Irish and English descent, but spent his youth in a Michigan orphanage, lonely and unwanted until two spinster Jewish sisters named Esther and Ida Osterberg walked in and decided that 14-year-old James was the child who most needed a home. They nurtured and loved him, and paid for his education, before passing away in quick succession: one in mourning for their lovely house, bulldozed to make way for a highway, and the second for her adored sister. James appreciated the break he'd been given late in life and worked hard at school. A keen baseball player, he later played in the minor leagues and tried out for the Brooklyn Dodgers, although he never obtained the contract card that designated professional athlete status. Like many of his generation, James Osterberg's education was interrupted by the war, but his obvious college potential meant he was trained as a radio operator in the Army Air Force (in later years he would still remember his missions over Germany and warn his son off the place). After the war James Senior toyed with studying dentistry and osteopathy, before training as a teacher of English and moving to Ypsilanti to take a job at the high school on Packard Road, a four-minute drive from Coachville.

James Osterberg Senior was regarded by most of those who knew him as a reserved, even severe teacher, who graded his students strictly. As well as teaching English, he assisted in sports. As a new teacher, he was more likely to teach the less academic pupils, in which case much of the emphasis in the English lessons was on public speaking. Many of his ex-pupils remember being intimidated by him during their school days, although as adults they've come to admire his tenacity and commitment; one pupil, Mary Booth, describes him as her most 'feared – and favourite' teacher. Around 1958 Osterberg landed a better-paid job at Fordson High,

in the Dearborn district, an area on the outskirts of Detroit dominated by a huge Ford plant. The bigger paycheck meant the family
could move from their Spirit trailer to a much bigger New Moon,
all futuristic and Jetsony. At Fordson, Osterberg was respected as a
committed, dedicated and fair teacher, who would occasionally
unleash a quick, dry humour. 'Mr O' was an idealist; sometimes
this made life difficult, notably when he unsuccessfully attempted
to found a teachers' union. According to Jim Junior, only one friend
backed him up, and the project was abandoned.

Not all of Mr Osterberg's charges remember his lessons, but
those who do retain huge respect for his dedication and persever-
ance. Patricia Carson Celusta was inspired to become a high school
teacher by his example, and credits him with transforming her
from a shy girl into a confident public speaker. 'He made you think
beyond yourself,' she recalls fondly, remembering that this inspirational figure helped impart 'truths that have sustained us all'.
Now retired after her own long career as an English and speech
teacher, Patricia Celusta hails James Osterberg as 'the very definition of a teacher', and still treasures a battered old copy of the
English textbook from which he taught. Mr O inculcated confidence and the power of the spoken word into his successful pupils,
as well as encouraging their understanding of wider cultural and
literary issues. Many other ex-pupils back up Patricia's description of him as committed, capable and fair. So does Osterberg
Junior. But this was the 1950s, and Jim Senior was a military-
minded man, and that intellectual rigour required a backbone of
discipline, which meant on several occasions he would resort to
using the belt or the hickory stick on his son.

While Jim Junior would disappoint his disciplinarian father
countless times over the following years, and often confront him,
sometimes with violent undertones, you could say the belt and
hickory stick worked. Like his father, Jim was a driven personality,
although in his case that drive was wrapped up in a charm and
wackiness that also betrayed the influence of his easy-going and
loving mom.

Around Coachville Gardens, Mr Osterberg was regarded as an intimidating presence, although a few people speculate that some of that severity came from necessity, given his job. According to neighbour Brad Jones, 'He'd only be severe if you let him get away with it.' James Senior's tough, no-nonsense attitude ('trailers make sense' was how he justified the family's unconventional abode) was reflected in his dress and military haircut. But he would also take Jim Junior on long idyllic drives into the country. When Frank Sinatra came on the radio, Osterberg Senior would sing along with him. Over fifty years later, his son remembers drives in the Osterberg Cadillac, listening to his dad crooning 'Young At Heart', and dreaming of becoming a singer.

Louella Osterberg, née Kristensen, was a cuddly woman of Danish, Swedish and Norwegian blood, who doted on the two men in the house and became a well-loved figure around Western Ypsilanti, despite working full-time in an office at Bendix, one of the main industrial employers in Ann Arbor. In later years she would preside over increasingly competitive arguments between father and son, but remained remarkably unfazed. Somehow, for all the male aggression on display in the tiny trailer in later years, there seemed little doubt that this was a happy, loving, if unconventional, family.

For many people in Coachville Gardens, the trailer park represented an American arcadia, where kids in bibbed denim overalls played happily in rolling fields, dreaming of Sputnik and Superman. Parents could leave their children to play around the park, safe in the knowledge they'd be watched over by friendly adults in the close-knit community. It was probably this family atmosphere, plus the postwar housing shortage in Ann Arbor, that initially drew the Osterbergs to the park; once there, though, they stayed put until the autumn of 1982, becoming some of Coachville's longest-term residents. There was green farmland all round, the nearest building being a stone, one-room elementary school on the other side of Carpenter Road. The Leveretts' adjacent farmhouse was the premier hangout for kids in the area, who could earn pocket money working at Chuck and Dorothy's vegetable stall or picking corn for them in the summer. For Osterberg Senior the presence of Pat's Par Three golf course, right beside the trailer park, was a major draw. Behind the trailer park a small track led to the railway lines. Young James could hear the mournful hoot of freight trains passing through at night, and in the daytime he could sneak down to watch them clatter past on their way from New York to Chicago.

On most days, kids from the trailer park played baseball or football around its snaking driveway. From the age of two or so Jim was a regular at the kids' birthday parties, although he spent more time in his trailer than most. Although not a snob, James Senior was careful about the kids with whom his son associated. He was particularly worried when Jim Junior wandered down to see the Bishops, who were 'different'. Jim would later describe them as 'bona fide hillbillies'; however, the Bishops were well liked, fun to be around and a natural focus for Jim's attentions. But when Jim Junior later developed a fascination with the precocious Diane Bishop, Jim Senior seemed to acquire an almost supernatural omniscience, and he inevitably turned up to whisk his son away from her. Osterberg Senior had no such concerns about Duane Brown and Sharon Ralph, whose parents had helped develop the site, and both remember childhood games around the park, although Sharon remembers, 'Jim didn't play out as much as the other kids, although you'd always see him at parties. His mom was popular, I liked to go over there, she always seemed so kind, calm and pleasant to be around.' In contrast, Mr Osterberg frightened the kids: 'I don't know why,' says Duane Brown. 'He was a very tall thin man with a marine haircut and I didn't like being with him. He never did anything that made us not like him, he just came across as very gruff.'

In the family atmosphere of Coachville, where stay-at-home moms nurtured large families, the Osterbergs, with two wage-earners and just one child, were out of the ordinary. Describing his earliest memories, Jim remembers mostly solitary images: sleeping and resting on a shelf over the kitchenette in his parents' 18-foot trailer, watching *Howdy Doody* in black and white on a tiny TV screen, or observing his dad chatting to a friend from the services in the back yard – a fully fledged cowboy in boots and Stetson: 'I'd never seen anybody like that and I really liked him.' As an only child who had recurring bouts of asthma, he was doted on by both parents, who took out the back seat of their Cadillac and built a big shelf in its place where the four-year-old Jim could walk about or lie in his crib as they drove around enjoying the countryside on Sunday afternoons, during their precious time together. Later on, although he might join Sharon or Duane for a walk into the fields or down to the railway track, he would also wander off alone for long walks or, more often, sit at home or at his babysitter's, Mrs Light, dreaming of science fiction, imagining himself as Superman or the Atomic Brain. Over these and subsequent years, he often missed school for extended periods due to bouts of asthma, and during these times he inhabited an imaginary world, which in his own mind set him apart from his schoolmates. When he was on his asthma medication, those imaginary worlds were even more vivid: 'It was ephedrine. They're cracking down now on pseudo-ephedrine, which is the basic ingredient for speed. I had real ephedrine, which was much better. It made me feel . . . great. It puts a bit of a poetic edge on things. And it stimulated my creativity, I'm afraid.'

Perhaps it was the attention he got from his parents, perhaps it was the verbal sparring and intellectual challenges constantly presented by his father, perhaps it was simply a result of measuring his intelligence against others, but it was obvious from the earliest days at elementary school that Jim Osterberg thought he was special. Quite a few other kids, and some of the teachers, shared that opinion. Slight in build, Jim Junior was full of energy, with a cheeky, slightly coy smile. He had a natural bounce in his step, and a kind of cute goofiness about him; he looked almost like an overgrown kids' doll, with a slim body, round head and enormous blue eyes with oversized lashes. His playful, almost coquettish charm seemed the perfect match to his looks. That cuteness allowed him to get away with a lot; most notably, it prevented the kid from a more educated household, with a bigger vocabulary and innate confidence, from being considered a smartass by his schoolmates. Instead he was a ringleader. Although for some kids those first days at school are a traumatic experience, Jim Osterberg, with his network of Coachville friends, had no such problems.

For nearly a century, Carpenter Elementary had been a simple one-room Victorian schoolhouse, directly opposite what became Coachville Gardens; Jim and his Coachville friends were the first kids to enrol at a much larger, newly erected brick and glass building nearby on Central Boulevard, which opened to students in 1952. Jim's network of friends soon included Sharon, Duane, Kay Dellar, Sandra Sell, Joan Hogan, Sylvia Shippey, Steve Briggs and Jim Rutherford – plus Brad Jones, who arrived from San Diego in 1956. They all regarded Jim as funny, energetic, smart and the leader of their gang, says Brown. 'He figured out how to get himself and the rest of us in trouble. One time in fourth grade he learned a new word, and that word was "fuck". He suggested I use that word to the teacher, I can't remember what he told me it meant, and got a bunch of us into trouble with our class teacher, Miss Connors.'

The young Osterberg frequently earned the formidable ire of his fourth-grade teacher, Rachel Schreiber, who'd occasionally swipe his knuckles with a ruler, but his obvious intelligence, most notably his verbal fluency and impressive vocabulary, ensured he was regarded with some indulgence and fondness by the teaching staff. By fourth grade, Jim Osterberg knew how to make people notice him. The blue-eyed boy was often described as 'cute' and was precocious around his teachers, but his eagerness to prove himself top dog – his ambition, even, if you could use that term for one so young – didn't hamper his natural charm. His manner was, says Brown, 'flirtatious. Connected. He understood what socially works to charm people.'

'Even at an early age, he was a character,' says Brad Jones.

'Always funny, always eclectic. But also very tortureable. We used to literally hold him down in class and tickle him and make him pee. You know, stuff that fifth and sixth graders do.' In class, Jim was particularly absorbed by the stories about America's frontier culture. They stimulated fantasies of being 'Daniel Boone and Jim Bowie. Jim Bowie, as tall as a big oak tree; I can do anything, and I have to be out there on the edge.'

It was easy to make friends and charm people at Carpenter Elementary, with its classes of fewer than twenty kids, all of whom lived just a short walk from each other. Carpenter was the centre of west Ypsilanti's social world. For kids, the school or the Leveretts' farm were the main out-of-hours hangouts; for parents, too, the school was a great place to meet their neighbours, at square dances and other cosy, countrified, family events; Louella Osterberg was a familiar figure at them, helping out on cake stalls and rummage sales at school bazaars – no mean accomplishment, as she was the only mom most people remember who also held down a full-time job.

Already the centre of his own tiny universe, from the age of six Jim Osterberg entered a new, bigger social circle after his father enrolled as a teacher and counsellor at Varsity day camp, a summer camp for middle-class kids established by Irvin 'Wiz' Wisniewski at Cordley Lake near Pinckney, Michigan. But these more middle-class boys who met young Jim and his Ichabod Crane dad outside their natural domain remember a very different creature from the confident Carpenter child. 'The counsellors would pick you up from your home,' remembers Mike Royston, who attended from 1954, 'and Jimmy would come with his dad. I remember him as excessively shy, and the picture that flashes in my mind is him cuddled next to his dad in the car, as his dad was driving us to and from camp. He was an unusual little boy with enormous blue eyes. Studying you, but in a shy, furtive way. He'd give you little side-glances. Did not maintain eye contact for very long. And his dad was excessively taciturn. Did you ever see the movie *Cool Hand Luke*? Well, if you can recall the guy with no eyes, just sunglasses, that was Jim's dad. He didn't say much, just kinda directed traffic. I don't remember ever seeing the guy smile.'

In subsequent years, Jim Junior would frequently moan to his new, more privileged schoolmates about his dad – his complaints were so vehement that most of them thought he was exaggerating. But in his happy, playful years at Carpenter, he stood out as an intelligent, charismatic, talkative kid. During summer evenings Wiz Wisniewski would often visit the family to spend pleasant hours at Pat's Par Three, and he would sometimes spend more time chatting with the son than with the father: 'Mr Osterberg was a somewhat reserved gentleman, but he enjoyed playing golf, and we had a very nice relationship with father and son. Young Jim was just learning, an active boy who played left handed, and we all enjoyed each other's company. I can still remember those evenings.'

For most American schoolkids, the transition from elementary to junior high school is a critical rite of passage. Untold numbers of movies, books, songs and poems record the shattered illusions, psychological traumas or long-treasured triumphs of those crucial early teenage years, which for many defined the shape of the adult life that would follow. Jim Osterberg managed this transition with enviable ease – in fact, he would leave his junior high celebrated by his schoolmates as one who would do great things. However, as an adult, Osterberg would term himself an outsider, someone marked out by the fact he was raised on a trailer park. The petty indignities endured at the hands of his comfortably middle-class contemporaries seemed to rankle with him for decades; in later years that belief would drive him, an abiding sense that he was an outcast. But for his one-time Carpenter friends, who watched as Jim graduated to hanging with 'the snooty kids', that belief seemed at best ironic – and at worst, completely ludicrous.

Duane Brown still recalls Jim's competitiveness: 'He was always trying to outdo the rest of us. And he was pretty good at it.' No one in his small group of friends resented Jim's need to prove himself the smartest – at first. '[Then] we got into junior high and high school, and I began to think, he thinks he's too good for us, and I don't know quite why,' says Brown. 'He just seemed a little stuck up, I thought, as he became an older child. It might be he didn't want any of the people he was associating with [at Tappan Junior High] to know any of us from the trailer park because we might blow his cover. But he had very little to do with any of us from elementary school after we got to high school.'

Sharon Ralph also looked on disapprovingly as Jim entered a new social circle with the move to Tappan in 1960: 'I don't know why he felt ashamed of being part of the trailer park – except that when we got to Tappan and Ann Arbor High, the kids were snooty, and he wanted to fit in with those. And he certainly did hang out with the snooty kids.'

Tappan Junior High is on Stadium Boulevard, near Michigan Stadium, in a green and leafy part of town known as Ann Arbor Hills. It's an imposing, elegant, spacious building, which must have been slightly intimidating to any child, especially one who took the bus down Washtenaw Avenue from an out-of-town trailer park. The presence of the University of Michigan ensured that Tappan, and the nearby high school it fed, Ann Arbor High, were both beacons of excellence in the American public-school system. Many parents worked as academics or administrators at the university; many of the teachers were exceptionally highly educated women who worked in the high-school system while their husbands studied for higher degrees. 'There wasn't a pressure from [Tappan] families about money,' remembers Jim's contemporary, Mim Streiff, 'but there was a lot of pressure about educational attainment – that was a real focus.'

Yet the scent of big money was inescapable at Tappan, thanks to the presence of a clique of wealthier kids from Ann Arbor Hills, which was where the city's architects, administrators, professors and company managers chose to reside. Most significantly, it was also home of a new generation of Ford management, who consciously aligned themselves with the liberal, sophisticated traditions of Ann Arbor. The Ford 'whiz kids' were a group of ten ex-US Army Air Corps officers headed by Colonel Charles 'Tex' Thornton, which included two future Ford presidents: Robert McNamara and Arjay Miller. Both McNamara and Miller chose to live in the intellectual, academic environment of Ann Arbor, a location that Miller – who later became a celebrated Dean of Business Studies at Stanford – still remembers fondly today: 'A lovely, very fine, very clean college town. The university is the centre of life there, it's separated enough from Detroit to have its own identity and culture, yet you could still get into Detroit for a major symphony or opera. I really enjoyed living there.'

The presence of two of the most important industrial leaders in the United States at Tappan Junior High concerts and other Ann Arbor events added a seductive frisson of power and money to the atmosphere – a tingle that surely attracted the 12-year-old Jim Osterberg, who would soon get close to its source.

For many kids enrolling at Tappan, its wealthy, cosmopolitan atmosphere was intimidating. So were some of the pupils. Rick Miller (no relation to Arjay) was a charismatic boy, a 'Mr Suave' who often sported a cigar, and was the idol of many boys and girls. But he also enjoyed making fun of kids, and one of the kids he chose to ridicule was Jim Osterberg. 'We used to take swimming class at Tappan, and you used to have to stand around naked for some stupid reason,' says Denny Olmsted, who was a friend of both Rick and Jim. 'Jim had a big dick, and Rick got hold of Jim's dick and pulled him around the shower room. We did make fun of Jim for that. He was embarrassed by it.' For many boys, Jim's prodigious dick was a source of envy, as was the fact he reached puberty earlier than most of them, but Rick's bullying turned a source of pride into embarrassment – for a time, at least.

George Livingston was another popular kid, who lived in an impressive house, designed by his architect father, in Ann Arbor Hills. Livingston and his friend John Mann were experts in stripping down Chryslers, and together won a state prize for troubleshooting Plymouths. 'George had a lot of bravado and often said what he thought before thinking of the other person,' says John Mann, who remembers Livingston mocking the Osterbergs' choice of residence on at least one occasion. 'Making fun of someone's zit or their trailer was just the way George was.' Most kids learned to laugh and move on; for Jim Osterberg, the insult rankled.

For the future Iggy Pop, Rick Miller and George Livingston would become symbols of the casual cruelty of white, American, middle-class kids – despite the fact that, as far as most of his peers were concerned, Jim Osterberg was in fact the epitome of white, American, middle-class privilege. That impression was symbolised by his friendship with Kenny Miller, son of Arjay Miller and godson of Robert McNamara. Even for the sophisticated, academic residents of Ann Arbor Hills, the Millers were classy people. And as it turned out, Jim Osterberg had the knack of making friends with classy folk.

There was always something going on at the Millers' house on Devonshire, in the heart of Ann Arbor Hills. The dance lessons were what really impressed the neighbours: a private teacher tutored Kenny and his classmates in foxtrots and waltzes in a spacious studio at the back of the house – the kids dressed in formal attire for the lessons, right down to skirts and gloves for the girls. At Christmas, a professional choir entertained the guests; there were tasteful artworks on the walls, while the house itself – all clean red brick and redwood sidings, with balconies overlooking its wooded setting – was a case study in understated, contemporary style. The colour TV in the lounge was the first one most of the Millers' guests had ever seen, but the Millers never seemed to brag. Chauffeurs would whisk the kids round to golf, football, or a coke and hotdog at the Howard Johnson Hotel on Washtenaw Avenue. On the way back from the hotel one time, one of Kenny's friends spilt a milkshake in the back of the Lincoln. No one from the family batted an eyelid, but the next day the chauffeur arrived to pick up his charges in a brand new car.

While the Millers' maid, Martha, was the one who spent most

time with the kids, Kenny's mom, Frances, was always interested in her son's friends. Arjay, too, seemed approachable; remarkable behaviour in a man who shouldered the heavy burden of turning round a company that was in severe financial straits. Arjay was company comptroller over a period that saw infamous debacles, such as the launch of the ill-fated Edsel. Several senior Ford executives based in Ann Arbor succumbed to stress or alcoholism over that time, but Arjay calmly negotiated his way through the Ford jungle, succeeding to the company presidency after fellow whiz kid Robert McNamara was lured away by John Kennedy to become Secretary of Defence, and later overseeing the launch of Ford's biggest money-spinner, the Mustang. In the course of his busy life, Miller got to know Jim Osterberg well enough that he remembers him to this day, although he politely declines to elaborate on the time Jim spent round at his house.

Within a short time of arriving at Tappan, Kenny Miller – an unassuming, friendly and rather gangly boy – had become firm friends with Jim Osterberg, to the extent, some say, of having a schoolboy crush. Early on in their friendship Kenny asked his mom Frances to invite Jim around to play; Frances got the name confused and asked Jim's alphabetical neighbour, Denny Olmsted, around by mistake. As Olmsted remembers it, Kenny opened the door and said, 'I don't want to play with you, I want to play with Jim, I like Jim better!' before bawling out his mom as the crestfallen Olmsted shuffled away.

Kenny Miller and Jim Osterberg were the nucleus of a small group of kids, including Livingston and John Mann, who spent long evenings playing golf at Pat's Par Three. They exemplified Jim Osterberg's ability to network with Ann Arbor's most influential people, as did his girlfriend in eighth grade, Sally Larcom; Sally's father was the city administrator, her mother a professor at Eastern Michigan University. Both parents were charmed by Jim Osterberg: 'He was definitely one of the good ones, that they liked me going out with.'

Although Jim was definitely not a stereotypical fratboy – he was too smart and too funny for that – he was clean-cut, with short hair, always dressed neatly in a polo shirt and slacks. His build was slim, wiry and muscular, which made up for the fact he was slightly smaller than average, and he was definitely an intellectual. He was also confident and opinionated, ready to engage adults in conversation, but always with a touch of humour. In the time they dated, Sally and Jim would mostly go golfing together; if there was anything about Jim that irritated Sally, it was probably the fact he was so opinionated – 'Authoritative, almost.' He was also noticeably obsessed by status, constantly ranking boys and girls in the class. Jim was cute, sexy even, with just a touch of angst that made him seem all the more attractive. The angst seemed to come from the fact that, despite being popular, he wasn't quite as popular as the football players or prom queens in the class. But Sally saw no trace of an inferiority complex: 'It was more a superiority complex; just one that didn't sit with his life situation. I don't mean that as a criticism, more that that's what drove him.' Cindy Payne, who went out with Jim a couple of years after Sally, retains almost identical memories of Jim's charm, the ease with which he impressed her father – who was a doctor – the same angst that seemed to underlie his ambition, as well as Jim's remarkable 'confidence. He was an amazing young person, a real go-getter.'

By the end of his first year at Tappan, Osterberg was well known, and his natural exuberance seemed to expand. Certainly, his classmates remember him as funny, analytical, always ready to challenge prevailing wisdoms. Several of the teachers were undoubtedly charmed; his impressive vocabulary and use of idiom endeared him to his English teacher, Mrs Powrie, and there were suspicions he was her teacher's pet. Several of his contemporaries recall him using phrases they'd never heard before – 'men of the cloth' or 'hoi polloi' – and today note the fact that he used them correctly, too. That ability to pluck words out of the air was memorable and helped him ultimately make the school debate team, the home of most of Ann Arbor's brightest kids, although his talent for swimming and golf prevented him being regarded as a geek. Most tellingly of all, says John Mann, 'His sarcasm was great. I just remember looking at him and having to think, what did he say? Then you realised he was being sarcastic. Most seventh and eighth graders weren't ready – he was way over our heads at the time.'

For all Jim Osterberg's presence and charm, the jibes of kids like George Livingston and Rick Miller did have an effect; while confident in his own abilities, Jim seemed excessively ashamed of his background. Most of his acquaintances were more struck by how often he mentioned the trailer park than by the living conditions themselves; there was another large trailer park on Packard Street with its share of middle-class residents, and James Osterberg Senior's status as a high-school teacher was an extremely respectable one in a town that set such store by education.

Nonetheless, Jim Junior seemed sufficiently ashamed by his background to invent – as, perhaps, do many schoolkids – a more impressive one. Tappan pupil Don Collier remembers one occasion when Osterberg was talking about 'his neighbourhood, the area of the very rich: Ann Arbor Hills'. Collier was impressed until the afternoon, a few years later, he offered to give Jim a lift home from high school. Only as Collier began to turn left into Ann Arbor Hills did Osterberg ask him to continue up to Carpenter Road and then to Coachville trailer park. Jim seemed matter of fact about the dramatic change in his living conditions. Perhaps he'd forgotten his impulsive fib about where he lived, three or four years before.

By 1961, when Jim reached ninth grade, most kids in his junior high school class would have considered the notion that Jim was regarded as an outsider or a dork as faintly ridiculous. Instead, he was widely regarded as an impressive figure who was undeniably part of the classy set. In a preppy environment, Jim was more preppy than most, always nicely turned out in loafers, slacks, button-down shirt and nice sweater. It was a look to which many at Tappan aspired, but Osterberg managed it to perfection, and he convinced many that he was the product of inherited poise and fine breeding. Rather than being mocked for his trailer park origins, in these years he was more likely to irritate his peers with his sheer slickness and confidence: 'Jim Osterberg?' says fellow pupil Dana Whipple. 'He had the highest quality line in BS of anyone I ever knew. He learned early on that you only had to keep one step in front of the other idiots in order to impress them.'

Osterberg certainly looked around at his classmates and envied their middle-class charm, but it didn't seem to occur to him that behind that façade they too had their own problems. For, as conversations with many of the kids who went through the school reveal, some of those confident exteriors had been erected to hide stories of shortages of cash, drinking problems and the anxious awareness that hard-won status could be easily lost.

The 14-year-old Jim Osterberg possessed, in fact, a sense of what would impress his colleagues that was almost supernatural. His abilities were demonstrated by his campaign to become class vice president in ninth grade. Jim's political platform was brave, for in a staunchly Republican environment he chose to champion Jack Kennedy and support unionisation – whatever his hang-ups about his father, he shared his liberal political convictions. Denny Olmsted, who was also a popular figure in the class, decided to run for class president, but was struck by Osterberg's political sophistication: 'He would've run for president, but he was a realist. He told me no one would win against Bill Wood, a popular guy who was running for president, but that he could make vice president. And he was absolutely right.'

Olmsted, with Brad Jones running his campaign, put up a strong fight. But Osterberg knew exactly what would play with the Tappan audience: 'I gave a speech,' says Olmsted, 'and there was this bit at the end where I walked away from the podium, and did this gesture with my eyebrows – it was something funny taken from a commercial. And it just infuriated Jim. He took me aside and said, "You had Bill beat, you had a better speech, a better presentation, then you did that stupid eyebrow thing and that's gonna lose you the election!"' Osterberg's instincts were spot on; he waltzed into the vice president's spot, a real feat considering his platform was based on restraining 'evil big business', while Olmsted lost to

Wood. By now Jim had convinced many classmates that he was a potential future President of the United States.

It was around ninth grade that Jim's interest in music surfaced. Like many of his contemporaries, he became obsessed with Sandy Nelson and the Ventures, and in 1962 he formed the Megaton Two, a musical duo in which he played drums alongside a friend from the choir, Jim McLaughlin. McLaughlin, a sweet, unassuming boy, was a pretty decent guitarist, and for a time would be Osterberg's closest friend, replacing Kenny Miller, who left for a private school. As we shall see, in Osterberg's private life music was starting to become a dominating passion, but at Tappan it seemed strictly a secondary interest. Today it is his talent for politics, rather than his musical ambitions, that his contemporaries remember – dozens of them still recall his support for John Kennedy, and his prediction that he would be in the White House before the age of forty-five ('He would be a huge improvement on what we have today,' laughs fellow pupil Dan Kett).

In 1962, during his final year at Tappan Junior High, Jim Osterberg was voted the boy 'Most likely to succeed' by his classmates. He signed dozens of his friends' yearbooks, often with a joke, but the inscription on Ted Fosdick's yearbook was serious. It was signed, 'From the 43rd president of the United States: Jim Osterberg.'

By the time Jim and his classmates reached tenth grade and moved down the road to Ann Arbor High, he was a well-known character at the huge new school, which was situated in impressive grounds directly opposite Michigan Stadium. The baby boom meant Ann Arbor High (more recently renamed Ann Arbor Pioneer) was packed to overflowing, with over 800 pupils in junior year, but even in this huge crowd Jim was widely recognised. A select few knew by now that an interest in music accompanied his obsession with politics. Rock 'n' roll would eventually become the new vehicle for Jim's ambitions, but any pupils who bumped into him in the sleek, clean corridors of Ann Arbor High – another elegant, *moderne* building, so high-tech that it even boasted its own planetarium – would still have taken him for a pillar of the establishment. 'Straight', was how a younger Ann Arbor High pupil, Ron Asheton, described him.

In his junior year, Osterberg secured a coveted place as an entrant to the American Legion's Boys' State program. An intensive summer course based at Michigan State University in Lansing, it drew five or six pupils from each of Michigan's most competitive high schools, all of them 'selected for outstanding qualities of leadership, character, scholarship, loyalty and service to their schools and community'. Many of the schools had intensively trained their entrants for the event, which was modelled on the state's political structure; each boy was assigned a dormitory, which took the role of a city, all of whose inhabitants would run for public office. Mike Wall was one of Jim's companions from Ann Arbor High, and ran for lieutenant governor; Wall made it through two or three rounds while Jim's campaign just kept on rolling. 'He looked at this thing,' says Wall, 'and said to me, Hey, I've got this figured out. I'm gonna run for governor of the state of Michigan!'

Up against boys who'd arrived with a party organisation and carefully constructed manifestos, Osterberg vanquished his opponents with almost embarrassing ease. He boasted formidable skills as a public speaker, but his progress through the system called for much more complex talents: 'He had to be cunning, and really sophisticated,' says Wall. 'In any political convention you've got different coalitions, guys who are gonna throw their votes behind you. He was very shrewd, very cunning, and had the skills to capitalise on the moment.'

It was at a Boys' State conference in Little Rock just one year earlier, 1963, that a young boy from Arkansas named Bill Clinton had taken his first step to political fame, becoming the state's delegate to the Boys' Nation conference in Washington DC. Osterberg seemed to be destined for a similar distinction and made it through every round, finally winning his party nomination to compete for the top slot. Says Wall, 'It was an incredible feat. He manoeuvred all the way through. He didn't win governor in the end, that went to the other party, but it was an amazing achievement. But was that Jim? Hell, no. It was basically, Fuck you guys, I'm having fun. 'Cause I'm not a mainstreamer and you're gonna vote for me anyway.'

Perhaps it was the sense that he'd secured admission to the upper tier of high school kids that made it easier to turn his back on them, for in his last couple of years at school the boy 'most likely to succeed' no longer seemed so painfully reliant on the approval of his peers, and the snobbery of his junior high years seemed to disappear. Ricky Hodges was one of Ann Arbor High's few black students. On his first day at the new school he was staggered by the wealth on display: 'At that time the high school had two parking lots – one for the students, and one for the teachers. And if you were to drive into the student parking lot you'd think it was the teachers' parking lot because the students had all the better cars!' Hodges assumed that Osterberg – or 'Ox', as he called him – was one of the wealthy, 'ritzy' kids, but was surprised to find that, in a school where black and white communities co-existed without any interaction, Jim would often come over and chat, 'and that was unusual. No doubt about it.'

For the first time, there were signs of physical fearlessness, of standing up for people. In Jim's junior year, there was an end-of-term talent contest in the spacious, wood-lined auditorium. One girl was singing a cappella when an older student started to heckle: 'Something about it being a stupid, mushy song,' says Ron Ideson, who was sitting next to Osterberg. 'Jim swung round and hit the heckler as hard as he could with his fist, three or four times, angrily saying "Shut up!" Jim cared nothing for his own safety, he was standing up for the performer on stage, and I doubt he knew her personally.'

The ex-Tappan kids noticed a change in Jim's demeanour, the fact he was not quite as consciously trying to join the establishment. He ran once more for student office in 1965, this time shooting for the position of president. His campaign literature listed all of his achievements: participation in the swimming, track and golf teams, membership of the AC math, English and history programmes, his role in the Ann Arbor High debate team and his participation in a recent State Model United Nations assembly. For this election, however, he boasted a new distinction: the fact he played drums in a 'professional rock 'n' roll band', namely the Iguanas, an expanded version of the Megaton Two. Whether it was the fact he was aiming for higher office, or that he was regarded as slightly more left-field than was the case at Tappan, this year his political talents proved inadequate to the task, and he lost the election to David Rea, a tall, handsome, football-playing, valedictorian BMOC – Big Man On Campus.

In a time of conflicting influences, the academic pressure from his parents, the lure of politics and the excitement of The Beatles, whose arrival in 1963 attracted his attention, Jim's desire to achieve was obvious but still unfocused. Jannie Densmore was Jim's girl-friend at the time, and she recalls 'vague memories of his home life not being that great. And he was an overachiever, I remember his devotion to his music and also political things, being a leader. I always thought he would do something larger than just grow up, marry, live and die in Ann Arbor.'

In the months that she went out with Jim, before she left to join her mom's new husband in New Orleans, Jannie was never invited back to Jim's trailer. The same applied to his other two or three girl-friends from junior high and high school. For some reason, Jim had been nervous about asking Jannie out in the first place, enlisting Clarence 'Rusty' Eldridge as a co-conspirator and raiding the Eldridge family's drinks cabinet before their first date: 'We got an empty Miracle Whip jar, poured a little bit from the top of each bottle into the jar, filled it up with orange juice, went over to Jannie's house and ended up getting plastered,' remembers Rusty.

One evening, after telling his parents he was going down to the Colonial Lanes bowling alley with his friends, Jim headed instead for a romantic *tête-à-tête* at Jannie's house. He raided the drinks cabinet, only to be caught as her mother returned early. The half-loaded

Osterberg and girlfriend fled for the bowling alley, where they ren-
dezvoused with their alibi, Jim McLaughlin: 'He was totally drunk,
and he loved it. He was smiling, giggling, off in his own little
world. She wouldn't even look at him or me – she was so mad she
couldn't even sit still!'

With both Jannie and Jim McLaughlin, Jim Osterberg seemed to
maintain a certain degree of separation, of control; both were aware
of his incredible ability to be different things to different people. It
was possibly instinctive and, engagingly, sometimes had no other
purpose than to entertain. For in an environment where 'jocks'
would mock weedy kids in the shower, or a 'goon squad' would
victimise kids with long hair (sometimes, according to Ann Arbor
High pupil Scott Morgan, administering forced haircuts on the
spot), Jim Osterberg was increasingly seen around the corridors
and classrooms in the guise of 'Hyacinth', an alter ego developed
from a poem he'd written, in which he had imagined himself as a
flower. 'It would just crack you up,' laughs classmate Jimmy Wade.
'He would walk out, have his arms outstretched, and just look at
you like he was a flower, bend a little, shake his arms as if there was
a slight breeze, do it in a manner that you had to laugh!' Lynn
Klavitter concurs. 'It was pretty crazy! But that's the way he was!'
By 1965, the 18-year-old Jim's hair was just a little bit longer and
flopped over his forehead. It wasn't long enough to identify him as
a greaser or rocker, but just enough to mark him out as not purely
an aspiring schoolboy politician any more.

Fortunately, Hyacinth's eccentricity was complemented by Jim
Osterberg's position within the school hierarchy, and his role on the
executive committee organising the graduation talent show meant
that his alter ego was engaged as MC for the event on 10 March
1965. Ricky Hodges (whom Jim describes as 'a very funny black
guy, not unlike a local Chris Rock') was co-presenter, but he claims
his role was simply that of straight man. After a couple of rehearsals
at Ricky's house and at 'Ox's' trailer, Hyacinth and Hodges opened
the show. Ricky produced a watering can, and sprinkled imaginary
water over his partner, who slowly unfurled and then blossomed

into life. Hodges and Hyacinth proceeded to transfix the 2,000 pupils who filled the auditorium, trading jokes and improvising lines; Hodges's humour was quick-witted, while Hyacinth was simply surreal, prancing around, giggling, skipping across the stage. Today, of course, it sounds quite camp, and Jim Osterberg is slightly defensive of his pioneering alter ego ('I didn't even know what a gay person was!'), but it was a hilarious, brave performance that had the high-school audience doubled over with laughter.

One younger boy, soon to become one of Ann Arbor's hottest singers, was mesmerised by the performance. He enjoyed the couple of numbers that Jim played with his band the Iguanas, who were also on the bill, but he was most impressed by Hyacinth's prancing, offbeat antics: 'Nobody expected anything like this,' says Scott Morgan. 'Hyacinth was so entertaining, so charismatic. It was like a preview of what he was to become.'

Three years later, Morgan would see Jim Osterberg's public unveiling of Iggy Stooge at Detroit's Grande Ballroom. He would remember Hyacinth, and realise he'd seen this all before.

Four decades on from that talent show, the class of '65 weave their way tentatively through the banked seats filling Ann Arbor High's huge auditorium. The area is in semi-darkness, thanks to holiday restoration work on the electrical system, but it's still possible to make out an impressive, beautifully designed performance space, which puts to shame many provincial theatres or arts venues. The night before, Jim Osterberg's reunited class members had met up at Colonial Lanes bowling alley for their forty-year reunion; tonight there will be a formal reception. Very occasionally you can see flashes of old high-school rivalries, the odd mention of 'snooty Tappan kids', but it's an overwhelmingly warm, textbook friendly event, rich with tales of people happily wed to their high-school sweethearts, or who've indulged themselves with early retirement, or who've gone on to successful careers in academia, engineering or the law.

Most of Jim's classmates smile at the mention of his name, and recall his political views or his goofy humour; perhaps two or three recall him as a misguided, eccentric creature whose music could never hold a candle to their favourite Detroit rocker, Bob Seger. Many of the women spontaneously volunteer recollections of his engaging wit and entrancing blue eyes, and maintain that his accounts of being an outcast, or a dork, are quite simply 'bogus', as one classmate, Deborah Ward, puts it: 'Let's face it, he wasn't Eminem.'

Mim Streiff is an elegant, ebullient woman who in her high-school senior year dated Sam Swisher, one of the tallest, wealthiest and classiest boys in Jim's year. She shares her schoolmates' warm memories of Jim, a 'super-smart' boy, 'a natural, in the top echelon', who claimed he would one day be President of the United States. But as we walk along the dark, brick-lined hallways, with their impeccable terrazzo floors and art deco signage, Mim smiles, before she dissects Jim's achievements forensically – almost brutally: 'I think Jim tried *everything*. He was not quite the best at golf; he wasn't quite an athlete. He wasn't quite the best at swimming. He was good, but he wasn't the top debater. He wasn't the coolest guy, and he didn't date the coolest girls. But he still wanted to be the coolest. He kept trying . . . but he never quite made it to the top.'

There was one kid at Ann Arbor High who back in 1965 was undoubtedly aware of this brutal truth; one kid who had a burning belief in himself, and a fierce desire to succeed, and that was Jim Osterberg, the boy who'd finessed his way so often, but only ever to second place. But still he knew that he was special. He would get to first place in something. All he needed to do was find out what it was.

CHAPTER 2

Night of the Iguana

The most respected guru of Chicago's blues and jazz scene hadn't expected this cold winter evening would turn out to be such an ordeal. A champion of black music, the patron of fast-rising young blues turks like Magic Sam and Junior Wells and the owner of Chicago's hippest record store, Bob Koester generally found that even the most ornery musicians would treat him with affection, or at least respect. But tonight, one of the most engaging, intelligent musicians he'd ever encountered was out to torture him, and soon he would find the limits of his endurance.

From the moment Koester had met Iggy Osterberg, he had been charmed by the young drummer's intelligence and enthusiasm. He was sufficiently enthused by the aspiring blues drummer to hire him for a gig with bluesman Big Walter Horton, who was playing a demonstration set at Oak's Park swanky Frank Lloyd Wright-designed Unitarian Temple, to accompany a talk by Koester on the blues in front of an admiring, middle-class audience. Iggy had acquitted himself well musically, while his tact and intelligence were demonstrated by the way he'd charmed some of Chicago's toughest bluesmen. But on this cold evening, at Koester's apartment on the ground floor of 530 North Wabash, in the winter of 1966, that charm had disappeared. In its place was malevolence.

It had all started when Iggy had asked Koester, who'd been putting him up for a week or so, if some of his friends could drop by. His friends were what Koester termed 'psychedelic dudes', but there was little peace and love in the vibe they brought. Of the five of them, Vivian Shevitz was OK, but now she'd disappeared in search of her friend Sam Lay, who was in hospital after accidentally shooting himself in the scrotum. The Asheton brothers, Ron and Scott, were a nasty pair; Ron's party-piece was a Gestapo interrogation routine, where he'd shine a light into Koester's face while sneering, 'Ve haf vays of making you talk.' Scott was more physically intimidating, a handsome, broody youth who resembled a young Elvis Presley and seemed to enjoy playing frisbee with Koester's precious blues 78s. The fourth psychedelic dude, Scott Richardson, was a Jagger-lookalike singer who professed to like Howlin' Wolf, but he was equally indifferent to Koester's blues guru status. He joined the others in taunting him, wrestling with each other, walking round the apartment shouting, mocking Koester or laughing at Iggy – or Ego, as Koester had started to nickname him – as the drummer danced naked with his dick folded back between his legs, shouting, 'I'm a girl, I'm a girl!'

By now, the headache that had been coming on over the evening made Koester feel like his skull was clamped in a vice, and his young charges were cranking up the pressure. Cradling his head in his hands, he asked Iggy if he could pour him a glass of water. For once, Iggy seemed sympathetic, and headed for the bathroom with a glass. Reappearing, he passed the full glass to Koester, who raised it to his lips before the warmth and retch-inducing reek of its contents alerted him. The little shit was trying to get Koester to drink a glass of piss! Enraged, Koester threw the glass at Osterberg, who held up his hand to protect himself as the glass shattered, cutting his finger and splattering its contents over the apartment. Incandescent with rage, Koester screamed at the young fucks to get out, bundling all of them out of the door and into the freezing Chicago night.

As they walked round the Loop in search of an all-night cinema, Iggy seemed strangely unconcerned. Teeth chattering, he confided to Ron Asheton that he'd abandoned his ambition of being a blues drummer. He wanted to form a band. And he wanted Ron and Scott to join him. He had an idea that they could come up with something different.

It was the drums that called James Osterberg away from politics. Trained in the school marching band, he later graduated to the orchestra proper, and right around the time the first stirrings of rock 'n' roll reached Michigan, he enrolled in a school summer camp and brought his marching-band side drum with him. One morning the seventh and eighth graders were being called from their dormitories to the assembly area, and Jim took it upon himself to lead them through the tree-lined paths, like a paradiddling Pied Piper: 'Jim was playing really, really well, and the kids just lined up and started marching,' says Denny Olmsted. 'He didn't have a shirt on and looked really healthy and fit; he had a flat-top haircut, like all of us. It sounded great, and everyone just followed him in formation and marched down the path.'

It became a ritual that was repeated over several consecutive days. And whatever his ambitions of emulating John F. Kennedy via his ample gift for public speaking, it was with this basic, primal beat that Jim Osterberg first became a leader.

Over subsequent months, visitors to the Osterbergs' trailer, like Brad Jones, noticed he had acquired a drum practice pad – modest circles glued to a piece of plywood – but it wasn't until 1961 that Osterberg, then fifteen, had his first brush with rock 'n' roll, after he met up with, he says, a 'not particularly popular, not particularly anything, but nice' kid called Jim McLaughlin, in the school marching band. McLaughlin's dad was a radio tinkerer, like a local Leo Fender, whose house on Hermitage, near Tappan, was always littered with microphones and amplification equipment, and it was there that Osterberg first heard Duane Eddy, Ray Charles and Chuck Berry. 'And I was like, Holy Christ, this is some serious shit.'

McLaughlin became Osterberg's closest friend, and the two spent long hours after school at the trailer in Ypsilanti, McLaughlin working out boogie riffs on guitar and Osterberg accompanying him on his tiny three-piece drum kit. An intelligent, unassuming man who now works in trade exhibitions, to this day McLaughlin is impressed by his childhood friend's confidence and his 'utter fearlessness'. He was also taken aback by the fierce rivalry between the Osterberg males: 'They had the most incredibly adversarial relationship in the world, they were at each other's throats every second – oneupmanship, who could cut the other person down, who had a quicker wit. They would take golf trips down to North Carolina, play every day and just go to war. It was such a paradox, because the guy also inherited this literary interest from his father and obviously the golf and the athletics, too.'

McLaughlin was nervous about the rock 'n' roll duo's public debut, but his new bandmate talked him into playing at a Tappan Talent Show in March 1962; they played two numbers, Sandy Nelson's 'Let There Be Drums', and then a self-written 12-bar using a bunch of Duane Eddy and Chuck Berry cast-off riffs. Introduced as the Megaton Two by Osterberg's friend Brad Jones, they took to the stage, and their rendition of Nelson's drum showcase aroused a decent spattering of applause. By the second number, 'People went nuts, they were dancing in the aisle, the teachers were running round telling 'em to sit down,' says McLaughlin. After the show, one of the high-school jocks went up to the drummer and gruffly congratulated him. '"Hey, Osterberg, that sounded good, your band's pretty cool," sorta thing. And girls liked us a little bit. And that was how it started off.'

As casual as it was, that jock's comment, the first modest acclaim, together with the subtle approval of Tappan's schoolgirls, would launch a fateful career – one in which future audiences' responses would veer from rapture to violence. It would be another two years before Osterberg's musical ambitions took obvious priority over his status as a classroom politician, but there was a good reason for the switch. As a politician, Osterberg relied on his verbal facility, his reading of audiences and his sheer audacity. Every one of those skills was also vital to his musical career, which demanded sustained hard work too, but music would become the one pastime he loved for itself, rather than for its ability to impress others.

From now on, he would practise incessantly with McLaughlin after school, and when the pair moved up to Ann Arbor High the work intensified as the line-up was augmented with sax-player Sam Swisher, the son of an Ann Arbor real-estate agent who lived over the road from the McLaughlins, and, in 1964, bassist Don Swickerath and guitarist Nick Kolokithas, who knew McLaughlin via a local guitar teacher, Bob Richter. Osterberg named the band the Iguanas, after what he claimed was the 'coolest' animal, and over the following two years, as they played the local high schools and frat parties at the University of Michigan, their set changed in tune with Michigan's musical vibe, with frat-band sax-led songs like 'Wild Weekend' or 'Walk, Don't Run' being supplanted by numbers from The Beatles, the Stones and the Kinks, as their stripy surf-band shirts made way for matching sharkskin suits.

McLaughlin and Swickerath were regular visitors to the Osterbergs' trailer, in contrast to Jim's girlfriends, Jannie Densmore and then Lynn Klavitter, who never got to see his home or meet his parents. From Swickerath's viewpoint, Osterberg had 'a lonely life. Before school his mom and dad would just sort of shake his foot, say, Jim, get up, and it was up to Jim to get up, get breakfast and get himself to school, as his parents took off for work.' What was unusual then is of course conventional today. But Osterberg's upbringing, and only-child status, undeniably contributed to an independent – solitary, even – streak. And a persona that, even in those innocent times, was being noticeably affected by the advent of drugs and rock 'n' roll. It was towards the end of his time at Ann Arbor High that girlfriend Lynn Klavitter noticed when he 'started taking overdoses of his asthma medicine. I remember one place we went with the Iguanas, some resort, where he bleached his hair, and I knew something was changing about him. He was doing extravagant things that he normally didn't do.'

Over those high school years, Jim's preferred social setting moved from the golf course to Ann Arbor's Discount Records. The store's manager was Jeep Holland, a well-known svengali on the local scene. He steered blue-eyed soulsters the Rationals to chart success, and built up a thriving booking agency based from a payphone, scaring off other potential users with his scary speed-freak glare. Holland took a liking to young Osterberg, even though the Iguanas were rivals to his own charges. Holland eventually hired him to work in the store after school, checking in and out Discount's stock of Stax and Volt 45s: 'But he was always late, never on time. Then I noticed that so many girls were hanging around him that nothing was getting done. So in the end I had him do all the stock work in the basement.' An expert in soul and R&B, in which he schooled all his charges, Holland enjoyed mocking Jim's Beatles-loving band – and over that year got into the habit of shouting 'Iguana Alert!' whenever Jim emerged from the basement.

It was during those after-school hours working at Discount that Osterberg first noticed two kids, fellow students at Ann Arbor High, hanging around on Liberty Street outside the store. Ron Asheton was a wannabe rock star with a Brian Jones haircut, who'd first met Jim in the Ann Arbor High school choir; Scott Asheton, Ron's younger, taller brother, was a charismatic young hood with a dark, glowering air. The pair had moved to Ann Arbor with sister Kathy and their mother, Ann, soon after the death of their father on 31 December 1963. Today, Iggy still recalls Scott Asheton looking 'magnetic, like a cross between a young Sonny Liston and Elvis Presley'. Many years after their first meeting, he commemorated that first sighting in his song 'The Dum Dum Boys', remembering the way 'they used to stare at the ground'. But over the next few months their conversations would be limited to muttered hellos in the corridors of Ann Arbor High.

It was with by now typical Osterberg bluster that the lead Iguana described himself as a 'professional drummer' in flyers for his unsuccessful presidential campaign of 1965 – his instinct for self-aggrandisement had reached new heights. Literally – in that spring's talent contest he overshadowed his fellow Iguanas by appearing on top of a ludicrous, seven-foot-tall drum riser. (Fellow student and fan, Dale Withers, one of the school's taller pupils, pondered if this was a classic 'Napoleon complex'.) But in July 1965, after Osterberg, Swisher and McLaughlin's graduation from high school, that exalted 'professional' claim became true, when the band secured a residency at Harbor Spring's Club Ponytail, in what several of them would recall as the most idyllic summer of their lives.

An elegant resort nestling close to Little Traverse Bay on Lake Michigan, Harbor Springs was studded with beautiful, sprawling Victorian mansions that were owned or rented as summer homes by the Midwest's wealthiest industrial magnates – many of whom had daughters who were keen to party the night away. Recognising the opportunity, local businessman Jim Douglas opened a teenage nightclub at the Club Ponytail, a Victorian mansion that had reputedly once served as a base for Detroit bootleggers during Prohibition. The Iguanas would be the bait for these society debutantes – and before long, it became obvious that Jim Osterberg was their biggest attraction. Located down a two-lane road, and advertised by a huge wooden cut-out of a blonde with a pert turned-up nose and a ponytail, the Club Ponytail's two dance floors soon became the hottest spot in town.

For five nights a week, the Iguanas would belt out a set that included several Beatles songs – 'I Feel Fine', 'Eight Days A Week', 'Slow Down' and more – plus the Stones' 'Tell Me', Bo Diddley's 'Mona' and, several times a night, that summer's smash hit, 'Satisfaction', most of the numbers sung by McLaughlin or Kolokithas. By now, Osterberg had decreed that Sam Swisher's saxophone was superfluous, and the real-estate agent's son was relegated to bashing on a tambourine (invariably on the on-beat) and looking after the band's money. According to Sam's girlfriend, Mim Streiff, Sam compensated for his humiliation by exerting financial control over his bandmates, advancing them money from the next week's earnings and deducting a lucrative 20 per cent. Naturally this earned the further resentment of his drummer, who glowers at the mention of his name to this day.

Honed by their two-sets-a-night, five-nights-a-week routine, the Iguanas became a tough little outfit, their voices roughened and funky from constant wear. Cub Koda, later the leader of Brownsville Station, saw the Iguanas many times over that summer, and describes them as 'a great, greasy little rock 'n' roll band'. Jim was a good drummer, who'd lie back on the beat and slash away at his ride cymbal, which was studded with rivets for a sleazier sound. 'And, man, you'd watch those rivets dance,' says Koda, who was also struck by the Iguanas' low-down versions of 'Wild Weekend' and 'Louie Louie'; Osterberg would customise them with his own dirty lyrics, which Detroit bands loved trading with each other. Michigan teen band the Fugitives claimed to have introduced the word 'fuck' to Richard Berry's garage-band classic 'Louie Louie' back in 1963 but, after dire warnings from Douglas, McLaughlin learned to hover by the microphone's volume control during the offending song, ready to protect the vulnerable teens of Harbor Springs from lines such as 'Girl, I'd like to lay you again', or 'Her ass is black and her tits are bare'.

McLaughlin liked and respected Osterberg, but was convinced that such obscenity could never win over an audience. Normally, the drummer got so carried away he didn't even notice his screamed vocals weren't audible. Neither did it bother his audience of apprentice teenyboppers, whose ecstatic response encouraged him to try another brief vocal spot, singing the jingle of a then-popular sugar-laden cereal, Sugar Crisp. As their drummer imitated the TV commercial's wacky cartoon bear singing 'Can't get enough of that Sugar Crisp', Jim's fellow Iguanas were aston-ished to see that the resort's female population had brought boxes of the sugary puffed-wheat concoction to the club, and were throw-ing it onto the stage as if at some cute performing monkey.

By the middle of that summer, McLaughlin, Swickerath and Kolokithas noticed that on their weekends off, when they would return to Ann Arbor to see their parents, or girlfriends, Jim invariably remained in their chalet at Harbor Springs, where by now he had been given his own room in a vain effort to stem the tide of mouldy peanut bars and rotting apple cores that accumulated behind the communal sofa. Much of the time, Osterberg stayed indoors, playing two LPs over and over – Dylan's *Bringing It All Back Home*, and *The Rolling Stones Now*. 'Not a day went by that I didn't listen to those things for hours.' But his bandmates had no knowledge about what else he got up to during his weekends off until, one weekday evening, he invited the others up to an imposing mansion overlooking the bay. Ushered into a large dining room, Swickerath and Kolokithas were astonished to be greeted by a distinguished-looking businessman, who was introduced by Osterberg as 'Mr Reynolds – he owns the Reynolds Aluminum Company'. The friendly industrial magnate chatted to the assembled Iguanas, telling them what a fan his daughter was of their music, before handing each of them a chisel and asking them to inscribe their names into a huge aluminium table that dominated the room. Soon it transpired that Jim hung out with the daughters of the Wrigley's Chewing Gum family too, while on other weekends he had worked his charm on Chuck Bowbeer, owner of the Depot House, an arty coffee bar based in a railway carriage, and persuaded him to host Jim's poetry readings. They never knew whether Jim invited girls other than Lynn Klavitter back to their quarters, but McLaughlin, who at one point had shared a bed with Jim in their tiny chalet, decided to change the arrangement after noticing some fresh stains on the sheets. 'Sorry about that,' Osterberg informed him with typical bluster when McLaughlin complained. 'It was either that or fatherhood.'

Osterberg worked his magic on visiting musicians too. When famed bouffant-haired girl group the Shangri-Las came to town, most of the Iguanas were in a cold funk at the prospect of backing such legends. 'I was terrified,' says McLaughlin, 'but Jim said, this is going to be great, screw the practical side, man, we're on with the Shangri-Las.' After an hour of practice in the afternoon with the band's 'greasy lead-guitar-player slash manager slash roadie-guy' they hit the stage, with McLaughlin babbling, 'Which one is the candy store one, what are the chords, this is going to be a disaster!' But: 'Jim was perfect. He had the confidence, he knew no one would notice if we made any mistakes. And they didn't.'

McLaughlin and band disliked the Shangri-Las' brunette back-up singers, but they suspected Jim had something going with the blonde one. He had a knack of getting on with whatever band they worked with, whether it was Bobby Goldsboro – 'so nervous he was shaking, then onstage he was totally relaxed' – or the Four Tops, despite the fact that, according to Nick Kolokithas, Osterberg had spent much of his time off teaching Nick's parrot Zorba the Greek to shriek the phrases 'fuck Sally' and 'niggers', terms which the diligently schooled bird mastered just in time for the Four Tops' visit to the Iguanas' chalet. Kolokithas admired Osterberg's drumming, but wasn't a fan of his animal husbandry, not least Jim's habit of running his fingers along the bars of Zorba's cage to create a metallic clang, waking the bird from its slumbers.

Not for the last time, however, nature wreaked its revenge. One fateful day Kolokithas heard unearthly shrieks coming from the living room, ran to investigate and discovered Osterberg and Zorba locked in a deathly embrace, the parrot's beak firmly clamped on Jim's finger as the drummer leapt about the room, attempting to shake him off. Finally, Zorba fluttered away, happy to have had vengeance. Nick never discovered who it was who'd unlocked the door to the parrot's cage. Frankly, there were too many suspects.

Basking in the adulation of the town's youth, the Iguanas all felt like celebrities, and would often get pestered for autographs on the main drag. But the authorities started to take notice too. There were complaints from the Harbor Springs Council of Churches over the obscene lyrics of 'Louie Louie'. When the Kingsmen – who took a paternal interest in the young musicians – played the Ponytail, they mentioned how they liked to run around town in their underwear. This planted a seed in Osterberg's mind; shortly afterwards, the band protested against the gruelling work regime imposed by Jim Douglas by playing in their pyjamas. Osterberg talked Swickerath into a night-time pyjama-clad roar through the town on Don's motorbike, but when he turned up for the jape clad in a trench coat, it became apparent that Jim Osterberg's night-time wear was his birthday suit. After a quick blast through Main Street, during which Osterberg enjoyed a naked streak through the idyllic Michigan moonlight, the two sped back to their chalet opposite the Ponytail.

By the end of the summer, the restrictions imposed by Jim Douglas, who was stingy with both pay and perks, were starting to grate. Although they took some satisfaction in petty insubordination – Don Swickerath found a secret passage beneath the Ponytail which allowed him to steal ice cream from under the unsuspecting club owner's nose – they were all relieved when their contract came to an end, and they moved to Chuck Bowbeer's Depot House for a couple more shows. The proprietor was taken with both drummer and band, and boasted of his connections at Columbia and other labels. Encouraged by this news, and the growing fan base, they booked into United sound recorders in Detroit to record their cover of Bo Diddley's 'Mona'. The B-side of the proposed single provoked some of the band's first internal arguments. Jim wanted to use his own song 'Again And Again' – a dark, almost gothic affair, with shouted, Dylanesque lyrics ('I walk through a field of bleak death') underpinned by Kolokithas's doomy guitar chords – but the rest of the band opted for Nick's more conventional, Beatles-y 'I Don't Know Why'. 'We didn't get what Jim was trying to do,' concedes McLaughlin. 'He wanted to do more Dylan material, but we only liked his songs once they were covered by the Byrds.'

The Iguanas returned to Ann Arbor in September, with seve⁻ ⁻ more high-profile shows lined up and, for most of them, an imminent return to college. Swickerath and Kolokithas already attended the Eastern Michigan University in Ypsilanti; Jim Osterberg had secured a place to study anthropology at the more prestigious University of Michigan, set in gorgeous Victorian buildings in the heart of Ann Arbor. Michigan had a generous entry policy for local students, who could secure a place with a B+ average, and qualify for Michigan Higher Education Assistance Authority grants towards books and tuition. There had never been any doubt among Jim's peers that he was destined for the university; as McLaughlin put it, 'He could be wild, but he would knuckle down to it when necessary. For instance, can you imagine how much discipline you needed to write poetry?'

In the heady days of early 1965, the Iguanas had been one of the hippest bands around Ann Arbor. But as summer gave way to autumn, their major-chord, British-invasion sound was sounding trite and last season. Michigan's musical climate was changing fast. Local bands like Johnny and the Hurricanes, who'd enjoyed big instrumental hits in the late 1950s, had sounded cheesy on record but they were notoriously tough-sounding on stage; other Detroit acts like Billy Lee could hold their own with Detroit's black soul outfits; Billy Lee even recorded an R&B single for the gospel label Carrie, before recruiting a band called the Rivieras and later choosing a new name – Mitch Ryder – from a phone book.

Other local entrepreneurs were schooling their own talent. Jeep Holland was nurturing Ann Arbor High student Scott Morgan in the Rationals – the band would hit big with their single 'Respect' in 1966, attracting the attention of Detroit's future first lady of soul, Aretha Franklin. Meanwhile, Dave Leone and Ed 'Punch' Andrews had opened a pioneering club in Harper Woods called the Hideout, to showcase the Fugitives, a tough rock 'n' roll act based around the arrogant but fiendishly talented Quackenbush brothers, who would draw crowds of 700, twice a week. Other aspiring promoters, such as Pete Andrews, opened up venues like Mothers Teenage Nightclub, which he ran at Ann Arbor Armoury, and would pull huge greaser and frat crowds.

As the Michigan music scene exploded, one crucial concert electrified many of its key players. On 24 October the newly electric Dylan played Detroit's Cobo Hall, fresh off a European tour that had seen him taunted as 'Judas', only to respond with some of his toughest, angriest speed-freak music to date. The Detroit audience was just as ill-prepared for Dylan's electrified assault as were the cardigan-clad English folkies, and when Dylan hit the stage for his electric set, dolled up in a four-button flannel suit and Beatle boots with a black Stratocaster, all hell broke loose. Osterberg was in the crowd with Jim McLaughlin, and watched as Dylan walked onto the stage with his back to the band. After guitarist Robbie Robertson counted them in, the band kicked into life, and Dylan executed a perfect jump turn, 'Just like a classic high-school greaser band,' remembers Osterberg fondly. 'I knew that move from the greaser bands around Ann Arbor, beetle-browed guys with pompadours leading these really tight bands.' Dylan's rocker cool increased Osterberg's identification with his hero, but even as Dylan and the Hawks rocked through 'Like A Rolling Stone' and 'Subterranean Homesick Blues', cries of 'Sell out!' rippled through the crowd. Osterberg was transfixed; both by the music, and the way Dylan was way ahead of the audience and seemingly didn't give a damn about their reaction. 'It made such a huge impression on Jim,' says Jim McLaughlin. 'He was really shaken. It wasn't just the music, it was the way the crowd booed him. And how Dylan had taken all this abuse, and didn't seem affected.'

One Ann Arbor band boasted a special affinity with this revolutionary, controversial music. The Prime Movers had formed that summer, and were led by Michael and Dan Erlewine, together with pianist Bob Sheff. Michael Erlewine was a confident, ambitious, self-styled intellectual – 'I was forceful, a bit of an asshole' – who had hit the road with Dylan in the mid-1960s, a beat scholar who had already experimented with marijuana and acid; guitarist Dan was a skilled musician (a guitar-playing 'machine' according to the Iguanas), who was friends with Chicago's Butterfield Blues Band – the musicians who had backed Dylan's first excursions into electric music. Sheff was an intriguing, eclectic musician who epitomised the new artistic atmosphere blossoming in Ann Arbor. Born in San Antonio, Texas, he'd won a BMI Student Composers Award and been offered a scholarship at Juilliard, but rejected its stuffy academic ambience and caught a bus to Ann Arbor. Intellectual, gay, schooled in Texas and Delta blues, he had already performed in, and in some cases premiered, works by John Cage, La Monte Young and Yoko Ono, and was soon a key member of the Once Group, an avant-garde multimedia art collective, led by architecture lecturer Joe Wehrer, with architect Harold Borkin, film-maker George Manupelli, painter Milton Cohen and composers Robert Ashley and Gordon Mumma.

With their talk of the Beats, vanguard art and Hegelian philosophy, and a purist blues set list drawn from songs by Little Walter and Junior Wells, the Prime Movers saw themselves as a bunch of intellectual heavyweights compared to British-invasion bands like the Iguanas: 'We didn't care for them much,' proclaims Michael Erlewine. And they let the Iguanas' drummer know it, every time they bumped into him at Discount Records, or clubs like Mothers; like Jeep Holland they teased Osterberg, calling him Iguana, or Iggy for short. 'It was derogatory at first – Iguana,' says Erlewine. 'Then when we became friends it became Iggy.' By November 1965, when the Prime Movers' first drummer Spider Wynn left the band, Michael Erlewine had no problem in persuading Osterberg to leave the Iguanas and team up with his pioneering outfit. Jim played a big University of Michigan freshman orientation dance with the Iguanas before informing McLaughlin and the others that he was leaving. Although he had once been Osterberg's closest friend, McLaughlin was not surprised: 'Jim was hard to get to know – he kept himself to himself. Over the years I guess our conversations had been limited to music and the band. He didn't give me much information about why he was leaving, but it wasn't a shock. I knew he was getting bored and frustrated with our conventional sound and approach.'

In the Iguanas, Jim had definitely been a leader. In the Prime Movers, he was 'very much a follower,' says Michael Erlewine. But his year with the band was crucial for two reasons. First, it would teach him about commitment. Second, it would give him a name.

The Iguanas had been an intimate, cosy outfit, all clanging chords and major-key optimism. But by the end of 1965 their music was comparatively archaic; the Prime Movers' cynical, bohemian attitude was in tune with the zeitgeist, as music got heavier and druggier. This attitude encompassed more than just music, for the Prime Movers' social circle included witty, intellectual quick-thinkers like David 'Panther' White – who arrived from Shaker Heights, Cleveland that autumn – and Lynn Goldsmith, later to be a celebrated photographer. Panther was a natural comic with a wicked, freewheeling Lenny Bruce-style wit, who made prize-winning art films and would soon, with his friend Jesse Crawford, become involved with the White Panther party and MC5 operation. Ron Asheton, Jim's old high-school acquaintance, started hanging out with the Prime Movers too, auditioning on bass guitar and surviving for a couple of gigs before being demoted to roadie and general helper. Ron and others observed that Iggy 'was in total competition with Panther', but Panther was usually prepared to go further than the Prime Movers' new drummer, such as the time he told Dan Erlewine he had scored some especially fine weed and handed him a pipe. Panther, Ron and the rest of the band watched Dan take a deep toke and then freak out: 'It was DMT – a terrible fuckin' drug, it's like peaking on acid, inside about five seconds,' says Ron. 'Panther was one guy who wouldn't take shit from anybody.' It was Panther who ensured the Iggy name became a permanent fixture. The drummer didn't complain about being saddled with the name of his uncool former group; it could have been worse. Ron Asheton, who had a spotty teenage complexion, was given the name Javalina – a midget warthog found in Texas, an animal which, according to naturalists, you can smell before you can see.

Three months out of high school, the 18-year-old Osterberg seemed keen to lay waste to his former straight, fratboy image. And where he'd made a real effort to fit in at high school, impressing fellow students with his intellect, his attendance at the university was desultory, and seemingly confined to hanging out at the library and the coffee shops. Lynn Goldsmith had bumped into

Iggy standing in line on their enrolment day at the University of Michigan; there was an instant erotic attraction between them and they arranged a rendezvous for later that day – to which neither turned up. When they met again, each of them admitted they were still virgins and had chickened out. 'Iggy was cute. Girls like cute guys, it's that simple,' says Goldsmith. But she remembers that where Panther was naturally unique, 'Iggy worked at being unique. He used to go in this coffee shop on the campus, and he'd sit there, pick his nose and eat his boogers. But only when people were watching him. That was my take.'

When eyewitnesses remember Jim over that period, the adjective 'coy' occurs again and again. Janet Withers had had a crush on 'Ostie' ever since she'd been introduced to him by her sister Dale at high school, and would hang around the university campus and Discount Records in order to catch a glimpse of this elusive creature. She kept a diary of her sightings, describing how Ostie would look her up and down as they talked, then look away, a true coquette. 'He's about my height [5' 9"], has a thin but very good build, black hair in a long Beatle [cut], large, large, beautiful blue eyes and a long straight nose,' she confided to her diary. 'His mouth is naturally appealing and just the right proportions. He has muscles, of course, and man! just the ideal guy for me.' Janet's crush was never consummated – but then none of them was. 'Jim was very coy and flirty, very come-on, but nothing to back it up,' says Dan Erlewine, who shared a one-room apartment on State Street with his drummer in 1966. 'But that's not bad, that's just being shy.' The shared bedroom gave Dan more of an insight into Iggy's character than he would have liked, particularly as Barbara Oliver, who was a couple of years older than Iggy and supposedly going out with Dan's brother Mike, was a regular visitor. As Dan vainly attempted to get to sleep, he would hear Jim tease her with the phrase, 'You can look, but you can't touch.' Jim getting girls over and teasing them with 'his thing' became quite a regular ritual. 'I wouldn't have done that with him in the room,' says Erlewine, 'but he would with me.' Both Erlewine brothers agreed that Osterberg's generously sized 'thing' was a crucial part of his self-image. It was no surprise when he announced that his featured vocal with the band would be 'I'm A Man'.

Seducing (or tantalising) Michael Erlewine's girlfriend underlined Jim's Oedipal relationship with this father figure. Later, Jim would denigrate the Prime Movers as effete bohemians, but throughout 1966 Erlewine's influence was crucial. '[Iggy] was a sponge, I think he soaked up ideas,' says Scott Richardson, then the singer with the Chosen Few. 'Michael was a very bossy figure, but a very influential one.'

Bob Sheff observed Iggy from close up, both in the Prime Movers and the Stooges, and he felt that Michael Erlewine was 'not a mentor exactly, but he made him. The [Prime Movers] experience was important to Iggy in an emotional way. Michael liked very emotional situations and he put that into the music a lot. Iggy's the same way.'

An intellectual, inspiring, often infuriating character to this day – it's sometimes hard to extract his opinions of other people, for he's far more interested in himself – Michael Erlewine was ruthlessly committed to his music. But this wasn't a selfish commitment, for he was devoted to bringing the audience with him – sometimes literally so. There was one late-night Prime Movers' show at Clint's Club where he worked up the audience into such an exalted state that after their final song he led the band and twenty kids from the audience through the streets of Ann Arbor, preaching and encouraging them to contemplate the beauty of the everyday objects around them. They stayed up until six o'clock in the morning, sharing the spirituality of the night turning into the dawn, before bundling into a 24-hour Greek restaurant for more earthly sustenance. 'It was an incredible experience,' remembers Sheff. 'A charismatic experience.' Few other performers would have taken such risks, but Michael's commitment in stimulating and challenging his audience was a crucial lesson. And one in which the pupil would eventually outdo the master.

There were some respects in which Iggy was already way ahead of his mentor, though, for as with the Iguanas, a substantial chunk of the Prime Movers' audience was there to follow the drummer. Kathy Asheton, sister of Ron and Scott, was one of them: 'I gathered up a couple of my girlfriends and we concocted a fan club, played the screaming-fan roles. I had a huge crush on him. There was a time we would walk down the street, holding hands, a real innocent thing, or sitting on his bed . . . for me this was very sophisticated.'

Joan Boyle was another Prime Movers fan who, despite Jim's habit of doing things to gross people out ('saying obnoxious things, sticking his tongue out'), saw him as sweet, considerate and 'sensitive. Definitely. He helped me get together with my husband [Dan Erlewine], gave me counselling on how to snag him.' Iggy's attraction to women inspired his agony-uncle column in the otherwise rather staid Prime Movers newsletter – the effect is rather akin to seeing a Page Three boy in a Stalinist propaganda leaflet. In it he would dispense wisdom to lovelorn teenagers, handing out sage advice.

> *Dear Iggy,*
> *I just wanted to know if you think a girl should kiss a boy on the first date.*
> *Love Veronica*
>
> *Veronica,*
> *That depends on where you kiss him.*
> *Love Iggy*

Happy to exploit his attraction for the opposite sex, Iggy nonetheless exhibited an unexpected humility, which deepened his charm. Dale Withers attended the University of Michigan with Jim, and she often saw him making his way from booth to booth in the semi-subterranean Michigan Union Grill. 'Jim would come through and stop at each booth or table, saying humbly with downcast eyes, and I remember him saying these exact words, "Please please please please come to our gig."'

To Dale, such humility seemed rare among men in general, let alone aspiring rock stars. It was all the more alluring in someone so naturally extravagant. Iggy himself recalls how his attitude to the audience differed from that of his bandmates. 'I remember once in the Prime Movers, we were on a break, we were playing in a bar, and the [Erlewine] brothers were going on and on about how fat and ugly the two girls in the front were. I just told them, "Are you guys crazy? You have two fans there! I don't give a damn what they look like. This is a treasure, you have two people paying attention to you!" You know?'

This faithful compact with an audience is something that would, in its unconventional way, endure in Jim Osterberg's life – even if this notion would seem ridiculous to some of his peers, including Pete Andrews, who regularly booked the Prime Movers into Mothers Teenage Nightclub. He regarded Iggy as a 'solid, sound' drummer but was staggered by some of his antics, particularly one evening when he checked the stage at showtime, only to see it empty but for a cheesy-looking cardboard phone booth. Then he saw the drummer, dressed in some kind of superhero outfit, break his way out of the ludicrous contraption, climb up a rope to the balcony where the entire band was set up and get to his kit just as the band fired into the intro. 'We were just going, Jeez,' remembers Andrews.

After dropping out of the University of Michigan by the second term of his anthropology course – he claimed he learned more as an autodidact, researching in the university library – Jim moved on from his apartment share with Dan Erlewine behind Herb David's guitar shop to a room across the road in Blakely Court, and finally to an apartment in the basement of a rundown Victorian building, which he shared with Scott Richardson. Lynn Klavitter, his girlfriend from high school, had moved to California, but went to search him out on her return in the summer of 1966. She was shocked at the transformation from the boy she knew from the previous summer: 'I'm sure he was heavily into drugs, he was wrapped in a blanket, the place was a total disaster.' Lauri Ingber, who'd served on Jim's High School election committee, saw him around the same time, and is convinced to this day that the previously clean-cut school kid was by then on heroin. But his dishevelled state was more to do with poverty than the marijuana that was the drug *du jour*, and which he only smoked 'when force-fed', as it exacerbated his asthma. By now he was living on his meagre earnings from the Prime Movers and Discount Records, along with handouts from his parents. 'We were poor, and we were starving half the fucking time,' says Scott Richardson. 'We had our clothes hanging on the water pipes, newspapers on the floor, we were living like Kurt Cobain underneath a freeway. But I remember laying with him all night and talking about stuff. It was such a tremendously exciting time. And it was that painful period when you're young, don't know who you are yet, with all these influences around.'

For a short time, the Ann Arbor svengali Jeep Holland took control of the Prime Movers. His control freakery was excessive, and the band began to bridle at his insistence that they perform dressed in suits. But Jeep's megalomania was a godsend in a genuine crisis, notably the spectre of military service in the Vietnam war. Ominous letters started dropping on the doorsteps of many of Ann Arbor's musicians from 1966 – by which time Iggy, who'd dropped out of university and therefore lost his student deferment, was vulnerable, as was his friend Ron Asheton. Fortunately Jeep saw the military's predations on his musical empire as a personal affront, and he masterminded a counter-attack that was inspired in its audacity and frightening in its attention to detail.

The guiding principle, Holland explained to Ann Arbor's apprehensive musicians, was psychology. Creative, vulnerable psyches were by their nature incompatible with the rigours of a military campaign or the claustrophobia of life in a platoon. Jeep's tactics were to accentuate the charming personality foibles of his charges, and even amplify them, often with the use of his favoured drug methamphetamine, until the establishment was compelled to view these innocents as deranged psychopaths.

Jeep would work closely with his subjects for a week before their fateful draft examination at Ann Arbor Armoury (the cheek of the Army, subverting a rock 'n' roll venue for this charade!) and his evangelistic fervour would help all their fears evaporate. One example he liked to cite was that of Glenn Quackenbush, keyboard player with greaser band the Fugitives, and later the Scott Richard Case, or SRC. 'Like most organ players, Glenn felt superior, and didn't really like people very much,' he explained. Over the years Glenn had nonetheless attained a basic mastery of the niceties of human behaviour. All Jeep had to do was remove this, 'to take away all the little things you develop so you can get along with other people'. By the time Quackenbush got in line at the Armoury, Jeep proudly boasted, 'The lines on either side had a gap of four people, because no one would stand near him, they just knew something was very wrong.'

Iggy Osterberg's performance was a little more baroque, but still satisfying. After they had completed a questionnaire, the draftees were required to strip down to their skivvies in readiness for their physical examination. Osterberg duly lined up, but kept his hands down his pants, 'holding his dick', only to be admonished by the military police who were keeping order. 'No one is touching my dick!' Osterberg yelped, as the MPs counselled him gently, 'Don't worry son, no one will touch you.' Finally two of the burlier MPs grabbed his elbows and attempted to pull his hands away from his genitals. 'But Jim was a drummer, and he had arms of steel!' cackled Holland. 'They lifted him right off the ground, but couldn't get him to take his hands off his dick! He was out of there in half an hour!'

Holland calculated that he saved twenty-one musicians from the draft, including most of the future Stooges, the Rationals, and future members of the SRC. Many of their contemporaries were not so lucky. Two of Jim's close friends, Ricky Hodges and Dennis Dieckmann, were drafted, but survived their tours of duty. Several other Ann Arbor High classmates were maimed or killed in the South-east Asian conflict.

Liberated from military service, the Prime Movers could dedi-

cate themselves to their mission of converting the masses to their
own brand of authentic blues. They were sufficiently evangelistic –
or masochistic – to take their music to the heart of Ann Arbor's tiny
black quarter around Ann Street, playing a residence at Clint's
Club every week for over a year. They were tolerated by the clientele, who appreciated that they were making an effort, and any
mockery tended to be good-humoured. Often a set would finish in
silence until some wag shouted out, 'Let's give these guys the clap.'
('Meaning gonorrhoea, of course,' says Erlewine.) Sometimes at
the teen nightclubs like Mothers they met with similar incomprehension, but for a select few they were the coolest band around –
Chosen Few guitarist and future Stooge James Williamson
describes the Prime Movers as 'the best band Iggy was ever in'.
'What they were doing was relatively esoteric,' says Dale Withers,
who along with her sister, Janet, and future husband, Larry, was
one of the band's more committed fans. 'But we thought they
would really move on up, like the Stones did.' The band members
were formidable musicians. They would often throw unexpected
gospel numbers into their set; Sheff's adept, inventive keyboard-
playing anticipated the sound of the Doors by a full year, while
Dan Erlewine was one of the first US musicians to use a Gibson Les
Paul to achieve an authentic, overdriven, blues grittiness. Iggy
himself was becoming an impressive drummer, and he made a
decent fist of the songs on which he sang lead – 'Mystery Train'
and 'I'm A Man': 'I remember him singing that song as "I'm A
Tricycle",' says Bill Kirchen, later a revered interpreter of roots
music. 'He did it totally straight, like Muddy Waters, singing out
the letters "T-R-I-C-Y-C-L-E". I was impressed!'

Notwithstanding such japes, Iggy's stage demeanour was
restrained compared to his Iguanas persona. 'They were actually
quite shy on stage,' remembers Dale Withers. 'Not too much banter
or extravagance. But they had a mystique about them.'

The Erlewines' friendship with the Butterfield Blues Band, who
had revitalised the American blues scene the previous year with
their debut album, gave them a direct link to the source of Chicago

blues: the band's original rhythm section, drummer Sam Lay and bassist Jerome Arnold, were stalwarts of Howlin' Wolf's band, but had been lured away by the prospect of more money. Sam had become the best blues drummer of his generation, working countless sessions with Muddy Waters, Junior Wells and others, and he was also the inventor of the 'double shuffle' – a tricky variation of a standard blues beat, which Lay jazzed up, inspired by the sound of the tambourine players in a sanctified gospel chorus. It was a tricky beat, and when Iggy mastered it after hours of practice, with Ron Asheton standing in on bass, it was a source of pride to him. But despite such breakthroughs, the musical environment that had once felt liberating was starting to feel constricting. Although still regarded as a junior member by his bandmates, Iggy was ready to move on. And in the autumn of 1966 he spotted an opportunity to further his ambitions, when Vivian Shevitz, assistant manager at Discount, and bassist of R&B band the Charging Rhinoceros of Soul, became friendly with ex-Butterfield drummer Sam Lay. He recognised this as a unique opportunity to learn blues drumming from one of its greatest masters.

Iggy decided to break the news that he was leaving the Prime Movers to Dan Erlewine, rather than to Michael himself – a sensible move according to Ron Asheton, who explains that 'Dan Erlewine was like Goering to Michael Erlewine's Hitler – which is pretty funny for two Jewish guys!' (Unfortunately for Ron's historical analogy, the Erlewines were in fact Roman Catholics.) Dan describes their leavetaking as tearful: 'He was afraid to tell my brother, because Michael's a real taskmaster, there would have been a real confrontation. And he'd left it real låte, so he was, I'm leaving tomorrow. I was, I don't believe this. And that was it.' The next day the young drummer squeezed into Vivian's red MGB with her friends and fellow blues fans Barbara Kramer and Charlotte Wolter for the 200-mile drive to Chicago. They drove around the South Side looking for Sam, before they finally ran down their quarry at Curley's Club on the West Side.

Curley's, at Madison and Homan, was an archetypal West Side

club, distinguished by its 'upscale' cuisine and music by some of Chicago's younger generation of bluesmen, who would often hit the stage at three in the morning and then watch their audience leave for work, complete with lunchboxes, at seven fifteen. The club was rumoured to be owned by the mob, and it was a regular haunt of Otis Rush – who'd had his own run-ins with the Chicago mafia and was a regular, unwilling witness to shootings and stabbings. 'It wasn't the club's fault,' says Sam Lay, 'but I call that area the Wild Side, not the West Side, 'cause that's what it was. Infested with hookers, robbers.'

'It was a heavy place,' agrees Barbara Kramer, 'but we were luckily too young and too stupid to be scared.' Charlotte Wolter thought that Iggy seemed 'a wide-eyed innocent' about the whole trip, 'As we all were.'

The teenage blues fans arrived at the club expecting its clientele to be flattered by their interest. Instead they were greeted with amusement or suspicion, but luckily the only patron who threatened physical violence chose to pick on the three girls, rather than Iggy, and was hustled away by more sympathetic clubgoers. It was only when Sam Lay, tall, polite and dressed for the gig in tux and tie, arrived and ushered them protectively back to his dressing room that the Ann Arbor quartet could relax. He listened indulgently and supportively as they told him how excited they were to hear the music in its spiritual home. The four went back to see Sam again the next night, sharing a room in a run-down hotel by the lake, by which time Iggy had convinced the drummer of his mission and secured his support. 'The little I saw of him, I knew I could trust him,' says Lay. After making a few phone calls, Sam established that his previous harmonica player, Big Walter Horton, was in need of a drummer, and invited Iggy to sleep over at his place.

Sam and Elizabeth Lay's one-bedroom apartment on Flores was already cramped; their six-year-old son, Bobby, slept on the couch in the living room. The aspiring bluesman was allotted a space on the kitchen floor. He was the perfect guest, packing away his few belongings so as not to clutter the flat, making himself scarce and charming the neighbours, who were somewhat bemused by this new character in the street.

In late 1966 the parlous existence of the average Chicago blues-man was becoming rather less endangered thanks to figures like harp-player Paul Butterfield, who'd established new, better-paying white venues like Big John on Wells Street on the North Side, and record-industry figures such as Bob Koester and Sam Charters, who'd exposed old and young blues players to a new white audi-ence. Walter Horton and other bluesmen discovered that playing white venues could almost double their income. Even better, employing white musicians cut down on their overheads, as they could be counted on to ask for less money. Horton didn't even bother to audition the young drummer – instead, driving to the gig, Horton blew out a riff on his harmonica and asked Iggy to tap along. According to Iggy, Horton chose to motivate his new employee by brandishing a knife and asking him if he was *sure* he could keep up. Unfazed, Iggy shot back, 'Look old man, I can do anything you can, give me a break.'

Over the following weeks Iggy played more dates with Horton, plus J.B. Hutto – a previously obscure slide player who'd been showcased on Charters's album – and James Cotton, an amiable, easygoing harpist who'd played with Howlin' Wolf as a kid, and was now enjoying a modest career revival thanks to Chicago's new white audience. Through Vivian Shevitz, Iggy found a sympathetic patron in the person of Bob Koester, who was championing the new soul-influenced West Side bluesmen such as Buddy Guy and Magic Sam on his Delmark label. Koester had shown many blues fans around the city, including Michael and Dan Erlewine; a widely respected figure, he schooled a whole generation of future record-company bosses, as well as helping countless musicians, most notably Big Joe Williams, a cantankerous Delta bluesman who'd finagled a key to the basement of Koester's Record Mart store. Williams played kazoo, harmonica and nine-string guitar, nailing metal plates or beer cans to his amp to add a distorted, dissonant edge to his eerie, almost African laments. Occasionally, when the trek upstairs to his third-floor apartment in the Record Mart building was too much bother, Williams would crash in the basement. Sometimes Koester, his employees and his customers would be locked out until Williams rose from his slumbers and condescended to unbolt the door.

The Record Mart basement became a crash pad for many employees and blues fans, including Iggy. The drummer's enthusiasm and honest demeanour charmed the record company boss, who helped team him up with J.B. Hutto and would sometimes buy him lunch at the café round the corner from the Record Mart. It was at the café that blues fan and Wayne State University dropout John Sinclair was introduced by Koester to the as then-unknown drummer. Iggy was 'kinda raggety, a skinny little rock kid', and Sinclair was sufficiently impressed by the clear-eyed young musician to make a note of his name. 'He wasn't brazen or brash. But he was interesting.'

Koester today paints a different picture of his young charge. 'He was egotistical. He was talking about Mitch Ryder, and was saying if his record made the Top Five, he would join him. Later I made a slip of the tongue and called him Ego. Which seemed appropriate.'

Koester remembers Iggy staying at his two-room apartment over two separate periods, between which the drummer spent some time sleeping rough in the Chicago Loop. The area was busy and heavily developed, with elevated train tracks, and the banks of the Chicago River were lined with swanky apartments, as well as water, electricity and sewage works, all of them powering the bustling metropolis. It was there that the drummer walked down around twenty steps to sit on the dock. He thought about the time he'd played with J.B. Hutto at a club on 64th Street, sweating to keep up, focusing on his drumming while simple but profound riffs dripped like honey off JB's fingers, seemingly without him even thinking. Iggy smoked a fat joint he'd scrounged, and for the first time inhaled deeply as he contemplated the river. Then he decided that he was not destined to be a blues player. But in that simplicity lay 'a vocabulary'.

It was a notion that would take a full year of gestation to develop into a musical manifesto. But he knew his time in Chicago was up, and he phoned Vivian Shevitz and Ron Asheton to ask if they could collect him. In the meantime he'd be staying at Bob Koester's.

It would take Bob Koester a long time to get over the experience of having Iggy, Ron and Scott Asheton, Scott Richardson and Vivian Shevitz as guests. Vivian was no trouble; she left after the first night to check on Sam Lay. Sam had recently gone out armed to a Chicago club after hearing that a harmonica player, just out of prison, was planning to cut up Sam's bandmate James Cotton, whom he accused of messing with his wife while he was inside. Tooled up to protect his friend, Sam sat down at a table with the Colt automatic in his pocket and the pistol went off accidentally, discharging a .45 round straight through his scrotum. 'Vivian was so gone, because Sam was in hospital,' says Scott Richardson, 'so she didn't pay any attention to what was going on.' What was going on was the baiting of Bob Koester. 'He was just sorta mincing around, and that got to everybody,' Richardson explains. 'It was sheer punk sadism, that is all.'

Koester ascribes the tension to the fact he'd asked the 'psychedelic dudes' not to smoke drugs in his apartment. Iggy hints darkly at sexual predations by Koester and blames Scott Richardson for what ensued. Ron Asheton cheerfully admits that all of them were freaked out by their conviction – ridiculous, says Koester – that Koester was gay. And without a doubt, Jim Osterberg was also trying to show his new friends that he was as tough as they were.

'We were goading him,' remembers Ron. 'It was bad, but we were just kids.'

'We were like the Droogs from *A Clockwork Orange*,' explains Scott Richardson. 'We didn't care what anyone thought.'

There had been one relatively subdued night, where the five listened to Koester's rare records and tapes then barricaded themselves into their room with cushions. The mood turned nasty on the second night, as the Ann Arbor quartet started drinking Bali Hi wine, 'and getting him drunk too,' says Ron. 'And teasing him.'

The Asheton brothers, Scott and Iggy set out to confuse and torture Koester, walking around naked in Iggy's case, wrestling or piling on top of one another on the floor then jumping up as the confused record-company boss tried to work out what the hell was going on, or shining a desk light in his face to dazzle him. 'They were doing all kinds of stripteases I had no interest in, I had specified I wanted no drug activity, and I had this viral infection and was feeling shitty . . . it was like a horrible nightmare.'

When Koester, incensed at being handed that glass of piss, threw all his guests out, it proved a strangely bonding and cathartic experience for the future Stooges. They recount that tale as if it's slightly shameful but nonetheless a memory they seem to relish: 'That was the beginning,' says Ron. 'That was when Iggy said, we should be in a band, and start something.'

CHAPTER 3

The Dum Dum Boys

It is Saturday 5 July 1969, a clear, balmy day in Pottawatamie Beach, and as the Stooges finish their opening number, the brilliantly lamebrained '1969', Iggy Stooge looks blankly at the Saugatuck festival audience and announces, 'I'd like to dedicate the set today to Brian Jones, the dead Stone. Oh well, being dead's better than playing here.'

As they battle their way through their set, perhaps a quarter of the audience – high-school dropouts, a smattering of intellectuals, assorted misfits – is entranced, the remainder indifferent or actively hostile. One fan, Cub Koda of the band Brownsville Station, stands by the side of the stage to admire the spectacle of the freeform feedback-saturated jam which closes their twenty-minute performance. As uncontrollable shrieks squeal out of the PA stacks, Dave Alexander takes the neck of his Mosrite bass and jams it into the gap between two Marshall cabinets, then starts to hump them. Ron Asheton, in aviator shades and leather jacket, tosses his Fender Stratocaster to the stage; it moans and howls as he bends the whammy bar with his foot. Drummer Rock Action pounds out a Bo Diddley jungle rhythm on his tomtoms before suddenly losing the beat and, in a fit of childish frustration, starts kicking over the kit.

Iggy Stooge, meanwhile, simply writhes on the floor, in what looks like some shamanic trance, or even an asthma attack, blood trickling from his bottom lip where he's smacked himself with the microphone.

Koda looks on, entranced, as Iggy leans over and starts to throw up in the middle of the stage, when suddenly he senses someone leaning behind him, trying to get a better view. He glances behind and sees it's Muddy Waters, the grand patriarch of Chicago blues, who will be playing the headlining set in a couple of hours.

Muddy watches, fascinated and perhaps appalled, for a few seconds. Then he shakes his head, points at the stage and shouts over the feedback: 'I don't like that. Those boys need to get themselves an act!'

'Muddy!' laughs Cub. 'That *is* the act!'

For a generation of kids, 1967 was a pivotal year. Jim Osterberg was one of them, for it was over that extraordinary summer that he lost his virginity, dropped acid and left home for good. But there was a more crucial rite of passage. Over this period, this ambitious, solitary figure became part of a raggle-taggle band of brothers, influencing their path through life and, in turn, having the course of his life, and even the shape of his own personality, irrevocably altered. For better or worse, the Stooges were the making of Jim Osterberg.

The Stooges could only have existed in Ann Arbor, for no other town was as smart and as dumb. They originated at a place where high art met greaser thuggery, where the intellectual met the dysfunctional. And that collision was exemplified by the moment that Jim Osterberg teamed up with the Asheton brothers; the moment when the Boy Most Likely To became, as he boasts, 'corrupted!'

There are people who saw the Stooges up close who suggest that Iggy's bandmates were programmed by their leader. 'They were his stooges. Teenage glueheads, I'm not trying to slander them,' as John Sinclair puts it. Others maintain the Asheton brothers had just as profound an effect on their leader, who adopted their values and tough-guy persona. Some fellow musicians, such as Scott Richardson, contend that 'for the people that *really* understood, Ron Asheton was the creative force behind the whole thing'. Ann Arbor High student, Bill Cheatham, later a Dum Dum boy in his own right, describes how Jim Osterberg 'felt he was an outcast. [But] Ronnie, Scotty and I, we *were* outcasts.' And without doubt, much of the alienation, boredom and gonzo humour that pervades the persona of Iggy Pop originates from his fellow Stooges, Scott Asheton and Ronald F. Asheton Junior.

Ann Asheton had brought her two sons and daughter from Davenport, Iowa, to Ann Arbor in December 1963 immediately after her husband Ronald's death; her life was a struggle, for Ronald Senior's pension was too meagre for the family to survive, forcing her to take a job at the Ann Arbor Ramada Inn, in addition to looking after three intelligent but feisty teenagers.

Ronald Asheton Junior believed, like Jim Osterberg, that he was destined to achieve something significant in his life, a belief reinforced by his 1960 encounter with John Kennedy when the Democratic nominee was campaigning in Davenport, Iowa. Dressed in his cub scout's uniform, young Ronald was propelled forward by a surge in the crowd and ended up with his face in the future president's crotch. As a Secret Service agent attempted to tug him away by his cub-scout scarf, the future president intervened to save the unfortunate scout from being throttled, ordering the agent to 'leave the kid alone'; Ronald's fingers brushed those of the charismatic candidate as he was bundled away, star-struck. John F. Kennedy joined Ron's pantheon of showbiz heroes, alongside Adolf Hitler and The Three Stooges. Soon that select band was joined by The Beatles and the Stones, inspiring Ron to drop out of high school, along with his classmate Dave Alexander, and travel to London, hoping to see John Lennon or Mick Jagger walking down Carnaby Street. He settled for the more than satisfactory alternative of seeing the Who at their superviolent mod peak, bringing home a shard of splintered Rickenbacker as a souvenir. The Who's Pete Townshend would become his inspiration, although he started out on the bass guitar. After getting kicked out of the Prime Movers, Ron joined Scott Richardson's snotty English-flavoured R&B band, the Chosen Few, and would soon enjoy the distinction of playing the very first notes to be heard at Detroit's Grande Ballroom as a live rock 'n' roll venue: his bass intro to the Stones' 'Everybody Needs Somebody' launched the Chosen Few's opening set for up and coming band the MC5 in October 1966.

Scott Asheton, too, was a crucial Dum Dum boy, an aspiring drummer who at one point played with Ron, Dave Alexander and Bill Cheatham in a garage band called the Dirty Shames. As a kid, he'd spent countless hours with his dad discussing plans for racing go-karts and building V8 hot-rods, only for his whole world to fall apart with the premature death of his father. After that he became a wild child, thrown out of the house by his mom, hanging out with his hoodlum-looking friends on State and Liberty, spitting on passers-by. It was his tall, Brando-esque good looks and tough guy cool, together with the wickedly cynical Asheton sense of humour, that first entranced Jim Osterberg.

Iggy and the Asheton brothers returned from Chicago at the precise moment that a psychedelic revolution was engulfing Ann Arbor. Its huge student population, cosmopolitan atmosphere and Democrat administration contributed to a liberal ethos which meant that its fines for drugs possession were lower than neighbouring Detroit, and before long the town possessed its own mini Haight-Ashbury in the form of a gaggle of headshops around Liberty and State, at the edge of the university campus.

Jim, Ron and Scott Asheton had decided to form a band together. They hadn't by this point decided who would play what – at first the plan was for Scott Asheton, the most physically magnetic of the three, to sing, and Iggy to stay on drums. And as there was no immediate prospect of making money from their music, they needed a source of income. Fortunately, Ann Arbor's embryonic hippie subculture would become the perfect outlet, as they established their own little niche on the drug-supply chain, buying marijuana plants and drying them to sell on as grass. Jim had moved back into the family trailer on his return from Chicago, and he and Ron discovered that Coachville's communal laundry and service area was the perfect location to dry the leaves. Unfortunately, they often got high on their own supply, and left the plants drying for so long that they started to cook, filling the building with the distinctive smell of burning grass. Beating a retreat to the trailer, they had to plead ignorance as James Osterberg Senior sniffed the air and asked what they were up to.

Jim Osterberg was still firmly tethered to the parental purse-strings, particularly when major purchases were required for the trio's musical experiments. Early in 1967, Jim had his eye on a Farfisa organ and embarked on a campaign to persuade James Senior and Louella to finance the purchase. Eventually Louella agreed on condition that Jim cut his hair; there were complicated negotiations about what constituted a sufficiently short haircut, which revolved around the collar length. Negotiations concluded, Jim opted for a style which was short at the back with long fringe up-front. The results were so bizarre that, according to Ron, Jim attracted the attention of the Ann Arbor police. 'He was wearing baggy white pants, came here to my mom's to practise, and the cops stopped him 'cause they thought he was an escaped mental patient. That is how weird he looked, with that little haircut and those big eyes.' It was a 40-minute bus ride from Coachville to the Ashetons' home on Lake, and according to Jim, even when he got there, with Ann at work, it was often a long wait until the brothers awoke from their morning nap or marijuana stupor and let him in.

Over those early months, Ron, Scott and Jim recruited the Ashetons' friend, Dave Alexander – 'A spoiled child and a wild thing,' according to Scott – to assist in their musical experiments. Once the ever-tolerant Ann Asheton started to bridle at the incessant rehearsals at her house, the quartet moved to the Alexanders'; Dave would supply Ron, Scott and Jim with Colt 45 malt liquors as they crafted an embryonic rock opera. At first, they had debated a line-up with both Jim and Scott on drums; after the purchase of the Farfisa, Jim switched to organ, while Ron fed his bass guitar through a fuzz box and wah wah, and Scotty played drums on a 45-minute instrumental epic, which they named 'The Razor's Edge'.

It was the summer of 1967 when the tiny crew moved into their first band house, a Victorian building on Forest Court, in the heart of the campus. It was being sub-let by a group of University of Michigan students, who naively thought that the earnest Jim Osterberg and his chums were a better prospect than their other applicants, 'a bunch of broads. But woe betide the day those frat dudes let us in,' enthuses Ron, "cause we totally destroyed the building.'

Forest Court was where the band's distinctive lifestyle evolved, summed up by Kathy Asheton as 'Crazed, pig-style, crazed bachelors, fun times.' Jim Osterberg was often recognisable as his wide-eyed, charming self, but equally often the entire band could be found slumped, stoned, in front of the TV until early in the morning, giggling at horror movies or rerun comedies. Slowly, they evolved, like cavemen, their own language. At first, after Jim had cleared out the basement, the three worked on developing their embryonic songs, but after incessant complaints from the neighbours about the noise, they found other diversions. Sometimes they would descend like a marauding tribe on family or neighbours, and denude their houses of everything edible. Frat parties around the campus were other useful venues for loot and pillage – the four could fill their stomachs and disappear with armfuls of drink before the hosts realised what was happening. Yet for all the squalor of their living quarters, the group boasted a certain glamour. 'They were pioneers – cool, special,' says Kathy Asheton. 'They got a lot of attention, they got the girls, they were cool guys, people wanted to be around them.'

Both Ron and Jim lost their virginity during that psychedelic period. Both were essentially well-brought-up Midwest boys and had delayed that fateful moment, but one friend of the band, Mary Reefer, was an older woman who was taken with Jim's wide-eyed charm. She embarked on a campaign to seduce Jim, and finally succeeded with such memorable results that young Osterberg rode his bike back to the band house in a kind of trance, utterly transported. So transported, in fact, that he cycled straight into the path of a car, bounced over its hood and then landed on his feet. He arrived back carrying his mangled bike, a beatific grin on his face.

By the end of their stay at Forest Court, acid had become the band's new obsession. The four had an older adviser on its use in the person of Ron Richardson, a handsome, slightly nervous, intellectual character, who taught in Ypsilanti's Sumpter Townships, and who had been the manager of the Chosen Few. Little by little he was persuaded to take on Jim and Ron's band. Ron boasted two vital qualifications: he owned an old Plymouth Washer Service van, and was involved in University of Michigan tests on LSD, and located a supply of the then-legal compound via a medical school acquaintance. Richardson took such a serious approach to his students' induction to acid that he required them to complete a rigorous reading list before they took their first trip. Soon, their collective psychedelic experiences became a vital part of the band's fraternal bonding. Ron, Scott and Jim went first; then later, Dave Alexander's induction into the band was formalised by a trip with Jim, during which they flashed on *The Wind In The Willows*, and realised that Dave was Rattie and that Jim was Toad.

Regular acid trips became a staple of the band's cultural diet, which also included Dave Alexander's books on the occult, the Mothers of Invention's *Freak Out*, Jimi Hendrix's *Are You Experienced?*, Pharoah Sanders' *Tauhid* albums, Dr John's album *Gris Gris*, and the constant background noise of late-night TV, including Ron's particular favourite, *The Three Stooges*. Ron was devoted to the comedy trio, whom he had gone to see at the Illinois State Fair as a child, and his own humour, whether dry, gonzo or black, defined the atmosphere of the band house. Ron claims it was he who that summer declared, 'We're like the Stooges, but we're psychedelic. Let call ourselves the Psychedelic Stooges!'

Around the rest of Ann Arbor there were ripples of interest stirred by what Jim Osterberg and Ron Asheton were cooking up – Jim's role in the Iguanas and the Prime Movers meant he was well

known in the musicians' community, and the extended gestation
period of his new project became a talking point. 'I bumped into
Jim in the middle of the summer and asked what he was doing. He
just said, practising!' says ex-bandmate Jim McLaughlin. 'He'd
been practising for six months, which was hilarious, 'cause I
couldn't remember him rehearsing for more than fifteen minutes
with us!' Other bands on the scene, like the Rationals, and the
SRC – a local supergroup formed by the alliance of Chosen Few
singer Scott Richardson with hit greaser band the Fugitives – were
intrigued, as were other local figures including Jeep Holland, who
by now managed both the Rationals and SRC, and the hottest new
partnership on the local scene, the MC5 and John Sinclair. The
toughest, highest-energy band to come out of Detroit, the MC5 had
realised they needed to hitch themselves to the hippie revolution
engulfing the US, so they joined up with Sinclair, Detroit's psychedelic guru, in August 1967. Together, they aimed to revolutionise
Detroit and the rest of the country with a manifesto based on loud
rock 'n' roll, dope, and fucking in the streets.

The Psychedelic Stooges boasted a hotline to the MC5 in the
form of Ron and Scott's sister, Kathy Asheton, who had attracted
the attentions of MC5 guitarist Fred 'Sonic' Smith; Wayne Kramer,
the MC5's leader, had known Jim from his Prime Movers days,
and at one point had considered enticing him into his own band.
Hence, when the Psychedelic Stooges decided to unveil the results
of their music experiments, it was natural that Sinclair and the '5
would be invited. And as 1967 rolled on, it was decided that All
Hallows Eve, which marked the onset of winter and the time when
spirits walked the earth, was a well-starred date. The buzz spread
around town for several weeks beforehand.

The chosen venue for the Psychedelic Stooges' public debut was
Ron Richardson's house on State Street, a short way out of the
centre of Ann Arbor proper. Richardson was responsible for overseeing the guest list, while his wife Nausika was assigned the task
of assisting with Jim's costume. After fighting with him over a
Victorian nightdress at an Ann Arbor thrift shop, Nausika admitted

Jim's need was greater; she spent several days cutting aluminium foil into strips and gluing them to a rubber bathing cap to make Jim a metallic silver wig. Influenced by American avant-garde composer Harry Partch, who specialised in bizarre home-made instruments, Jim spent much of his time stoned, looking in the garbage dump at the back of Ron's house for promising junk. Scott Asheton prepared for his public drumming debut by decorating his improvised drum kit, which was fashioned from oil cans rescued from the dump. He decorated his 'kit' with symbols that were the perfect metaphor for the Stooges' mix of high and low art. In bright colours he painted the om, the winged eye of Horus, and other spiritual symbols from Dave Alexander's books on Eastern mysticism, then wrote words like 'shit' and 'pussy' in ultraviolet paint that would only be visible under black lights.

October the thirty-first was a busy night on the hippie calendar, and many of those who attended the party were on their way to or from another celebration. Bill Kirchen, of the psychedelic band the Seventh Seal and later Commander Cody, perhaps best sums up the ambience when he points out that 'DMT was the dominant drug, that night especially. Of all the drugs I've ever done, that was definitely the one that most made you worry you'd done something permanent to your brain. You'd have to have someone hold the pipe for you and rest your head back on something so you wouldn't fall over when you did it, it was so gnarly.'

Dozens of people drifted in and out of the band's debut party; most of Ann Arbor's beautiful people were present, including John Sinclair and his friends Michael McLatchy and Jimmy Silver, Panther's friend Jesse Crawford, and the MC5's Rob Tyner. The room was festooned with tapestries, the aroma of pot hung heavy in the air, and the noise when it started was casual. Iggy sat cross-legged on the floor playing a Hawaiian guitar with every string tuned to E. Ron played his bass through a variety of effects boxes, while Scott maintained a basic Bo Diddley beat. Dave Alexander's role was restricted to twirling the amplifier dials, or smashing Ron's Kustom amplifier against its cabinet, sending reverberating roars echoing through the room – and surrounding neighbour-hood, for the volume at which they played was, everyone agrees, simply staggering: 'They were long instrumental pieces, and it must've been like being badly beaten to listen to them,' Iggy remin-isces fondly.

Bill Kirchen was unmoved by the spectacle ('I thought, this will never play'), but the people the band needed to impress, John Sinclair and crew, were convinced. 'I loved it, because it was out there, but in a rock 'n' roll context. Taking this sterile European avant-garde stuff and translating it into a thing kids can listen to,' remembers Sinclair, who was shaken – both literally and metaphor-ically – by the deafening sound levels in Ron Richardson's living room, and impressed by the variety of drugs circulating in the tiny audience. One of Sinclair's friends had brought a small carrier bag with nearly a hundred joints, all wrapped neatly and passed out freely among the party goers; everyone crammed into the kitchen was getting loaded on Freon propellant, spraying aerosols into bal-loons and then inhaling the contents, or getting high on amyl nitrate poppers. The disorientating mix of pharmaceuticals was exacerbated by the aural onslaught. Ron and Scott's rhythmic backdrop occasionally faltered as Ron's overloaded amp kept blowing fuses, while Iggy moved from the Hawaiian guitar to coax noises out of more improvised instruments, including a vacuum cleaner and the appropriately named Osterizer – a Waring blender half filled with water, into which he'd insert a microphone to pro-duce rippling white noise, like a waterfall, or a Theremin, the ethereal, spooky sci-fi instrument familiar from the Beach Boys' 'Good Vibrations'.

By the time Ron's amplifier finally gave up the ghost after its last fuse blew, many of the audience had fled, some of them, like Sinclair, in a psychotic state: 'I was paranoid I was so high, con-vinced they could hear this noise at the police station two miles down the road.' Instead, it was left to Brother J.C. Crawford – later best known for his hip preachers' intro to the MC5's *Kick Out The Jams* album – to close the performance, by announcing, 'This is a

magical night, the first night of Zenta New Year.' Despite his early
exit, John Sinclair was taken with the band. Iggy's charisma, even
the ex-drummer's dancing ability, made a real impression on
Detroit's foremost hippie visionary, but the MC5 guru also came
away with the conviction that the Psychedelic Stooges needed 'a bit
more insulation between them and the rest of the world'. He meant
the sound, but his remark could equally have applied to the band's
brittle egos.

Crazed, loud and drug-drenched, the Psychedelic Stooges' debut
performance was unsurprisingly regarded as memorable, and the
reaction was positive enough for the band to start planning their
next show. But this was not the music that would later be associated with the Stooges. By now Ann Arbor's alternative arts scene
was well established, and the Once Group – a loose collective of
avant-garde musicians, performers and film fans – had overcome
the suspicions of the University of Michigan and started to draw
like-minded intellectuals from around the US. The Stooges' out-
there experimentation and improvised instrumentation fitted
perfectly into this arty, intellectual niche. To most observers, Jim
Osterberg was an intellectual first, a rock 'n' roller second. Russ
Gibb, a high-school teacher who'd been inspired by Sinclair to open
the Grande Ballroom, the venue that nurtured both the MC5 and
the Stooges in their infancy, was introduced to Osterberg by Rob
Tyner and the MC5 that fall, and was instantly impressed with the
earnest, impassioned youth. 'The MC5 were working-class kids
from the industrial suburbs of Detroit. Iggy's dad was a teacher at
a beautiful high school, and he came from Ann Arbor, from a much
higher class status.'

  Gibb was a crucial connection, one of the main players in
Michigan's fast-moving rock scene. He was equally capable of getting what he wanted from stoned revolutionaries like John Sinclair
or straights like his bank manager, and like many people who
could charm the pants off others, he appreciated the skills of
another such operator. 'He was a charming man. Iggy played

second fiddle to the [MC] Five, deferred to them. But he was no one's fool.' According to Gibb, while he had some dealing with Psychedelic Stooges manager Ron Richardson, there was never any doubt it was Iggy who was running the show, and there was an open offer to the Stooges to play at the Grande whenever they felt ready.

Although Ron Richardson was a wise, intellectual character, he was also an unworldly one. He was christened 'the Mad Professor' by Ron Asheton's grandma, and was always tinkering with gadgets and attempting to repair things that simply couldn't be fixed. He was skilled at cramming knowledge into supposedly difficult kids in a poor part of Ypsilanti, but being 'camp counsellor' to the Psychedelic Stooges was a much tougher challenge. After Ron, Nausika and band moved to Toad Hall, a farmhouse on Vreeland Road out in Ypsilanti, Richardson made futile attempts to stem the neighbours' incessant complaints about the noise by gluing egg cartons to the wall. It seemed to Ron that the entire band expected to live off his teacher's salary, although Jim earned some cash waiting tables at the Virginian restaurant, while Ron Asheton worked at a local headshop, the Pigments of the Imagination, where he would spend much of his time stoned, looking on benevolently as the customers rifled the shop. Eventually, Richardson's tolerance became exhausted. One day when his and Nausika's food had disappeared from the refrigerator, he decided to cut off the heating until the perpetrator owned up, but he was subject to an amplified mutiny as Iggy picked up a microphone and led the others in a chant of 'We hate the Mad Professor'. 'They were sucking me dry,' the professor concluded, 'and I was beginning to freak out.' The confrontation did, however, have a profound musical implication, for Jim Osterberg would later claim that the band's heavily amplified chant was the first time the Stooges mastered an intense, threatening musical groove. This new discovery combined with the influence of Doors singer Jim Morrison, who had entranced Jim as he staggered around drunk for his show at the University of Michigan on 20 October 1967, howling like a gorilla and 'enraging the fratboys', says Jim. Morrison's antics and provocation of the audience convinced Jim that he too could be a singer, inspiring his move to fronting a more conventional line-up, with Ron switching to guitar and Dave Alexander playing bass.

For all his truculence, Jim Osterberg was smart enough to have already identified a successor to the Mad Professor, in the person of Jimmy Silver. A close friend of John Sinclair, Jimmy came from a talented Jewish intellectual family – his father served in the Johnson administration as Deputy Assistant Secretary for Health – and had come to Ann Arbor to enrol at the University of Michigan's School of Public Health. Jimmy had already been approached by Ron Richardson to assist with his troublesome charges and had declined. The band's singer, however, was much more persuasive. 'He sold it to me perfectly, that I would be part of this great mission.' Silver's first job was to inform his predecessor that his services were no longer required – and also to persuade him to let the Psychedelic Stooges retain the use of his Plymouth Washer Service van. Happy to be relieved of his burden, the professor readily agreed.

Intelligent, forceful and charismatic, Jimmy Silver, aided by his wife Susan, proved the ideal person to steer the Psychedelic Stooges. He was a paternal figure who could impose some degree of organisation. He could negotiate their always complex relations with what became their 'big brother' band, the MC5, and sweet-talk often reluctant local promoters into booking his charges. He even ministered to their nutritional needs, improving their health with a macrobiotic diet which he and Susan had researched. But it was still a tough job – 'Like herding cats,' he recalls. 'They were completely immature in most ways. Then they could drink alcohol and take drugs and get even further over the wall.'

Jim was both a leader and a follower to his bandmates. He learned from his fellow Stooges, and frequently, as in the episode with Bob Koester, set out to outdo them, to validate his membership of their gang. Hence he was quite capable of being, as Jimmy Silver observes, 'a wilful and destructive child'. But in quiet moments – particularly during the occasional weeks when Jimmy and Susan would wean him off drugs and alcohol and nurture him on a macrobiotic diet to eliminate his asthma – he demonstrated the preternatural insight he'd demonstrated at school. 'One of those days when we were looking after him I realised what a brilliant, analytical mind he had. He had an ability to identify what attracted people – and what would make them want to do what he needed or wanted.' After some months, Silver realised that in some respects he was the one being managed; that Jim would set aside 'quality time' to nurture their relationship, to bond with Silver, 'or allow me to feel like I was bonding with him'. Yet Jim did it in such an honest, open fashion that it never felt calculating or manipulative. Only in retrospect did Silver realise how Jim had managed to entice him into managing the Psychedelic Stooges by offering him the chance to be a part of something bigger than himself – intuitively, he'd worked out what was the driving force of Silver's life.

From early in 1968, Jimmy and Susan lived with the Psychedelic Stooges at close quarters, moving in with them to what would become the fabled Fun House, a large wood-framed farmhouse at 2666 Packard, some way out of Ann Arbor toward Ypsilanti, which had been spotted by Ann Asheton. The farmhouse was up for rent at a bargain price because it was due to be demolished to make way for a highway (in forthcoming years its owner, Farmer Baylis, aka the Bear, would drive over and mournfully survey its increasingly decrepit condition). It would become the seat of the Stooges empire, and was christened Stooge Hall, or the Fun House. The name was appropriate, for it was a location that local girls and boys couldn't wait to visit – although the girls in particular faced the prospect of being chased round the farmhouse in complete darkness to the music of Harry Partch, a fiendish sensory-deprivation technique that today would doubtless qualify as cruel and inhuman treatment.

In those early months, the Psychedelic Stooges worked fitfully, spending perhaps half an hour in the evening rehearsing at mind-boggling volume. Jimmy Silver, who heard all their practice sessions, observed that they possessed a surprising musical sophistication, demonstrated by their brilliant pastiches of their Ann Arbor rivals: 'They could perfectly mimic the style of bands like Bob Seger, the Rationals, Ted Nugent – but they sounded even better than those bands could sound themselves in their own style!' Silver thought this surplus material could become a lucrative sideline, and tried to persuade them to demo their material for other bands to record, but his suggestions were rejected. Instead, Jim and Ron concentrated on developing music that bore no relation to any existing style, music that existed on a completely unconscious, unmediated level, unrestricted by conventional structure. It would be the perfect collision of highbrow and gonzo. Jim drew on all the avant-garde precedents he'd learned about from Bob Sheff, while Ron and Scott drew on their honest, rock 'n' roll dumb aggression. Yet that interaction was rendered more complex because, as Jim points out, 'Ron has an elegance as an instrumentalist and a writer that I lack.' Although in later years there would be disputes about who had written what in the Stooges, with Iggy Pop claiming to have written every single note of the music, it's clear that most of the early songs derived from Ron's ideas and riffs. Asheton's guitar style was simple, its intelligent minimalism and intense delivery heavily influenced by the ultraviolet guitar assault he'd seen Pete Townshend unleash back in London. But sculpting songs out of the chaos of ideas was a slow process. As Jimmy Silver recalls, the band's musical stamina was such that even rehearsing for more than forty-five minutes was a strain, 'and they couldn't physically play for more than fifteen minutes, twenty at the most'.

Although the band usually recall their first professional show as opening for Blood Sweat and Tears at the Grande Ballroom on 3 March 1968, their debut in fact was on 20 January, replacing the Amboy Dukes on a bill headlined by Scott Richardson's new band, Scott Richard Case. The hippie kids and heads attending that evening could have had no clue what was about to hit them.

For the first Grande dates, Jim Osterberg finally left the

Hawaiian guitar at home and made his debut as a frontman. Jim himself describes those early performances as being naive, heavily derivative of his heroes Mick Jagger and Jim Morrison: 'Jim Morrison and Mick Jagger, that's who I wanted to be. In fact, it was so obvious that they should have called me Mick Morrison!' But Jim Morrison never appeared on stage in a white Victorian night-dress, wearing a home-made metallic silver wig and white make-up, towing a vacuum cleaner in his wake. Indeed, the Psychedelic Stooges looked so ludicrous that on the 45-minute drive to the gig, according to Ron Asheton, several rednecks attempted to run them off the highway, while the security guard at the Grande took one look at Iggy, bedecked in his aluminium finery, and asked, 'What *is* that? Some kind of mechanical man?'

Once at the venue, owner Russ Gibb was nonplussed by the singer's costume ('He looked like the tin man in *The Wizard of Oz*'), and listened patiently as Jim Osterberg explained the practical dif-ficulties of amplifying 'the Osterizer', which Russ thought was some kind of toilet bowl. Open-minded and enthusiastic, always ready to indulge anything that 'the kids' might go for, Russ came out of his office to watch the band open their set. He found it thrilling. Based around high-energy rock 'n' roll in the vein of the Who, Hendrix – or, indeed, the MC5 – this was way more freeform. Iggy would sing into the vacuum cleaner, vocalising lines that were then picked up by Ron and Dave in long, repetitive loping riffs, while Scott Asheton kept up a Bo Diddley-influenced tribal beat, bashed out on 55-gallon oil cans, augmented with a set of timbales and battered cymbals.

The 'heads', like John Sinclair – and even the 'greedheads', as Sinclair half affectionately described Russ Gibb – were entranced. 'Shamanistic is the word to use about Iggy's performance,' says Sinclair. 'People talk about Jim Morrison being shamanistic but this was much farther out.' The MC5, most of whom were in attend-ance, thought the performance was 'simply amazing', says Becky Tyner, girlfriend and later wife of MC5 singer Rob Tyner. The 'kids', however, were less convinced. Over the next few months, Iggy would become familiar with the sensation of watching the audience frozen in horror, their only discernible reaction being to laugh, or leave. Russ met one of the first of them, a young girl who went into his office later that evening to ask what the hell he was doing booking someone so 'weird! He was a little too alternative for those suburban kids,' he explains. 'I guess the closest she'd ever got to something exciting was a Doris Day movie.' Fatefully, while the crowd was unmoved, a local reporter, Steve Silverman, named the Stooges as the most exciting thing to be seen at the Grande, while he damned the slick, covers-based Scott Richard Case with faint praise. The Stooges, as Silverman termed them in their first published review, 'played electronic music which utilized controlled feedback, wah wah, slide guitar and droned bass as well as scat-like singing and neo-primitive howling'.

Over the next few weeks, the Stooges returned to the Grande again and again, supporting Blood Sweat and Tears, Sly Stone and Junior Wells. Most often, though, they shared the bill with the MC5, who were already capable of drawing 800-strong crowds to the old Victorian ballroom, and became champions of what they called 'our little brother band'. The messianistic fervour that John Sinclair had built up around the MC5 organisation, with which Jimmy Silver and his charges were informally allied, was infectious, particularly for musicians who, says Silver, 'saw themselves as stars from day one' – and who were also, for much of the time, high on dope or acid.

But acid could be a cruel mistress as well as a beneficent one, and there is no better illustration of its highs and lows than 21 April 1968, a day that marked the completion of Jim Osterberg's twenty-first year on the planet; a day that harboured a beatifically good trip for the Stooges' guitarist, and a devastatingly bad one for its singer.

Ron Asheton remembers that day for its windy, sunny afternoon, when he flew a kite with a beautiful girl, both of them gently high on acid and seeing faces in the clouds. That afternoon he lost his virginity, and as he and his lover basked in their psychedelic high back at the Fun House, they listened to the Byrds' new album,

The Notorious Byrd Brothers. The gentle whimsy of songs like 'Goin' Back' or 'Dolphin Smile' was perfectly fitted for the faultless afternoon, and a day so unspoilt that Ron would never take acid again, for he knew no future trip could ever live up to that one.

But not every song on that Byrds album was so distinguished; one of its least successful tracks was 'Tribal Gathering', a forgettable piece of hippie indulgence in 5/4 time, heavily influenced by Dave Brubeck's 'Take Five'. The song meanders along, aimlessly, until one minute in the musicians seemingly get bored and switch beat and mood to play a tough, simplistic two-note riff for eight bars. This fragment of an otherwise forgettable tune would lodge in Ron's psychedelicised mind.

The evening looked as promising as the afternoon, for the band were playing again at the Grande, supporting the James Gang, on a bill that had originally featured Cream. As with all their performances so far, the band had planned a completely new set for the occasion, while Jim Osterberg had cadged a lift to the venue earlier that week to bring in a five-foot-tall oil-storage tank which Jimmy Silver was delegated to 'play', and place it in front of the stage. To celebrate the event, Iggy decided to drop two hits of Owsley Orange Sunshine. But as the band launched into their set, they discovered that instead of the expected all-conquering roar of sound emanating from their Marshall amplifiers, a problem with the power hook-up reduced the output to a pathetic weedy murmur: 'It was like the aural equivalent of erectile dysfunction,' says the singer with a shudder. As the opening number faltered to a premature halt, the band decided to stop the set until they could get the amplifiers back to full power. Growing increasingly restless, the crowd started to chant, 'We want the Cream! We want the Cream!'

Deciding to confront the audience, Iggy climbed to the top of the huge oil-storage tank and posed, like a renaissance statue on a massive plinth, 'just to be a lightning rod for this hatred', as the crowd's chanting grew louder and more aggressive. Finally the Marshall amplifiers spluttered back to life, and the band resumed the show.

'But it was not a good set,' says Iggy, who, despite his initial bravado, found the crowd's hostility profoundly disturbing, particularly in his 'sensitive' hallucinatory state.

Grief-stricken, he returned to Ann Arbor to stay overnight with Dave Alexander and his parents, but even the birthday treat of a cheeseburger with a candle plonked on top couldn't erase his sense of failure. 'And if ever I was going to give up, that would be the time. I was not encouraged.'

This was the point where a sensitive hippie would have given up. But Jim Osterberg was not a sensitive hippie. He was the boy most likely to, and he would face down this hatred.

But how do you confront hatred?

Jim Osterberg says he reacted by becoming 'more brazen. So they could bill me as The Guy You Love To Hate.'

Jimmy Silver says that Jim Osterberg built up a kind of psychic armour. 'He had to. Because there were all those people that hated him. Plus there was the potential [of them] physically attacking him.'

Cub Koda, fellow musician and fan, observed that 'the audience's rejection of that pop art performance brought out the meanness in him – made him go out and physically provoke the audience into responding, one way or another'.

Kathy Asheton, friend and later lover, points out that 'He knew the viciousness of people. And it's hard not to build an attitude after a while. He did not set out for shock value, it just naturally happened.'

This new man, brazen, indestructible, mean, confrontational, was Iggy Stooge.

The idea of an alter ego that takes on a life of its own reaches back through time, was formalised in nineteenth-century gothic fiction, and reached new popularity in the postwar America that nurtured Jim Osterberg, the boy who dreamt of being the Atomic Brain. For a twenty-year-old performer confronting a hostile audience, being able to call on a superhuman alter ego might enable survival. But as we know from countless cheesy horror movies, alter egos can get out of control.

Over the coming years, those people who were close to Jim Osterberg mostly came to respect Iggy Pop, as he would later rename himself. They'd enjoy sharing a stage with Iggy, or going for a meal with Jim (heaven help anyone who got the combination the wrong way round). They'd learn to forgive behaviour from Iggy that would simply be unforgivable from his charming creator. Ultimately, Jim Osterberg created what many people regard as the greatest rock 'n' roll frontman ever to command a stage. But this Iggy creation would subsequently become the focus of all the attention on the Stooges and, ultimately, the morality of the cheesy horror movie could not be ignored. As Ron Asheton puts it, 'It was an act for a long time: sincere, wholesome emotions that made him be Iggy. Then it spilled over. To where he could not separate the performance from his real life.'

As Iggy, once a term of abuse, became an official stage name, it was obvious that this superhero needed his own costume. Inspiration came, according to Jim, when he was engaged in his own research in the undergraduate library of the University of Michigan, which he'd still occasionally visit: 'I was looking at a book on Egyptian antiquity. And [I realised] the Pharaohs never wore a shirt. And I thought, gee, there's something about that!'

Of course, for any casual observer, the notion that the Wild Man of Michigan rock found inspiration for his outfit in a tome on tribal anthropology seems ludicrous. But it's true, as Psychedelic Stooges roadie Roy Seeger testifies: 'We'd often get together and smoke some weed while Jim would tell us about anthropology, and how ancient people were. He was fascinated in how the human race was when we were real primitive, closer to the animal kingdom and nature. And he did definitely use that in his music.'

Performing stripped to the waist obviously fitted the Psychedelic Stooges' primal ethos, but Jim also decided to opt for something more spectacular in the trouser department, inspired primarily by the flamboyant stage gear of the MC5. In early 1968, the Stooges were regular overnight visitors to the MC5 and Artist Workshop offices overlooking Detroit's John C Lodge Freeway, and often 'babysat' the MC5's wives and girlfriends, who lived in fear of some of the heavy local characters who'd previously broken into the building. Becky Tyner and Chris Hovnanina, the partners of Rob Tyner and Wayne Kramer, had become expert costume designers working for the '5, and Becky volunteered to make a pair of stage pants for Jim in cheap, leather-look PVC. The pants were tailored, via trial and error, to fit Jim's 'wonderful body', says Becky. The eventual hip-hugging design they decided on was 'very, very low – the top of them just came to his pubic-hair line. And they were very, very tight.'

Purpose-built stage clothes seemed perfectly appropriate for the moment when the Psychedelic Stooges were expanding out of the Grande Ballroom into the small clubs scattered around the tiny rural and industrial towns of Michigan. One such club, Mothers, had been launched in Romeo, Michigan during the summer of 1968 by Luke Engel, and on a visit to Ann Arbor, Luke dropped in to see Jeep Holland, who by now was operating his A2 (aka A-squared) agency out of an office, rather than a payphone. Despite not having high hopes for the Psychedelic Stooges after seeing an early 'rehearsal', Jeep was helping them out with bookings, and on this day Jimmy Silver happened to be in the office. After nearly an hour of sweet-talking, Engel was convinced by Silver's blandishments to book the Psychedelic Stooges as support act to the Jagged Edge, on 11 August 1968.

After the band arrived for the evening's performance in roadie Roy Seeger's Pontiac station wagon, Engel had a pleasant chat with an alert, soft-spoken 'little guy in low-cut pants', but as the band started up playing their elemental music he was surprised to see the youth, who he'd assumed was a roadie, walk up to the microphone and sing into it – only to grimace, as no sound came out of the PA system. Disgusted, he tossed the offending mike onto the stage, then watched the Jagged Edge's roadie walk on and retrieve it, switch it to the 'On' position, then leave the stage. A slightly chagrined Iggy resumed the performance, dancing in a 'demented' fashion before confronting the indifferent crowd. 'He jumped off the stage, began approaching girls and humping them, much as a large dog might have!' recounts Engel, who remembers with delight how the local farmboys stood stock-still, their fight-or-flight instinct hopelessly confused. Soon the crowd was transfixed by this 'seemingly psychotic little person'.

By now Iggy had stripped off his shirt, then he suddenly twisted into a trademark move, arching himself backwards into a seemingly impossible contortion. And at the very last degree of the arc, his PVC pants, stretched beyond their limits, popped down and Iggy's penis made the first of its many public appearances. 'The club was buzzing with concern and confusion,' says Engel, 'and the two off-duty sheriffs who provided my security were making haste towards me as I ran to find Jimmy Silver and tell him he had to pull the band!'

Within moments the club was swarming with cops, all of them alerted, believes Engel, by a rival club owner, and the now naked Iggy fled out of the back door, accompanied by roadie Roy Seeger. As local and state police rushed around, Jimmy Silver located the superior officer and, using his considerable powers of persuasion, negotiated a deal that guaranteed his charge wouldn't be beaten up by the irate cops, who were convinced they'd busted some kind of perverted homosexual strip joint. Deal concluded, Iggy was persuaded out of his hiding place in the back of Seeger's station wagon, and admitted into police custody.

As neither band nor manager had enough cash to bail out the unfortunate singer, Jimmy Silver was forced to summon James Osterberg Senior for assistance. Mr Osterberg arrived the next morning to stand bail for his son. With commendable promptness, the case was heard the following morning by Justice Shocke, who fined the offender $41, with $9 costs. Osterberg Senior paid the fine, and seemed remarkably good-humoured about the escapade, once Jim Junior offered to take him out for a round of golf at Pat's Par Three.

The notorious gig was the subject of one of the band's first press reports, making the front page of the Romeo *Observer*. Sadly, its PR value was limited, as the newspaper described James Osterberg as a 'dancer and entertainer', making it appear the cops had managed to close down some lewd homosexual strip club. The infamy Luke Engel attracted for hosting this display inspired the club owner to pull his lease the next day, and the aspiring promoter left town soon afterwards.

Because of – rather than despite – such displays, the Psychedelic Stooges started to attract a hard core of fans, most of them, according to Jim, 'high school and junior high kids who either were bad – or wanted to be. Plus a few of the more musically informed people.' Those groups epitomised the polarity of the Psychedelic Stooges' appeal, for the music was brutal and anti-intellectual, while the spectacle itself was theatrical and confrontational. Dave Marsh, later a celebrated writer for *Creem*, and one of the Stooges' main supporters, saw a performance at the University of Michigan in Dearborn where a 'straight-looking, fraternity couple got up to leave and were confronted by the singer: he begins to do this routine haranguing them, getting right in their faces – which resolved into a song called "Goodbye Bozos".' The confrontation was thrilling, 'deeply theatrical' and anticipated a controversial play, *Dionysus 1969*, later filmed by Brian De Palma, which experimented with similar psycho-dramatics, confrontation and nudity. However, the Stooges didn't look as if they were acting, and the brutal monotonous riffing added to the sense of danger. When it didn't fall apart, that is, because for the few local musicians who actually enjoyed the music, the Psychedelic Stooges' semi-competence was an intrinsic part of their appeal. Embryonic songs, like 'Asthma Attack', had memorable riffs but no worked-out endings, and would often simply fall apart. Crowds might be treated to the sight of Iggy and Scott Asheton having an argument mid-song about a drum pattern that would culminate in Iggy taking up the sticks and showing a scowling Scott what to play. Or they might watch Iggy incense the crowd by simply lying on his back as yet another song ground to a halt, and crooning an a cappella rendition of 'Shadow Of Your Smile'.

Brownsville Station's Cub Koda shared many concert bills with the Stooges, and remembers, delightedly, how: 'A lot of the bands like Ted Nugent or the Frost, who thought they were superior, didn't like sharing a bill with the Stooges. With us it was: Great, it's the Stooges, what's gonna happen? 'Cause they could do twenty minutes and be brilliant, then all of a sudden the set would go to hell in a handcart. All the stuff that happens on the *Metallic KO* record, even though it's a different band, was what those perform-ances were like – 'cause they could really fall apart in mid-song. And because you had a leader who was no leader, who was a leader of chaos, the band would just stand there looking at their shoes waiting for their next piece of direction.'

For all the chaos, for all the ridicule, the Stooges, four Midwest nobodies with huge egos, entertained no self-doubt. They had cast their fates to the wind, they said, and they would see where it would take them, outcasts against a world they considered shallow and banal. Jim Osterberg, the schoolboy politician, was perhaps the only Stooge who could have lived in this outside world. But according to his confidant, Jimmy Silver, rejoining that would require him 'putting on a face he no longer wanted to bother with. He had made this decision to play this music. That's what he was. That's what drove him. That's what called him.' And there was no going back.

Nowadays, when the late 1960s Detroit scene is revered as a hotbed of tough garage rock, it's easy to forget the hippie evangelism that nurtured the Stooges. Perhaps the most effective reminder is John Sinclair, at the time a high priest of the Detroit arts scene, and today a tubby, avuncular DJ in New Orleans.

Sinclair's greatest fame came when he was adopted as a cause célèbre by John Lennon when the authorities gave him 'ten for two': ten years' jail for two joints of marijuana. Sinclair was victimised for his establishment of the White Panther Party, whose claimed exploits included blowing up a CIA building in Detroit. Grey-haired, with a hip hoarse-voiced jazz jive in the style of Dr John, today Sinclair looks like a cross between a dress-down Santa Claus and one of the lazy hippies from Gilbert Shelton's Fat Freddy's Cat cartoon. In the daytime, he makes a living via his oldies show on New Orleans public radio. At home, he sits late into the evening playing rare old vinyl records by Albert Ayler or Charley Patton.

He's an engaging, smart, inspiring raconteur, but as our conversations continue over several drawn-out, generous New Orleans lunches of catfish and okra, it becomes increasingly obvious why Amerika was never consumed by revolution. For all his charm, he's a self-absorbed, unworldly figure, overflowing with ideas but always complaining he's out of cash.

Sinclair was a crucial influence on the young Jim Osterberg, putting him in contact with Elektra records, tutoring him in free jazz and helping the Stooges score their Marshall stacks. But he was the making of the Stooges in a more crucial way, too. By encouraging their art-rock experiments, he unwittingly engineered their rejection by Michigan's unheeding, untutored audiences. What started out as an optimistic, avant-garde hippie experiment would become something altogether darker and ultimately confrontational. This confrontation would have a profound, painful effect on Iggy and his Stooges. But it would also make for some great music.

CHAPTER 4

Oh My, Boo Hoo

'It was Sunday, the twenty-second September, when I heard the Stooges. I know that was the weekend because it's my parents' anniversary. I stopped in the doorway and did a mesmerisation moment. What is this? You don't get too many moments like that in your life. Some movies, some passages of books, like *Catcher in the Rye*. You live for moments like that. Well I do. And this was one of them.'

An engaging, flirtatiously energetic character with a mordant sense of humour, Danny Fields has occasionally been described as Jim Osterberg's brother, and more consistently been credited as Iggy Pop's discoverer. The man who finally exposed the Stooges to New York, and ultimately to a worldwide audience, the maverick who championed revolutionary music that no one else could comprehend, he would be rewarded for his crucial contributions with ingratitude, endless early morning phone calls and huge credit-card bills. Despite the fact that, in the main, his greatest protégés caused him nothing but trouble, the visionary who helped them record their most radical albums recounts their story with grace and wit. And a lot of sex, drugs and revolutionary mantras.

In the mid-1960s it was compulsory for any record label to

recruit a 'company freak' – a hippie who knew what was down with the kids and could help the label make money out of them. Elektra Records founder Jac Holzman was hugely interested in recorded sound, had established his label recording folkies like Phil Ochs and repackaging European music, but hit gold-dirt when he happened on Danny Fields, who established his credentials in grandstanding style in 1967 when he insisted that the Doors' 'Light My Fire' should be the band's breakthrough single. Unfortunately for Fields' career with the label, those credentials would be comprehensively shredded by his involvement with the Stooges, and confrontations with Elektra's management.

It was John Sinclair's messianic zeal that inspired the MC5 and Stooges' hook-up with Elektra. After a couple of years of intimidation by the police and other rednecks, Sinclair and the MC5 moved from Detroit to the far less repressive bohemian enclave of Ann Arbor, where they set up their organisation at 1510 and 1520 Hill Street around May 1968. Together with John's brother David, who managed the Up, and Jimmy Silver, they established Trans Love Energies, a loose management cooperative. Sinclair issued endless press releases and manifestos from his sprawling Victorian headquarters, and eventually piqued the interest of DJs and music writers Dennis Frawley and Bob Rudnick, who hosted the Kocaine Karma radio show on the pioneering independent radio station WFMU in New Jersey. When Sinclair dropped off a copy of the MC5 single 'Looking At You/Borderline' in the summer of 1968, the two put it on heavy rotation. One of the first people to notice it was another head and fellow WFMU presenter: Elektra's Danny Fields. Enthused both by the single and by Sinclair's radical polemics, Fields flew to Detroit to see the MC5 at the Grande on Saturday 21 September, 1968. He thought they were 'terrific . . . very show business' and agreed to sign the band to Elektra, convinced the act would be a huge money-spinner.

Only when Fields was in Detroit did Sinclair and Wayne Kramer mention their 'little brother band', the Psychedelic Stooges. 'The Stooges weren't something you could send a promo kit out on,' says Sinclair. 'Sending out a demo tape would be like sending them a vacuum cleaner, there was no way you could understand what the Stooges were like without seeing them in performance.' The Stooges played on an all Trans Love bill, featuring the Up and the '5, the next afternoon, at the university's union ballroom. 'It was twenty minutes of brilliant shit,' says Sinclair. 'And once Danny saw the Ig, he understood. He was gone.'

'I didn't know their songs, I couldn't recognise any intro or chord thing or anything,' says Fields. 'It was all pretty free form. I loved the sound. It was like Beethoven finally got here, or Wagner. It was so solid and so modern and so non-blues. How long did it take me to recognise this was something special? Five seconds.'

Immediately after the performance, Fields walked into the tiny dressing room, which was crammed with stacked-up chairs, and proclaimed, 'You're a star!' to Jim Osterberg. The singer's reaction was that Fields 'just wanted to pick me up'. (Fields is obviously and very openly gay.) Ron Asheton's reaction was, 'Who is this asshole?'

It was only after Fields spoke to Jimmy Silver that the band realised that this interloper was the Elektra Head of Promotions, and represented their shot at the big time. But the misunderstanding was fateful, for it helped plant the idea that Fields' excitement was inspired by the Stooges' singer, and not their music. That idea, Fields insists, is a fallacy: 'It was the music I liked more than his charisma or him.' Nonetheless, relations between Elektra and the Stooges would subsequently hinge on the relationship between Danny Fields and Jim Osterberg and Iggy Pop. And as Iggy Pop was drawn into Danny's extravagant milieu, the Ashetons would be left to glower, resentfully, from the sidelines.

Fields had gone to Ann Arbor with the specific intent of signing the MC5, and had discussed the size of advance with Sinclair on the Saturday night. On Monday, Fields called Holzman, and told him that not only were the MC5 all he'd hoped, but that he had another band he wanted to sign too. According to Fields, Holzman replied, 'See if you can sign the big group for twenty thousand dollars and the little group for five.'

Silver and his charges were not in the least fazed by being offered a deal so early in their career. 'My expectations were so unrealistic that it didn't seem that out-there. The boys did feel like second-class citizens about the size of the advance – but they had a We'll Show Everybody attitude anyway.'

Although Sinclair announced in *5th Estate* magazine that both bands signed to Elektra on the next Thursday, there was no signing of any paperwork until Elektra founder Jac Holzman and Vice President Bill Harvey saw both bands for themselves the following weekend at the Fifth Dimension, a hip club built in what had been a bowling alley. According to Jim, in the intervening week he'd become so nervous about the audition that he was bedridden with asthma, hence the Stooges wrote two songs 'specially for that show': 'I'm Sick' and 'Asthma Attack'. 'We played these two songs, I [just] flopped around on stage, and we got the deal,' says Jim. 'They just thought, well they're crazy, people want crazy things, and maybe this guy has some sort of charisma or something, so let's sign him.'

According to Fields, Holzman and Harvey were 'completely stupefied by the Stooges. The MC5 they could [understand] because it was a more conventional, traditional approach to rock 'n' roll.'

Holzman himself readily admits that he signed the Stooges to humour his Head of Promotions. 'Danny was very high on the Stooges, and I just said yes. I have always liked things that were odd but interesting, and they certainly fit that bill. But yes, the Stooges were an afterthought for Elektra.' Holzman was an intelligent but relatively unassuming man, who for a record-company boss was remarkably young and hip; he dressed in slacks and polo-neck sweaters but never patronised his artists by pretending to be 'down with the kids' – he left that to company freaks like Danny. Elektra's deal with the band was concluded on 4 October 1968. On the contract, they were simply titled 'the Stooges', although the

'Psychedelic' tag remained on the band's stationery and posters for another month or so. 'I think Jac Holzman told us the kids wouldn't think the word was hip any more!' laughs Jimmy Silver.

The Elektra signing inspired a whirlwind of activity for the MC5's organisation; the MC5 recorded their debut album live at the Grande on 30 and 31, while early in November Sinclair announced the formation of the White Panther Party – a white counterpart to Huey Newton's Black Panthers. Meanwhile, according to Jimmy Silver, his own charges proceeded in a rather more sedate fashion. 'They were pretty lax. They spent a lot of time thinking about stuff and talking to each other. In terms of what they could have been doing to perfect their ability to present what they wanted to present, I felt like they were, I won't use the word lazy . . . I felt they were shortchanging themselves.'

Silver kept the band's live regime light, worried they would tire themselves out, while rehearsals were always limited to just twenty minutes per night, invariably conducted at mind-boggling volume. Instead, the focus was on building a band mentality, establishing a shared vocabulary of 'in' words and developing the 'O-Mind' – best described as the collective band vibe (or drug stupor) and soon Stooges slang for anything that was tolerable. Jimmy and Susan Silver, tolerant and well balanced as they were, found the O-Mind occasionally disturbing. 'People who work in hospitals will tell you about the full moon, which is the time when all the crazy stuff happens. And I could relate to that. Soon I could see every full moon, they would want what they called "the hat trick – narc, 'tutes and 'cohol" – drugs, girls and alcohol. And as it came round, like the tides, they'd want money so they could score dope and everything else. It did kinda freak me out. Ultimately it *totally* freaked me out . . . They were four corky guys.'

Quite often Jim Osterberg was totally lucid, and would explain that the slow pace of activity was optimum, or at least as much as his comrades could sustain – that pushing them harder would ensure everything fell apart. But Jim could be every bit as slothful and irrational as his peers, and his intake of weed in particular exacerbated his asthma to the point it sometimes became Jimmy and Susan's primary concern; they nursed him on a macrobiotic diet, medicating his asthma with lotus-root tea, and wrote updates to Danny Fields, delaying the album sessions until he returned to health.

With the first small advance cheque banked, life was comparatively cushy at the Fun House; the living quarters were now well established, with Jim ensconced in the attic, Jimmy, Susan and new baby Rachel (aka Bunchie) in a self-contained apartment on the top floor, while Scott had a room nearby; Ron and Dave lived on the ground floor, handily close to the communal TV room, which was decorated with posters of Malcolm X, Eldridge Cleaver, Brian Jones, Elvis Presley and Adolf Hitler, plus an ad for Ron's old band, the Chosen Few.

In the autumn, a new resident took over the basement of the Fun House: John Adams, a friend of Jimmy Silver's from the University of Illinois. Adams came from a wealthy Chicago family who'd made their money in the railroads; he was a fan of Damon Runyon, fancied himself as an ace pool hustler and had a fascination with the underworld. 'It's like Conrad said in *Heart of Darkness* – the fascination of the abomination – and John was really into that,' says Jimmy Silver. Silver discovered Adams had acquired a heroin habit since they were fellow students, but had subsequently kicked it. His friend was 'tremendously intelligent, tremendously loyal and willing to work hard', and so the band offered him a refuge and a job as a roadie. Once established with the band, he grew out his wiry red hair, which bounced up and down over his ears and gained him the nickname Flaps. 'But he had the most nicknames of anyone I ever knew,' points out Bill Cheatham, who joined as roadie shortly afterwards. 'We also called him the Hippie Gangster, Nickels, Peanut, the Sphinx, Goldie and the Fellow.' By now, Jim too had gained an additional nickname – Scott, Ron and Dave had christened him 'Pop' (none of his fellow Stooges ever called him Iggy, except when referring to his live performances). The name came after Jim shaved his eyebrows, and was therefore reckoned to look like an Ann Arbor character called Jim Popp, whose hair had fallen out. But for professional purposes Jim was usually titled Iggy Stooge.

In comparison to his charges, Fields was frenetically busy, overseeing the mechanics of recording the MC5, and also investigating a producer for the Stooges' first album. Soon Fields thought of John Cale, who had just contributed a stunning sequence of arrangements to *The Marble Index* by his fellow Velvet Underground refugee, Nico. With his intimate knowledge of the avant garde and high-volume amplified rock 'n' roll, he seemed like the perfect choice, so Fields called and invited him to the MC5's recording date at the Grande. A few days later, Cale was in Detroit, watching both bands.

'I *hated* the MC5!' he emphasises today, in his rich Welsh tones. 'Heartily! Not because they were conventional rock 'n' roll but because of the violence. It was like a Nuremberg rally! I was like, holy shit, the fuckin' Nazis are alive and well.' The support act was a different matter: 'Here was this spindly little guy in the middle, a tremendous sense of humour, and it was really delicate, but aggressive – and self-parodying, in a happy kind of way!'

Fields' confidence that Cale would 'get it' was vindicated. But while the tall, authoritative adopted New Yorker 'got' the music, the Stooges' lifestyle was a shock. Visiting Ann Arbor to discuss the project, he took a look around the Fun House and opened the refrigerator to see 'dozens of bottles of Bud. And no food. I said, what do you fuckin' eat? Iggy said, Whatever, you know.' Cale was taken with the band's proto-slacker attitude; the Ann Arbor outfit were similarly impressed by his intellectual demeanour and the fact he wore black bikini briefs and drank wine, both of which seemed to embody his urban sophistication. 'He was this commanding, intellectually strong person – but also a whack job,' says Silver. 'He was married to [the designer] Betsey Johnson but would chase girls around, he was into drugs and drink but could take it or leave it, it didn't seem to make any difference.' As a 'whack job',

Cale recognised a kindred spirit in the young singer, notably when he picked up the lap steel that had featured in the Stooges' Halloween Night party debut, and realised that all six strings were tuned to one note – a technique the Velvets had experimented with on an early song, 'The Ostrich'. Informed by its owner that he would play the instrument while high, plugging it into a huge bank of Marshall amplifiers, the dark lord of the New York avant garde thought, 'It must have sounded horrendous!' Simultaneously, he concluded, 'Man, this is in the raw. Let's go!'

John Cale and Danny Fields' enthusiasm for the Stooges would help make them the darlings of New York's hip society, and a couple of weeks after Cale's visit to Ann Arbor, the band flew to New York, where Danny Fields introduced them to the city's cornucopia of delights. They took in all of Fields' hangouts: Andy Warhol's Factory, Steve Paul's The Scene nightclub and Max's Kansas City, the haunt of various Warhol acolytes and, it seemed, just about anyone of sophisticated artistic sensibilities and exotic sexual predilections. According to Danny, however, Iggy needed little introduction. 'He was born sophisticated and confident. He was a star before he was a star. He was Iggy. By that time he was already famous in the backroom of Max's.' Iggy moved with ease through Max's various factions, the most crucial of which were the Drellas – the nickname for the Warhol crowd. The Miseries were 'all these thin pregnant women in black, who always looked unhappy,' says Fields; the Bananas were gay Cuban exiles. 'The Phoebes were the busboys,' says Danny; 'I called myself Phoebe'; and then there were inevitably intriguing characters of indeterminate gender and orientation from John Vaccaro and Charles Ludlam's Play House of the Ridiculous set. Not that Ron and Scott were impressed, says Ron: 'Being Midwest naive people, we never fell for that bullshit, man, it's supposed to be great that you are some scumball, or some derelict, so Iggy and Scottie and myself are always like, fuck that.'

The Scene, the club run by Steve Paul – a canny, frighteningly smart friend of Danny Fields, invariably dressed in blue – was the other main hip location, and it was there that Jim met Nico, the

Germanic icemaiden, whose recent album had attracted critical plaudits, but only marginal sales. Before long, says John Cale, 'Nico was in love with Iggy. For Jim Morrison reasons. As usual.' The pair, with their disparate backgrounds, were fascinated with each other, although Jim's fellow Stooges sniggered at the sight of the couple: 'Jim looked like the black dwarf next to her!' laughs Jimmy Silver. The two, over a few brief nights, became the star couple at Max's, where Iggy was the focus of everyone's attention – boys and girls. Leee 'Black' Childers, one of the Warhol crew, was chatting to Jaime Andrews – an actor who went on to work for MainMan – when the two of them spotted Nico standing next to Iggy, with her hand down his pants. 'I wonder if I could do that?' Andrews said to Childers, before walking over to the couple. Nico pulled her hand out; Andrews put his in. Iggy stood there, enjoying the attention.

Nico became so enamoured of the young singer that she told him, 'I vont to get out of the city, I vont to come to Detroit.' A few weeks later, she flew to the city, and the two lovers spent two weeks sequestered in the attic of the Fun House. 'It was totally bizarre,' says Jimmy Silver. 'This striking regal being, who somehow didn't look real, living up in the attic.' Nico charmed the Stooges – who were disturbed by the presence of a foreign woman disrupting their boys' club – by lovingly cooking vegetable curries and leaving opened $25 bottles of wine for them to taste. Despite their suspicion of such effete European pursuits, the band were eventually won over. Jim, too, cheerfully admits 'she had no problem corrupting me' – although, in these as yet innocent times, the corruption consisted of drinking European wines and learning to eat pussy. In the last few days of her stay, Nico was joined by François de Menil – scion of the Texas oil-drilling and art-collection dynasty – who brought a small crew to shoot a promotional film for Nico's song 'Evening of Light', shot in the cornfields behind the Fun House. The three-minute short was, according to de Menil, shot on spec rather than as a record company-financed promo, and looked like a cross between a European art-house movie and a low-budget horror flick: Nico plays the brooding icemaiden in a chill Michigan landscape studded with dismembered mannequins; Iggy revisits his white-face mime-influenced look, while moustachioed roadie John Adams wanders around with a flaming cross in suitably post-apocalyptic fashion. A few days later, Nico was gone, having left a beautiful Indian shawl for Jimmy and Susan Silver in thanks for their hospitality – and eventually she fled for Europe. Jim reverted to his former, carefree bachelor state. However, around that time, it transpired that Jim was to become a father, with Paulette Benson, a friend of Sigrid Dobat, who was MC5 guitarist Fred Smith's girlfriend. Jim's son, named Eric Benson, was born on 26 February 1969. For perhaps obvious reasons, Paulette decided to bring up her son without Jim's help; she moved to California, and Jim would have little contact with the child over the next decade.

Over the spring of 1969, the Stooges worked on developing enough songs for their debut album. John Cale had agreed to produce the band on the basis that they 'make the record and forget about what's on stage'. For that reason, apart from tantalising clues, no true record remains of early Stooges performances, and those early freeform 'songs', including 'I'm Sick', 'Asthma Attack', 'Goodbye Bozos' and 'Dance Of Romance', were abandoned or reworked. In three months of twenty-minute rehearsal sessions, minimal songs were sculpted, piece by piece, from the primordial matter of those early riffs.

The standout song was crafted from the fragment of Byrds riff that Ron had first heard on his last acid trip back in April. It would become the perfect illustration of the maxim 'talent borrows, genius steals', for the Byrds' simple two-note guitar line was lifted whole-sale to become the basis of '1969'. But where any other band, including the Byrds, would feel the need to embellish something so simple, the Stooges unlocked its primitive beauty simply by leaving it unadorned. The song was remarkable as much for what was left out as what was included; where convention would suggest augmenting the song's basic two-chord structure, or resolving it by escaping to a third chord, the Stooges simply repeated themselves: 'Another year for me and you. Another year with nothing to do.' The musical dead-end, trapped within two chords, perfectly expresses the boredom and claustrophobia of the song's deadpan disaffection.

'I Wanna Be Your Dog' was carved out of another riff that Ron had started playing in his room; Jim had instantly spotted 'that's a goodie'. It was another simple motif, similar to a standard blues riff from Yusuf Lateef's 'Eastern Market', a staple of the Stooges' listening, but set against a musical drone it transforms into something elemental, inexorable and far more malevolent. Jim would later claim that its basic lyrics were romantic, expressing the simple yearning to lie in a girl's lap, but the song's sado-masochistic overtones undoubtedly betray the influence of the Velvet Underground's 'Venus In Furs'. 'No Fun', which the band were playing live by the spring, was based on a simple chord change familiar from Question Mark and the Mysterians' garage staple '96 Tears' – in this instance, though, it was shorn of its seventh-chords to make it, as Danny Fields put it 'un-Blues'. Meanwhile, the dirgy 'Dance Of Romance' – what would today be called a classic 'stoner riff' – gained a lyrical, romantic opening, a vehicle for Jim's desire to sing the words 'I Love You'. It was given the title 'Ann', partly in tribute to the ever-tolerant and motherly Ann Asheton – although the gossip at Hill Street, according to White Panther Minister of Culture official Hiawatha Bailey, was that it was inspired by Anne Opie Wehrer, the charismatic, blue-blooded doyenne of Ann Arbor's avant-garde scene: 'She was an amputee, had lost one leg to cancer, and when Jim would see her stranded in the audience he would drop his wildman persona and carry her, tenderly, to where she needed to be.'

As the Stooges worked with what was, for them, unstinting zeal, there was troubling news from New York. At the end of January, Danny Fields was gossiping in the company's New York office about the company vice president, Bill Harvey, a man who had always been Fields' nemesis: 'He was a good art director, but the opposite kind of person I found attractive on this earth.' Harvey heard Fields speculate that Bill's daughter's upcoming marriage was a shotgun wedding, 'and smacked me in the head!' says Fields. 'He had been waiting for the opportunity [to sack me] for a long time.' And he did.

With Fields gone, for a new job in publicity at Atlantic records, his major signings had no one to champion their cause at Elektra. Then on 13 February, Sinclair placed an advertisement in the Ann Arbor *Argus* proclaiming 'fuck Hudsons', in protest at the Detroit record store who had pulled the MC5's *Kick Out The Jams* album from their shelves because of J.C. Crawford's use of the word 'motherfucker'. Holzman decreed that the '5 were bringing the label's name into disrepute, and dropped them. The spat produced a short-term benefit for the Stooges, for Jimmy Silver realised that Holzman might be intimidated by the loss of another high-profile band, and decided to push for a bigger advance. 'Jon Landau (the writer and future MC5 producer) was in Ann Arbor to see the MC5 and he put me onto this fantastic lawyer called Alan Bomser, who was nicknamed Bomser the Momzer – Bomser the bastard – because he was so tough.' Silver and Bomser went to see Holzman in New York, and when the Elektra boss started huffing about his 'responsibility to his shareholders', Bomser asked Silver to leave the room. 'Five minutes later Bomser calls me back in, and says Jac's agreed to what we've asked, $25,000. I've no idea how he talked him into it. Maybe Alan had a picture of Jac fucking an aardvark!'

The Stooges' many detractors would not have been surprised to know that the band's first recording session started on April Fool's Day, at New York's Hit Factory, at one in the afternoon. The studio was situated on Times Square, over a peep show, according to Jim. There was conflict from the off when an engineer told the band their Marshall amplifiers were too loud, and that Hit Factory owner Jerry Ragovoy always had his soul musicians record with smaller amps. Iggy's negotiation tactic was to have a tantrum: 'I took a deep breath, and said I don't care who the fuck Jerry Ragovoy is, you don't know anything about *this*! And that was always my attitude: stay away, get back. And then we set up the full stack.'

Ron Asheton remembers the band staged a sit-down strike and sat in the corner smoking hash until John Cale suggested they turn the amps down from full to nine, in order to get the performance on tape without too much leakage. But still there were problems. 'It was very hard to get those tempos up,' Jim remembers. 'With an audience the tempos would come up because we were nervous. In fact, we'd all be shitting our collective little pants. But without the audience the dope took over.' Finally, Iggy and Cale realised that if the singer danced in the studio as the backing tracks went down, the band would speed up somewhat from their pot-induced torpor.

The Stooges had arrived with '1969', 'No Fun', 'I Wanna Be Your Dog' and 'Ann' prepared, and realising that this would be insufficient, worked up the dirge-like 'We Will Fall', based on a chant by Indian guru Swami Ramdas, whose biography Dave Alexander had borrowed from Jimmy Silver. In addition, they also recorded a freeform jam – a chaotic assemblage of wah wah guitar and wordless moans – that would languish in the Elektra vaults for many years, and is quite possibly a version of 'Asthma Attack'. Each song featured a lengthy freak-out, and together the six songs made up well over half an hour, plenty for a vinyl album, thought the Stooges. But Holzman disagreed after hearing the first mixes, and asked if there were any more songs. 'I said, yeah, we've got more,' said Ron, and the band returned to the Chelsea Hotel and wrote 'Little Doll', 'Not Right' and 'Real Cool Time', 'in an hour', according to Ron. 'That was the magic Stooge time, when I could just sit down and come up with the shit.' In every case the lyrics were drawn from Stooges slang. 'Little doll, real cool time, those were words we used every day,' says Ron. 'Real Cool Time' and 'Not Right' recycled the basic chords of 'I Wanna Be Your Dog' to great effect; 'Little Doll' was a straight lift from a bass line that appears halfway through 'Upper And Lower Egypt' by Pharaoh Sanders – the ex-Coltrane sax player and new jazz pioneer who, coincidentally, shared an interest in ancient Egyptian anthropology with the Stooges' singer.

According to Cale, the recording sessions at the Hit Factory were too frenetic for Nico to visit for long, but Jim still retains a memory of her 'sitting in the control room, with a very severe expression, knitting, while [Cale] sat there in a Transylvanian black cape. It set up an atmosphere.'

Although Cale was undoubtedly the dominant presence at the sessions, the first-time producer was actually slightly nervous: 'I was wet behind the ears running a studio session and it was really difficult. I found myself just wanting to be part of the band.' Jimmy Silver remembers Cale as being committed, communicative and full of suggestions. 'Jim described a sound he wanted, and Cale goes, That's a Cuban instrument called a guiro, there's a 24-hour music store near here, do you want me to send out for one? Then they got into the Stooges' mentality, and it was, Oh that's too much trouble, don't bother.'

Nonetheless, Cale managed to get the Stooges' 'monosyllabic slab of noise' on tape, while adding his own more literate, European sensibility. But when he attempted to bias the mix to give Iggy's voice more of a Kurt Weill 'art' edge, there was a confrontation. 'I was trying to characterise Iggy's vocal, make it a little more evil,' confesses Cale. 'I decided I was going to work the [mixing] board and went after this idea to the horror of Jim, who was sitting there listening to his vocals get thinner and thinner.' For a studio novice, Jim was very specific about what he wanted – in fact, today he maintains that after a major fallout he remixed the album himself, without Cale, assisted by Elektra boss Jac Holzman. Cale remembers he abandoned his approach and that engineer Lewis Merenstein helped broker a compromise mix. Today, Holzman has no memory of a remix, while Lewis Merenstein – a celebrated producer in his own right, responsible for Van Morrison's *Astral Weeks* – concurs with Cale: 'It is as John said. I certainly know that without John the album would not have happened.' Nonetheless, Iggy would later claim, 'John Cale had little or nothing to do with the sound. He shouldn't have been there,' a sentiment that Danny Fields dismisses as 'unworthy'.

As it was, Cale demonstrated commendable commitment to his

charges, who overran on their five-day booking at the Hit Factory
and had to move to Mastertone studios on 42nd Street. Richard
Bosworth and his band Jennifer's Friends were booked into
Mastertone and were forced to sit and wait as this session over-ran:
'John Cale refused to relinquish the studio! He was a very intimidating presence, and no one was going to argue with him. But
there was a big confrontation, a fist fight, because John wouldn't let
their recording time be cut short.' One of the first people outside
the Stooges privileged to hear their debut recording, Bosworth's
reaction would anticipate that of most of the American public. 'It
seemed *totally* alien. Disturbingly different, raw, with screaming
vocals. It was very, very different from anything I'd heard before,
and I remember thinking, This won't fly.'

Iggy's subsequent denunciation of Cale was a classic Oedipal
sentiment, a need to prove he was superior to his mentors. But in
many respects the Stooges, Jim included, were not as worldly-wise
as they would later make out. Joel Brodsky was commissioned by
Bill Harvey to shoot the album cover at the beginning of May. Once
the band arrived at his studio on 27th Street he found them uncommunicative and unresponsive. But he'd heard that the singer, Iggy,
was 'physical', and asked if he'd fancy jumping up in the air for the
shoot. 'OK, no problem,' was the reply. Brodsky finally captured an
image of Iggy leaping in the air with no thought of how he would
land, while Ron and Scott wince at the prospect of his imminent
fall – which was, inevitably, flat on his face. Brodsky rushed the
singer to St Vincent's emergency room, where he had five stitches
put in his chin. The stitches were airbrushed out for the final album
cover, which was a straight rehash of Elektra's sleeve for the Doors'
debut LP.

The recording over, and with a release date scheduled for later in
the summer, the band returned to Ann Arbor buoyed up by the
supporters they'd found in New York, who included Josephine
Mori and Natalie Schlossman – soon to be known as Natalie
Stoogeling – from the Elektra press office, and Steve Harris, vice
president in charge of promotions and marketing at Elektra. In the

summer of that year, the Stooges became a regular on the festival circuit, and crowds from outside of Detroit were treated to the sight of them for the first time. On 23 May, Ben Edmonds, a fan of the MC5 who'd heard about the Stooges via Danny Fields, persuaded the Delaware, Ohio student union to book the Stooges at the Grey Chapel, a large college venue that held 2,500 people. The Stooges walked on to the huge stage to see around a dozen people in the entire auditorium. 'It was a magical performance,' says Ben Edmonds. 'The three Stooges just stood there on this huge stage, while you could see Iggy checking out all that space and working out what to do with it.'

Dressed in cut-off jeans, in a page-boy haircut, with no shirt, Iggy launched into his dance, and the small crowd, not one of whom knew the band's music, were transfixed. 'I didn't know any of the music, and couldn't distinguish any songs apart from one that went "no fun, my babe",' says Edmonds, 'but I was totally mesmerised by Iggy. I'd never seen anybody move like that before.' The singer seemed transfixed by the elemental music, so much so that at one point he picked up the shards of a broken drumstick and started scraping it, almost absentmindedly, over his chest. 'He apparently increased the pressure with each stroke,' remembers Edmonds, 'because red welt lines soon became visible, which then discharged trickles of blood down his torso. I was dumbstruck.'

After the show, Edmonds watched as the singer donned a white T-shirt and blood began to ooze through the fabric. 'Watching that made me more queasy than even committing the act,' says Edmonds. 'This was mild compared to the damage he'd later inflict on himself, but this, it turned out, was the first time he'd ever done such a thing.'

One audience member who was also shocked by the spectacle came up to speak to Jim after the performance. Her name was Wendy Robin Weisberg. Nineteen years old, and an ex-girlfriend of Panther White, she came from a wealthy suburb of Cleveland, Ohio, and had met Jim via Panther during his one term at the University of Michigan. He'd been struck by the slim girl, with her long dark hair, the first time they met. Now that he was a professional musician, with a record deal, she seemed all the more intrigued, and the sight of him bleeding on stage had confused and stimulated her. Soon Jim established that Wendy 'was a virgin. I just had to have her.'

What transpired, say Jimmy and Susan Silver, epitomised Jim's obsession with getting what he wanted: 'There was no logic to it. Remember, you're talking about a guy who later nearly killed himself with drugs and addiction – not someone who makes good choices in life!' Jimmy and Susan went up with Jim to visit Wendy and her parents. 'They had a very nice house in a rich suburb, and for some reason I remember her father was friends with Jayne Mansfield.'

Wendy's father, Louis, had played sax with the Ted Lewis big band in his youth, and had worked for the American Meat Company before building up a chain of fifteen Giant Tiger discount stores around Cleveland. Like Jim, Louis was a keen golfer, and Louis and wife Jeannette were at first quite taken with the intense, well-spoken singer, until it became obvious that Jim's advances towards their daughter were getting serious. Within a few weeks Jim was obsessed with Wendy, and would take her to sunbathe that summer on the beach at Silver Lake, Michigan, the resort town where he used to take Lynn Klavitter; inevitably, he became the butt of the Stooges' humour. 'Everyone would laugh about the whole thing, and she'd be pouting. She was a pretty little thing, but I think they were all a bit too much for her,' says Laura Seeger, who was living with roadie Roy Seeger. 'The joke was that she wouldn't dish out,' says Kathy Asheton. 'He was gonna marry her so he could have sex, and so he took a pretty good chiding from the guys.'

Jimmy Silver tried counselling his charge. 'I didn't think it made sense, he and I talked about it, and like everything else it was just something he wanted to do.' He tried counselling Wendy, too. 'I think I said, Do you have any sense of what you're getting into, living in the attic?' but Wendy was also intent on getting married, primarily, thought the Silvers, to rebel against her conservative Jewish background. Ultimately, arranging Jim's wedding turned out to be another of Jimmy Silver's many responsibilities, and the Stooges' manager accordingly sent off to the Universal Life Church, which offered mail-order ministries in the back of *Rolling Stone* magazine. Duly ordained, Jimmy officiated at the wedding of the happy couple, with Susan providing a macrobiotic spread, on the lawn of the Fun House, on 12 July 1969. The Stooges and the MC5 attended the wedding, as did the MC5's new producer, Jon Landau, and Mr and Mrs Osterberg. The Weisbergs stayed home. Russ Gibb telephoned the Fun House and put the call on air on his radio show. Ron Asheton presided as best man; showing commendable sympathy with Wendy's Jewish heritage, he elected to leave the SS uniform that he normally sported on festive occasions in the closet, and opted for a Luftwaffe officer's uniform ('they were soldiers, not political') with sword, Knight's Cross with oak leaves and riding boots.

The nuptials were a blissful occasion for all concerned, bar the MC5, who were disgusted there were no burgers or steak on the strictly macrobiotic menu. 'Of course we all wound up getting real drunk,' says Ron. 'I remember I fucked some girl, then I came back out in my uniform and passed out with her on the front porch. It was a historic party.' Kathy Asheton made a more surprising conquest. 'I decided to show up in this dress. I didn't wear dresses. And the day of Jim's wedding was the day he chose to make his advance on me. Which I decided was not a good sign!' Bill Cheatham attended with Dave Alexander: 'Dave looked at Jim's new tennis shoes and said, I bet those tennis shoes outlast the marriage.'

For just a few weeks, Jim remained up in the attic with Wendy, who tidied up Jim's slovenly apartment and furnished it with tasteful wicker furniture from her father's store. The Stooges, meanwhile, mocked her ceaselessly, particularly after they formed the theory that all she ever ate was potatoes. 'She was a pretty girl, but they all referred to her as the Potato Woman and said she looked like a potato,' says Silver. Meanwhile, says Ron, Dave and Scotty would raid the couple's room during their absences, pilfering food, earning the unfortunate Wendy's enmity. 'Then Iggy realised it was her or the boys, he decided to start hanging with us again, so she got fed up with him and split.' The Ashetons remember Wendy's tenure as lasting less than a month; when it became obvious that the marriage was a failure, Louis Weisberg reportedly pressured for an annulment, so that Jim Osterberg would have no claim on the family wealth. 'It was all done on the pretext that [Jim] was a homosexual and the marriage was never consummated,' says Ron. 'That was the deal, so he would not be privy to any money.'

Soon after the annulment, Jim was sitting with Kathy Asheton in the TV room at the Fun House. They waited for everyone to go, then held hands and went up together to his attic room. 'We both got up, went upstairs, and he was very sweet and very nice. We kept it private – he was very respectful because it might cause problems with my brothers. He was always very attentive, and one of the few people I could rely on.'

Kathy knew enough of Jim to understand that a long-term love affair was simply not on the cards. They would remain friends, even as she saw him and her brothers go to 'a dark place'. But in that summer of 1969, the Stooges' existence seemed blissful. The band were aware there was an envy of their mystique, but felt 'untouchable', remembers Ron; even though their live shows were often still greeted with bewilderment or disdain, nothing could disturb the Stooges' magical aura, their conviction that their music was unique, and the belief that one day the world would realise this fact.

Even hostile, awkward encounters had their own share of comedy. When the band played the Delta Pops festival in July, at the Delta Community College just north of Saginaw, Michigan, there was a huge stir when Iggy confronted one woman in the audience, scooped her up from her seat, and started carrying her around the auditorium. Pete Andrews, the promoter of the festival, which included the MC5, the SRC, Bob Seger and others, was watching the performance 'standing next to the administrator of the university. And it turns out the girl was this guy's daughter.' Andrews says he crawled across the floor of the venue to reach the singer, and held quite a lucid conversation with him. 'I said, it's a bit serious, could you put her down and stop this? He said, Oh gee, I'm sorry, put her down and went back to the stage.' Even though he claims he withheld the Stooges' $300 fee, and his acts were instantaneously barred from the college, Andrews was privately indulgent of the band. They had a pretty good act, and they'd never hurt anybody. The story of 'The Dean's Daughter' would become a staple of press articles about the Stooges, and Iggy would subsequently claim he had become 'obsessed with the chick' and bit her – and that ultimately the college had backed down and paid his $300.

As the Stooges' debut album finally reached the pressing plant, the band's mood was one of cautious optimism. 'We were happy – it was like a stepping stone was in place,' says Jimmy Silver, and that optimism would be borne out by reviews that were generally supportive. Lenny Kaye, later a celebrated writer, and guitarist with Patti Smith, was one of the first in print, suggesting in *Fusion* magazine that the album's rootlessness and lethargy perfectly captured the mood of the times, and that '1969 may well be the year of the Stooges'. The *Rolling Stone* review, which ran in October, described the Stooges as proof of 'the causal relationship between juvenile delinquency and rock 'n' roll': the statement was a compliment, rather than a criticism, and writer Ed Ward concluded, 'I kind of like it,' although his employers were unconvinced. Nonetheless, the nation's radio industry, and most of the public, generally ignored the album, which sold a just about respectable 32,000 copies in its first year and scraped to 106 in the US album charts.

In retrospect, the Stooges' debut album was an album out of time, an artefact that was about as admired as an African tribal painting would be at an exhibition of Victorian pre-Raphaelites.

Released the same week that the Woodstock Festival took place, into a world that was obsessed with surface detail, technical proficiency and peace 'n' love, it was regarded as stone-age and retrogressive. Later it would become revered as an early punk classic. Both interpretations are equally simplistic. For *The Stooges* today actually sounds fresher and more contemporary than most of the punk, alternative, glam and thrash-metal material it allegedly spawned. The album took rock music and stripped it down to its barest essentials: simple three-chord riffs and unforgettable tunes, underpinning deadpan, bored lyrics. No one else had ever attempted to put this kind of anomie to music. The songs too seemed brutishly simplistic; the generally slow pace meant they were all the more immense and imposing. At a time when rock music was becoming positively baroque, it was no surprise that this simplistic manifesto met with general incomprehension. It would take a full decade for its importance to be recognised, as the Sex Pistols and other UK punk bands recorded cover versions of songs like 'No Fun', treating *The Stooges* as both a musical and lyrical primer.

Critics have often used the term 'dumb genius' when discussing the Stooges' debut. Much of the album's appeal comes from its flat, bored, cynical lyrics – lyrics that were a straightforward depiction of life in Ann Arbor: 'Last year I was twenty-one. Didn't have a lot of fun.' Yet the minimalism of the lyrics derives from high ambition, not a small vocabulary, crafted by the boy who had impressed his school contemporaries with his gift for memorable phrases. The musicianship, too, is frequently stunning: Scott Asheton (or Rock Action, as he'd started to term himself) is arrestingly unconventional, his drum patterns echoing Iggy's vocals, rather than simply marking out four beats to the bar. Ron Asheton's guitar playing, meanwhile, was unique; some of the basic chord patterns obviously came from the band's garage band roots, but there were ringing, droning open notes that added to the claustrophobia and monumentality of the music, and at points where other musicians would have resolved a sequence by switching chords, Ron would

OH MY, BOO HOO

resolutely avoid convention. John Cale spotted the outlandish overtones of Ron's playing and emphasised it by adding a droning
viola or piano here and there. Bob Sheff, now a respected avant-
garde composer under the name of 'Blue' Gene Tyranny, describes
the results as: 'So ahead of its time – it captures the simplicity of the
blues, yet those minimalist, droning effects on songs like "I Wanna
Be Your Dog" were very cutting edge. It paralleled the approach of
composers like Terry Riley.'

It was this bizarre mix of disconnected, enigmatic themes (no
other band had ever sung about wanting to be a dog), simple,
monolithic riffs and unconventional tonalities that ensured the
Stooges' debut album would become revered in many different
quarters. Yet while the album was underpinned, to a far greater
extent than is normally realised, with an intellectual thesis, much of
its dumb, bewildered confusion was genuine. It was this lack of
worldliness that would soon tear the Stooges apart.

It's a sparkling-clear night, with the Milky Way crowding in from
dark horizon to dark horizon, and the wind rustles gently through
the trees that shade the modest, middle-class houses on the west
side of Ann Arbor. Outside one, a neat wood-clad two-storey building, a Cadillac El Dorado rusts in the drive, in forlorn hope of
eventual restoration.

Inside, Ron Asheton watches TV into the early hours, devouring
an eclectic cultural diet that encompasses serial killers, the design
of battleships, the Third Reich and alien visitations. On warm
nights he ventures out on vigilante patrols, hunting for aliens with
his Chinese AK-47 ('The greys, with the big eyes, are cool, but don't
mess with the insect ones'). It is 1996, and Ron still lives with
mother Ann Asheton, his lifestyle hardly changed from the golden
days when the Stooges were planning their assault on the world.
Today, though, the Stooges are a bittersweet memory. Every couple
of weeks, he drives down to the Party Store on Packard Avenue,
opposite where the Fun House used to stand, to pick up his
favourite Canadian cigarettes. On occasion he sits in the car,

remembering the old days, when he'd wait for Jim, Dave Alexander or his brother to emerge carrying boxes of Miller High Life beer.

Bouncing around enthusiastically, apologetic that our meetings took so many months to set up, Ron is chubbier but still instantly recognisable as the arrogant young punk staring out of the cover of the Stooges' debut album. He is, by turns, lovable and scary. He ministers after you caringly, making coffees, doling out generous supplies of grass and cocaine, then brings out the first of a disconcertingly comprehensive collection of automatic weapons. He lovingly tends a collection of ageing, incontinent cats, then remarks how the SS General Reinhard Heydrich was his hero. He boasts of his youthful looks, then stares deadpan at the wall as a brochure for a toupée supplier falls out of a photo album.

Of all the people who've been ascribed a pivotal role in Iggy's career, Ron is the most fascinating and the most crucial. He cofounded the band that made Iggy famous, wrote many of their best-known songs, and was co-conspirator in many of the Stooges' triumphs. But, most crucially, Ron was also the co-creator of Iggy Pop, along with his friends Jim Osterberg, Dave Alexander and his brother Scotty. In a brief aside, Ron claims Iggy is 'the channeler of what we all are. Iggy is what he has absorbed and taken from Dave Alexander, my brother . . . our personality and our feelings and our outlook on life and our contempt for establishment and bullshit.'

At times, his voice rises in anger, as he contemplates the predicament of his brother Scotty, who has made failed overtures to the Stooges' one-time singer, and is being, Ron feels, unjustly ignored. 'Scotty was Marlon Brando – and Iggy wanted to be Marlon Brando and James Dean. The closest he could be was my bro' and Dave Alexander. He took, like David Bowie took from Iggy. Psychic vampires.' Meanwhile, he laments, people like Dave Alexander remain forgotten footnotes. 'He was the catalyst for so much of the Stooges, he was so ahead of his time . . . Iggy was a straight-laced puppy-dog frat high-school regular dude when Dave Alexander was a fuckin' true rebel, man. Dave Alexander was a big fuckin' part of . . . I was gonna say perverting us, maybe that's true too.'

Then, at other times, his voice softens, as he recalls a recent encounter and remembers, 'Wow, it was great to see Jim again,' before reflecting on how 'people believe in Iggy and not Jim. It is hard for him.' Talking about Jim Osterberg, there is love and empathy; discussing Iggy Pop, there is a consistent thread of bitterness that 'when [Jim] believed in Iggy Pop then there was no more group'. At times, there's a palpable grief that Jim Osterberg, like his dead fellow Stooge Dave Alexander, seems irretrievably lost. But there's no possibility of closure while the spectre of Iggy Pop is there to taunt him. And, as we speak, through the night and into the dawn, when Ann Asheton rises to attend a collectors' fair in Illinois, the possibility of reconciliation seems more and more remote.

Although Ron is likeable, funny, warm, slightly deranged, it's a rather depressing encounter: that sense of loss, that claustrophobia. The knowledge that, while Ron helped capture the frustration of another year with nothing to do in his music, it's a predicament that he hasn't managed to escape. Although there has been talk of a Stooges reunion, escaping the wreckage of their personal relationships seems like an impossible prospect.

CHAPTER 5

Fun House Part I: I Feel Alright

Iggy was the most beautiful thing many women, and men, had seen. Now it seemed he was making love to all of them. With guitarists Ron Asheton and Bill Cheatham shooting out high-energy riffs like machinegun bullets behind him, he was high on the electrifying music and his own sexual energy. Again and again he threw himself into the crowd and let them close over him, gave himself up. No one could work out what was going on while he disappeared but many observers were sure it was sexual, that he was being interfered with.

Then he rose up out of the crowd, squirming, dozens of hands grasping and lifting him, and stood straight up, on their hands. He pointed, striking poses like a bronze of a Greek athlete, defying gravity, and never looking down for a second. In the wings of the Cincinnati stage, as the TV cameras captured the moment at which Iggy Stooge ascended into the pantheon, the Stooges' roadies and fans were transfixed with a beatific feeling. This was the moment: 'The zenith,' Leo Beattie confided to Dave Dunlap, who knew that the album they'd just watched the Stooges make would assure their immortality. This was why they'd left their previous jobs to join up as the band's roadies. This was why they had their pick of the most beautiful groupies in Michigan. This is what an English rock star named David Bowie would attempt to emulate, only to tumble to the ground. And this is what Jim Osterberg was born to do: 'I know I'm at the beginning,' he would tell people, with almost religious intensity, 'but I know I will always be involved with this beautiful thing.'

That beautiful feeling would last for just two blissful months. Eight weeks later, Iggy would look down. And then he would jump. It would be six years or more before he stopped falling.

At the beginning of 1970, the Stooges were the people everyone had to hang with. Many local musicians mocked the band, whom they still saw as hopelessly incompetent, but the girls of Ann Arbor knew who they liked best. As Kathy Asheton points out: 'There was an envy of the band, because there were musicians who thought they couldn't play, yet they created all this excitement. They got the attention, they got the girls, they were cool guys, people wanted to be around them.' Soon two of the SRC's road crew – Zeke Zettner and Eric Haddix – came over to the Stooges camp, while roadie Leo Beattie's defection to the Stooges from the MC5 signalled that the Stooges were on the point of overtaking their big brother band. The Stooges were less conventional, and simply more fun. There was the band's shared humour, their self-parody and the way they all collaborated in brilliant deadpan mockery of those who didn't get them. Then there was the nightly entertainment of seeing which of his nine different Nazi uniforms Ron Asheton would decide to wear for the evening. 'The Stooges always seemed to have better-looking, more exotic women around than the '5,' Leo Beattie remembers fondly. 'Models, interesting, intelligent women. Iggy was a sex symbol and brought them in, and Ron would also have these beautiful women around. It was a great atmosphere. We all felt that we were gonna go bigger than the MC5. Everything was in place, Ron was coming up with great riffs, Iggy had that sex appeal. We were sure it was gonna happen.'

Jim's 14-year-old girlfriend, Betsy Mickelsen, somehow epitomised the optimistic, almost innocent atmosphere. Betsy was
blonde, intelligent, street-smart and literate. In her company, Jim
always seemed child-like and sincere – so sincere, in fact, that he'd
managed to win the consent of Betsy's family to the relationship.
The approval of Dr Mickelsen, who lived in a large house five
minutes away on Adare Road, was essential, and not just for cosy
family reasons; for if Jim were to take Betsy out of the state of
Michigan he risked being charged under the Mann Act for trans-
portation of an underage girl. As one member of the Stooges
household points out, this meant that 'if you [don't want] to get
arrested, then you're gonna have to sit around with the family
and play cards with the old man – and they're gonna have to
decide you're OK'. As far as most of the onlookers could see, Dr
Mickelsen seemed to be charmed by the young singer, although
it's likely he felt he had little choice, and consequently elected to
have the relationship between his 14-year-old daughter and a man
eight years her senior go on in plain view, rather than behind his
back.

Despite the age difference, in many respects Betsy seemed more
mature than Jim. 'She ruled the relationship in a lot of ways, and he
enjoyed that,' thought Ron Asheton. Within the band, Jim was the
one in control; with Betsy, he was free of responsibility and seemed
to enjoy behaving in a naive, childlike manner, as they walked
around holding hands, talking in almost baby language. When he
was faced with Betsy's wrath – which was signalled by her calling
him Iggy, rather than Jim – he would be genuinely disturbed, and
when Betsy disappeared to her parents after a particularly bad
falling-out, his distress was apparent to everyone around the
house.

For most of the time, Jim and Betsy's relationship seemed to be
an idyllic one, and the general happiness was shared around the
Fun House. There were no factions within the household – unusual
for a rock band – although the roadies were, as custom dictated,
seen as belonging to a lower caste. John Adams, aka the Fellow, was

head of the 'below stairs' contingent – in an English country house he would have doubtless been a butler – and the Fellow became responsible for more direct supervision once Jimmy, Susan and Rachel Silver moved out of their small apartment on the second floor into a house on Brookwood late in 1969, to make more room for the band (and to escape the deafening rehearsals). Within the main household, Jim – or Pop, to use his band title – was seen as the titular head, with Ron, whose nickname was Cummings, an autonomous lieutenant, who would often call practices independently of Jim. Scotty, aka Rock Action, and Dave Alexander, aka Dude Arnet, were less visible, and as time went on, Alexander, who had always been shy, seemed to retire more and more. Even Dave's girlfriend, Esther Korinsky, considered Dave 'very, very withdrawn' – he liked to keep an aura of mystery around him, and forbade Esther from looking at any of his books on the occult. But Dave's musical contributions were valuable, most notably the riff to a song that would become 'Dirt', as well as a circular, repetitive bass melody that would eventually underpin the song 'Fun House'.

Indeed, where the Stooges had struggled to come up with enough material for their debut album, the new songs came thick and fast. The object, says Jim, was 'to forge ahead. We realised we had another album to do and I wrote them all, one by one.' 'Down On The Beach', written as a love song for Wendy, was reworked after her departure into 'Down On The Street', while the savage guitar riff of '1970' was written by Ron, as was 'Loose'. Although in his more megalomaniac moments, Iggy would claim to have written every single note of the band's set, he later described the material as all essentially 'variations on a theme by Ron'. But over this period the band's compositions, like their lifestyle, were totally communal. Even roadie Bill Cheatham was drawn into the musical mix, recruited as a kind of apprentice to Ron. The two would practise on guitar together up in Ron's first-floor apartment, which had been inherited from the Silvers and given an Asheton makeover with display cases housing Ron's Nazi uniforms, helmets and bayonets. Surrounded by artefacts of the Third Reich, the two worked on intricate guitar voicings which allowed Ron to perfect his overdub parts for the imminent second Stooges album.

Although Elektra had taken their sweet time arranging the band's debut, with the MC5 gone Jac Holzman and Bill Harvey paid a little more attention to the little brother band, and the sessions for a follow-up were being planned by January 1970. The choice of producer was critical – in typical Stooge fashion, the band, Iggy in particular, were already badmouthing John Cale's work on their debut – and Elektra's first two suggestions, Jackson Browne and Steve Miller-keyboard player Jim Peterman, were rejected after cursory consideration. The third contender, who'd recently been recruited by Jac Holzman as a producer based in the label's West Coast office, was Don Gallucci, who'd just racked up his first production hit with Crabby Appleton. A charming, diminutive Italian-American guy, Don's expensive suits and impressive vocabulary were both a surprise considering his first musical break was playing keyboards on the Kingsmen's proto-punk classic, 'Louie Louie'.

In February 1970, the Stooges were booked for a two-night run at Ungano's, a hip club on West 70th Street named after its founders, Arni and Nick Ungano. It was the band's first New York gig since an August 1969 showcase at the State Pavilion with the MC5, at which the Stooges had been overshadowed by their 'big brothers'. Jac Holzman sent Gallucci a plane ticket just a few days before the show, and told him there was a band he needed to check out. No more information was forthcoming.

Neither Gallucci, nor most of the audience, had any clue what would hit them. Many of the Max's Kansas City crew were present, to see the boy they'd met in the back room. Every one of them, boy and girl, wanted to know what it would be like to fuck this exotic creature: 'Isn't it great that so many of them got to find out!' laughs Leee 'Black' Childers.

As the Stooges hit the stage, Gallucci was mesmerised by the sheer wall of noise. Up to now, every band he'd ever seen had decorated their music with lots of chords, or flash solos. But he thought this sounded like 'machine music' – a deconstructed, minimalist slab of sound. For the past four months the Stooges' skills had been honed by an intensive performance schedule booked by their new agency, Detroit's DMA, and their playing was at a peak: the momentum of Ron, Dave and Scott's instrumental onslaught did not let up for a moment.

Iggy, sporting his new customary outfit of threadbare Levi's, black boots and elbow-length silver lamé gloves, confronted his audience from his first moment on stage. As the band broke into 'Loose', inviting them to take a ride 'on the pretty music', most of the audience were transfixed by the lascivious lyrics – 'I'll stick it deep inside'. The sexual tension was heightened as Iggy danced with his back to the audience; *East Village Other* writer Karin Berg speculated how one could enjoy a performance solely on the basis of watching his muscles move under his skin. Some rival critics were not as impressed. One beer-bellied, suited, bespectacled *Billboard* writer sat stage-front, impassive; Iggy walked up, tickled him under the chin, then sat in his lap, head resting intimately on his shoulder. Moments later he slowly pulled a girl out of the audience by her leg, then grabbed her by the head, before dancing off again over the tables, swinging off electrical piping on the low-slung ceiling, backflipping off a table and jumping back onto the stage. At some points the music stopped, at another it morphed into a backing for Iggy's improvised 'I am you' chant. One moment the atmosphere could be intimidating, at others intensely erotic, the next it could turn to farce, as Iggy would accidentally split his lip with a microphone and sing, laughing, 'My pretty face is going to hell.'

The New York audiences were divided by this spectacle. Some were disgusted by the 'hype'. Others were besotted, like Berg, inspired by how the band broke through the 'ennui and boredom' of white America; Rita Redd and Jackie Curtis printed an awed conversation recollecting the show in *Gay Power*, and concluded, 'Rock is gone . . . Iggy's performance is proof of it.' Gallucci was both impressed and shaken by the spectacle of the band playing

live, but when Holzman called him the next day to see if he'd produce their album, he turned the assignment down with a typical
record-company cliché: 'Great act, but you'll never get it on tape.'

Holzman's response was simply, 'Let's do it.' As Gallucci was a
full-time employee of Elektra records, that meant he had the assignment whether he liked it or not. Fortunately the Stooges, TV
addicts as they were, were enthusiastic because they'd seen
Gallucci on the Dick Clark afternoon show, *Where The Action Is*,
with his band, Don And The Good Times. By March, with each
new song being slotted into the set one by one, the Stooges had
enough material for a complete album. 'Then finally,' says Jim, 'we
played the Armoury in Jackson [Michigan], and they were all in.
We fucked up a couple but it was starting to string together.'

Jim in particular seemed to be approaching the imminent recording with almost messianic fervour, a fervour that was intensified by
some of the Stooges' most powerful performances to date. In
Cincinnati, on 26 March, the band shared an impressive bill with
Savoy Brown, Mountain and others, and were forced to follow the
MC5 on stage. Fellow Detroit musician Cub Koda chatted with
them before they went on, and sensed their nervousness, but then
watched as they walked on and 'tore the place apart'. For the first
time, Iggy plunged into the enthralled audience, was lifted up and
walked on their hands.

Dave Marsh spent several days with the Stooges for a *Creem*
story; he was struck by how driven the band's singer seemed. At
times there was seemingly intense mental manipulation, as Iggy
turned the interview back on Marsh and started asking him questions. The confrontation seemed a set piece of how Jim Osterberg
could use his mental agility and mastery of reading social situations. At times he was sensitive and vulnerable, detailing how his
life had lacked any meaning until he'd teamed up with the Stooges
and his very existence had 'flowered'; at others he was frighteningly focused, loftily dismissing those who didn't understand his
vaunting ambition. Marsh was, from moment to moment, moved,
impressed and totally disorientated – sensations heightened by the

supply of hash they were both smoking. There is little doubt that Iggy was also mythologising his own history – 'but the thing about all those interviews, is I never had a sense that he was telling me anything but the truth, or that it mattered,' Marsh points out. 'At some level or other it was true enough.'

Over March 1970, when Marsh was staying at the Fun House, a new Ann Arbor musician was pulled into Osterberg's orbit. Steve Mackay was the most in-demand sax player in the city, playing with Bill Kirchen and Commander Cody, Vivian Shevitz's Charging Rhinoceros of Soul, as well as leading his own avant-garde duo Carnal Kitchen – which occasionally featured ex-Prime Mover and future Stooge Bob Sheff. One night he looked up from a Carnal Kitchen performance at a Beaux Arts Ball to see the Stooges' singer in the audience. A few weeks later Jim walked into Discount Records, where Mackay worked, and invited him out for a coffee: 'He's already got *Fun House* written in his head,' says Mackay, 'he knows there's gonna be sax on it, and he already knows he wants to take me to Los Angeles to record – but I was the last one to know.'

Mackay played one performance with the Stooges, and was given the obligatory nickname – Stan Sax. Then in mid-April Jim called to tell him they were leaving for Los Angeles in two days. He postponed his college exams, convinced he'd be back in a couple of weeks.

For the Stooges, their followers and their publicist, the recording of *Fun House* was the most blissful period of their existence. The band flew into Los Angeles on Jim Osterberg's twenty-third birthday, 21 April, and promptly moved into the Tropicana – a universe of sex and drugs and rock 'n' roll in one shanty motel.

Situated on Santa Monica Boulevard by the heart of the Sunset Strip, the Trop was owned by legendary Los Angeles Dodgers pitcher Sandy Koufax. It was LA's premier down-market rock 'n' roll location. Andy Warhol was a regular (he would film *Heat* there in July 1971), Jim Morrison had only recently moved out after a two-year stay, and the day the Stooges moved in, Ed Sanders was on-site writing *The Family*, his disturbing, shockingly detailed story of the Manson murders that had horrified Los Angeles the previous summer. The four main Stooges commanded a suite each round the central swimming pool, where Jim would spend the early mornings building up an impressive suntan. The rest of the entourage, including new boy Mackay, road manager John Adams, plus roadies Bill Cheatham, Leo Beattie and Zeke Zettner, shared crummier six-dollar rooms at the edge of the motel. The first night at the Tropicana, Scotty found a sap in his room; Jimmy Silver found a gun in his rental car. In the evening after the gruelling recording sessions finished, the band wandered the garish neon-lit Strip, or wandered down to Long Beach (where Scotty got a tattoo), hung out in diners and picked up actresses who aspired to the Hollywood big-time but paid the rent doing porno flicks. Andy Warhol stopped in to say hello – Jim obliged, although most of the other Stooges thought he was creepy and avoided him. The place was full of groupies, and people who had good – 'and bad' – drugs. Whoever you saw, girl or boy, the possibilities were endless. 'You walked down Santa Monica Boulevard to pick someone up and said, "I have any named drug. Let's go back to your suite",' remembers Danny Fields, fondly, who still helped out the Stooges as a publicist despite the fact he was now employed by Atlantic. 'The whole place was like that. Free wheeling.'

Every afternoon, the band would tuck their guitars, drumsticks and saxophone under their arms and walk the few blocks to the Elektra West Coast offices on La Cienega. Don Gallucci, the man who had initially refused to record the Stooges, would work them hard, right from their preparatory rehearsals at SIR studios on Santa Monica. But he would also, along with engineer Brian Ross-Myring, show heroic dedication in his mission to record the unrecordable.

The Elektra Sound Recorders studio, situated within the company's West Coast office, was a cosy bleached-wood set-up, perfectly suited for Elektra's wistful folk troubadours. But it was hopeless for recording scuzzy rock 'n' roll. The floors were draped with tasteful rugs and the walls were covered with baffling, to deaden the sound and ensure acoustic instruments could be recorded with utmost clarity. Holzman's interest in audiophile technology also meant that the mixing desk was a state-of-the-art Neve all-transistor design, which gave a totally clean, clinical sound. The moment the band set up their Marshalls and started playing, Gallucci shuddered, and realised, 'This is a nightmare!'

Gallucci is a talkative, voluble soul, although today he describes himself as 'naive. I'd started young and I missed a whole lot of emotional cues.' He was also faced with a remarkably truculent, uncommunicative bunch of musicians. Where Jim Osterberg was normally the conduit between the outside world and the Stooges, during these sessions Gallucci mostly dealt with Ron Asheton, and found the Stooges' singer twitchy and nervous. There was a simple explanation for these communication problems: Iggy had decided to celebrate recording the album by dropping a tab of acid at the beginning of every day's work.

In the face of such mutual incomprehension, it was quite remarkable that Gallucci elected to throw the rule book out of the window, and the sonic baffling and rugs out of the studio. After a couple of days of trial and error, he allowed the band to set up all their equipment in the same room so they could feed off each other's performance. Finally, in an unprecedented move, Gallucci and Ross-Myring decided to record the entire band live, with Iggy singing through a hand-held microphone and amplified through a PA system set up on the studio floor. For Gallucci and Ross-Myring – a respected British engineer who had just come from a Barbra Streisand session – this would ordinarily have been anathema but for the fact that if they tried recording the band in conventional fashion 'it simply sounded stupid. There's no other explanation.' By now, according to Jimmy Silver, there was a certain amount of bonding going on, thanks to Don Gallucci's wife – 'a white witch, with that gothic look, nearly twice as tall as Donny' – who took the band to see Bela Lugosi's old house. By 11 May the band had progressed to recording a set of promising run-throughs – the sonic leakage contributed to an unrelentingly

intense onslaught of sound, while Iggy's voice was simply electrified, distorted and fiery like a Chicago blues harmonica. Thereafter,
Gallucci dictated the band should work like a jazz outfit, recording
one song per day, in the order of the Stooges' live set.

A couple of days into recording proper, the Stooges took a weekend out for a trip to San Francisco, to headline for two nights at The
New Old Fillmore, supported by Alice Cooper and the Flamin'
Groovies. By now Iggy's reputation had spread within the city's
gay community, and on Friday 15 May the audience was packed
with members of the Cockettes, the city's outrageous theatre
troupe, who sat on the floor, hypnotised by the spectacle of Iggy in
tight jeans and silver lamé gloves. The singer, too, was transfixed
by the outrageous gay posse, and it seemed to Rumi Missabu, a
founding Cockette, that 'He was playing just for us, looking just at
us.' After an exhilarating show, the singer came over to say hello,
although it soon transpired that some of Iggy's interest was
inspired by Rumi's companion, Tina Fantusi. Tina was a 14-year-
old wild child, a regal beauty of Latin and Scandinavian blood,
who'd moved into the Cockettes' household a year before. Iggy's
fascination was reciprocated; Tina found him ravishing: 'He was
the first guy I'd ever been attracted to physically like that – an
absolutely beautiful body.' Iggy tried to entice Tina back to his
hotel room, only to be told by her mentors, 'No way. You can have
her, but you're gonna have to come with us.'

Hence, that evening Iggy Stooge followed Tina, Rumi and the
others to the Cockettes' communal house on Bush and Baker, a
location far more exotic than anything Jim had encountered in the
Midwest. The Cockettes had at that point only staged a couple of
performances, but that summer their outrageous, camp, draggy
revues would sweep them to notoriety. Soon, Jim and Tina disappeared into her bedroom on the ground floor for what felt to Tina
like a romantic tryst – 'almost like a school love affair, very romantic, while he was sweet, sensitive and rather vulnerable'. Tina
found Jim earnest, almost child-like, and the difference in their
ages felt irrelevant: 'It's possible he didn't even know I was

fourteen, as I could pass for a lot older. It was different then, people took care of each other, it wasn't dark at all.'

For all the peace and love that still endured in San Francisco, however, the mood had turned darker with the killings at Altamont that past December, and heroin had joined the cocktail of drugs that were readily available in the city – and also in the Cockettes' commune, where many of its members had already experimented with it. 'It was a Saturday-night kind of drug, which a lot of us flirted with,' says Tina, 'and I think unfortunately we're the ones that turned him on to heroin.'

Cradled with Tina in the house on Bush and Baker, nestled in the warm embrace of heroin for the first time, Jim was also subject to the attentions of the various Cockettes, who tramped in, many of them in all their finery, to admire the visitor. There was plenty to admire; Rumi still remembers Cockette Tahara's stage-whispered aside as he contemplated the naked singer: 'Check the size of that organ!' It was a ravishing, disturbing, but exciting experience which seemed to echo the mood of the Stooges' increasingly intense music.

Tina joined Jim back in LA for a couple of days at the Tropicana, as the recording hotted up for its last week. Although the band occasionally bridled at Gallucci's insistence on recording multiple takes, they appreciated his commitment and there were many lighter moments: Ross-Myring joking on tape, or Bill Cheatham performing skits in the character of wrestler Red Rudy (afternoon wrestling shows were naturally a staple of the Stooges' TV diet). But behind the scenes, according to Cheatham, dark clouds were gathering. Now that Jimmy and Susan Silver had a one-year-old baby to look after, they were becoming less enamoured of playing babysitter to a set of 20-year-olds and were spending much of their time in LA round the corner at the Erewhon macrobiotic store on Beverly, which was run by a couple of old friends. In their place, the Fellow – John Adams, the band's road manager – started to take a more central role. And in LA, Adams' 'fascination with the abomination', as Jimmy Silver termed it, was given free rein. Cheatham roomed with the Fellow, and noticed he was fascinated by their next-door neighbours on the sleazy side of the Tropicana, a gay couple in their forties or fifties, both of them cokeheads. 'One guy's septum was completely burnt out,' shudders Cheatham, 'and for some reason that set John off. He saw this older guy who'd been doing drugs for years, and John just wanted to be that, I guess.' Adams declared that he too had to track down some cocaine; but the one-time heroin addict wouldn't stop there.

Over the same period, the Stooges' singer was also sampling new drugs. He'd been given his first taste of cocaine by Danny Fields early in the sessions, but had told his publicist, 'I don't feel *anything*!' – then a few days later climbed in Fields' motel-room window to beg for some more, before hoovering up all his supply. Towards the end of their stay, freelance photographer Ed Caraeff came in to shoot the album cover and photographed the band sprawling around the studio: 'And it was, oh, you want the band to look perky for the shoot,' says Steve Mackay, 'so we all took a whole bunch of cocaine.' Jim Osterberg today still recalls the 'charming hippie photographer' fondly, as well as his pink cocaine from Peru and psilocybin, in pill form (although today Caraeff recalls no cocaine use during the sessions). For Iggy and John Adams in particular, cocaine soon became an obsession.

On Monday 25 May, the band recorded twelve takes of 'Dirt', deciding the final one was the keeper, before embarking on the final song, a freakout that they'd generally referred to as 'the hippie ending', or occasionally 'Freak' and would eventually be titled 'LA Blues'. The hippie ending normally followed on directly from the song 'Fun House', but rather than attempt to record twenty minutes of material in one go, Gallucci decided they should record the freakout as a standalone. To get in the mood, and to celebrate the album's conclusion, all five Stooges, bar Ron, dropped acid. Ross-Myring rolled up his shirt sleeves and manned the board. 'You could tell the Edge Patrol was finally getting to him,' says Gallucci, 'but still, he figured, if we're going out the box, let's go all the way.' Steve Mackay still remembers lying on his back on the studio floor, wailing away on the sax, feeling out on a limb, looking over at 'Pop' and feeling freaked out: 'Does he hate me, this is scary, all that stuff. You know.'

Finally, the Stooges had recorded the unrecordable.

As if to consummate their sleazy love affair with LA, the band played two nights at the Whisky-a-Go-Go. The feeling was mutual. Their performance, like that at Ungano's, shocked and awed the audience; even Gallucci was shaken when he saw Iggy pick up one of the wicker-clad Chianti bottles, which served as candlesticks at the Whisky, and pour hot wax over his midriff. Photographer Ed Caraeff, too, was astonished, but not so much that he missed the shot. The story of this new outrage became legendary, so much so that fans who saw Iggy in New York, San Francisco and countless locations across the US claimed to have seen him do it at their local club. In fact, it probably happened only at the Whisky, but like so many moments in the Stooges' brief career, it would be obsessed over for decades.

A few days later, on Memorial Day weekend, Dave, Scott and Steve flew back to Detroit, with Jim and Ron following a few days later. When he returned, Jim looked healthier than anyone could ever remember, tanned and relaxed. But according to several denizens of the Fun House, when Jim hit Ann Arbor, so had cocaine, almost as if it was planned. (In some respects it was; Nixon's Operation Intercept, launched in late September 1969 to cut down the supply of marijuana, had inspired Michigan grass-smokers to seek out alternatives, initially opiated hash, sourced from Canada, then cocaine, and finally heroin.) Within a few weeks, even his fellow band members were calling Iggy a 'coke whore', after he started hanging out at a local dealer's, Mickie B, washing her dishes in the hope of scoring more white powder for free.

Over the summer, the Stooges seemed untouchable. Major stories in *Rolling Stone*, *Creem*, *Entertainment World*, *Crawdaddy* and more attempted to address this new phenomenon. Then on 13 June in Cincinnati, at the Summer Pop rock festival, the band reached their zenith, performing their *Fun House* set at a peak of intensity. Iggy, who had taken to wearing a dog collar, which emphasised his blending of choirboy innocence with animalistic depravity, plunged into the crowd again and again, in a glorious, exhilarating interaction. No performer had ever been this open, this confident, and singer and audience collaborated in an unforgettable event. Lifted above the crowd Iggy laughs, sings, poses, and at one point takes a tub of peanut butter and throws its contents at the audience. Iggy had practised this impossible feat at Cincinnati just a few months before, but now there were TV cameras present, to prove this was real and not just a figment of overwrought fans' imaginations. Broadcast by NBC as *Midsummer Rock* at the end of August, a tantalisingly brief snippet of film, just over five minutes in length, remains the best record of the Stooges at their height.

As if to seal that compact with their fans, the release of *Fun House*, in August, would be the grand statement of the original Stooges. It would be one of the most uncompromising albums of the 1970s, an assault on the senses that remains exhilarating today. The album sounded dense and claustrophobic, with Iggy's distorted vocals fighting to be heard above repetitive, almost funky guitar and saxophone riffs that would occasionally explode into thrilling climaxes. Where their debut was all deadpan restraint, *Fun House* was aggressive, outgoing and, at times, almost expansive and cocky. For a group whose technical prowess was often derided, the musicianship was deft: spooky and gothic on 'Dirt', strutting and greasy on 'Fun House', lamebrained and thuggish on '1970'.

Today, *Fun House* is the Stooges album most consistently cited by musicians, for instance Jack White, of the White Stripes, who reckons, 'In my mind, *Fun House* is the greatest rock 'n' roll record ever made. I'll always feel that.' Eventually, this music would spawn the dark gothic rock of Nine Inch Nails or Jane's Addiction, but for many contemporaries, *Fun House* seemed to prove the Stooges were simply deluded. There was impassioned support from *Creem*'s

Lester Bangs, who wrote a huge feature on the album that was serialised over two issues, and many others. Even industry bible *Billboard* weighed in on their behalf, although the positive review must have irked the singer by crediting 'Steve Mackay and his magic saxophone' as the leader. Even so, the album was generally reviled, in particular by the radio industry. Steve Harris, senior vice president in charge of marketing at Elektra, was a fan of the Stooges and pushed the record hard, but received an unequivocal reaction: 'Oh my God! Isn't Elektra a company of beautiful and wonderful and classy music? What are they doing with *this*?'

CHAPTER 6

Fun House Part II:
This Property is Condemned

The end would be swift, but not particularly merciful. There were several portents. The first came from the city of Ann Arbor, who in June 1970 served notice that Stooge Hall – the Fun House – would be demolished in a year, to allow Eisenhower Parkway to be turned into a highway. The same month Jimmy Silver was offered a job at the Erewhon Natural Food company; he felt drawn to the challenge, believing that the Stooges were now in a good position, and that his old friend John Adams was well placed to take over.

The third portent was Goose Lake, a hellish festival on 7, 8 and 9 August 1970, which well and truly telegraphed that the 1960s were over. Most people who were there describe the atmosphere as post-apocalyptic, like something out of *Mad Max*. Bill Cheatham, finally promoted to rhythm guitar, remembers the show as 'a blur, there was a huge amount of cocaine around'. Bill Williams, a music fan, was working security and saw vendors openly dealing heroin from trays slung round their shoulders, as if they were cinema usherettes selling ice cream; Hells Angels were dispensing a range of drugs from their bikes backstage. Roadie Dave Dunlap saw one boy who was so high he was picking up mud and eating it; Leo Beattie saw another kid fall from the PA stack, bounce on the ground, then get up and start dancing.

The Stooges' performance was similarly on the edge, thanks to an order from the promoters that the singer was not allowed to dive into the audience. Williams and another 19-year-old security guard were ordered to restrain Iggy, and as the singer headed for the fence that separated him from the audience, they grabbed him by the arms and pulled him back. Iggy retreated to the stage, and as the Stooges riffing rose to an almost psychotic intensity, started screaming, 'Tear it down! Tear it down!' Williams was terrified. 'Two hundred thousand people were there, and they were going *nuts*! They were ripping planks off the fence, we were trying to hold on to it, it was insane!'

At some point – no one seems to agree on when, or how – Stooges bassist Dave Alexander simply became overwhelmed by the spectacle and lost his place. Some say he lost the beat, others, including Iggy, that he forgot every song. The singer felt naked, exposed, and after the performance demanded that Dave was sacked. The others objected, according to Ron, then finally gave in. The first of the Dum Dum Boys was gone. Perhaps it was a coincidence, but at the same time Jim Osterberg announced that his professional name was no longer Iggy Stooge. From now on, he would be known as Iggy Pop.

Some of the Fun House residents thought that Dave's fuck-up at Goose Lake was just a handy excuse; that Jim was irritated by Alexander's reclusiveness, or even by his physical frailty. Years later, sitting outside his beautiful, peaceful house in Miami, the singer ponders his decision: 'I've been reminded since that at one point I said, No, I won't work with Dave any more on bass, and that . . . the whole thing began to slide apart. But there I was out on stage, and there was no bass – he just had a complete mental lapse, was too stoned, he didn't know what he was doing. And that's traumatic, for somebody that . . . erm, I was serious about this shit. So . . .' he continues, sadly, 'the group never had a focus after that.'

On 11 August, just as Alexander was being ousted by his old high-school chums, Iggy was a guest on DJ Dan Carlisle's WKNR radio show. On the recording, the voluble, talkative Jim Osterberg is absent; you can hear Dan Carlisle losing the will to live as he attempts to extract a coherent sentence from the distant, uncommunicative Iggy Pop. There is a disturbing lassitude about him: the singer sounds flat, as if in the grip of depression. It's likely that Jim was already beset by drastic emotional swings, an affliction familiar to many musicians or artists who speed towards a deadline on an almost manic high, then hit a trough of despondency when the work is finished. Those emotional swings were undoubtedly exacerbated by Iggy's ingestion of acid, hashish and cocaine – and the latter was, as Iggy's close observer, writer Nick Kent, points out, 'absolutely the worst drug for him. It sent him absolutely crazy.'

A few days later, in New York, another connection was made that would intensify the evil miasma that was gathering round the Stooges. The band was booked into Ungano's for a four-night run in mid-August to showcase *Fun House*, with roadie Zeke Zettner – a quiet, sweet blond boy, who often played with his back to the audience – promoted to playing bass. When the band hit New York, their acting manager, the Fellow, had a single obsession: scoring heroin. It was all Adams could talk about; most of the junior Stooges with whom he hung out were unenthusiastic, but the Fellow kept at it, telling them, 'No no, you don't understand. This is the best high.' Adams described the effects of heroin, says Billy Cheatham, 'as if it was Coleridge. It was a place he wanted to be.'

The Fellow shared a room at the Chelsea Hotel with Steve Mackay, and as the band checked in, there were twin drug obsessions. Iggy wanted cocaine; John wanted heroin. Chatting with Mackay, Adams told the sax player, 'A weird thing happened to me. I was standing on the corner waiting for a connection for junk. And I found one.'

That evening John Adams returned to the loving embrace of

heroin, sharing 'a snoot' of his new haul with Steve Mackay; meanwhile, Iggy approached Bill Harvey of Elektra and explained that if the Stooges were to perform, he needed $400 to buy cocaine. Although Harvey usually seemed hip to the presence of soft drugs – and is said to have had an official 'lawn-keeping allowance' to purchase the other kind of grass – such effrontery was guaranteed to enrage him, as he was no fan of the Stooges. Reluctantly, Harvey handed over the $400, but although the band had the cash, their dealer was late. Showtime came and went; finally they decided they could wait no longer and made for the stage, only to run into the dealer on their way through Ungano's kitchen. Then it was 'Zoom, back to the dressing room,' says Mackay, where the Stooges gleefully opened up a huge tinfoil package, snorting up 'a mountain' of cocaine, before they finally hit the stage, hopelessly late. That night was, by most accounts, a good show – 'All glistening and sparkly,' says Mackay – which featured lengthy improvisations, including a new song, 'Going To Egypt'.

A recently discovered tape of one of the Ungano's shows sounds terrific; the following nights' performances were apparently inspired, too, memorable for more than just the sight of Iggy's penis, which he waved at the audience on the final night. Indeed, over the same period the Stooges headlined over the MC5 in Asbury Park, went on last and demolished their one-time big brothers. But, as Scotty Asheton puts it, the evening in New York finally 'woke up [John's] worm. And it was like a sledgehammer in the head, memories after that, 'cause it was all downhill. All of a sudden, heroin was cool.'

In the autumn of 1970, heroin was starting to flood Detroit. As the MC5's leader Wayne Kramer points out, 'One day heroin was like some exotic jazz musician's drug, and the next day everybody could get it – cheap. It was plentiful, and it was potent.'

The MC5 succumbed to heroin just before the Stooges; for Wayne Kramer, it eased the pain of the awareness that the MC5's career, their hopes and dreams, were on the wane. For Jim

Osterberg, heroin brought welcome ease. 'I always felt the group could work harder . . . I always felt it incumbent on me to do certain things for everyone and there was a resentment. It became a weight. And a great excuse. And it's only an excuse. Honestly, there were tensions at that time, the amount of acid I was taking, things like this . . . it became a burden on the psyche, frankly. Heroin was a great way to calm down. And it was around.'

In the early days of the Stooges, it had been Jim Osterberg who'd turn up for rehearsals and struggle to get his fellow Stooges out of bed. Now it was Ron who attempted to keep the band together, like a mother hen. In the grim heroin roll call, Adams and Mackay went first, in New York. Then the Fellow had a package of heroin sent to the Fun House, and Jim went next, following his first experience of mainlining back in San Francisco. Scotty and Bill followed – 'sniffing first, then skin-popping' – followed at some point by Zeke. Inevitably, the band split into factions – with the Asheton brothers on opposing sides. It seemed that Ron was irrevocably sundered from his singer and, worst of all, his brother. 'There was no relationship,' says Ron. 'Scotty was in the Iggy sphere. I was totally shut out and alone.'

When Jimmy Silver had handed over the financial reins, with John Adams taking day-to-day control while Danny Fields oversaw operations from New York, there had been a healthy surplus in the Stooges' bank balance. Within a few weeks, the money was gone, and the band was being paid in drugs: instead of their weekly $50 in cash, Mackay and Zettner were given $15, plus a bag of weed and a dime bag of China White heroin. Mackay was not so stoned, however, to ignore that he, like Dave, was being ousted. But when the call came from Pop, it was a merciful release. 'There was never a job I ever wanted to be fired from more than that one. I'd got to snorting smack every day for maybe two weeks, then when I got frozen out of the band I lost my connection. For about two months I couldn't sleep through the night, I had these pains in my arms, so I went through a minor withdrawal. If they'd sacked me two months later, I'd have had a full-blown habit.' As it was, Mackay managed to persuade Discount Records boss Dale Watermolder to give him his old job back.

With Mackay gone, the Fun House was becoming a charnel house. Ron would turn up for rehearsals and sit there, alone and brooding. Sometimes on their mostly weekend gigs the band would get paid in heroin; occasionally the singer would flirt with danger by openly snorting heroin on plane flights. But Iggy was a good actor. When he got on the phone to Danny Fields, who was still attempting to oversee the Stooges while holding down a publicity job at Atlantic Records, he could always convince him that he was straight, and change the subject to the new songs he was writing. And there were new songs, for as Iggy maintains, 'Even as we were falling apart we were coming up with great riffs.' One such song – an anthem of dumb defiance – was 'I Got A Right': 'Any time I want I got a right to sing.' It was one of Jim's first entirely solo compositions – that's if you don't count Doc, his incontinent parakeet, who sat on his shoulder as Jim worked out the tune. For a variety of reasons, most fundamentally that one of them was a junkie, and the other wasn't, Ron and Jim's songwriting partnership was at an end. And some time in November 1970, the man who would take Ron's place arrived on the scene.

When you talk to the dozens of people who knew the Stooges in late 1970, the word 'dark' appears again and again. Often it describes the general atmosphere. Often it describes a person: James Williamson, the hotshot guitarist who joined the Stooges just as they headed for self-destruction. There is a striking unanimity to how some people describe him.

> Natalie Schlossman: 'James accelerated the drug use, he accelerated the craziness, he accelerated the make-up and just all the bizarro. The Stooges were in the Bizarro Zone.'
> Danny Fields: 'I didn't like him. I didn't understand why he was there. He was such a contrast to the sweetness of the Asheton brothers that he seemed like a malevolent presence there to me.'

Scott Asheton: 'I told James to come on over to the house
and set up in the practice room and jam. It was my fault.
Damn my eyes for doing it, damn my soul, damn me for
ever . . .'

James Williamson was intense, intelligent, talented and troubled.
Born in Casterville, Texas on 29 October 1949, James had lost his
father at the age of four; his mom remarried an army colonel, who
hated long hair and rock 'n' roll. After moving to Detroit, James had
briefly joined Scott Richardson's band, the Chosen Few, but then
the colonel gave him an ultimatum: 'Cut your hair or go to a juvenile home.' A big fan of Bob Dylan, James did what he figured Bob
would have done in the same situation, and told the colonel to get
lost. At the juvenile home they cut all his hair off on the first day.
James had been schooled in guitar by Oklahoma country musician
Rusty Sparks, who'd invited him on his TV show. At the juvenile
home, he was schooled in rebellion, and when he finally joined the
Stooges, according to Scott, he was 'a wild, on the street speed-
shooting guitar-playing maniac'.

In fairness, by the time James Williamson replaced Bill
Cheatham, who reverted to his role as roadie, every one of the participants in the Stooges' psychodrama had a whole zoo-full of
monkeys on their back. For, as Williamson points out, few of the
people who found him so threatening ever got to know him properly, 'and with respect to the heroin usage, I got in the middle of
this situation – I certainly wasn't leading it.' Williamson accepts
that he was an 'intense person, who focuses on what he is doing at
the time. To that degree, I was always pushing the band to do
better, play better, be better. So if that makes me a villain, then so be
it . . . I don't see it that way.' And it was Iggy, desperate to find any
way forward, who engineered Williamson's ascension to notoriety, spotting that the young Texan's psychotically intense
guitar-playing represented a new direction, and inviting
Williamson into the band to play alongside Ron on guitar. Iggy
had become frustrated with what he saw as Ron's laziness, he

MOST LIKELY TO SUCCEED

KATHY KIMBALL   JIM OSTERBERG

Jim Osterberg, self-styled outsider, was a consummate school politician, vice president of the school council and voted 'most likely to succeed' at Ann Arbor's competitive Tappan Junior High school.

PHOTO CREDIT: RACHEL SCHREIBER

James Osterburg

Jim as a 'bright, alert' second grader, 1955

PHOTO CREDIT: DUANE BROWN

A party at Coachville, the Ypsilanti trailer park set in cornfields.

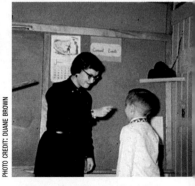

Carpenter Elementary school teacher Mrs Tedesco 'scolds' Osterberg for the camera, 1957.

PHOTO CREDIT: BOBBIE LAM

Above: Jim Osterberg, second left, parties in 1961 with, from left, Bob Hallock, Dennis Gay, Mary Jane Lyndon, Kenny Miller, Denny Olmsted. Kenny Miller, godson of Defence Secretary Robert McNamara, son of Ford Motor Company president Arjay Miller, and Jim's best friend, exemplified Osterberg's ability to charm the rich and powerful.

Below: Jim Osterberg, second from right standing, on the Ann Arbor High debate team, 1964. Classmates like Jim Carpenter, bottom right, still recall the way he'd drop phrases like 'hoi polloi' or 'men of the cloth' into the conversation.

PHOTO CREDIT: BOBBIE LAM

Osterberg's drumming debut, with Jim McLaughlin, Tappan Junior High, March 1962, as The Megaton Two.

Below: 'they were a great, greasy rock 'n' roll band'; The Iguanas, 1965: from left, Nick Kolokithas, Sam Swisher, 'Osterberg', McLaughlin and Don Swickerath.

Club Ponytail

Teen & Collegiate Nite Club

Harbor Springs

PRESENTS

The SHANGRI-LAS

Leader of
The Pack

Give Him A
Great Big Kiss

Give Us
Your Blessing

Plus THE FABULOUS IGUANAS

OPEN 7 NIGHTS
LARGEST PATIO IN NORTHERN MICHIGAN
Dance Under The Stars
Casual Dress Continuous Entertainment   8:00 p.m. – 1:00 a.m.

By 1966, the Iguanas (Jim holds the snare drum in the photo above) had turned professional, playing night after night at the Club Ponytail in the upmarket resort of Harbor Springs, home to many Michigan industrial magnates – whose daughters seemed to adore Osterberg the singing drummer, and his obscene versions of garage classics like 'Louie Louie'.

Left: Jim's high school girlfriend Lynn Klavitter. Together they survived a car crash that left Jim, he said, feeling destined to achieve something unique.

Below: Jim with the 'bohemian' Prime Movers, who nicknamed him 'Iggy'. From left, Bob Sheff (a future Stooge), Jim, Michael Erlewine, Jack Dawson and Dan Erlewine.

PHOTO CREDIT: LYNN KLAVITTER

PHOTO CREDIT: ANDREW SACKS

PHOTO CREDIT: BARBARA KRAMER

Iggy, the aspiring blues drummer, on the first night of his Chicago pilgrimage to see Dylan and Butterfield Blues Band drummer Sam Lay, next to him, at Curley's Place in the West Side. He is accompanied by, from left, blues fans Charlotte Wolter, Barbara Kramer and Vivian Shevitz. The trip would end in trauma – and inspire the formation of the Stooges.

The 'Dum Dum Boys', as Iggy would later term them. Ann Arbor High pupils Dave Alexander, above, and Ron Asheton, right, both shown in 1968, would 'corrupt' the young Jim Osterberg, and help create his Iggy persona; a persona, believed Ron, that would ultimately get out of control.

PHOTO CREDIT: LENI SINCLAIR

Stooges drummer Scott Asheton – aka 'Rock Action' – with MC5 singer Rob Tyner, probably in the MC5's Hill Street headquarters, Ann Arbor, autumn 1968. Scott's hoodlum cool would influence Iggy's antics; the MC5 and their evangelist manager, John Sinclair, gave crucial assistance to the Stooges, their 'little brother band'.

PHOTO CREDIT: LENI SINCLAIR

Signing party for The Stooges, the MC5, and Elektra executives, at 1510 Hill Street, Ann Arbor, late September 1968. From left, standing, Elektra's Jac Holzman, Danny Fields, John Sinclair, Fred Smith, Ron Asheton; Iggy Stooge is seventh from left. John Adams, aka 'The Fellow' is sixth from right, Stooges manager Jimmy Silver and wife Susan third and fourth from right, near to Electra VP and Stooges' nemesis Bill Harvey (far right, in sports jacket).

PHOTO CREDIT: LENI SINCLAIR

PHOTO CREDIT: NATALIE SCHLOSSMAN, PER NILSEN COLLECTION

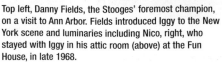

Top left, Danny Fields, the Stooges' foremost champion, on a visit to Ann Arbor. Fields introduced Iggy to the New York scene and luminaries including Nico, right, who stayed with Iggy in his attic room (above) at the Fun House, in late 1968.

Iggy Stooge, Jim Osterberg's indestructible alter-ego, at the Grande Ballroom, Detroit, late 1968.

PHOTO CREDIT: JOEL BRODSKY

Main photo: Iggy heads for a fall as the Stooges wince during the shoot for their debut album, May 1969. 'I'd heard he was physical!' says photographer Joel Brodsky, who took the singer to St Vincent's Emergency Room. Iggy's stitches, left, were airbrushed out of the album cover, below.

PHOTO CREDIT: JOEL BRODSKY

would say later, but there were undoubtedly simpler, pharmaco-logical reasons for their growing estrangement. Yet even in his narcotic fog, Iggy kept pushing, encouraging Williamson to work on a stuttering, vicious guitar riff that became the song 'Penetration'. That Christmas, Iggy took a brief trip to Jamaica with a tape recorder, Framus bass and a Mosrite guitar in an attempt to clean up and write an entire new repertoire.

By the beginning of 1971, Ron Asheton's alienation from the rest of the Stooges was increased when Scotty, Iggy and James moved to University Tower, a newly built high-rise in the centre of Ann Arbor which made a more convenient stop-off for the band's dealers. Ron says he was 'an outcast. Because I was not going along on the death trip.' Zeke Zettner had now been sacked, replaced by Jimmy Recca, who'd played with James in the Chosen Few. Leo Beattie and Dave Dunlap had left back in December, when no paychecks had materialised for Christmas presents, and roadies with better drugs connections were recruited to replace them. While a penniless Ron and Jimmy Recca lived on vegetables grown in the Stooge Hall garden, his brother and the other band members lived out their rock 'n' roll druggie fantasies. Scott and James were now close buddies and shared a room on the seventh floor; Iggy was on the top floor. 'And it was cool,' says Scott. 'We had a great time. We had two maids that came in once a week, both of them foxes, to clean the apartments and we had great wild sex with them. It was happen-ing, man, we were on top of the world. Well, we weren't on top, but we were . . . on the seventh floor, bro, it was cool. And we were both supporting habits.'

On his regular phone calls, Fields continued hearing glowing reports from the singer. Although it was 'uncool' to address people's drugs habits back then, Iggy had the knack of leaving Danny encouraged as he put the phone down, convinced a major new breakthrough lay round the corner. In true Warhol style, Danny taped many of his phone calls; replaying the tapes in later years, Danny would remember how there had only ever been one occasion on which Iggy seemed close to breakdown or betrayed any sense of crisis. The phone call came early in the morning.

Jim Osterberg: 'I really have to talk to you. I came home last night from practice and my bird is dead and I'm like, freaked out!'

Danny Fields: 'What happened? I remember I had a bird that died once and we never knew why.'

JO: 'Well yeah, that's it. We thought it was a little sick but nothing serious. He had his feathers ruffled and his eyes closed, and I don't know what it was, he came down plop – he must have had a stroke or a heart attack, that's a common thing with birds . . . Well, anyway, he dropped right off his perch like a stone and landed on his back with his little feet up in the air, you know, just like in the Raid picture where they kill the little ants.'

DF: 'Ohhhhh . . . Was it a parakeet?'

JO: 'Yeah, a yellow parakeet. And we tried to give him water, and we had to put the water right up to his beak and he'd go [makes little bird drinking sounds] and finally like after ten minutes I started freakin', I started crying, I didn't know what to do and I just called my mom. And finally, uh, we heard these tiny tiny little coughing sounds [makes tiny coughing sound] that he was making. And he was just dead. So we're keeping him here tonight and then we're just going to bury him tomorrow.'

DF: 'Oh that's crummy. Are you OK now?'

JO: 'Yeah. We're keeping him here tonight and then we're just going to bury him tomorrow. And we've been practising, it sounds real nice, and ummm we've got this thing together for the fifteenth . . .'

Sitting in his Greenwich Village apartment, in 2006, Danny Fields shakes his head: 'Over all those years, that was the only time I remember Jim being upset about another being. A parakeet.'

In truth, Iggy was, as his bandmates put it, 'a tough little son-of-a-bitch survivor', overcoming disaster after disaster over the course of 1971. He'd built up a lucrative heroin-dealing business with Wayne Kramer; Kramer knew a source in Detroit, while Iggy provided the customers in the form of his own 'heroin acolytes'. Then one day Kramer returned from an MC5 tour to find the singer in the hospital, presumably recovering from an overdose; the heroin and the money were gone. Determined to wreak his revenge, Kramer enticed Jim to Inkster, a notoriously heavy area of Detroit, and told him to bring some cash. Then Kramer pulled out a gun, took the money and left Iggy penniless and stranded (and wearing, some say, a pink tutu). 'It was a dark time,' says Kramer. 'But that's what people with the mental disorder of drug addiction do.' Many times Iggy went into convulsions at other people's hangouts, including one near-fatal overdose at the apartment of MC5 bassist Michael Davis. Often Betsy was in tow – and Betsy was looking terrible, too. Then there was the gig at the East Town ballroom in May when Scott was driving the equipment out of Ann Arbor and decided to drive the twelve-foot-high rental truck under a ten-foot railway bridge on Washington, just near University Towers, peeling the top off the van like it was a sardine can, and smearing Scotty and two roadies over the road. 'I missed getting under that bridge by a clear two feet – smack!' laughs Scott. 'I hit that sucker so hard it wasn't until I was laying out on the road and stopped rolling that I realised what happened.' With Scotty in hospital, the band called Steve Mackay to play drums in his place. Struggling to master a new set with an unfamiliar drum kit, the sax player had to endure the drawn-out humiliation of Iggy Pop stopping in the middle of each song to complain about his drumming. 'Meanwhile, there's this hometown crowd,' he says, 'and they're screaming, come on Iggy ya motherfucking junkie, come on, let's see you puke, asshole.'

James Williamson points out that, 'It was hard to distinguish my own chaos from that of the band,' while sanguinely noting that the Stooges' desperate straits didn't preclude the presence of a constant stream of women. Eventually Danny Fields had a moment of realisation, at a Chicago show in April 1971. 'Iggy's supposed to be on stage, you're pulling a needle out of his arm and there's blood squirting in your face. Meanwhile Alice Cooper and his band are adjusting their false eyelashes and powdering their noses in the same room. And I'm thinking, those Alice Cooper guys are not as good as this band, but they're pros. That was sorta the metaphor. Both bands are playing for $1500, and there's one that looked poised for stardom. And one poised for the floor of the bathroom.'

Some Stooges diehards enjoyed their final shows. Leee 'Black' Childers savoured the infamous performance at New York's Electric Circus in May 1971, where Iggy looked particularly psychotic, covered in baby oil and glitter. Gerry Miller, the one-time topless dancer and star of several Warhol movies, shouted, 'Let's see you puke!' at Iggy, in her squeaky Mickey Mouse voice. 'So he did!' laughs Leee. 'Right on her!' Some of Danny's live recordings, too, show that when the band got their act together they were still potent, the music based around incessant, headbanging high-energy guitar, and by now they had developed a set of all-new material, including songs titled 'You Don't Want My Name', 'Fresh Rag' and 'Big Time Bum'. Although Elektra records were aware of Iggy's drugs problems – Jac Holzman wrote to Danny Fields recommending a rehab clinic that had presumably been patronised by some of his other artists – Danny believed there was still a good chance that the company would pick up their option for another Stooges album. It was not to happen. But the decision had little to do with the band's collective smack habit. Instead, much of the responsibility for the Stooges' sacking would lie, not with heroin, but with the Third Reich.

As far as the Stooges were concerned, the man responsible for dumping the band from the Elektra label was Bill Harvey, arch-enemy of

Danny Fields. But in reality, the decision fell to another Elektra executive, who by supreme irony was also the producer who had nursemaided the band's greatest recording. For according to Don Gallucci, who went with Bill Harvey to listen to the Stooges' new material at the Fun House, it was he who made the decision to reject the band.

Today, Gallucci runs a successful real-estate finance business, although he looks back on his production of *Fun House* as one of the finest moments in his musical career. But in 1971, the album was anything but a feather in his cap. Gallucci was, he explains, emotionally naive but politically adept. He was acutely aware that the album he produced with the Stooges had not troubled the Billboard Top 100 albums, yet he also knew no opprobrium attached to him for this failure – for the decision to press the button had been Jac Holzman's. But if Gallucci elected to produce the band a second time, the responsibility for failure would be his alone.

When Don Gallucci and Bill Harvey arrived in Ann Arbor to audition the band's material, they were aware of the band's drug abuse, and the two of them took Steve Mackay for a drive to pump him for information about his ex-bandmates. Mackay was noncommittal, and as Gallucci tells it, he had no conception that the Stooges were involved in anything worse than the hashish he had seen them smoke incessantly at the Elektra studios.

Gallucci didn't want to be out in Michigan, which he considered a god-forsaken location, nor in a falling-down farmhouse with a bunch of people with whom he felt little rapport. But he had to go through the niceties, and in any case enjoyed the company of Ron Asheton, whom he considered the most 'reach-out' and PR-savvy of the Stooges. Consequently, he was happy to join Ron on a tour of the Fun House, until they reached Ron's room. For Gallucci, the slick savvy exec in an expensive sports jacket, was horrified by the Nazi uniforms, by the books on concentration camps, the swastikas, the lightning-bolt logos and the photos of atrocities that he says he saw in Ron's living quarters. Shocked, he asked Ron why he was fascinated with the Nazis. Ron explained that when he was a child, Ann Asheton used to wash and then blow-dry his hair, says Gallucci, 'And then Ron said, "In the noise of the dryer going *wheeeshhh, wheeeshhhh,* I could hear voices going *Sieg Heil . . . Sieg Heil . . ."'*

What was perhaps typical Asheton black humour completely weirded Gallucci out. And then he sat down to listen to a couple of Stooges numbers, played live in the Fun House. James Williamson remembers Harvey and Gallucci being 'appalled' by the music, but the producer maintains that while the music perhaps seemed derivative of their earlier material, that was the last thing on his mind. 'I thought I was in nut land, I hated the whole Michigan middle of nowhere thing and I wanted to get out. And now we're gonna do another album where the first one didn't make it? And I think I said some fairly unkind things in front of them, to Bill Harvey, something like, Cream is the London Philharmonic compared to these guys, something really asshole.'

Gallucci's abandoning of the Stooges' cause gave Bill Harvey ample justification for telling Danny Fields that, as far as the new material went, 'I hear nothing.' The label would forgo its option on the Stooges' next album. More seriously, on 21 June, Elektra demanded the return of $10,825 that had been advanced to the band. According to Jim Osterberg, Jac Holzman was apologetic that things hadn't worked out, and gave him a Nikon camera as a farewell present, but over the same period Bill Harvey was writing to Danny Fields, demanding that all the fees for Stooges live performances be paid directly to Elektra, to recoup their debts. Holzman, it transpired later, was interested in retaining the services of Iggy Pop as a solo artist, but the loss of all their income from live shows was the death sentence for the Stooges. The band failed to show at dates booked over late June and early July; Ron, Scott and Jimmy Recca played one last show at Wamplers Lake, enlisting Steve Richards, from River View, Michigan, to sing in place of Iggy; meanwhile, James, who had contracted a nasty case of hepatitis, went to recuperate at his sister's in Detroit.

As his band finally splintered, Iggy was making plans with a junkie's deviousness. Although the band's Elektra bank account had been closed, Iggy would regularly walk over from University Tower to Discount Records, brandishing the band's cheque book. Steve Mackay, who was behind the counter, was suspicious, but Dale Watermolder was sufficiently star-struck by Discount's famous ex-employee to allow him to cash the cheque. For ten days, Iggy kept returning, each time with a cheque for around $200, until finally the bank informed Watermolder that all the cheques, over $2,000 in total, had bounced. A shamefaced Jim Osterberg finally came in with his father, who paid all of his debts, saving his son from facing any criminal charges.

Around July 1971, Jim Osterberg took refuge in the Adare Road home of the Mickelsens. According to Hiawatha Bailey, a friend of the family, Iggy made himself at home in their comfortable house, sprawling imperiously in the lounge with Betsy in his lap, and regally gesturing his approval should Dr Mickelsen walk into the room to pour himself a drink. Hiawatha, a Trans Love employee, was obeying a summons from Iggy to bring over the Up's old Chevy van, and on his arrival was invited to sit down and offered a glass of wine from the Mickelsens' cabinet. Then Iggy told Hi, 'What I want you to do is go over to Stooge Manor [aka the Fun House], and these are the things I want you to pick up. I want you to get the Marshall stack, I want you to get the Echorette, I want you to get the drums . . .'

Hiawatha pauses for a moment. 'When Iggy sent me over there . . . he was sending me to break up the Stooges.'

They bulldozed the Fun House a couple of months later.

It is a sunny day, and Billy Cheatham and I are sprawling on a small grassy bank in the centre of Ann Arbor, watching aeropla ·⸱ɔ track slowly overhead as Billy explains the mechanics of heroin addiction. As apprentice to the Fellow, Billy charted the progress of the drug as it wreaked its havoc among the Dum Dum Boys. Later he himself took the red wine cure, one of a bewilderingly wide range of folk remedies to wean users off Sister Morphine. Billy is a thoughtful, placid, thick-set man, and he speaks fondly, dreamily, of Dave Alexander – 'a crazy kid, and a great guy' – and of Tommy 'Zeke' Zettner and his brother Miles, both of them 'lost to . . . that damned heroin'. Together we mourn the Dum Dum Boys, a mourning more poignant for the fact that, a few years later, I would hear that Billy, too, died prematurely.

Perhaps no friendships really survive fame. Perhaps few of them survive heroin. Perhaps it's simply that no man is a hero to his roadie. But when Billy's conversation turns to his one-time singer, his tone becomes precise, and cold. When Billy and Iggy were bandmates, they would hit the Detroit ghettos together to score. But drug buddies they were not. Even as the Dum Dum Boys went missing in action, says Billy, their leader found them expendable. 'There was a movie on the other day by Elia Kazan, called *A Face in the Crowd*, where Andy Griffith starts out as a radio personality and starts climbing and climbing and gets more and more power, and he gets uglier and uglier.

'I can almost see that happening to Jim, in that the more popular he became, the less likeable and friendly, and less admirable he became to his friends. Like he thought, I'm the one that does this, you're along for the ride. I don't know if that was the smell of power, or the drugs, but I did see that happening. I didn't care for it too much.'

As the Dum Dum Boys retired, hurt, to family houses across Ann Arbor and Detroit, their singer kept on moving. As he describes it, there was 'no operatic sense of doom'; instead he was busy trading on his new contacts, of whom by far the most promising was Steve Paul, the ambitious, canny proprietor of New York nightclub The Scene. Paul was a member of Danny Fields' intimidatingly smart gay circle; he had made his first fortune, according to Iggy, selling pimple remover, he dressed only in the colour blue, and was force-fully steering the career of Johnny Winter, extracting a then unprecedented $600,000 advance from Columbia Records for the albino Texan guitarist. Paul paid Iggy and Betsy's fare to New York so the blue-clad svengali could discuss overseeing his career. The conversation advanced to the point where Paul decided he had to inform his close friend – and Iggy's existing manager – Danny Fields, who by now had spent his entire life savings attempting to bankroll Iggy and his band.

Their conversation, sitting on a hill in Central Park, did not go well. Fields was overwhelmed with grief and jealousy. Danny's mortification and sense of betrayal was intensified by his conviction that Paul, for all his persuasiveness and eloquence, presided over music that was retrogressive and empty – flashy guitar masturbation. Resolving to himself, 'If Steve makes Iggy the star I always knew he could be, I'll kill them both,' Fields told Paul to go ahead and do whatever he wanted, and that he had no interest in knowing what went on.

Steve Paul's plan was to unite Iggy with another of his charges, Rick Derringer. Derringer had scored his first number-one single, 'Hang On Sloopy', with the McCoys when he was just seventeen and was an adept blues-rock guitarist, who also played with Johnny Winter and his brother Edgar. Today, Paul downplays his ambitions for the ex-Stooge singer, maintaining, 'It wasn't a svengali plan. Just an honest instinct about finding a guitar player that he was comfortable with.' Derringer was open-minded about the partnership, although unimpressed by the fact that a couple of days after moving into his apartment on 30th Street, the singer disappeared to Miami, ostensibly to play golf – although while he was there Iggy called his agent at DMA, Dave Leone, to ask for a hundred bucks for methadone treatment. (Leone sent him the money, and told him never to call again.)

Derringer was unfazed by the evidence of Iggy's heroin addiction, and found the down-on-his-luck singer pleasant enough to talk to. Rick's wife, Liz, liked Iggy's 15-year-old girlfriend, Betsy, who was young, waif-like and vulnerable. After the couple returned from Miami around the end of August, Jim confided in Liz and told her that Betsy had recently had an abortion and needed to rest; she too was invited to stay at the Derringers' apartment.

To this day, however, Liz Derringer remains disturbed by Iggy and Betsy's stay. A couple of days in, Liz and Rick had taken Jim to see a movie when Betsy, who'd been left to rest in bed, turned up at the cinema. 'My first thought was, Oh my God! She's left my door open. I have to go back. I knew the door would be wide open because she didn't have a key. Then I walked in and I noticed that something was not right. I think it was a day or later that I was looking for my jewellery and couldn't find it.'

Liz realised that a jewelled heart, a Star of David, a small diamond and some rings were missing. Convinced that Betsy had stolen them, she went to Max's Kansas City that evening, and started telling all of those present about the new low to which Iggy Pop and his girlfriend had sunk. Later that evening, Liz, Rick and a friend were at home when they heard the doorbell ring. Looking through the peephole, they saw Iggy. 'I was terrified!' says Liz. 'He has crazy eyes, and I was convinced he was going to stick a knife through my heart and kill me.'

Eventually, Liz's friend Geraldine opened the door, and Liz emerged from the bedroom where she had been hiding, to hear Jim Osterberg tell her, 'I need you to tell me exactly what's happened.' Liz told him her jewellery had been stolen and described exactly what was missing; Jim – scarily intense, but coherent and profusely apologetic – promised he would find and return the missing items. Over the next few days he called Liz repeatedly, updating her on his attempts to reclaim most of the jewellery from New York's pawn shops. Eventually he returned most of the pieces, but by that point any idea of a collaboration between Rick Derringer and Iggy Pop, whether or not it had been a serious prospect in the first place, was dead in the water. The theft represented the death-blow to Jim and Betsy's relationship, too, and the 15-year-old fled to her parents in Ann Arbor. It's difficult to track poor Betsy's progress from then on, for it was scattered and hazy; in later years she called her friend Hiawatha Bailey, telling him that she was suffering from terminal cirrhosis of the liver, and that Jim was the love of her life. Her family, according to Bailey, harbour undying resentment towards Jim Osterberg, and since her death refuse to talk to outsiders.

Cast adrift once more, Jim called Danny Fields, who found him a refuge with Terry Ork, who happened to be housesitting an elegant Upper East Side apartment and had already taken in Gerard Malanga – another member of the Warhol circle, best known for his exquisite photos of Edie Sedgwick and for his leather-clad appearances cracking a whip on stage with the Velvet Underground. Jim was an ideal houseguest; he travelled light, with just the jeans and shirt he stood up in, and came and went quietly, sleeping in one of the penthouse's two bedrooms while Malanga took the couch. Those few days, sitting around as the sun streamed in through the penthouse's large windows, were a brief respite from the mayhem that had surrounded Iggy, and one morning, as he emerged from the bedroom, he sashayed over the living room's parquet floor and started moving and stretching, going through the exercises he'd always used to limber up before his stage performances. Seeing him caught in the mid-morning light, Malanga picked up his Nikon and clicked off four or five frames as Iggy cavorted, throwing shapes. Iggy peeled off his shirt as Malanga moved around him as if in a ballet, then Malanga instructed him: 'Strip down to nothing.' Iggy obliged; posing naked and calm in front of the white wall; thin, but physically fit, vulnerable, but unbowed, confident in the face of all his travails.

A couple of days later Jim moved in with Danny Fields, who was delighted to resume the 'don't worry, I'll take care of everything' regime to which they'd both become accustomed. They were both watching TV, on 7 September 1971, when the phone rang. It was Lisa Robinson, the rock writer who with producer husband Richard made up Max's hippest rock 'n' roll couple. She told Danny, 'We're here with David Bowie.'

'Oh, David Bowie,' Fields drawled in reply. 'He's the only person outside of the United States ever heard of Iggy.' Danny registered something about the fact they were on their way to Max's Kansas City, and David wanting to meet Iggy, before he dozed off again.

Appropriately enough, David Bowie had discovered Iggy on his first trip to America the previous February, when he'd alighted in San Francisco looking disconcertingly like Lauren Bacall, according to writer John Mendelssohn, who'd been persuaded by a friend at Mercury Records to write a feature on the then-unknown English singer. Mendelssohn felt protective towards this exotic, fragile creature, carrying his luggage and accompanying him to San Jose for a radio interview. After a brief, unenlightening chat with the disdainful hippie DJ, Bowie was asked to choose a record to play; Mendelssohn spotted a copy of the Stooges debut album, and suggested they cue up 'No Fun'. Bowie was instantly 'amused'. That December he nominated Iggy as his favourite singer in *Melody Maker*. When he hit New York early in September, Bowie was 'absolutely intrigued' by Iggy, according to Robinson, who was at the centre of this social nexus.

The phone rang again. Again, it was Lisa and Richard, telling Danny they were waiting for him. Danny dragged Jim away from his TV movie, *Mr Smith Goes To Washington*, cajoling him, 'C'mon, he's been nice to us, we'd better be nice to him.' And they stepped outside for the four-block walk to Max's.

CHAPTER 7

Street-walking Cheetah

No one could work the back room at Max's like Iggy. And when he walked in to sit down at a table with David Bowie, Tony Defries and Tony Zanetta, with Richard and Lisa Robinson looking on, there was no doubt as to who was the high-voltage character. Iggy Pop was living like a cat, staying on couches across town, trying to kick heroin; his girlfriend had just split after being accused of stealing a prominent New Yorker's jewellery. And he was on top of the world, ma. He walked into the room ready to impress, according to Tony Zanetta, who was sitting by Defries: 'He knew they were waiting for him. And he was Up For It. He was immediately entertaining. He practically did a tap dance there and then.' For the first time, but not the last, Iggy Pop showed himself unbowed by the slings and arrows of outrageous fortune. In fact, he traded on his travails, turned them into his own narrative – one in which he was the indefatigable hero.

The last time David Bowie had visited the US he had been an apparently fragile creature, travelling alone. This time he had an organisation with him, in the form of Tony Defries, a one-time solicitor's clerk who boasted the most brilliant improvisational management style to hit the Big Apple in years. Defries had an acute mind and a fearless negotiation technique: he would go straight to the chief executive of whatever company he was dealing with, unintimidated by anyone's reputation, would score a great deal – and make the other guy feel good about it, too. Earlier that evening, Defries had blitzed through the social scene of New York, wining and dining RCA's executives at the Ginger Man restaurant, guided by the proprietors of all that was hip in New York, writer Lisa Robinson and her husband Richard, the producer who as A&R at RCA had brokered the deal with Bowie. At the Ginger Man, Defries and Bowie had also met up with David's other American musical obsession, Lou Reed, and talked about a production deal.

That night at Max's, David Bowie seemed low-key in comparison to Iggy and Defries. He was sympathetic, curious, a good listener: 'very canny; self-possessed – and a not unkind person' was Iggy Pop's first impression. David asked intelligent, incisive questions, drawing out the star-crossed singer in a manner that was almost innocent. In comparison, Iggy was the one who seemed more calculating, but that impression was counterbalanced by the fact he was so engagingly honest. He simply enjoyed charming people. To Tony Zanetta, who'd met Bowie and Defries while playing Andy Warhol in a London production of the play *Pork* a few weeks before, and had instantly been recruited to what would become the MainMan circus, it seemed like David was trying to impress Defries with this exotic, exciting creature, almost as if Iggy were a work of art the two could add to their collection.

In retrospect, to many people this meeting seemed calculated, a collaboration hatched via mutual exploitation. It would indeed profoundly affect the lives of both David Jones and Jim Osterberg. In reality, there was an innocence about the encounter between the two 24-year-olds, one seemingly down and out, one on the way up. On Bowie's part there was an almost naive enthusiasm, a fascination for rock 'n' roll and theatre – and Iggy represented a one-stop shop for both of those interests. For Iggy, the main attraction was that of joining the circus and simply seeing where it would take him. So he readily agreed when Defries and Bowie asked him to come round the next morning for breakfast at their tenth-floor suite in the Warwick Hotel. (Although a favoured haunt of Liz Taylor and Cary Grant, the Warwick was chosen by Defries for the symbolism of its association with The Beatles, who had stayed there on their all-conquering debut American tour.)

The next morning, over one of Defries's habitual drawn-out English breakfasts – he'd sit around half dressed, smoking cigars, taking several phone calls at once – the manager made his pitch. Iggy's performance was as classic in its way as anything seen at Ungano's or the Electric Circus. Defries was a tower of strength, an operator who left his audience in no doubt he could take care of business; Iggy was flip, entertaining, and knew instinctively how to trade on Bowie and Defries's fascination with Americana, telling them how he grew up in a trailer park, or describing his methadone treatment in minute detail. Bowie, in turn, discussed the music, and how he could find Iggy a new backing band over in London. Even before Defries was fully dressed, the manager guaranteed he could negotiate a new record deal, and Iggy agreed to sign to Gem, the management company for which Defries handled business affairs. Defries instructed Jim to return to Ann Arbor and continue his methadone treatments, and that he would be 'summoned' when a record deal was imminent.

Linking up with Bowie and Defries was a risky throw of the dice – Bowie had enjoyed just one quirky hit single – 'Space Oddity' – in the UK and star status in America for such an unconventional artist was anything but guaranteed. But there was an irresistible energy about Defries, his love of showmanship, his conviction that he could beat the system. And a showman loves a showman.

Ironically, at the end of September Jim Osterberg was sent a letter from Bill Harvey, care of Danny Fields, telling him that Elektra wanted to retain his services as a solo artist. Elektra's move was possibly a reaction to Defries' interest in Iggy, but by the time

Danny received the letter, it was irrelevant. Jim was back in Ann Arbor, plotting his MainMan career with James Williamson. Ron Asheton would hear the news just a few days later, when he'd gone into town to see a Fellini movie but ended up instead at a party for the SRC. His friends James and Jim were there, but they avoided talking to him. Later in the evening he heard that Iggy had a new contract with David Bowie's people; he told his informant, 'Someone take a shotgun and blow my head off,' before walking home, crying all the way.

For Ron and many of his Ann Arbor buddies, Iggy Pop's abandonment of his high-school friend was a cold-hearted betrayal which would take decades to erase. It would mark the point at which Iggy first became a solo singer, rather than a member of a band. This move was partly inspired by Tony Defries, who only dealt with singers; his plan was to build a studio of stars, like MGM, and in this plan musicians were expendable, mere technicians. For Iggy, dropping the Ashetons was simple pragmatism; he had a musical manifesto to advance. Still, one senses echoes of the ambitious child who'd dropped his elementary-school pals when they'd outlived their usefulness. In the meantime, Jim and James plotted together; Iggy had not mentioned Williamson at September's breakfast meeting, but the two agreed that Iggy would go to work on persuading Defries to bring over his new songwriting partner.

Over that autumn, Defries worked at fulfilling his guarantee that he would find Iggy a record deal, and his best prospect turned out to be Clive Davis at Columbia. Davis was well on his way to becoming a legend in the American music industry. He had doubled Columbia's market share with a raft of new signings including Santana and Janis Joplin, and would later go on to found Arista Records. It was an easy sale – Iggy was well known in New York, and the notion, perhaps broached by Defries, that Clive Davis could succeed where Jac Holzman had failed appealed to the Columbia boss's ego. Defries sent Jim a plane ticket to New York so that Davis could meet Iggy in person. Iggy would dine out frequently on his description of how he won over Davis, recounting it thus:

Davis: 'Will you do Simon and Garfunkel?'
Pop: 'No, I won't.'
Davis: 'Will you be more melodic?'
Pop: 'No, I won't.'
Davis: 'Will you do what anybody asks you to?'
Pop: 'No, I won't . . . but I can sing, wanna hear?'

At which Iggy sprawled over Davis's desk, crooning 'The Shadow Of Your Smile'. Iggy maintained that at that moment Davis called his legal advisers and told them to draw up the paperwork, but according to Zanetta, who was present, 'The meeting was a formality. This wasn't Iggy the operator, on high voltage. When we walked in it felt like it was a done deal already, that it had already been sorted between Defries and Clive Davis.' The Columbia advance – which was for Iggy Pop alone, with no mention of the Stooges – was widely quoted as totalling $100,000; but this was typical Defries grandstanding, for that figure was almost certainly an advance against several albums.

Over the next couple of days Zanetta babysat Iggy in the Warwick Hotel while Defries attended to other business; although Defries wasn't particularly interested in Iggy's music, he focused on emphasising his star quality, and gave Zanetta $500 to take the singer out and buy him a pair of silver leather pants Defries had spotted uptown at North Beach Leather. Then the two sat around for a couple of days in a suite at the Warwick, before Defries concluded his business and was able to spend more time with Iggy. It was probably during this trip that Iggy persuaded his manager to let him bring James Williamson – 'the only man who understands me' – on his trip to London early the next year.

London in the spring of 1972 was thrilling, sleazy, glamorous and stoned on Mandrax and hashish. David Bowie and Marc Bolan were together sprinkling the final touches of fairydust to what would become glam; the charts were also full of the pompous college whimsy of outfits such as Jethro Tull, while in the clubs, bands like the Pink Fairies and Hawkwind purveyed trippy but tough hippie rock. And new boy on the scene Iggy Pop walked the streets, convinced he was better than any of them. *New Musical Express* writer Nick Kent, who had been in awe of the Stooges ever since he'd heard their debut album on John Peel's BBC Radio 1 show, wangled an introduction to his hero and realised that Iggy's sense of self-belief was 'staggering. There he was, walking round London, working out his plan to take over the world. He's one of those people. He believed he had this manifest destiny to throw his shadow across the world on a major level.'

It seemed appropriate that James Williamson, rather than the sweet, laid-back Ashetons, would become Iggy's accomplice for his new assault on the unsuspecting music industry. Like Iggy, James had become even more intense since the dying days of the Stooges, and was determined to leave his own imprint on the world. Tall, thin, pale-skinned and black-haired, with scars from childhood acne, James reminded a few people of Keith Richards' more evil, more manic twin. He wasn't the product of a warm loving environment, but he would get his own back. He had no track record, but was hell-bent on building one.

Iggy and James were roomed together at the Kensington Gardens Hotel, a sprawling stucco-fronted Victorian building set in a leafy west London square. They spent their time writing songs, chasing schoolgirls or watching TV, with equal intensity. On a couple of occasions they were invited to David and Angie Bowie's gothic headquarters in Beckenham, just outside London; Jim was impressed with Bowie's eclectic, Arts Lab-style operation. Angie was also somewhat taken with James Williamson, although as time went on she'd come to resent Iggy's demands on Defries' time and, as she saw it, David's money. Occasionally James and Jim would drop into parties or gigs, surveying London's 'counterculture' with general disdain, loftily dismissing most musical rivals apart from

Marc Bolan. Back in the hotel, Williamson would sit in their room, continuously spitting out riffs on his Gibson B25 acoustic guitar, a six-string stream of consciousness. When he hit on something memorable, he'd play it to Jim for his approval and together they'd work it into a song. As always, Jim, the boy with the knack for a memorable phrase, seemed adept at crafting arresting lyrics, although over this period his style changed, becoming perhaps more conventional, but certainly more intense, with more powerful imagery packed into every line. David Bowie was true to his word, calling around London's leading rhythm sections and asking them to audition for Iggy; often, like Pink Fairies drummer Twink, they would call up and be told the vacancy was already filled – for, as far as Williamson in particular was concerned, no English rhythm section was aggressive enough.

Early in 1972 ex-child actor Michael Des Barres was preparing his own grandiose rock 'n' roll project, Silverhead, at the subterranean Kings Road rehearsal complex ACM when he encountered Iggy in the studio corridor. With bare-faced effrontery, Iggy asked him, magisterially, 'Do you want to watch my rehearsal?' Des Barres walked into the damp, dingy studio, with old Pink Fairies posters peeling off the wall, and was dazzled by the sheer noise and spectacle. 'It was truly a life-changing moment. He was standing there in jeans, no shirt, he grabbed the microphone . . . then this raw, this three-dimensional noise hit me.' Where London's decadent cliques affected a kind of Edwardian dandyism, to Des Barres this was a much tougher spectacle, delivered with unprecedented aural brutality. 'They made everything else sound effete.' Des Barres was just as taken with the image of James Williamson, who was determined to make his mark. 'He was an unbelievable guitar player. And also he had a huge cock, by the way, that was the thing about the Stooges. That's why the girls liked them.'

Williamson, according to most who met him in London, was more openly arrogant than his singer. According to Jim, it was Williamson who invariably objected to the musicians Bowie suggested, telling the singer, 'These English people wear funny clothes, these are not serious musicians, there's no groove!' By now, David Bowie's career was taking off in the wake of *Hunky Dory*, and Defries was maddeningly distracted, branching out with his own artists, principally Bowie, to launch MainMan – a Defries-owned offshoot of Gem, in which Gem owner Laurence Myers retained a slice of the turnover. But by the early summer MainMan were planning a showcase performance for all their acts, with Iggy Pop playing back-to-back with Lou Reed's first performance in London. And it was James's idea, fatefully, to reunite the Stooges by bringing Ron and Scott Asheton over to London. James had been close to Scott – they had been, after all, drug buddies at University Tower – and was taken with his musicianship, if not his brother's. 'Then I suggested that Ron get moved to bass,' says Williamson. 'So this is where there's sour grapes about it from Ron's perspective. But at the time he was damn happy to have a job.'

The demotion of Ron Asheton from guitar to bass would be devastating for the one-time lead guitarist of the Stooges – 'It was chump city for me and my brother, we were reduced to being sidemen in our own band.' Yet it would also kickstart a period of hectic creativity. On 6 June, Ron and Scott were flown over from Detroit (Scott brought his own supply of toilet rolls, convinced there was a shortage of them in London). For all their misgivings about London plumbing and band politics, the Asheton brothers loved being in the city; the band borrowed Laurence Myers' house in Little Venice (which was of course eventually trashed) and by the end of the month were rehearsing feverishly at Underhill Studios in Greenwich, a favoured venue for Gem's acts as it was en route to the Bowies' Beckenham HQ. Lou Reed was rehearsing his own new band, the Tots, in the studio the same month, while the Spiders From Mars were also preparing for their July shows. London band England's Glory were rehearsing in the adjacent studio, and drummer Jon Newey was struck by this unknown band: 'You knew they weren't English,' says Newey. 'No English rhythm section was as aggressive as that. They were playing with such intensity, the same superheavy riffs played again and again, getting it down perfect.'

The night before Iggy's first ever show outside of the USA, Lou Reed made his London debut at the same venue, King's Cross Cinema. James and Iggy went to see their rival, whose show was attended by Roxy Music and other members of the Glamorati. Lou was clearly out of it on tranquillisers, or alcohol, or some combination thereof; Iggy and James could be seen snickering at each other, especially the moment when Lou's sequinned trousers started to fall down. 'James was nudging Iggy, and Iggy looking at James and they pointed to it,' says Nick Kent. 'It was, ha ha, Lou, you aren't so cool. We're going to kick your arse.'

Iggy Pop made his public debut the following night, 15 July 1972. In keeping with MainMan's concentration on stars, rather than bands, the billing read 'Iggy Pop, ex Iggy and the Stooges'. Creem's Dave Marsh was one of several writers who'd been flown over to see Bowie's Aylesbury show, in a pioneering MainMan propaganda operation, and managed to watch Iggy, too. He'd seen the old Stooges, but found this performance, in the black-painted theatre that had been recently converted from a sleazy porn venue, far more dark and forbidding. 'All the things that I'd never took seriously in my Id were coming to life. And there was no Buffy in sight to slay the vampires.'

The show left many onlookers shaken, disturbed or inspired. Mick Rock, who was then just starting out as a photographer, had to track the singer, in his silver leather pants and silver hair, like he was chasing a big cat over its home territory; he was stunned by the attitude and physicality of the singer, and the sheer rawness of the sound. The crowd was smaller than that for Lou, but possibly more influential. A 16-year-old boy called John Lydon attended with his friend, John Grey; Mick Jones, later a founder of the Clash, thought, 'The full-on quality of the Stooges was great, like flame-throwers.' Music industry press officer Richard Ogden was contentedly observing the show from his seat in the balcony when suddenly

Iggy climbed up and deposited himself in his lap, pulling Ogden's hair, bellowing into the microphone and splattering sweat and melted make-up over his mortified victim, as London's journalists giggled at Ogden's discomfort. Williamson's guitar playing was rough in places, but Nick Kent for one felt that this was the most cataclysmic show he'd ever seen. 'A lot of new genres were created that night, musically. One song was the first time I ever heard what became known as Thrash Metal. This was where I understood what rock 'n' roll was all about, because it simply dripped from their fingers.'

Two days after the King's Cross performance, the Stooges went into London's Olympic Studios with engineer Keith Harwood to record more rehearsals. Together with other early demos from Trident Studios, and tapes from R&G Jones rehearsal studio, where they'd start at midnight and play until dawn, they document a period of insistent creativity and a sound that was profoundly different from the previous Stooges. Any vestiges of art rock or the avant garde were gone, replaced by a more conventional but infinitely more aggressive bug-eyed guitar assault. At times the recordings simply dissolve into white noise, as Williamson's Wagnerian rumble drowns out Iggy on songs like 'I Got A Right': psychotically intense, taken at a dizzying pace, the song vindicated Nick Kent's assertion that he'd witnessed the birth of Thrash Metal. On other songs the music is simple and sweet, notably 'Sick Of You', a crooned dissection of Iggy's relationship with Betsy – 'sick of hanging round your pad; sick of your mom and sick of your dad' set over limpid arpeggios that lull the listener into a false sense of security before the sucker punch of Williamson's rattling powerchords launch a nasty rant that makes the Rolling Stones' 'Under My Thumb' sound sensitive and retiring.

The recordings, magnificent as they are, capture the work of someone almost literally manic, obsessed with being faster, louder and treblier than any magnetic tape could capture; an impression Jim Osterberg would bear out recently, pointing out how: 'My insanity bar was raised so high at that point that nothing sounded bent enough – ever.'

For the other Stooges, those early days in London were comparatively idyllic. Ron, for all his change in role, felt blissful that the band was reunited, and spent much of his time wandering around Lambeth's Imperial War Museum. Scott recalls an eclectic drugs regime, which included the odd grain of pure brown heroin ('the strongest, best I ever had'), beer, hash, Mandrax, Quaaludes and Valium. According to Ron, Williamson also appreciated the fact that in the UK, codeine was available over the counter. Many times they would call a limo to take them down to Defries' Gunther Grove apartment to hang out. The studio flat, with its impressive mezzanine and inevitably 'colourful' inhabitants, was the centre of the MainMan empire, which by now included Mott the Hoople, Dana Gillespie and Wayne County. But the MainMan circus, for all its flash, was a slow-moving operation. In January, David had unveiled his Ziggy Stardust persona; the fact that this grandiose rock superhero was openly based on Iggy was flattering, as was the fact that Ziggy had attempted to emulate his hero by walking on his audience's hands at Imperial College in February, only to tumble to the floor. But as the *Ziggy Stardust* album started to take off following its 6 June release, it was obvious that this fictional creation was occupying all Defries' attention – much to the resentment of the real people left standing in the wings. Wayne County saw his own career become hopelessly stalled, and in the endless weeks of hanging around MainMan, observed why that didn't happen to Iggy. 'The joke going round was that Tony gave Iggy to Bowie to play with. But he refused to be exploited. He could be the sweetest thing in the world but if he thought somebody was fucking with him, fucking with his life, fucking with his career, he'd be, "I'm gonna take you, motherfucker".'

Today, Angie Bowie attributes cynical motives to her then-husband's championing of Iggy. 'If he had all the people that were cool, then did that not make him more cool than the most cool?'

Many others credit Bowie with a more sincere respect for Iggy's music, but by now the Ziggy bandwagon had a momentum of its own and the Stooges, for better or worse, were left to their own devices. MainMan director Hugh Attwooll block-booked London's rehearsal studios for them, but there was a limit on how much time they could spend rehearsing and, for a group of characters devoted to watching midnight TV screenings of *Night Of The Living Dead*, the British way of life – notably the fact that television shut down at 10.30 – seemed cruel and inhuman. Those who first met the Stooges in June found them 'chipper' and optimistic. But Nick Kent, one of Jim and James's few regular visitors in the early days, noticed that even though the two had kicked serious drugs, 'Jim would talk about his heroin days, James would too . . . and there was a longing in the way that they addressed the subject'. Kent sensed an inevitability that Iggy would follow that route again; and he would be proved right.

In July, Angie Bowie was allotted the task of finding the Stooges a new home, and selected a mews house at 19 Seymour Walk in Kensington, five minutes from MainMan's office, which belonged to novelist and screenwriter Frederic Raphael; Angie also demonstrated her efficiency by managing to recruit a maid who was also an expert macrobiotic cook. On the summer afternoons, Iggy would walk around Hyde Park in shades, wearing his leather jacket with a cheetah on the back, reading magazines. During one such ramble early in September, after he noticed a *Time* magazine feature headlined 'Search and Destroy', Iggy snorted several rocks of Chinese brown heroin and decided the phrase would make a great song title. The song's inspiration was the search-and-destroy missions of the Vietnam War, which was constantly in that summer's headlines. Ironically, the subject of the article was the global depradations of heroin.

The lyrics featured as its narrator and hero 'a street-walking cheetah with a heart full of napalm'. The phrases perfectly fitted a scything James Williamson riff worked up at R&G Jones, which the guitarist used to punctuate with the exclamation, 'Kill it, gooks'.

('The Stooges are really horrible people, politically incorrect,' laughs Jim.) It was the perfect manifesto, the war cry of the 'world's forgotten boy'. But the subtext was obvious to the Stooges' singer, if no one else. Search-and-destroy missions were a notorious failure. For all his bravado, Jim Osterberg felt his new venture was doomed: 'I knew we were going down and I knew no one was going for this,' he murmurs today, matter-of-factly. 'Because there were all sorts of weaknesses. The lyrics to "Death Trip" are my way of saying, I know what is happening to us, I know what we're doing, here's why . . . and I'm gonna sing about it.'

When Iggy first arrived in London, David Bowie had offered to produce what would have been his solo debut, but Iggy had declined the collaboration – which might well, as with Mott the Hoople's Bowie-penned 'All The Young Dudes', have yielded a hit. Instead, Iggy had insisted on producing the album himself, along with Williamson. Today, Williamson concludes the insistence was probably a mistake. The two of them – for all Iggy's claims that he, rather than John Cale or Don Gallucci, had produced the band's first two albums – were inexperienced in the studio, and overlooked many basic errors and sonic glitches. But from the moment the sessions started on 10 September at CBS's studio on Whitfield Street, just under London's sparkling, futuristic Post Office Tower, the entire band were focused on their task and worked doggedly to ensure that, even if this was their last chance, they would go down fighting.

In retrospect, it's apparent that with the album that became *Raw Power*, Iggy and the Stooges were attempting to stick to certain conventions. Unfortunately – for their commercial prospects at least – they were simply incapable of doing so. The album follows a completely formulaic structure, suggested by Tony Defries: uptempo opener for each side, followed by a more romantic ballad, a classic rocker and then a moody, significant closing number. Many elements were far more conventional than anything from the band's first two albums: twelve-bar blues forms, rockabilly references and chugging riffs that bore the influence of Marc Bolan.

But for all that, the Stooges remained deliciously warped. Their romantic song, 'Gimme Danger', was based on a luscious, intricate Stonesy guitar riff, but the lyrics detailed how Iggy wanted to 'feel your disease'. One song's glammy strut resembles T-Rex. But where Bolan's chorus went 'get it on, bang a gong', Iggy's lyrics informed his girl that 'your pretty face is going to hell', while his vocal performance is simply deranged. Opening side two, 'Raw Power' is introduced with a belch, before James Williamson's exquisite sledgehammer guitar makes its entrance. The album's closing song, 'Death Trip', sketches out Iggy's past and his future in an almost documentary fashion: 'I'll stick you, you'll stick me, we're going down in history.' This was music from people on the edge. Bolan or Bowie were happy with a veneer of decadence, to update a musical structure based on the Yardbirds and vaudeville values shared with Lionel Bart (the composer of *Oliver*, another Defries client). The Stooges were decadent right through to their sweet, Midwestern hearts.

By 6 October, *Raw Power* was finished. Only for nothing to happen. On 10 September, David Bowie had sailed for New York on board the *QE2* (he'd famously become terrified of flying after his plane ran into an electric storm on the way back from Cyprus in December 1971). Tony Defries flew over a few days later, to oversee Bowie's tour from the MainMan New York office, which had been set up (literally, including painting and decorating) by Tony Zanetta. That same month, Cherry Vanilla, another cast member of *Pork* and, according to Zanetta, the only MainMan employee with any experience of running a business, arrived to handle PR. MainMan's centre of gravity had moved, it seemed permanently, to the US.

Deciding to *chercher la femme*, Jim flew over to Detroit in pursuit of Bowie and was met by Leee Childers, who'd been co-opted into the MainMan operation as a photographer, manager and babysitter, and given the title 'Vice President, MainMan USA'. A few days later, after visiting Jim's parents and rendezvousing with Bowie, who was playing Detroit's Fisher Theater, Leee and Jim flew to Los

Angeles to stay with Bowie and his entourage, who were all ensconced at the Beverly Hills Hotel (and, in a typical MainMan sleight of hand, charging their food, limos and groceries to RCA). Jim arrived, the stress of recording well behind him, looking bright-eyed, blond-haired, happy and on a healthy vegetarian diet. He was different from the early days, more self-sufficient, less wide-eyed. He was calm and optimistic. It wouldn't last.

CHAPTER 8

She Creatures of the Hollywood Hills

In their short, messy career, the Stooges had been assailed by many perils. They'd survived ridicule and hostility, but they couldn't handle being ignored. So they went crazy, like bored suburban housewives, stranded in a swanky house high up in the Hollywood Hills.

The first clue to what would happen when employees dropped off the MainMan radar came with the fate of the remaining Stooges. Before Jim had flown off in search of Bowie, the remaining Stooges were told to 'keep rehearsing' and then were simply abandoned. For a couple of days they trucked down to a subterranean rehearsal studio in Blackheath, before deciding to stay home and get high. Frederic Raphael's tasteful mews home was trashed – Hugh Attwooll had to placate the irate author about the fag burns and unidentifiable stains on the carpets – before Angie Bowie took pity on them, and flew them back to Ann Arbor on RCA's dollar. She and James briefly became lovers: 'I loved James. Ron was sweet; James was smart. He knew when to shut up. When asked about a particular song on David's new album, he'd find one positive thing and leave all the negatives. Same when he talked about Iggy. It was the juice of the survivor.'

In Ann Arbor, Angie Bowie met the SRC's Scott Richardson, became enamoured of him, and took him back to England (where, according to Angie, Scott and David became cocaine buddies). A few days later the Stooges followed their singer to the Beverly Hills Hotel, where James was just in time to drop in on Jim and David Bowie, who were mixing *Raw Power* at Western Sound in Hollywood.

In the years to come, Bowie and Iggy would engage in public sniping about Bowie's mix of *Raw Power*. Iggy, down and nearly out a couple of years later, would allege that 'that fuckin' carrot-top' had 'sabotaged' his album. Bowie himself would mock Iggy's production 'technique', maintaining that, of a 24-track master, just three tracks were used; one for Iggy's vocals, one for James's lead guitar, and the remaining one of the band, all mixed together. Without a doubt, Bowie's version of events was closer to the truth; both the pre-Bowie mix and Iggy's own remix of 1997 bear the same murky, confused imprint, with Ron and Scott's bass and drums submerged under a wall of battling guitars and vocals. By any conventional standards, the eventual results were a mess; as Cub Koda points out, 'No one could work out how, even if you took that much drugs, a record could sound that bad – and still get released.'

The Stooges' debut had been a masterpiece of minimalism and simple eloquence, like a Picasso squiggle on neatly framed white paper. *Raw Power* was, in comparison, a sprawling, abstract expressionist canvas, with sound splattered over every square inch. *Raw Power* would be the album that, more than any other, defined the inarticulate assault of punk rock, its raw excitement deriving both from the wealth of ideas and the confusion with which they were expressed. Bowie's mix – a touch of delay from an exotic device called the Time Tube, the sudden emphasis on shouted backing vocals – added a quirky edge to that confusion. Which, in hindsight, was as much as anyone could have done, says James Williamson: 'I could never stand the guy [Bowie] personally . . .

but I wouldn't hold it against him. I was one of the people saying I didn't like the mix, but in retrospect it was actually a good job.'

By now, the pressure was telling on Bowie too, for he had to squeeze the three-day remix into a punishing live schedule, with dates dotted apparently randomly across the US right through until 10 December, when he sailed back to England on RHMS *Ellinis*. His trip was fruitful, both for the huge press interest, which established the foundations for future superstardom, and the inspiration he gained for his next album, *Aladdin Sane*, including 'Panic In Detroit', inspired by Jim's stories of the 1967 Detroit riots, and the tale of the screaming and bawling 'Jean Genie', who was based partly on Bowie's increasingly troublesome protégé.

With Bowie and Defries gone, RCA eventually bridled at the huge hotel bills being run up by the Stooges and the band was given its marching orders. Rumbled, Defries ordered Leee Black Childers to 'find a place where Iggy and the band can live – an apartment. Because we're going to open up MainMan's West Coast office'.

Childers started searching for a suitable location, Iggy telling him, 'If I'm to rehearse, I need a swimming pool. I can't write without a pool.' Thinking to himself, well, this is California, Childers went to view several apartment complexes, only for Iggy to point out that this would create problems with noise; finally the singer upped the ante such that Jim himself located a spacious, five-bedroom house on Torreyson Drive, rented for $900 per month. By Christmas, Jim, James, Ron, Scott and Leee were happily established in the sprawling, low-rise building atop the Hollywood Hills, from which they could see the twinkling lights of Los Angeles spread out below. Each Stooge had his own room, while Childers could monitor comings and goings from his bedroom over the garage. The pool, at the rear of the house, was the centre of most of the social activity. It also overlooked Errol Flynn's old house at 3100 Torreyson, which had been purpose-built for the notorious actor back in the 1940s, complete with one-way mirrors in the bedroom so Flynn could observe his guests' sexual couplings. Flynn's description of his own house soon proved apt for its neighbour: 'Strange people wended their way up the hill to the Mulholland house; among them pimps, bums, down-at-the-heels actors, queers, athletes, sightseers, process servers, phonies, salesmen – everything in the world.'

For five years now, Iggy had forged on; often distracted, often confused by a haze of hashish, acid or heroin, he'd still maintained the drive that sustained him from the very first days of the Stooges, when he'd taken the early bus from the trailer park to rouse Ron and Scott from their slumbers. Now, with an album ready for release and a new set ready to be unleashed on an audience, he was forced to sit and do nothing. Many evenings Jim would talk late into the night with Childers, analysing his predicament. It was impossible to know for sure whether he was being pampered or punished. In the early days Defries had appealed to Iggy and James's natural arrogance: 'Make yourself unavailable. Make yourself mysterious,' but that cover story was now becoming less and less plausible.

In the meantime, the Stooges threw themselves into rehearsing at Studio Instrument Rentals, a huge complex on Santa Monica Boulevard, where Leee had negotiated a cut-rate deal from the starstruck management. Day after day they would step in the MainMan Cadillac for the fifteen-minute drive down Mulholland, spending hours rehearsing on the six-foot-high stage in front of a huge mirror, as Iggy and James directed their efforts. Poignantly, for a band who would eventually be celebrated as born losers, their work was unstinting. Even while their existing album languished in limbo, they worked towards a new one, before emerging in the evening and wandering down to Rodney's English Disco, a couple of minutes away on Sunset, for a little R&R.

Perhaps more than any location before or since, Rodney Bingenheimer's English Disco perfectly epitomised Hollywood's enchanting intermingling of innocence and depravity. Rodney's artless, naive demeanour and frank adoration of celebrity ensured that when he first came to Hollywood he was nurtured by a succession of teenage girls on the Strip, then adopted as a sidekick by Sonny and Cher. As a PR man at Mercury Records, he'd become one of David Bowie's first champions in LA, and was so obsessed with the magic of English glam rock that he opened Rodney's English Disco at 7561 Sunset Boulevard. It boasted a mirrored dance floor, Watney's beer on tap, and was the only location in California to serve that English delicacy, sausage rolls ('absolutely dreadful', according to Annie Apple, who worked at the club), all calculated to make visiting English rockers feel as if they were back in Blighty. Soon it became a hangout for every girl from the Valley who owned a pair of platforms, and Rodney became the gate-keeper, as Rodney's regular Michael Des Barres puts it, of 'a posse of pussy'.

The girls who hung out at Rodney's were either wild rich kids or desperate street kids, and 'there was very little distinction between the two', according to Kathy Heller, one of the former. Some of them sipped Coca-Cola; a few shot up heroin in the tiny toilets. Some liked just to hang out with visiting English rock stars; some liked to get in their pants. When Iggy and the Stooges arrived at the end of 1972, the queen of the LA scene was Sable Shields, aka Sable Starr, a self-styled 15-year-old groupie and wild child offspring of a wealthy family from Palos Verdes in south-eastern LA. Sable was often accompanied by her older, sensible sister Coral, who was more reserved, but equally beautiful; with Sable's curly blonde mop, and Coral's waist-length dark hair, they reminded many onlookers of Snow White and Rose Red. Coral and Sable had prob-ably first met Jim and James via their friend Evita Ardura, whom James had noticed one day as he drove in the MainMan limo past Hollywood High where the 15-year-old was attending school – he won her over by taking her, Coral and Sable to Disneyland, and seemed a powerful, mysterious presence, despite his obvious dis-taste for funfairs. Along with their friend Lori Maddox, these diehards of the postage-stamp-sized VIP area at Rodney's gravi-tated towards the West Coast offices of England's hippest management company, MainMan. And Leee Childers found his babysitting responsibilities just got a whole lot more challenging. One of the key roles of the MainMan vice president was to watch closely for any signs of drug use; demeaning as it was, he was ordered to search the band's room while they were down at SIR. And week by week, he found more dirty spoons and other paraphernalia.

Even as their consumption of drugs increased to help ease the sheer boredom of being stranded up in the hills, Jim, James, Ron and Scotty worked more consistently than ever before. Finally, it was announced that there would be a showcase performance, promoted by MainMan, at the end of March in Detroit. Over the spring of 1973, they continued piecing together songs like 'Head On The Curb', based round an intricate riff lifted from the Doors' 'LA Woman', and 'Cock In My Pocket', a fast Eddie Cochran-style number that, with its salacious lyrics and traditional blues structure, may well be the only Stooges composition obviously indebted to Bowie and the Spiders. Later came 'Johanna', a song about Iggy's main girlfriend, with whom he was involved in a bizarre heroin ménage à trois, and 'Open Up And Bleed', a dark and sombre epic. The song's conversational delivery paralleled the Stones' 'Sympathy For The Devil', but where Mick modelled himself on Satan, Jim was playing Jesus. In earlier interviews, Jim had already compared his audience to the first Christians, the world's downtrodden. Now, his message seemed even more overtly messianic – that he was offering himself up as a sacrificial victim, in the belief that his music would somehow endure. But if Jim Osterberg really felt doomed, he felt little self-pity at his predicament. 'If he did get maudlin, it was when he was drinking,' says Childers, 'but it was never, Why me? It was about the world being fucked up.'

As the weeks went by, the Stooges household took on a warped little routine of its own. From his apartment over the garage, Leee watched as the scene came to resemble a Hollywood movie set, with teenage girls running around, visitors being thrown in the pool, a motley assortment of drug dealers and teenage runaways coming and going in flash cars. Sable was the loudest and most outrageous of the girls, and was rapidly becoming notorious around Hollywood. She also had fantasies of becoming a conventional housewife, so every now and then you could see Hollywood's most celebrated groupie washing the mountain of dirty dishes accumulating in the kitchen.

'Everyone was in love with Jim at the time,' says Lori Maddox, who'd often hang out with her friends Sable and Coral at Torreyson, 'and everything was pretty crazed, so there was a lot of passing girlfriends back and forth.' Sable had a fling with Jim, who eventually moved on to Coral, who was the more responsible child and often looked out for her younger sister. Sable was 'funny, always on it, very quick-witted, that was why men liked being with her,' says Lori, 'but she would decide to do things absolutely out of nowhere; like maybe in the middle of night decide to put on Hollywood underwear and a garter belt and drive around town. She would do things no one else would even consider, things that Coral would never do. It was very crazed, and it was right at that period that Sable was becoming notorious.' During the same period, Jim's relationship with Johanna was warped and druggy. 'It was a junk thing,' remembers Ron Asheton. 'She had a boyfriend who was selling junk, Iggy was giving the guy a bunch of dough. I stayed out of that crap. He loves to be hurt. Thrives on the chaos.'

Ron and Scott's demotion to mere sidemen by now seemed to absolve them of any responsibility for their singer, and many times they would look on indifferently as Iggy floated motionless in the pool. Leee Childers realised it was down to him to rescue MainMan West Coast's premier star, drag him out of the pool and ensure he was breathing. It happened so often over those twelve weeks that Leee learned to swim in the process.

By March, rumours of the band's increasingly debauched behaviour were getting back to MainMan's New York office; Cherry Vanilla started to get suspicious about incessant requests for money to buy new equipment and other vague expenses. When Wayne County dropped by, with even his extensive knowledge of excess, gained in the backroom at Max's, he found the situation surreal.

Before Wayne arrived, Leee briefed him. 'Whatever you do, don't bring any drugs. Don't give Iggy money. Don't give him alcohol. Don't give him *anything*.'

Arriving in the house, which seemed forebodingly dark inside, Wayne saw Jim and the Stooges in a line, sitting on the couch, immobile and unresponsive. Only Sable seemed interested, giggling and flirtatious; eventually it dawned on Wayne that 'she wants to fuck, fuck, fuck, and she even wants to fuck me!' In his melodious Blanche Dubois drawl, Wayne informed her, 'Honey, are you barking up the wrong tree,' and watched calmly as LA's most celebrated groupie slashed her wrists and took a melodramatic leap into the pool. Feeling contented and warm, thanks to a couple of Quaaludes, Wayne watched Sable splash around, until Leee Childers assumed his lifeguard duties once more and fished Sable out of the pool. The cuts were, it transpired, only surface scratches, and Leee salved Sable's wounded pride by telling her, 'Wayne is not like Bowie or Iggy, that is a freak but who's still gonna fuck you – Wayne is a real queen!' Subsequently Wayne and Sable became best friends, sharing tips on make-up.

Even after a short-term exposure to life at Torreyson, Wayne County was worried whether his friend Leee would emerge unscathed. As for Iggy, his one-time hero, a man he'd always considered intelligent and cultured, he was now simply 'a lunatic. A charming, lovable lunatic, but definitely a lunatic.'

Iggy's fellow Stooges apparently believed that his increasingly erratic behaviour derived from his craving for attention – reassuringly, he could still keep his act together in the rehearsal studio. But Nick Kent, Jim's confidant from London, wangled his way over to Los Angeles to interview his hero in the middle of March and was shocked at what he saw. Physically, Iggy seemed in the best of health, tanned, with centre-parted bleached hair, looking like a Californian Brian Jones. But Kent observed Iggy going into 'crazy states. And it wasn't even the quantity of drugs he was taking. Sometimes it would take just one Quaalude to completely bend his mind and other times he'd take twenty and they'd do nothing to him. He had a nervous system that had been shot and he'd never taken the time to mend it.'

Several people who hung out with Iggy on Sunset share the same memory of watching him lost in his own reflection in the mirror at Rodney's English Disco, coiling and uncoiling like a snake, wrapped up in a narcissistic dream, or adrift on planet heroin. The drug didn't make him a nicer person. In public he was frequently paranoid, nasty or superior. '"Hey, I'm Iggy Pop. Remember that. I'm the boss,"' says Kent. Evita remembers that he was like 'a bad child. It's not like it was calculated or intentional . . . he loved Coral but he would fuck her sister 'cause she was there. He would go with anyone if they offered him drugs.' Many of the Rodney's girls share recollections of Jim as being charming, 'humble' or 'a gentleman'. But dig a little deeper and there are darker stories, such as that from Lonnie, a friend of Coral's, who remembers Iggy as a lost, Little Lord Fauntleroy figure who maintained an innocent demeanour even as he attempted to turn her on to heroin: 'Jim used to do it a lot with my friend. Then, at some club, we went in the bathroom, they tied that rubber thing around my arm and he shot me up with heroin. I spent the rest of the night in Denny's parking lot and bathroom throwing up.'

Jim's mental state was plainly careening out of control, and no one close to him was immune to the effects of his alarming mood swings. But there was one segment of his life that Jim still seemed to hold inviolable: the music. Some time in February he had called Bob Sheff, pianist from the Prime Movers, who was now teaching at a music college in Berkeley, to ask him to augment the Stooges' line-up, adding a rootsy edge with his blues piano stylings. He was to be ready for the band's Detroit homecoming on 31 March, the first of a projected three or four shows. They spent a long time chatting, overlooking Errol Flynn's house, and Jim was plainly ambitious about his music, even as he talked dreamily of the temptations of heroin.

Throughout March the band worked intensively in SIR. On some songs they were obviously attempting to move the music in precisely the opposite direction of Jim's original musical manifesto, towards heavy blues rock – evidence of a readiness to experiment, or perhaps desperation. Jim was excited about the forthcoming release of *Raw Power*, taking tapes of his earlier mix to WABX for the Detroit radio station to give the album its first public airing. By 18 March Jim and the band were back in Ann Arbor, rehearsing at the recording studio on Morgan Road that the SRC had sensibly bought with their first advance from Capitol records, ready for their flagship show at Detroit's Ford Auditorium.

For all the frustrations of waiting for the MainMan machine to lurch into operation on behalf of the Stooges, everything seemed set for a triumphant return. Cherry Vanilla was calling her contacts to send round acetates of the new album, and a couple of days before the Detroit performance Iggy appeared on Mark Parenteau's afternoon radio show on WABX to preview the album.

Iggy seemed positively joyous, Parenteau thought, and after a couple of songs started to sing along with the album that he'd waited so long for the world to hear. In between they chatted, fooling around in the tiny studio converted from an old dentist's office, up on the thirty-third floor of the David Stott skyscraper. After two or three songs, Iggy undid the one button of his bright red trousers, revealing he was wearing no underwear, stepped out of the pants and started to dance as he sang along. Parenteau started giggling uncontrollably as he realised Iggy's penis, flapping against his stomach, was clearly audible over the radio. Every now and then he caught sight of WABX admin and other staff peering through the narrow strip of glass in the studio door, as Parenteau hinted to his radio audience what was going on. After the show finished, Parenteau had to sit and listen meekly as WABX general manager John Detz declared the singer would never be allowed on the radio station again.

To some of the MainMan staff in Detroit, who were well aware of what the Stooges had been getting up to in Hollywood, the radio show became another example of Iggy's unreliable behaviour. Cherry Vanilla, who by now was keeping Defries informed of the shenanigans at Torreyson, observed that the MainMan supremo was losing his enthusiasm for 'the Ig', as he had once fondly termed him. Jim and James conspired to accelerate that process. According to Jim, James forced him to approach Defries immediately before the Ford Auditorium show and tell him, 'James is strung out on heroin, and we want to move the band to Florida [where James's mother lived] because we're strung out and we need to kick.' Today, Williamson describes Jim's account as ludicrous. 'I wasn't strung out, and furthermore my mom lived with the Evil Colonel, who would never have done a thing for us.' Leee Childers, who detested the guitarist, maintains Williamson soured the Stooges' relationship with MainMan and that the guitarist was difficult and unprofessional. It's a view few onlookers seem to share, for in the later days Williamson seemed by far the most together Stooge, but Childers would get an opportunity to vent his spleen.

That evening's show, according to all who attended, was a triumphant homecoming, to a crowd of diehard fans – including Mr and Mrs Osterberg – who packed the swanky, all-seated venue, which with its wood-lined interior and chandeliers normally housed the Detroit Symphony Orchestra. Augmented by Bob Sheff, with James Williamson clad in full Mick Ronson attire – most notably a pair of towering, thigh-length silver platform boots – the band played a set drawn mostly from *Raw Power*, augmented for the occasion with 'Cock In My Pocket' – which, Iggy announced, was 'co-written by my mother'. Iggy looked lithe and fit, and although perhaps the presence of Tony Defries imposed some restraint, the singer dry-humped a girl in the front row, spat on some of his fans and used a lot of 'sour' language, some fans remember. The audience's response to the show was ecstatic, although there was irritation and a few catcalls when the Stooges, at Defries' insistence, refused to do an encore.

It was probably Iggy's frustration at not being allowed to perform an encore that soured the atmosphere at the lavish after-show party. Defries worked the room as if he was a major politician or local union boss. Nick Kent looked on as Iggy greeted his fans. Then one girl, slightly the worse for a couple of drinks, came up, cooing, 'Iggy, you look great!' before attempting to give her hero a hug. Irritated, the singer pushed her away, towards a nearby stair- case. 'She almost went backwards down a whole fucking flight of stairs,' says Kent. 'This caused a bit of a ruckus in the house because she was a friend of one of the people giving the party. It was a horribly despicable thing to do as well. It really shocked me.'

Defries was mortified by Iggy's behaviour, which nearly turned a triumphant show into a disaster. But it was James Williamson who was made a scapegoat. Leee Childers hated the guitarist, and when James had a messy argument with Leee's friend Cyrinda Foxe after getting her pregnant, Childers set out to claim Williamson's scalp. On the band's return to LA, Childers per- suaded Defries that Williamson was the cause of the Stooges' behaviour, and the MainMan boss gave Jim an ultimatum: either James was sacked, or the Stooges would be dropped. The remain- ing Stooges and Leee Childers all voted: Leee went first, then the Ashetons sheepishly sided against their nemesis. And then finally Iggy agreed to sack his friend and songwriting partner. James was thrown out of the house, not allowed even to take his guitars or his platform boots. Distraught at the betrayal by his friend, who'd 'pushed me under the bus for the sake of his career', James disap- peared to Hollywood, where an employment centre directed him to a job working as a projectionist at a porno flickjoint.

Iggy was apparently undisturbed by the loss of his collaborator. Ricky Frystack played in a blues band called Moonfleet, and had gone to Westchester High with Danny Sugerman, a fast-talking 18- year-old who hung around the Doors office and later assisted with their press. Sugerman was 'very aggressive' about getting involved with MainMan, says Frystack, and pushed his friend to audition with Iggy. After a brief chat, Iggy suggested Frystack bring his guitar to the house. On the appointed day, Ricky showed up to see Iggy reclining by the pool, cradling a glass of Courvoisier, with Sun Ra's *Atlantis* album being played at cacophonous volume over a huge PA system. 'It was a total eye-opener,' says Frystack. 'We jammed for a couple of hours, then hung out for a few more.' Iggy seemed in his element, 'really happy', living out the ultimate rock fantasy life, hanging by the pool.

Iggy, in fact, was investigating many potential new partnerships. Earlier in March, Tony Defries had chatted with Kim Fowley, record producer, Lurch lookalike and celebrated denizen of Rodney's English Disco, and there had been vague talk of Fowley working on an Iggy solo album. For a time, Fowley became Iggy's confidant, and they worked on a set of songs that would have been Iggy's second album for MainMan, including a new composition called 'She Creatures Of The Hollywood Hills'. Fowley was asked to cast around for a replacement for Williamson. The lanky, droll-faced producer picked on Warren Klein, who'd attracted a modest amount of attention on the LA scene with Fraternity of Man, a psychedelic blues outfit in the vein of Moby Grape; their biggest claim to fame was getting one song on the best-selling *Easy Rider* soundtrack. Klein was a 'Tony Curtis-looking guy with a shoe salesman personality', according to Fowley; the guitarist kept quiet but laughed in all the right places when the lead singer spoke. This, together with his rootsy blues style, apparently qualified him for a job in the Stooges. To give him a little more glam cachet, Warren was renamed Tornado Turner, and he was hurriedly enlisted into the Stooges. But if it was Tony Defries' belief that eliminating James Williamson would make Iggy and the Stooges behave, he was soon disabused of that notion. Early in April, Defries had joined Tony Zanetta in Japan for Bowie's tour there. The bad news that by now flowed in a steady stream from the Torreyson Drive house became a constant preoccupation. Zanetta heard reports of a robbery, which they assumed was a put-up job to score money for drugs, and demands for money for an abortion for one of Iggy's teenage girl-friends (which was almost certainly a fiction, although it's impossible to know who made up the story). 'And every phone call there was another disaster to sort out.'

Tony Defries had reached the end of the road with Iggy Pop, the all-American boy who had once charmed him. As Childers points out, 'Tony always fell a little in love with the people he worked with. Until, like a love affair, it starts to go sour – and then it really goes south fast. Then it was fury like a manager scorned.' In Detroit, there had been little Defries could do about Iggy's behaviour; he'd signed him at Bowie's behest, and he couldn't drop him without David's assent. Now, just a few days into his first, tumultuous Japanese tour, David was forced to sit and listen as his manager explained why MainMan would have to drop his friend. 'Defries was talking and talking to David about it,' says Zanetta. 'And David felt bad, because he really didn't want to let him go. But he was on the brink in Japan, and preoccupied – there really wasn't anything he could do. So, reluctantly, he agreed that they should let them loose.'

Back in LA, Leee Childers informed the Stooges that they had been dropped. He expected a scene. But like naughty children who know they've been rumbled, there were no complaints. Leee jumped into the pool and paddled around forlornly as he watched them gather their clothes and leave.

CHAPTER 9

Beating a Dead Horse

Ron Asheton: 'The whole thing was never-ending torture. Hanging on, somehow in the hope it will turn better . . . really, it was just beating a dead horse until it was dust.'

Jim Osterberg: 'There was some perverse pride in showing ourselves, but no. There were no good shows. It took a big person to manage the Stooges, and once we lost Defries, then . . . that was it.'

Scott Asheton: 'They threw all kinds of things. Cameras, bags of pot, pills, money, they'd throw all kinds of shit . . . not just bottles.'

Scott Thurston: 'Everyone knew it was doomed. But it was a pretty potent band, and a pretty potent thing to stand there and go through it. There wasn't really any bullshit about it.'

James Williamson: 'They say the definition of insanity is trying to do the same thing over and over thinking you're going to get a different result.'

The slow, painful, heroic death of the Stooges started with humiliation, and ended in a hail of bottles. The humiliation hurt more.

In early 1973, there were still a few Iggy fans scattered around Hollywood, and one of them was Danny Sugerman. Jim Morrison's death in July 1971 had left a void in Sugerman's life, Iggy looked to be the man to fill it, and after the MainMan axe fell, Danny was keen to start hustling on behalf of the Stooges. The band also lucked into a heavy-duty manager in the five-foot-six, pugnacious form of Jeff Wald, who had been turned on to Iggy by rock critic Lillian Roxon. Wald was husband and manager to singer Helen Reddy, who, like her friend Lillian, was an Australian expat and committed feminist. Her husband Jeff was, in contrast, a coked-up tough guy from the Bronx, whose typical opening line in a business negotiation might go: 'Don't fuck with me or I will hurt you.'

Before he could sign with Wald, though, Jim had to undergo a ritual humiliation at the hands of Abe Somers, the Doors business attorney, who witnessed the contract. 'You should count yourself lucky that a respected businessman like Mr Wald would even consider representing you,' Somers told a mute, listless Jim. 'You're not worthy even to kiss his feet!' Faced with such a tirade, Jim's legendary charm for once deserted him. This was the first time, Sugerman told his friends, that he had seen Jim cry. Others observed the psychic toll of such humiliations and Nick Kent, for one, believed that over the spring of 1973, Jim suffered some kind of nervous breakdown: 'A lot of bad things had happened to him and his nervous system simply couldn't take any more.' The fact that the MainMan money supply had finally dried up did have one positive consequence: Jim no longer had the money to maintain his renewed love affair with heroin. The bad news was that he would eventually become a trashcan drugs user, using whatever was going for free or for cheap, most notably the Quaaludes that seemed to be freely available in Hollywood.

There was another humiliation to come in the form of a Chicago show, probably booked by MainMan, on 15 June, which featured their new guitarist, Tornado Turner. Those who attended retain vague memories of a performance that was utterly professional and unbelievably tedious. Ben Edmonds, then an editor at *Creem*, was a Stooges fan and had driven all the way to the Aragon, a faded ballroom rather like the Grande. The performance was so dull that the only standout memory was of Tornado Turner's moustache: 'There was nothing there. It was like watching a bad covers band.' Both for the cash, and for their self-esteem, the Stooges needed to work; Jim threw himself into fevered activity, acknowledging that with Turner, the Stooges' magic was gone. As Jeff Wald hit the phones, hustling for live shows and calling Clive Davis to ensure the Columbia boss maintained his commitment to the Stooges, Jim swallowed his pride and called James Williamson, who was staying with Evita and her mom. James still believed in the music, but knew their relationship as friends was over. 'He doesn't apologise, he just goes on with things. So did I. But from now on I was watching my back.'

When Bob Sheff got the message that the Stooges were playing again, he sensed the change in their circumstances without needing to be told. Meeting Jim a few days later, he noticed that his old friend looked tired. The beautiful house was gone, most of the 15-year-old heroin molls had disappeared, there were rumblings about record-company debts and the road manager made a habit of going into the bank to cash cheques with a gun in his jacket pocket. And accommodation for the hired help now consisted of a crummy room at the Tropicana and, later, even sleazier accommodation with garish wallpaper at the Riviera motel, a rundown joint full of hookers and other shady characters where James and Evita had their wallets stolen one night as they slept. Still, considering what he'd been through, James Williamson seemed to be keeping things together. The guitarist and his girlfriend Evita treated Bob to a meal, talked about astrology, and discussed the progress of their rehearsals at SIR and an imminent live tour that would start with a residency at the Whisky-a-Go-Go on Sunset. Where Iggy seemed to be running the show back at the Ford Auditorium, this time round James was taking charge.

The band's run of shows at the Whisky started on 20 June, two shows a night. In the three years since the band had last played the

West Coast, it seemed like they'd picked up a huge new following, and the opening night was packed with younger kids who'd later form the backbone of LA's punk scene. Many of them were dumbstruck by the spectacle of this band, who were now living on the edge, but whose power was undiminished.

On the opening night, Bob Sheff had decided to unveil his own alter ego, the avant-garde creation called 'Blue' Gene Tyranny. He wore ripped clothing, and a string of red lightbulbs in his hair that twinkled brightly; backstage a couple of observers who were high became paranoid that he was on fire and attempted to pat out the flames. Sheff hit the stage first, pounding out the opening chords of 'Raw Power' on a decrepit piano stuck up in a corner above the Whisky stage. Then Williamson, the Ashetons and Iggy walked down across a gangway, behind a movie screen showing a silent loop of Lee Marvin assassinating Ronald Reagan from *The Killers*, and strolled onto the stage. The guitarists and drummer joined Sheff beating out the monstrous, repetitive riff. Iggy stood at the front of the stage, glaring at the audience as a couple of girls crouched in front of him with their hands down his bikini briefs, fondling his genitals. When he got bored of their attentions, he simply kicked one of them out of the way before picking up the microphone and launching into 'Raw Power'. Life was imitating art. He'd written about being doomed but for a driving rock 'n' roll beat, and now he was living out that message.

But those pile-driving chords couldn't sustain Iggy for ever. The main act was expected to play two sets a night at the Whisky, and within a day or so Iggy was simply too exhausted to complete the second performance. By the second night, Bob Sheff realised he had lent so much money to the other Stooges that he had only just enough cash left for his plane fare back to Berkeley. Sheff told road manager John Myers that he needed his pay for the show, or he'd have to quit and fly home before he was stranded with the Stooges for eternity. Myers' response was to offer him a lift to the airport. Sheff fled, and never spoke to Iggy again; the Stooges played without out a pianist for the next three nights.

Reports of the later performances are garbled, like messages from a battlefront, but several images linger. One is of Iggy threading the microphone stand through his bikini briefs and humping it for fifteen minutes without singing a note, as the crowd dwindled to twenty frazzled onlookers. Another is of Iggy being passed around by an ecstatic audience, in a joyful reminder of the Stooges' legendary Cincinnati performance. Still another was a backstage glimpse of Iggy passed out in the dressing room, his head cradled in Sable Starr's lap, as each Stooge sat mute in his own corner, long after they were supposed to hit the stage. 'We went backstage [because] we were so frustrated waiting for the second set,' remembers Don Waller, a fervent fan who saw practically every Whisky show. 'We're scratching our heads and couldn't work out what was going on. We didn't understand that they were that fucked up, that Williamson and Iggy were spiking so much.'

Columbia had finally released *Raw Power* in May, which was credited to Iggy and the Stooges, but without the prospect of being linked up with a hot management company like MainMan, the record company made little pretence of commitment. Steve Harris, who'd had the job of promoting the Stooges at Elektra, found history repeating itself when he became a vice president at Columbia and again attempted to enthuse a boardroom full of indifferent staff. This time round, it was markedly worse; the reaction was, 'Ha ha, Iggy – the guy's a joke.' Columbia were making more money from the three-years-old *Bridge Over Troubled Water* than from the Stooges. But Harris persevered, concluding that the only way to make New York radio stations take notice of the Stooges was to underwrite a series of shows that he termed 'Iggy at Max's at Midnight'. At first Jeff Wald was suspicious – 'You expect me to send Iggy to New York?' he roared. 'It's junk city out there!' Once Harris assured him he would watch the singer's every move, it was agreed the band would start a four-night residency on 30 July.

The Max's dates were strung together with a few Midwest and Canadian shows to make a ramshackle tour, for which the Stooges decided they needed to replace Bob Sheff. James Williamson again took charge, calling up Scott Thurston, a keyboard player he'd met while rehearsing at Capitol studios during his exile from the Stooges, joining him in LA for a brief runthrough of the songs and giving him a copy of *Raw Power*. A few days later, Thurston was on a plane with road manager John Myers for a show at the Ice Arena on St Clair Lake, just north of Detroit. Scottie's first meeting with the band was the ride to the arena; that night he shared a stage for the first time with Iggy, who was dressed only in kneeboots and bikini briefs. He was stunned. He remained stunned for some time. That evening was the beginning, according to many Stooge connoisseurs, of an era of unparalleled comedy. Fans could enjoy their chaotic shows as much for Iggy's ludicrous clothing and bizarre antics as for the intermittently thrilling music. 'They were funny, hysterically comical,' remembers Michael Tipton, a friend and fan whose tapes documented many of the band's final shows. 'You could fill a thousand pages and still not capture all the insanity.' Although the Stooges themselves were comparatively oblivious to their leader's troubles, seeing them as self-inflicted, other close observers, like Tipton and Natalie Schlossman, eventually realised there was a black underbelly to the comedy. 'It did become obvious Iggy needed professional help,' says Tipton. 'It got to the point where people around almost feared him.'

At St Clair Lake, Iggy dressed down for the show in black Soho knickers, a souvenir from his amblings around London's tourist haunts. It was a baking hot day, and the band had been eating watermelons backstage. As the Stooges, Thurston included, blasted out the opening chords of 'Raw Power', Iggy ran out on stage and hurled a watermelon into the crowd; it hit a girl in the audience, who was apparently concussed, causing ructions with the promoter later. A few songs in, Iggy felt an irresistible urge to empty his bowels and ran behind the Stooges' Marshall stacks to take a dump; Tipton watched Iggy run back on stage and start throwing 'stuff' at the crowd. Once he'd exhausted his ammunition, he took a cup of ice and emptied it down his Soho briefs, then fished it out piece by piece, sucking it provocatively or throwing it at the audience.

Thurston was shellshocked by his debut with the Stooges, transfixed by the power of the band in performance and appalled by the increasingly obvious hopelessness of their predicament once they left the stage. He would hang with James Williamson, the one band member attempting to be positive. 'He was circling the wagons, like we were under attack in a Western. The kind of Western where everyone gets a bullet, but maybe you can shoot somebody on your way out.' But no one, not even James, could change the path down which the Stooges were heading. 'Nobody was in control. It was complete anarchy.' Eventually Thurston got used to the doomed glamour of his new outlaw life, arriving at venues without any equipment, borrowing amplifiers from the support band, leaving hired Marshall backlines at venues to avoid paying rental fees and skipping out of hotels through the back door.

Once the band hit New York around 28 July, however, it felt like the good old days were back. Columbia gave the band free run of their rehearsal studios in midtown; a sedate, comfortable building that usually hosted acts like Tony Bennett, it was overseen by a union attendant, who looked on impassively as Iggy danced on the grand piano. One by one old friends came in to meet the band, getting ready for their prestigious engagement at Max's; Natalie Schlossman and her friend Pat, who had a thing for Ron, turned up, James's girlfriend Evita flew in from LA, Scotty's girlfriend Esther Korinsky arrived from Detroit, as did Esther's ex, Dave Alexander, the lost Dum Dum Boy. Dave looked healthy and slim, and sat in on rehearsals, telling the others how he was making a fortune playing the stock market. Over several days, the band worked on their set, augmenting their *Raw Power* material with new songs including 'Heavy Liquid' and 'Open Up And Bleed', to which Thurston added a wailing harmonica part. Jim himself seemed in decent shape, optimistic, working the band through the new material, although there were the usual lapses. He'd arranged to meet Coral Shields at Kennedy Airport the afternoon of the Max's show, but forgot to turn up. Coral was in a panicky state, without the money to get into Manhattan or any idea of where the band were staying; fortunately, a white knight appeared in the form of Led Zeppelin guitarist Jimmy Page, who'd met her back at Rodney's English Disco in LA. Page was about to catch a plane back to London, straight after Zep's triumphant summer tour had concluded with three sold-out shows at Madison Square Garden, and persuaded Coral to come back with him. Once in London, Coral would tell people like Nick Kent that she'd given up on Jim Osterberg, who was more interested in drugs than in other people.

The opening night at Max's was packed, with old friends like Danny Fields, Leee Black Childers, Lenny Kaye, Alice Cooper and Lisa Robinson in attendance, and a huge queue outside the club. There were problems with the PA, which meant Iggy's voice was swamped by the huge wall of sound generated by the rented guitar amplifiers, and James's guitar was occasionally out of tune. Some Stooges old hands sniggered at the clichéd make-up and at their ludicrous costumes, crafted by Hollywood designer Bill Whitten – James wore a glammy Star Trek outfit, while Iggy appeared at one point in a campily ridiculous gladiator costume. Despite the technical problems, the band was magnificent. Bob Czaykowski – Nite Bob – was hired for the Max's shows to look after the amplifier backline; his job was to get 'the clang': the ringing, physically brutal noise that would help beat the audience into submission. Nite Bob sat in for every Max's rehearsal and show, and realised that 'even though everything was really raw, you knew there was something going on. That's why we wanted to work for them. This wasn't a bunch of fading groovers who were going to fall into oblivion.'

In the confined space of Max's, the New York audience was transfixed with both excitement and fear, for as Bebe Buell, the Ford Agency model and celebrated girlfriend of Todd Rundgren, points out, 'There was that element of danger, because everybody had heard about his antics on stage.' The second night, the club was again packed, and as Iggy walked over the tables and chairs, glaring at the crowd, one chair either wobbled, or was pulled from under him; he slipped and fell onto a table top full of glasses, which shattered under his weight. As Iggy got up again, Nite Bob saw cuts on his chest and chin, and a puncture wound by one of his ribs; as Iggy staggered to the side and crashed into him, Bob noticed his own shirt was covered in blood and shouted, 'Let's pull it. Let's stop it, man. You can't do this!'

Iggy kept singing, the blood dripping down his chest. He discovered that if he pulled his left arm back, blood would spurt out in a continuous stream. 'It was horrible, like a Roman arena,' says Wayne County. 'I kept running up the stairs to look, going Aaaaggghhhhhhh, then running out again.' Bebe Buell remembers, 'We didn't see him go down, but when he got up there was an enormous amount of blood gushing from what looked like, from where we were sitting, a massive gash.' Nite Bob recalls, 'We had this saying that a piece of gaffer tape will fix anything, but he was bleeding so bad the tape wouldn't even stick.'

As Jim Osterberg explains today, the cut 'just happened. It was an accident.' (Evita, alone of the witnesses, is convinced that wound was deliberately inflicted, in grief and guilt at Coral's departure for England.) But where other singers would have left the stage, Iggy finished the band's seven-song set, and the blood trickling down Iggy Pop's chest would become a defining image in his career.

The streams of blood seemed the culmination of a process that had started the first time Iggy had been booed by Cream fans, back in April 1968. In those days, his confrontation of the audience had recalled the savage, physical theatrics proposed by Antonin Artaud in his Theatre of Cruelty – like Iggy, Artaud believed one could achieve a kind of purity by violently confronting or terrifying a desensitised audience. Yet now, revelling in his physical injuries, Iggy seemed to be going further still, into the realms of performance artists like Chris Burden, who had famously had himself shot in his 1971 art piece, *Shoot*. (Burden was later celebrated by Bowie, in 'Joe the Lion', from *"Heroes"*.) Without doubt, some of Iggy's behaviour was calculated, but in his volatile mental state there was no way of knowing how this escalation of confrontation would end.

Within days, it would be reported that Iggy had slashed himself over a star-crossed romance with Bebe Buell. As far as some long-time Stooges fans like Dave Marsh were concerned, the celebration of Iggy's blood was 'such a fucking cliché. It was like, have we really come to this?' Scott Thurston remembers the band's reaction as 'shock . . . I felt bad for Jim, and felt mad a little bit. It was kind of a protest against himself.' After this initiation, Thurston realised it was 'kinda the band vibe to be relaxed under any circumstances. It wasn't like we panicked . . . but it felt bad, and it was definitely a low point. But there were plenty more low points to come.'

As the Stooges finished their set, Alice Cooper pressed his way into the dressing room and insisted that Iggy needed professional medical attention, delegating his press agent, Ashley Pandel, to take him to hospital for stitches. Jim, stitched and bandaged, returned to the club later that evening, quite possibly to see Bebe Buell; later that evening photographer Lynn Goldsmith snapped a photo of the two together, with Jim staring adoringly at the lofty, WASP beauty. It's more than likely that the vulnerable singer exploited his injuries to enlist Buell's sympathy, and even encouraged the rumours that he had slashed himself over his unrequited love for her – which, given that they first met after the Max's performance, is a little far-fetched. However, Jim pursued his new love interest with his trademark combination of indefatigable charm and a certain craftiness.

Jim's injuries meant that the next two Max's shows were postponed, but rather than recuperate, the wounded singer wandered off to see the New York Dolls at Madison Square Garden's Felt Forum the next evening. The Dolls were fast emerging as claimants to the Stooges' status as pre-eminent icons of decadence, and that evening Iggy looked a forlorn figure; he collided with a glass door, cutting his head, and New York's glitterati were literally stepping over him, laughing at his condition. Fortunately, Bebe Buell had persuaded Rundgren along to see the Dolls and she saw the stricken hero leaning against a wall. She kneeled down to minister to him, tenderly wiping off the blood with a towel as Bebe's companions

Cyrinda Foxe and Cindy Lang giggled at her concern, while Todd was plainly getting irritated. His concern was justified, for by now Buell had concluded that Iggy was 'totally fucking gorgeous. Built like an Adonis. Plus he had these big blue eyes which were like saucers. He was a walking sex machine, he truly was. Maybe a fucked-up one, drooling and falling down, but any girl would wonder, "Hmmm what's he like after a shower and a good night's sleep?"'

Rundgren finally tugged Buell, tottering on her platforms, away from the scene, but in their brief conversation Bebe had mentioned where she and Todd lived, confident that in his confused state Jim couldn't possibly remember. The next day, a few moments after Todd stepped out of their Greenwich Village apartment to replenish his sock supply for a trip to San Diego, Bebe heard a knock at the front door and ran down to open it, thinking her boyfriend had forgotten his wallet. And there, bouncing with vitality, was Jim Osterberg, in a thin T-shirt and pants, smiling: 'You said fifty-one Horatio, right?'

Not long after Jim sat down and explained, with almost excessive politeness, how he had no money and needed a place to stay, Todd returned from his shopping expedition. Rundgren was rightfully suspicious of the rival musician, but it was too late to cancel his trip – a trip on which, Bebe believed, the revered producer and multi-instrumentalist was planning his own romantic assignations. Unable to do more, Rundgren issued a stern order to Bebe: 'Do not, under any circumstances, leave him in the place by himself. He'll steal everything we've got to buy drugs. And whatever you do, lock up the third floor, and don't let him anywhere near it.'

Assuring her boyfriend he had no reason to be concerned, and that she wouldn't let Jim near the third-floor studio where Todd kept his guitars and valuable studio gear, Bebe bade him farewell. She settled down with Jim to what would be a romantic few days, going to see *Paper Moon*, that summer's feelgood movie, walking around Greenwich Village, sitting in the park, or eating burgers laced with Tabasco at PJ Clarke's, the bustling mahogany-panelled saloon over on the Upper East Side. Jim was fortunately the same build as Todd, even if he was a good few inches shorter, so Bebe cut the legs off the lanky guitarist's pants so that her new beau would have fresh clothes to wear.

On 6 August the Stooges returned to Max's Kansas City to fulfil their two postponed midnight performances. Nite Bob had spent the intervening time assembling a huge PA system, and for the last shows Iggy's voice was finally audible, and the band were brutally honed, their energy levels almost unendurable in the confined space of Max's upper floor. Whatever Ron's disenchantment at being demoted to playing bass, he was one of the greatest exponents of the instrument before or since; melodically inventive, ruthlessly aggressive, he locked in faultlessly with brother Rock Action's clattering sturm und drang; his bass guitar leading the assault for extended instrumental passages during which the adrenalin never flagged. Over those two nights, the Stooges were in their pomp, their magnificence undimmed by their obvious travails. 'They were at their peak, like an American Stones in their *Exile On Main Street* period,' says Bob Czaykowski. Over those final two midnight performances, they continued to develop their new material, still in hope of working towards another album on Columbia; by the final night, 'Open Up And Bleed' was reworked with new lyrics and became an anthem of the band's turbulent residence. 'It was something special,' muses Steve Harris, who relished almost every aspect of what would be the band's last appearance in Manhattan. '[But] what's important was that it didn't make a dent in record sales.'

Nonetheless, the shows were seen as a triumph, widely praised by the critics, whose reviews Jim always studied minutely, although some of the New York writers, in particular Lenny Kaye, did have a sense that the Max's shows indicated the Stooges 'couldn't go much further . . . except by damaging themselves'. There was the odd dig, notably in *Rock Scene*, the hip photo-heavy magazine launched by Lisa Robinson – those in the know could infer the influential editor's feelings about James Williamson by the fact his photo was captioned 'Jones' Williamson. In the wake of the shows, Jim enjoyed a blissful New York summer holed up with Bebe Buell at Horatio Street. For their first couple of days together they simply talked and talked, with Jim acting cute in his puppy dog way, treating Bebe as if she were some pure-blooded Scandinavian princess before the inevitable happened and Bebe embarked on what would be her first affair since she'd moved in with Todd: 'When we finally made love it was, I don't want to sound like a sap, but it was incredibly beautiful, storybook. Then we were like, Oh my God! All we did was shag, seven times a day, everywhere, anywhere.'

Todd was an influential figure in the New York music industry, but Jim and Bebe were oblivious to his inevitable wrath. They were like awestruck adolescents, enjoying moments of what seemed like rare purity amid the chaos that threatened to engulf Iggy. In the mornings Bebe would sit on the huge round waterbed with him, admiring his ballet dancer's body – 'breathtaking, like a work of art' – while he would improvise songs, serenading her with smoochy lyrics in his best Frank Sinatra baritone. Over those waking hours, Jim Osterberg was the most considerate house-guest – cooking omelettes, vacuuming, keeping the place tidy, attending to Bebe's two dogs – although as time went on, Bebe noticed that sometimes after Jim disappeared in the afternoons for an unspecified rendezvous, Iggy would return in his place. And Iggy could be 'creepy and mean and nasty'. It seemed to Buell that Jim could switch on his Iggy persona easily enough, but he couldn't always switch him off: 'That is the problem; you can conjure the demon, but you can't always get rid of it.'

One morning Bebe had to rise early for a modelling assignment; Jim had been such a troublefree guest she felt it was safe to ignore Todd's specific orders, and she left Jim asleep, alone in the house. On her return in the afternoon she looked around, but Iggy had obviously left for one of his assignations. Seizing the opportunity of a good rest, Bebe walked up to the second-floor bedroom, sprawled out over the big round waterbed and within moments was fast asleep.

It wasn't long afterwards that Bebe was woken by the insistent splashing of water dripping on to the bed, and realised that water was seeping through the ceiling. Running up the stairs to the forbidden third floor, she entered the bathroom to see Jim fast asleep in the tub, his head resting gently on an inflatable pillow, his toes blocking the overflow, with Bebe's two dogs cradled one on each shoulder, both of them out cold.

Bebe pulled Jim's toes away from the overflow, then noticed a neat little row of blue pills lined up on the toilet cistern. She shook him awake.

'Jim, what have you done?'

'Nothing,' he replied, dreamily, 'just a little Valium, relax!'

'So what's wrong with Puppet and Furburger?'

'I just gave them a little Valium . . .'

Incandescent with rage and fear for her dogs, Bebe slapped Iggy hard, before gathering Puppet under one arm, Furburger under the other, and running out of the house. It was a two-minute sprint to St Vincent's hospital, up the ramp and into the emergency room.

'Help! Help! My dogs have OD'd!'

'Miss, we don't treat dogs here. This is the emergency room. This is for people . . . What did they take?'

'Two and a half milligrams each of Valium.'

'Don't worry, they won't die,' the helpful ER medic assured her. 'Take them home, and they'll wake up.'

Back on Horatio Street, an angry Bebe berated Jim, telling him he could have killed her precious dogs. 'I'm a dog lover!' he replied, soothingly. 'I know a lot about animals.'

Once her anger had subsided, Bebe did reflect that Jim obviously had a good working understanding of canine anaesthesia. And today she acknowledges that Jim did look cute, asleep with his furry bedmates, although it would be the next morning before Puppet and Furburger – both of them, fortunately, hardy and lively mutts – regained full use of all their faculties. Danny Fields located a handyman who repaired the damaged ceiling, leaving Todd unaware that his new love rival had trespassed onto the sacrosanct third floor.

Within a day or so, Jim had left for a string of Stooges shows in Canada and Arizona; the two kept in regular touch, on Todd's phone bill – for which there would, of course, be more recriminations – planning a rendezvous before the Stooges' show at the Kennedy Centre in Washington DC on 19 August. Jim mentioned to a few people that Bebe would be attending the show; it caused some concern, for as Natalie Schlossman points out, 'It was playing with fire, getting together with Bebe. I was worried about it. Everyone knew how influential Todd Rundgren was.' The Kennedy Centre was a beautiful, prestigious venue; Bebe's mom Dorothea was coming to the show, which was headlined by Mott the Hoople, while the Stooges savoured the fact they were staying at the Watergate Hotel complex, scene of Richard Nixon's notorious bugging of the Democratic National Committee headquarters. Bebe and Jim arranged to take the train together out of Manhattan – a plan that Jim seized on, believes Buell, because he fancied the thrill of an illicit shag on the train. Unfortunately, Bebe arrived with a woman she'd met via Alice Cooper's girlfriend, Cindy Lang.

When they arrived at the plush, modern theatre complex, Jim was still frustrated at having his train sex fantasy thwarted; when Cindy's friend walked into the dressing room he snarled at her, 'What the fuck are you doing here?' It was, perhaps, in a bid to make herself useful that the interloper doled out a huge line of what looked like cocaine to placate the irate singer, who hoovered it up, not realising it was PCP. He collapsed within seconds, occasionally burbling semiconsciously in response to who-knows-what visions as the powerful synthetic hallucinogen took effect. Bebe and road manager Chris Ehring slapped his face and attempted to walk him around the dressing room or get him to drink some liquid. As Jim's fellow Stooges smoked cigarettes, contemplating their leader slumped senseless on a commode, Don Law – the show's promoter, fast becoming one of the most powerful music-business figures in the area – walked in the dressing room, reminding them they were an hour late, and begged them to take the stage; finally, as he realised Jim was incapable of even walking, Law lost his cool, unbuckled his Rolex watch and smashed it against the dressing-room wall, screaming at the band, 'You fucking guys will never work in this area again!' The Stooges simply shrugged, by now immune to such abuse.

Eventually, Jim told them he was capable of singing, and the band rushed out on to the stage and started hammering out 'Raw Power', playing the opening riff again and again. And again; Thurston believes they repeated the opening chords for a full fifteen minutes before Chris Ehring carried Iggy on stage and dumped him there. Eventually Iggy managed to sing, mumbling the words at half speed, then decided to walk out into the audience, who were mostly dressed in crushed velvet suits and unmoved by the bizarre spectacle they were witnessing. Iggy returned and attempted to climb back onto the stage. His band laughed at his pathetic efforts until Thurston walked over to help him up – and then recoiled in horror: 'I saw his chest, it looked like he'd cut himself up really bad, there were bits of flesh hanging on him, it was ugly to see.' Disgusted, Thurston turned back to his piano as Ehring rushed over to investigate. A few minutes later, Thurston saw Ehring laughing as he discovered the gaping wound was in fact a peanut butter and jelly sandwich someone had crushed onto Iggy's chest.

The incident became yet another surreal episode in the Stooges' increasingly doomed drama. It contributed to a reputation for excess that meant they'd soon be thrown off tours for such minor incidents as eating a cake meant for the J. Geils band. For all the chaos – much of which, as with the THC, wasn't totally Iggy's fault – the Stooges still had a hard-working, Midwestern ethos, but little by little the number of venues willing to book them was dwindling. Bob Czaykowski would go on to work with a string of huge bands, including Aerosmith and Limp Bizkit ('Wimps!'), but would consider the Stooges one of the hardest-working bands he'd ever encountered. 'They wanted it. They wanted to play beyond their ability; they were trying to make some statement musically. And they were kind of pure. It was all about music and it wasn't about business, most probably to their detriment.' And even when things fell apart, there was little self-pity. 'Ron, for instance, even though he had issues with James, always had a can-do positive attitude. He'd sustain things with his humour: "Oh you know, the singer can't stand up and the drum set's on fire and I can't find my brother, but it's a normal day in the life of a Stooge."' Even when things were more obviously messed up, says James Williamson, it was customary to ignore it: 'Simply, we were young and we didn't know any better. Besides, what else were we going to do?'

With their dozen or so shows on the East Coast and Canada completed, the Stooges made their way back to LA. But with no base from which they could work, their lives were increasingly fractured, and Jim moved around from location to location, finally ending up at the Hyatt Continental – which had become famous as the Riot House during Led Zep's excess-fuelled stay there in June – hanging with Johnny Thunders after the New York Dolls arrived in LA on 29 August. Sable Starr was Johnny's constant companion over that week, while Coral had returned from her trip to London and made up with Jim, which meant Johnny and Iggy were now rock 'n' roll brothers-in-law. And their family relationship was celebrated, according to New York Doll Syl Sylvain, with Johnny's induction into mainlining heroin. 'Iggy and Johnny were always in Johnny's room, and that's when I saw Johnny finally high on smack. They were all doing it. It was in LA that I saw him change and he was never the same again.'

Thunders' dalliance with heroin was infinitely more serious than that of Iggy, who always liked to boast of his physical indestructibility. Thunders' life would soon follow an inexorable downward spiral; the guitarist was rarely off heroin or methadone thereafter, and would die in New Orleans at the age of thirty-eight.

By this point, scoring smack was a constant obsession of Iggy's. Late one evening Annie Apple, who'd seen Jim around Rodney's, answered the phone to hear: 'Hi, I think you know me, this is Iggy Pop.' Credentials established, he asked if she had any money, trading on his celebrity with relaxed ease. At around three that morning he knocked on her door at the Coronet, a once-magnificent Mediterranean Revival apartment building that had housed the House of Francis, an upmarket brothel, back in the 1930s. Now it was ramshackle, full of drug-dealers, hookers and artists, and was handily close to the Hyatt. Iggy was accompanied by Stan Lee, later the guitarist with LA punk band the Dickies, and Max, a well-groomed, suave European who was the main celebrity drug-dealer in Hollywood. It soon transpired that Iggy was planning to sell Annie his celebrated 'cheetah' jacket, in which he'd posed on the *Raw Power* sleeve, for $25, and Annie handed over the cash before Max realised what was happening. 'You're not hawking your jacket!' Max informed Iggy, before taking the jacket and returning Annie's $25. 'Thanks for helping me out,' Iggy told Annie politely before the three of them disappeared into the Hollywood night. (Lee would wear the cheetah jacket around LA for many years. It was slightly too small for him, and eventually fell apart.)

By now Iggy's freeloading was notorious – there was even an urban legend that he used to stand beneath a huge Columbia billboard for *Raw Power* on the Strip, pointing to his photo as he panhandled for dope – but there was also a keen intelligence to his behaviour. During his brief visit to Apple's apartment, Jim had recognised the potential of the Coronet, also known as the Piazza Del Sol, which was managed by Jerry Flanagan, an eccentric character who used to write hectoring letters to his tenants in exquisite longhand and sign them 'the Corporation'. Apple had been planning to move out of her apartment, number 404, but after returning from a short trip to San Francisco she opened her front door, painted in sky blue with cheery white clouds, to discover that Flanagan had given the keys to Ron Asheton. Apple managed to retrieve a few of her meagre possessions, but left the Stooges with her pots and pans, and even her little brother's sleeping bag – which Jim commandeered, sleeping on the plywood floor. It gave her an excuse to drop by every now and then and survey the activities at the Coronet. After James Williamson and Evita moved into their own apartment at 306, the run-down building became the Stooges' base of operations.

After their two-week lay-off, the Stooges returned to the Whisky on 3 September, for a run of shows that by now were being poorly attended, according to Don Waller and fellow fan Phast Phreddie Patterson, who put together *Back Door Man* magazine. 'When he came back in the fall there weren't nearly as many people,' says Patterson. 'Some days we'd go and there was just us and a couple of others.' Where on the previous runs the crowd had been so packed they could pass him over their heads, this time Iggy could dance out on the floor, just a few people around him. 'Just doing his Iggy thing,' says Patterson; at one point Iggy poured melted candle wax down his chest, just like the old days. Still, say Waller, Patterson and others, the band were on fire, playing more new songs, including 'Heavy Liquid', as well as baiting the audience most evenings. One evening Iggy announced, 'We can't be bought, not even in this town. Not by all the faggots in the world. Not by all the money in Israel.' It's tempting to speculate that Danny Sugerman and Jeff Wald made up the Jewish contingent in the audience that night; in any case, Wald decided to drop the Stooges over the course of their Whisky run, disturbed, he says, by Iggy's erratic antics, and worried that he would be tainted by their fast-growing reputation as losers. 'You are judged by your success and they weren't a success. I didn't want [them] to be my calling card, the artists by which they judge my management abilities. You could say it was a ruthless decision . . . I would prefer the word cold.'

Although Wald always insisted on firing bands in person – he wasn't the kind of manager who left his underlings to perform brutal tasks – he remembers Jim as being composed and not particularly surprised. However, there were still a fair number of bookings dotted across the US, and a few days later the band returned to their Detroit home turf for two shows at the Michigan Palace, starting on 5 October.

There was something about the venue's atmosphere that the band disliked, but the old theatre was packed, and by now the band were in their element. The Detroit audiences, more than anyone, appreciated the Stooges desperate, take-no-prisoners attitude and in-your-face aggression, and that night they received a raucous, enthusiastic reception, with the audience invading the stage at the end of the show. At some point, Iggy invited the crowd back to the band's hotel, the Detroit Hilton, for what might well have been the band's most gloriously depraved night in the city.

Michael Tipton and Natalie Schlossman, two of the band's closest friends, were staying at the Hilton but, like most of the hotel guests, got little sleep that night. At one point Michael Tipton was chatting with Scottie Thurston in his room when James Williamson knocked on his door, walked in with two friends, one male, one female, explained that his own room was packed with people, asked if he could use Tipton's bathroom, and the three of them disappeared inside. Twenty minutes later Natalie Schlossman arrived in search of James, and knocked on the bathroom door; after a pause, James and friends emerged, apologising to Tipton for the mess. Tipton looked in the bathroom and saw the walls were splattered with blood.

A couple of hours later Natalie got a call from Ron Asheton asking for a chat. She was about to take a shower and forgot to go down for some time. When she knocked on Ron's door it swung open and Asheton told her, 'Come on in, it's cool.' Inside were Ron and Scottie Thurston, both naked from the waist down, with one woman wearing an exotic wig and nothing else; the guitarist and mild-mannered keyboard player were 'both kind of having a go at her'.

Later in the morning, Natalie heard her phone ring twice, called the operator and heard two messages from Jim telling her, 'Come on down, pick me up and let's go eat.' She was already going for breakfast with Michael Tipton, and the two of them stopped at Jim's room on their way downstairs. When the door opened Natalie and Michael saw approximately twenty people in the room in various sexual combinations; another couple – or other combination – was copulating against the bathroom's glass door, banging against it so loudly Natalie thought it would splinter any moment. Jim stood there with shirt but no pants, a girl holding on to his legs. Politely, he told the pair, 'Sorry, I've changed my mind, I think I'm going to crash.'

Ten minutes later Tipton and Schlossman were tucking into their morning coffees when Jim bounded into the restaurant. 'I got rid of 'em,' he whispered, before sitting down for breakfast.

The following night's show was triumphant, too; the new, harder-rocking set went down better with the Detroit audience than the comparatively restrained Ford Auditorium show six months earlier; one Detroit fan, photographer Robert Matheu, remembers: 'We all loved "Cock In My Pocket", it became quite a local anthem for a while.' A few days later, the band settled into a residency from 8 to 13 October at a small club called Richards, in Atlanta, Georgia, for what James Williamson regarded as a string of their best performances. Several of the band's fans, including Ben Edmonds of *Creem*, conspired to raise their morale with an endorsement by Elton John. Elton was sweeping across the US on a hugely successful stadium tour that significantly outgrossed the performances by his friend and rival David Bowie, with whom Elton was engaged in semi-friendly sniping. Elton decided to signal his support for the Stooges, plus his own general zaniness, by renting a gorilla suit and planning a one-ape stage invasion during the Stooges stint.

Creem had prepared a photographer for the stunt. Unfortunately, no one had prepared Iggy. Indeed, the previous night he had disappeared with the usual local 'Rich Bitch', to use the Stooges' term of endearment. Early in the morning she brought him back to the band's hotel unconscious; he had gobbled down her entire supply of Quaaludes. Scott Asheton and a friend of the band, Doug Currie, were called to lift his dead weight out of her Corvette; carrying him into the hotel, they dropped him and were overcome with a giggling fit, seeing him peacefully sleeping, sprawled over a spiky Mediterranean bush.

He was still hardly conscious that evening when Doug and Scotty carried him into the club ('God knows what the poor club owner thought!' laughs Currie), and after a quick discussion of what to do, Doug announced he had some speed. James Williamson managed to find a syringe, and they duly shot their singer full of methamphetamine sulphate in order to get him on his feet.

Unsurprisingly, during the performance for which Elton had planned his jolly jape, Iggy was, he says, 'unusually stoned to the point of being barely ambulatory, so it scared the hell out of me.' For a couple of seconds, as Elton emerged from the wings in his gorilla suit, Iggy thought he was hallucinating, or else a real gorilla was raiding the stage. The *Creem* photograph documenting the event is hilarious, showing James Williamson transfixing the uppity ape with a malevolent glare that signals, he says, his intent to 'take him out. He lucked out, because he was smart enough to take his head off to let people know who he was, just in time.'

Once Elton discarded the ape mask and revealed his cheery face, Iggy realised what was happening and danced around with the fur-clad Elton for a song or so, and the event was duly plugged in *Creem*, with Iggy telling the magazine, 'Elton's a swell guy.' (Off the record, he would tell people that Elton had only pulled the stunt because he wanted to get into tough-guy guitarist James Williamson's pants.) Yet, although there would be ongoing discussions with Elton's manager, John Reid, and his record imprint, Rocket, the encounter failed to lift the Stooges' spirits, and soon the band was becoming more obviously frazzled. Around this time it seems many of the Stooges clung to pathetically poignant lucky mementoes. Iggy had a pet cuddly rabbit. Drummer Scott had a lucky towel, which he would wrap round his head at times of acute stress. Guitarist Ron had a treasured pillow which his mom had embroidered – if any of his fellow band members hid it, he went mad.

By the end of the year bookings had started to fizzle out, so the band switched agencies to ATI in New York. Rumours spread that the Stooges were about to split, or had split already, as the various members dispersed around Hollywood. In LA, regulars at Rodney's English Disco started claiming that Iggy was asking a New York promoter for a one-million-dollar fee to commit suicide live on stage at Madison Square Garden; Andy Warhol announced the event would happen at the Stooges' end-of-year show at New York's Academy of Music. The story reached the band themselves, but their reaction, according to Bob Czaykowski, was, 'We don't think he's strong enough to commit suicide.' Instead, the evening was remarkable mostly for Iggy's announcing every song as 'Heavy Liquid'. It was telling that by now no one, whether band or road crew, knew if he was putting on an act, or was under the influence of a new drug, or had literally lost his mind.

With increasing regularity, outsiders who caught sight of the out-of-it singer before the shows would ask the road crew, 'Do you really think he can make it?' The answer would be, 'Well, he always does.' But the New Year's Eve show marked a turning point, says Nite Bob. 'Before that, everybody seemed to be happy. And now everybody seemed to be unhappy. You could see the signpost up ahead, "The End Is Near".' News of the death of one-time Stooges bassist, Zeke Zettner from a heroin overdose on 10 November further darkened their mood. Up to now, James Williamson had been the one force attempting to push the band forwards, but even he was losing heart. 'The fact is that I already knew this, but I had to be taught many times about how unreliable Iggy really is. That band could have been a real [success] and . . . instead it was becoming a flop.'

By the time the Stooges returned to the West Coast in January 1974 for four shows at a club called Bimbo's in San Francisco, their audience had dwindled, with just a few dozen fans in the 700-capacity club, all of them clustered round the stage. Joel Selvin was there to review the show for the *Chronicle*; he remembers that despite the tiny audience, the band was ragged but on the rampage, and that Iggy was as committed as ever. At one point he jumped out into the crowd, whereupon a fan pulled his bikini briefs down and the singer shouted a running commentary over the microphone, 'Somebody's sucking my dick, somebody's sucking my dick!' Finally, bored of the attention, he screamed, 'Give me my cock back, you bitch!' and continued the performance. Selvin wrote up the incident in his review, with heavy use of asterisks. 'But I genderised the story,' he says, 'and wrote how the girl unhanded him, or something like that. The next day after the story runs I get a phone call from a guy who says, "That was no girl that did Iggy – that was me and my cousin Frankie!"' Annie Apple was at the show, and she wonders if Iggy was aware of what was happening and relished the experience: a sort of 'when-in-Rome-do-as-the-Romans-do thing.'

When the Stooges hit the Midwest again, despite the fact that supporters like Natalie Schlossman were there to look after him, Jim seemed to be in an even worse state. Physically he was in decent condition, still slim, surviving on a diet of burgers with Tabasco or even raw meat – which he loved to order in restaurants, freaking out the waitresses. Now, though, his face was puffy and careworn; glammed up with make-up and blond hair he looked scary rather than androgynous. Mentally, he was tired and listless. Columbia had recorded the end-of-year Academy of Music show with a view to releasing it as a live album, but in January they'd decided it wasn't worthy of release and that Iggy's contract would not be renewed. In Toledo, Ohio, the band was supporting Slade, who played good old-fashioned brickies' glam rock and detested the Stooges; before the show there was nearly a fight when the Brummie roadies insulted Natalie and her friend Pat; Rock Action threatened to take them all on, and the Brummies backed down. When it came to the show, Iggy, wearing pale make-up and a little bow tie, launched himself into the audience twice; each time the audience parted like the Red Sea and looked on smugly as he smashed into the floor.

The entire band were depressed by the audience's indifference; Jim was particularly disturbed, and that night Ron asked Natalie to look after him and put him to bed. Ron had hidden Jim's clothes in the hope that this would curtail his usual habit of cruising the hotel corridors for drugs in the middle of the night. Natalie spoke to Jim gently and reassuringly, as if to a child, until he fell asleep. After waiting another twenty minutes to make certain he was OK, she left. An hour and a half later there was a disturbance in the hallway; Michael Tipton and Scott Asheton ran out and saw Jim cowering naked as Slade's roadies pulled the fluorescent light tubes out of the elevator and threw them at him.

It is Ron who describes those last months as 'never-ending torture'. Jim Osterberg today displays very little emotion about his physical and mental travails. But by January 1974, this ambitious, driven man was regarded by everyone, even his closest bandmates, as a failure and a liability. And whatever drugs he was taking, says Michael Tipton, Jim knew exactly what was going on, and was suffering greater mental torture than any of his bandmates could comprehend. 'Everybody thinks he's not 100 per cent – but even when he's high, the little man thinks a lot. He knew.'

Over the next two weeks, the Stooges continued zigzagging across North America, from Wisconsin to Toronto to Long Island. A few days later, on Monday 4 February, the band was booked into a tiny club on the far West Side of Detroit, on the way to Ypsilanti. The Rock and Roll Farm, in Wayne, Michigan, was a tiny bar, with a capacity of 120 or so, that normally hosted blues or rock 'n' roll revival acts. The road crew started complaining the moment they realised how difficult it would be to cram the Stooges' amplifiers onto the tiny stage; several fans who turned up early started feeling worried when they saw how many bikes were lined up outside the venue. Robert Matheu was standing in the parking lot, smoking a cigarette in the freezing cold as he worked out how to blag his way in for free. Matheu brought a camera to most Detroit gigs, but knowing the venue, he'd left it at home. He knew that 'this wasn't a place where people were going to see the band. This was more like the Stooges were playing *their* bar.'

Bob Baker, another Stooges fan, had arrived early and found himself a good vantage point at stage right, on the edge of the dance floor. He too started feeling uneasy when he saw how many bikers were filling the bar. There were several dozen scattered around the audience, with a huddle of six or seven at the edge of the dance floor; heavy-set bearded guys, aged around thirty, most of them in dark denim jackets, several of which were decorated with the colours of the Scorpions, a West Side Detroit biker gang.

Baker loved the Stooges; this was the first time he'd seen them since the Ford Auditorium. This time round the music was more cutthroat and malevolent, and their look was far more extreme too; Iggy was prancing in a leotard, while James Williamson was a dark, powerful stage presence, who also seemed bizarrely androgynous – 'If you were too drunk you might not be sure he was a man.' It was not a combination calculated to appeal to the typical Michigan biker, and even as the Stooges launched into their set – which still opened with 'Raw Power' but was now augmented with more new songs, including another poignant doomed anthem, 'I Got Nothing' – there were scuffles at the back of the venue. Robert Matheu and his friend Mark heard shouted threats, and the word 'motherfucker' being uttered from the stage: 'And that is not a word you should say to a biker. Because they tend to take it personally.' As the violence continued, randomly across the crowd, it was impossible to see what was happening; Matheu and his friend Mark decided they'd had enough and left. Then at some point during the set, the group of six or seven bikers produced a carton of eggs and started throwing them at the stage.

What happened next would be heavily mythologised by the Stooges, especially their leader. The reality, witnessed from a few feet away by Bob Baker, was perhaps even more scary. He was used to seeing Iggy surge out into the audience as the mood took him, and he saw the singer head straight towards the biker gang. In Iggy's own retelling of the story over the years, his encounter would have an almost ritual air about it, as the crowd parted to reveal his nemesis, dressed in studded leather gloves, like Goliath confronting David. As Baker watched from a couple of feet away, the flurry of violence seemed more hurried, nastier and altogether more brutish. 'Iggy came into the audience, went right up to one of the bikers. This guy was big and heavy. And the biker just nailed him right in the face and he went flying backwards through the crowd. It's just a law of physics if you weigh 300 pounds and you punch somebody, that punch carries a lot more wallop than a 100-pound guy punching you. So when he hit Iggy he just flew backwards through the room, like something in a movie. And then they all just laughed.'

'I've heard how the biker was supposed to be wearing studded gloves or a knuckle-duster,' says Skip Gildersleeve, a teenage Stooges fan who saw his favourite singer being punched out. 'He didn't. He didn't need one.'

As Iggy staggered back onto the stage, he shouted, 'That's it, we're gone,' and the band scrambled out of the venue. 'We all thought we were going to die,' says Evita, who'd come up for the show, but they managed to face down more bikers as they cleared the dressing room.

Speaking today about the violent, scary confrontation, Jim sounds philosophical, as if conscious of the inevitability that one day his confrontation of the audience would invite revenge. But to his fellow Stooges, who had come to believe in his invincibility, the shock seems more profound. 'It did change everything,' says James Williamson. 'The invincibility of the band was shattered. Think about all the gigs we played and Iggy always did this crowd inter-action thing. Then somebody just knocked him down. It basically shattered our world.'

The Wayne show was on a Monday. It had been a mere stopgap to earn a little money before the Stooges played a much bigger show at the Michigan Palace, the once ornate, but now rapidly decaying 1920s movie theatre on Bayley, just off Grand River Avenue, on the Saturday, 9 February. In the days after the Rock and Roll Farm show, phone lines around Detroit burned red-hot with conflicting rumours: more predictions of Iggy's suicide, boasts that the Stooges would enlist another biker gang's assistance, spec-ulation that the Stooges wouldn't show. In reality, there was no

doubt that the Stooges would appear at the Palace; every member
of the band and crew desperately needed the $5,000 plus share of
the gate they were being paid for the show. What would later look
like heroism was, in fact, more like simple destitution. The band
was upset, scared and simply fed up; but that didn't stop them
from appearing on Detroit's WABX radio station and challenging
the Scorpions to show up at the Michigan Palace.

Jim Osterberg was known for his physical courage. Just as he'd
stood up for kids who were being bullied at school, there was little
doubt that he'd show up for his encounter at the Palace. But he
knew he was fast running out of road. Throughout the previous
five years, even though he'd abandoned friends like Ron Asheton or
James Williamson when it seemed expedient, he'd stayed true to his
music, refusing to compromise even when it would have made his
life easier. Now Jim, more than anyone, was aware that his music
was becoming a parody of its former self. Although there were still
flashes of brilliance like 'I Got Nothing', songs like 'Rich Bitch'
('when your cunt's so big you could drive through a truck') were
forgettable jokes. However, any confrontation of reality was surely
momentary, if a rumour from that time was true. Michael Tipton:
'We heard that when the band came home for a rest before the last
hurrah, Iggy somehow conned some people that were working at
the University of Michigan giving monkeys cocaine for a medical
test. He took all the monkeys' cocaine and was doing all of it. And
the monkeys were living on sugar water. Whoever it was got fired.'

In the weeks running up to the Rock and Roll Farm performance, there had been something close to contempt among the
Stooges for their singer, the man who'd commanded them imperiously for so long, but who now seemed to be blowing every crucial
show. Yet as they approached their Saturday-night show at the
Michigan Palace there was renewed sympathy. James Williamson,
an ambitious man, had seen Iggy trash his best shot at the big time.
Despite the bravado he showed others, Williamson felt he himself
was a failure. But as the Stooges prepared for the Michigan Palace,
he felt the singer's plight was worse than his own. And he, like Jim,

had quite simply had enough. 'We were all fed up with the rock 'n' roll thing. We'd been on the road for months and months and months, hand to mouth, and it wasn't working. I think for everybody this was it.' Scottie Thurston knew that the band was 'lost. Lost people, without resources mentally, financially or physically to try to group back together and make anything happen.'

There was defiance as the Stooges took the stage, apparently uncowed by their travails. Nothing would change about the Stooges' act; James still wore his slightly camp Bill Whitten Star Trek costume, but by now it was dirty and a little threadbare. Jim wore his leotard and ballet shoes, with a shawl wrapped round his waist. The evening was dank and depressing, with the sidewalks of Grand River Avenue coated in dirty slush, but still the hall, of around 1,200 capacity, was full, ensuring the Stooges would at least command a substantial fee. Hundreds of the Stooges' fans had turned up to champion what was, with the slow and messy demise of the MC5 over in England, Detroit's last great hope.

No Scorpions seemed to have turned up; so for their final show, the Stooges wouldn't even have the dignity of meeting a formal enemy who'd set out to destroy them. Instead, those who came to mock did so purely to indulge Detroit's traditional 'fuck you' attitude. 'It was nuts,' says Skip Gildersleeve, who'd followed the band around since their Ford Auditorium performance. 'There were people that you thought lived out in the woods and only came out once in a while. It was like Charles Manson's followers. The Michigan Palace at that time was always plagued with sound problems and power cutting out and little heat. It was frightening and it was cold.' All the psychedelics and grass that had sustained John Sinclair's attempted revolution were gone. Instead, all the survivors turned on each other fuelled on Jack Daniels and Quaaludes. 'The Detroit biker attitude was to give the Quaaludes to the chicks and drink the Jack Daniels,' says Robert Matheu, who notes that the more sophisticated clientele would have been dropping THC: 'It gave a nice solid buzz. I believe its history shows it was a horse tranquilliser.'

Even by Detroit standards, the event was scary, but the Stooges had enlisted the help of God's Children, a biker gang based in Ypsilanti, whose leader John Cole had often helped out John Sinclair and the Trans Love organisation. Cole looked on coolly at the carnage as the evening unfolded; he'd seen worse. Some Stooges fans, like Hiawatha Bailey, enjoyed the buzz of violence and the crunch of glasses which hurtled over the crowd the moment the Stooges launched into 'Raw Power'. Robert Matheu went up to the balcony where he could see the crowd throwing projectiles at the singer, who threw them right back. 'After a while it became like a theatre. Iggy was definitely prepared for it.' Fortunately, the Palace's lofty, large stage meant it was harder to hit the band with a bottle, although Scott Asheton and Scottie Thurston, both sitting targets, had more narrow misses. This is when Ron was cut by a flying coin, which gave him a scar he has to this day.

Michael Tipton was taping the evening and was convinced that Iggy knew it was all over. 'That's why he had fun with it, antagonising the crowd.' Over the last few months, if a record company executive was in the audience, Iggy could be guaranteed to fuck up. Now, with maybe half the audience baying for his blood, he revelled in the moment as he prowled the stage in his ludicrous costume, soaking up the hate. The sound was often ragged, the singing just a shout, much of the music simplistic aural thuggery, but the real performance was in Iggy's incessant insulting of the audience. The banter was drawn out, and any odd projectile – a coin, ice cubes, an egg – launched in his direction served only to prolong his speeches. Some fans threw objects as tributes: Bailey tossed an antique velvet neckpiece, which was greeted as a 'certified cock ring', and a quarter pound of grass which John Cole secreted in Rock Action's bass drum. Watching Iggy confront this hail without flinching, a few audience members thought this meant the band would survive. Others, like Bob Baker, who'd also seen the violence at the Wayne show, were convinced it was over. 'I was extremely depressed. You got the feeling that it was his farewell concert, although you didn't know for sure. It was such a hostile environment, people were obviously trying to mess with his head . . . I thought, This guy's not going to live to be very old.'

'I thought they'd given up,' says Skip Gildersleeve. 'It was the end of something really good.'

'Part of you was sad,' remembers Scott Thurston, 'and guilty, that you've seen something that probably was worthy of some respect [being] degraded. Otherwise you were just worried about getting hit with a bottle.'

After leaving the stage briefly, the Stooges returned for their last number, 'Louie Louie' – the song's message was that anything more sophisticated would be lost on such a deadbeat audience. Iggy improvised new, obscene lyrics to the garage band staple that he'd sung back in the Iguanas. And as the song reached its conclusion, more missiles showered onto the stage, one of them a large Stroh's bottle that shattered on Scottie's piano: 'You nearly killed me, but you missed again,' sneered Iggy, 'so you'd better keep trying next week.'

But there was no next week.

CHAPTER 10

Kill City

There were no decisions. There was no plan. Jim was cast adrift, like a piece of flotsam, pushed back and forth by the desires of the people around him, all the while contemptuous of them, yet painfully conscious that he was reliant on them for shelter, drugs and human fellowship. Worst of all, while still in love with the raw power of the Stooges, he was convinced there was a hex on them. The drawn-out disaster of the band's last tour had left him deeply spooked and his skyscraper ego was profoundly scarred by the knowledge that he bore the heaviest responsibility for the band's failure. This was a time when the best he could do was to grasp whatever chances came his way.

Throughout 1974 and 1975, Jim would be reliant on the kindness of strangers. There was no form to his wanderings, he would simply find refuge where he could – fellow musicians, aspiring managers, kindly groupies or rich heiresses. It would only be at the orders of the Los Angeles police that he would find some structure to his life, in the dormitory of a psychiatric institute. But before that would happen, there were a few vestiges of dignity that needed to be ripped away.

*

When Jim returned to Los Angeles in February 1974 and holed up with James Williamson in the Coronet, he had not quite abandoned the idea of the Stooges – who were, with customary irony, featured on the cover of *Creem* a few weeks later, with their long-term champion Lester Bangs proclaiming that their time had finally come, just as the news filtered out the band had finally split. Yet Jim's relationship with both of his one-time songwriting partners was crippled by mutual suspicion. Ron Asheton, still seething from the humiliation he'd suffered at his friend's hands, had left brother Scotty in Ann Arbor and returned to his apartment at the Coronet, where he worked on assembling his own band, New Order. James Williamson, too, was hustling around for ideas, and Jim was content to sleep at his apartment whenever necessary, even though he himself was suspicious of Williamson, who he thought had tried to take over the Stooges as his own personal fiefdom in the band's final days.

Still, there was a belief that the Stooges might reform, despite all their troubles, right up to the moment when James got trapped in a serious drugs bust. The LAPD had been keeping a dealer's house in Laurel Canyon under surveillance; James drove out there for his supply and was busted on the way home, with heroin concealed in a balloon inside his packet of Old Gold cigarettes. In jail, facing a charge for dealing with no money for bail or an attorney, Williamson called Evita for help. 'I had never known him be scared, but this time he was, he was going through withdrawal and telling me, I am going to die, you have to get me help.'

Evita's mom was a liberal attorney, who back in 1973 had consented to the 16-year-old living with James as long as he dropped her off at Hollywood high school each day – he'd managed it for two weeks, following which Evita had abandoned her studies. Mrs Ardura agreed to defend James, on the understanding that he and Evita parted, and her daughter return to school. The couple accepted the deal, and as James's attorney, Ardura even put up her house to stand bail. She got the charge reduced to mere possession, and James was soon back in the Coronet, alone. The harrowing experience had at least cleansed him of his drug habit, but from now on he had to be extra careful about hanging around with Iggy, lest he infringe the terms of his probation.

Hollywood loves winners, but it's a city where losers are meant to disappear into the background scenery. Yet Jim threw himself into playing a loser with the same conviction he'd displayed as the glamorous MainMan star. Indeed, there seems to have been a fascination with plumbing the depths, as if Jim, like his one-time fellow heroin devotee John Adams, revelled in living out the plot of a *noir* novel. And over the next year, his principal role would be as a kept man. Michael Des Barres, who had hit the skids at the same time as the singer he so admires, witnessed some of Iggy's decline, and even back then thought there was magnificence amid the sleaze: 'The idea of being a kept rock 'n' roll star was a very seventies one – these people would pay your way to give them[selves] credibility. And he was still this lithe, beautiful thing.' Occasionally, Iggy could be sighted in upmarket locations like the Sunset Marquee, reading the *Wall Street Journal*, or swimming back and forth in the hotel pool as a beautiful blonde sat waiting for him holding a bag of cocaine, a scene of almost mythological perfection (the blonde was a well-known character on the Strip, who'd left her husband in New Jersey and spent months cavorting with LA rock types until her money ran out and hubby came to reclaim her). Conversely, there would be the same scenario played out in the most pathetic of guises, such as the time that one teenager, a Rodney's regular and friend of Annie Apple, managed to bribe Jim out on a date with the offer of a couple of Quaaludes. It was possibly coldhearted calculation that made him encourage her to down her own supply early in the evening; a neophyte drugs user, she soon fell over and smashed her head on a car door, after which Iggy whisked her off to Apple's house, warning Annie's father, 'You see, sir, she's taken some pills,' before abandoning the teenager once he'd divested her of the remaining Quaaludes. 'She was mortified,' says Annie Apple. 'She'd been obsessed with Iggy for months, now she'd blown her big date while he managed to get the drugs and be done with us!'

Other participants in the increasingly dark drama believed that there were simple solutions to Jim's consistently erratic behaviour. Scottie Thurston found Jim an apartment in Venice Beach near his own, and tried working with him on demos for new material. The keyboard player thought that a little stability and focus, a chance to contemplate his own situation, might help Jim understand what was going on. 'I did try. But I was naive. There were much deeper-seated problems.'

Instead, it was a Los Angeles character with deep-seated problems of his own who'd assume the role of Iggy's new champion. Danny Sugerman had been hanging around the Doors office since he was just fourteen, was an occasional reporter for *Creem*, ran his own mimeographed fanzine, *Heavy Metal Digest*, and had pretty much started at the top of the music business by becoming manager of Ray Manzarek, the affable one-time Doors keyboard player. Now that Iggy needed a band, what could be better than to take over his management and team him up with Manzarek? It was a perfect plan, except that Sugerman was fast developing a drug habit of his own, and had nowhere near the emotional maturity to deal with the 27-year-old singer.

By the spring of 1974, Jim was rehearsing on and off with Manzarek's band at Wonderland Avenue, a rustic two-storey Spanish adobe house that was used as Ray Manzarek's office and practice space, as well as living quarters for Sugerman and, with increasing regularity, Jim, too, who was at one point on Manzarek's payroll. The keyboard player and singer got along well; Manzarek found Jim Osterberg a well-behaved, intellectual conversational partner, and had huge respect for Iggy Pop's 'Dionysian' energy. They worked with a small band of hip Hollywood musicians, including drummer Hunt and guitarist Tony Sales – the boisterous, crazed sons of comic Soupy Sales, who'd been playing profession-ally as a duo since Hunt was fourteen – and Nigel Harrison, who'd washed up in Los Angeles after his band Silverhead, led by Michael Des Barres, had crashed and burned. The group worked on complex, jazzy material, vaguely in the style of the Doors' 'Riders

On The Storm'. Manzarek in particular was amazed by Jim's genius at improvising lyrics, and the band worked up material in record time. The songs they crafted included 'Ah-Moon's Café', based on the bizarre characters who'd hang out at a Venice café that was a favoured haunt of Jim Morrison, and 'Line 91', about the bus journey from Venice Beach to Hollywood. Manzarek thought Jim was affable and easy to get on with. Except when he would 'Iggy out'. As far as Manzarek was concerned, this was a chance to liberate Jim Osterberg, with his versatile singing voice and intelligent demeanour, from his crazed alter ego. But Iggy refused to be erased.

Iggying out took many forms, but invariably it required someone having to come along and rescue him. Typical examples were his trips north to San Francisco, where he'd hang with the Pop Patrol, his own fan club made up of stalwarts from the Bimbo's and Cockettes scene. On his return, Iggy would usually be, as Danny Sugerman put it, 'feminised': hair dyed black, wearing mascara and foundation and a skimpy dress. The dress wasn't as much a problem as the fact that his San Francisco admirers would ply him with heroin and Quaaludes. On one occasion, Manzarek was called up by Sugerman, who begged him to come to the Hollywood jail to bail out his new bandmate. The two arrived and found, among the usual gang members, junkies and hookers, Jim Osterberg, in a long dress, with smeared eyeliner, bare-footed, drooling and mumbling. Manzarek, the only one with the necessary cash on hand, bailed him out.

Iggying out could also refer to his behaviour with Bebe Buell, who flew over to see him in April and took him to Hamburger Hamlet in her rented convertible. During a quick trip to the bathroom while the motor was being refuelled, Iggy doled her out a neat line of powder on the toilet cistern, which she inhaled in one go on the assumption it was cocaine, only for Jim to tell her that it was heroin. The pair took refuge in Ben Edmonds' apartment, where Bebe was sent off to puke in the bathroom. Jim gently showered her clean, while Ben yelled, 'Don't you clog up my drain with your puke, godammit!' from the living room. As Jim apologised, Bebe shouted at him, 'Go fuck yourself,' then got in her car and split.

Another typical Iggy trick might be to arrive at a practice two hours late, then walk into the rehearsal room stark naked. This sometimes happened when Ray was auditioning a new musician, for instance Alice Cooper's one-time guitarist Dick Wagner. A similar example was the time when Danny Sugerman had persuaded Clive Davis to come and check out Ray's amazing new band. Davis turned up at 2pm as arranged and started chatting with Ray. No Iggy. The conversation continued for another hour or so. Still no Iggy. 'Finally it gets to five o'clock, and Ray's run out of every Doors story he can tell Clive,' says Nigel Harrison. 'Then suddenly a yellow cab, which is rare in LA, shows up, and it's Iggy in his underwear, totally fucking buzzing on something.'

Clive Davis looked at Manzarek and smiled. 'Well, Ray, I guess some things never change.'

Ray Manzarek believes the psychological motivation behind Jim and Iggy's behaviour was simple. 'It was about: who are you? The problem was: am I Iggy Pop, the crazy wild man, doyenne of the Cockettes, or am I Jim Osterberg, the good poet, the good singer? He would have had to put that on the line in front of Clive Davis and choose one of those personas. And I think rather than confront that choice it was easier not to appear.'

When he wasn't crashing at Wonderland Avenue, Jim would find refuge anywhere across the Valley. Despite his wild mood swings and eccentric behaviour, he usually seemed conscious of what he could get away with. Some people speculated that, despite his apparent confusion, he was simply using Manzarek and Sugerman until something better came along. 'He was often out of it,' says writer and producer Harvey Kubernick, who crashed at the same house as Jim for a few weeks, 'but you also had the sense you were watching Rommel working out exactly where to place his tanks.' Kubernick was staying in the Laurel Canyon home of his friend Bob Sherman, and Jim intuitively understood Kubernick and Sherman's ambition to break into the music business. He charmed them, rather than exploited them, and when he cheerily welcomed Sherman with the words, 'Hey, Bob, let's go get a slab and a beer,' Sherman hardly resented the fact that when they ordered their spread, at Harry's Open Pit BBQ on Sunset, he was invariably expected to pick up the tab.

By the summer of 1974, Manzarek was openly floating the idea of producing an Iggy album, mentioning the idea to *Rolling Stone*, and Sugerman was keen to project his new charge as a responsible, reformed individual – despite the mass of evidence to the contrary. Over June and July, Iggy guested a couple of times at Manzarek's sets at the Whisky, singing on old Doors numbers like 'LA Woman' or 'Back Door Man'; he cut a respectable figure on stage, and a damaged, sad one off it. One night rock fan Jim Parrett and wife Dee Dee saw a ball of arms, legs and pink fur bouncing down the stairs of the Whisky. As the strange apparition hit the bottom it uncoiled and jumped up to greet them with a cheeky grin. 'Hi, I'm Iggy!' A couple of nights later he accosted Dee Dee backstage, asking her, 'Hey, wanna see me do a somersault,' and obliging, then boasting, child-like, 'That's nothing, here's a double whammy.' Another time, Kim Fowley invited Iggy onto the Whisky stage to introduce his latest creations, the Hollywood Stars. Clad in his pink feather concoction, Iggy commanded a beat from the drummer before improvising a monologue. 'I didn't useta like the Hollywood Stars, I useta like the New York Dolls, then I heard 'em play "Satisfaction", now I wanna sleep with 'em.' The crowd was impressed, until they realised he had no intention of leaving the stage; the Hollywood Stars' roadies vainly attempted to peel him off the microphone stand, before the band gave up and allowed him to guest on a couple of songs. After the show he accosted Jim and Dee Dee once more, his face puffy and lined, asking them, 'Wanna see my cock? Take as many photos as you want and send 'em to London. They love me there, you'll make a lot of money.'

The Parretts interviewed Jim for their fanzine, *Denim Delinquent*; in conversation he was coherent, but his mood was dark and defeatist, and his main hope seemed to be that he would be asked to sing in a reformed Doors line-up. 'He was so vulnerable, you wanted to wrap your arms around him and protect him, despite the bravado he occasionally projected,' says Jim Parrett, who sensed that the singer felt angry about how he was being portrayed, yet was incapable of doing anything about it.

There could be no better indication of the depths to which Jim had sunk than his first full post-Stooges performance. Jim and Ray had been working on a loosely themed piece, which pasted together a number of musical movements in the vein of the Doors' *Soft Parade*. 'Maybe there'd be acting, talking, girls on stage,' says Manzarek. 'The idea was to keep on expanding it.' The first anyone heard of actually staging this extravaganza was when Iggy turned up at Nigel Harrison's apartment just by the Whisky early in the morning ('which of course means he'd been up all night buzzing on something,' says Harrison) on 11 August. He sat down on the edge of the mattress where Nigel and his blonde Bowie-lookalike girlfriend Suzette were attempting to snooze, insisted Nigel pick up his bass, and started singing a simple riff, telling Nigel to keep playing a drone in F sharp. It transpired that Jim had worked up the song – which was based on the Velvets' 'Some Kinda Love' and revolved around the lyric 'put jelly on your shoulder' – with Ray, but that Ray had declined to participate in this 'premature artistic ejaculation'. Ordering Nigel to turn up at Rodney's English Disco at nine, and mentioning he was off to find a guitarist, a drummer and, cryptically, a virgin, Iggy disappeared onto the Strip.

He found his guitarist at the Coronet, knocking on the sky-blue front door of 404 to rouse Ron Asheton, telling him: 'You still got your Nazi uniform? Good, bring that, and you'll need to brutalise me, so bring a whip too.'

No one is sure where Iggy found his drummer, but, unsurprisingly, he found it impossible to locate a virgin, and instead had to settle for a gay youth who was dining at Denny's, just down from Rodney's. In the meantime, he ordered Danny Sugerman to phone up every journalist he knew and tell them to expect 'a landmark

PHOTO CREDIT: ROBERT ALTMAN www.altmanphoto.com

'The first truly beautiful man I'd ever seen': Iggy as the Stooges hit their peak, San Francisco Fillmore Auditorium, May 1970.

Communing with the audience in St. Louis, March 1970. Often he'd disappear into the crowd 'and I was sure he was being interfered with sexually,' said one onlooker; 'there was such an erotic charge about the whole show.'

PHOTO CREDIT: CRAIG PETTY, PER NILSEN COLLECTION

Tina Fantusi, of the Cockettes, in San Francisco around May 1970, with photographer Robert Altman. Around this time Iggy stayed with the Cockettes, sampling heroin for the first time, with eventually catastrophic results for the Stooges.

PHOTO CREDIT: TOM COPI/OCHS ARCHIVES

The zenith: Iggy lifted up by the crowd in Cincinnati, June 1970.

PHOTO CREDIT: LEEE CHILDERS

Ron Asheton is flanked by new boy Bill Cheatham (left) and sax-player Steve Mackay at Ungano's, August 1970. Mackay would sample his first heroin during this New York trip; all the other Stooges, except Ron, would soon follow.

The young James Williamson in Padre Island, Texas, *circa* 1968. A fiendishly talented guitarist, he was sent to juvenile home by his step-father, 'The Colonel'. He joined the Stooges in December 1970, as things started getting 'dark,' but would become Iggy's longest-serving collaborator.

PHOTO CREDIT: BRUCE DINSMOR, PER NILSEN COLLECTION

Above left and right: Iggy and the Stooges in Chicago, April 1971, with Williamson (far left) and Asheton (far right) on guitar, and Jimmy Recca on bass, just a few weeks before the band was dropped by Elektra Records: 'We were falling apart. But we were coming up with some great riffs.'

PHOTO © GERARD MALANGA

Photographed by Gerard Malanga in the Manhattan apartment of Terry Ork, late August 1971. Iggy Pop had lost his record deal, his girlfriend – but not his heroin habit. Within days, he would 'tap dance' into a meeting with David Bowie and relaunch his career.

PHOTO CREDIT: JAMES WILLIAMSON

Above: Iggy and James Williamson in London, *circa* June 1972, working towards their death trip manifesto, *Raw Power*, under the auspices of David Bowie and his manager, Tony Defries.

Left: Iggy with Bowie at London's Dorchester Hotel, 16 July 1972; MainMan mainman Tony Defries looks over Iggy's shoulder.

Below: stranded in Hollywood, Iggy immersed himself in the city's leisure pursuits. Here he's in the VIP area of Rodney's English Disco, LA's teenage hotspot, in early 1973, sitting between girlfriend Coral Starr and singer Michael Des Barres.

PHOTO CREDIT: RODNEY BINGENHEIMER

Iggy and the Stooges at Columbia studios, late July 1973. Dropped by MainMan, they were rehearsing for a promotional stint at New York's Max's Kansas City. Ex-Stooge Dave Alexander (sitting on flight case, below) visited; it was the last time many of his friends would see him. New Stooge Scott Thurston is just visible in the foreground of the live photo.

PHOTO CREDIT: ESTHER KORINSKY

PHOTO CREDIT: ESTHER KORINSKY

On the second night at Max's, Iggy slipped on broken glass. Many thought his injuries were self-inflicted, inspired by his star-crossed relationship with model Bebe Buell (right). After the show, he moved into the apartment Bebe shared with boyfriend Todd Rundgren.

The Whisky, LA, September 1973. It was the Stooges' second residence; the crowds were dwindling, Iggy's stamina was giving out. New manager Jeff Wald dropped them at the end of their eight-night run: 'You are judged by your success. They weren't a success.'

PHOTO CREDIT: RICHARD CREAMER/OCHS ARCHIVES

St. Louis, August 1973 (above), ere was defiance. By February 9, 74, at Detroit's Michigan Palace ght), after being attacked by kers on their previous show, Iggy d his Stooges had given up: 'We n't hate you. We don't even care.'

PHOTO CREDIT: ROBERT MATHEU

PHOTO CREDIT: JIM PARRETT

By summer 1974, with the Stooges splintered, Iggy teamed up with Doors keyboardist Ray Manzarek. Top left, a Whisky show marks Jim Morrison's birthday. On 11 August, Iggy branched out on his own with the bloodsplattered Murder Of A Virgin show. Danny Sugerman (in hat, upper right) publicised this pathetic spectacle; ex-Stooge Ron Asheton (in Nazi uniform) reluctantly brutalised his ex-singer.

PHOTO CREDIT: RICHARD CREAMER

performance' at Rodney's that evening, which would be entitled *Murder of a Virgin*. Sugerman spent hours on the phone, telling his contacts, 'Your name's on the guest list, and you better come because he's only going to be doing this once,' floating once again the delicious prospect that Iggy would commit suicide on stage.

Rodney Bingenheimer was delighted at the prospect of Iggy performing at his club – the singer told him 'he wanted to show the glitter crowd what real rock 'n' roll was all about' – and volunteered to resume his old job as radio plugger. Rodney duly picked Jim up in his black Cadillac convertible and drove him to KNAC, where they buzzed on the intercom – only to be told that Iggy Pop was not allowed in the building.

There was a line outside Rodney's for the show, although once inside the packed club it was impossible to see what was going on unless you were right at the edge of the mirrored dance floor, where Iggy, wearing a pair of Jim Morrison's leather pants borrowed from Danny Sugerman, declaimed in front of a huge drum kit. Nigel Harrison kept up a rhythmic pulse, and Ron Asheton, wearing his Afrika Korps uniform, complete with swastika armband, brandished a 'sconce' he'd carefully crafted from a length of electrical flex. The 'virgin', who was wearing some kind of sacrificial white robe, looked nervous, but it soon transpired that the victim would be Iggy himself. Iggy had brought along a hangman's noose and started waving a steak knife he'd borrowed from Sugerman's kitchen.

'Do you want to see blood?' he yelled at the Hollywood crowd.

'YEAHH!' they shouted back.

'Do you really want to see blood?' he asked again.

'YES WE WANT TO SEE BLOOD!' they shouted as one.

'Beat me with the whip!' he ordered Ron, who instead pulled on the noose, to choke him a little bit. 'No, whip me, hurt me!' he insisted, and Ron laid into him. 'Then he goes up to a black guy,' says Ron, 'and tried to make him stab him with this rusty kitchen knife. He wouldn't, so Iggy did it himself.'

'Then he carved an X into his chest,' says Nigel Harrison. 'I was really scared, because he'd mentioned he wanted to kill off Iggy Pop. But also I was worried he might get blood on my brand new Kensington Market polka-dot top.'

'We were not at all easily shocked back then,' says Pamela Des Barres, 'but that was really, really shocking. We were all very worried. Yet it seemed a logical next step for Iggy, letting us in on his anger and frustration.'

It was all over in fifteen minutes. 'Then they put him in a burlap bag, out of the club and into the gutter,' says Ron. 'It was horrible. He was fried.'

'I never really planned the blood,' says Jim today. 'Then as I got nearer I made the decision to use the knife. It was unnecessary. It didn't really work . . . it was bad blood, the blood at Max's Kansas City was nicer blood, much less cynical blood. I was desperate.'

When Jim Osterberg had created Iggy Pop, his alter ego had been the medium, to help him communicate his music. Now, Iggy was the message, and the music was irrelevant compared to the spectacle of his ritual self-harm, which at this low point seemed to be all he had to offer.

'He sacrificed himself for us at the rock 'n' roll altar,' says Kim Fowley. 'As they did in the Roman Colosseum every Sunday when the lions would eat the Christians. And Iggy Pop is both the lion, and the Christian.'

Danny Sugerman, the man who had publicised this spectacle, took Jim to the beach. 'So he could dive in the Pacific Ocean and bathe his wounds. I waited like an hour and he didn't come back. What was I gonna do? I wasn't gonna swim out there looking for him. So I went home, took a couple of Quaaludes and went to bed.'

The next morning, according to Danny Sugerman, he was woken by a phone call from a hysterical girl, screaming that Iggy was attacking her father's Maserati with a hatchet. Meanwhile, Sugerman, too, was struggling to keep a grip on his own problems. But when Manzarek called to ask Sugerman how everything had gone at Rodney's, Danny told him, 'Great!'

The weeks after the sad spectacle at Rodney's continued in much the same fashion for Iggy: confused living conditions, sometimes hanging with whatever women would give him shelter, sometimes crashing with fellow musicians, who by now were used to the sight of a Quaaluded Iggy at their door. 'He would regularly show up in a yellow mini-dress with this huge dick hanging out of it, and would go "I'm cold, I'm hungry," and empty your refrigerator. Then the next minute he would be trying to crawl in bed with me and my girlfriend. Between us. That's what it was like,' laughs Nigel Harrison. Even when Iggy lucked into more luxurious living quarters, such as a wealthy woman called Alex who had a pleasant house in Stone Canyon, he was still a creative scam artist, sticking Band-Aids over his face before he left the house, remembers Harrison, so he could hang out at the Rainbow and moan, 'I got beat up by two Puerto Ricans, I got no money!' hoping to beg some cash or drugs.

Unfortunately, real life soon conspired to imitate such scams, when Jim turned up to see David Bowie at LA's Universal Amphitheater at the beginning of September. He'd already suffered the humiliation of trying to find Bowie at the Beverly Hills Hotel, cadging a ride there with Ron's friend Doug Currie and realising his one-time champion was nowhere to be found. Now, walking through the parking lot, he and Sugerman were bounced by two surfers, who enticed Jim to a quiet corner with the offer of drugs, then beat the two of them up. Ron Asheton saw Jim sitting outside Wonderland Avenue the next morning, missing a front tooth and complaining that Sugerman had abandoned him to his fate. These weren't the only humiliations over this period. In the autumn, Iggy ill-advisedly popped up on Flo and Eddie's radio show. The KROQ DJs were celebrated for their witty lampooning, and when Iggy guested to chat and sing along to records, it was obvious his days of fast-talking repartee were behind him. Flo and Eddie, a hip duo who'd made their name playing with the Turtles and Frank Zappa, were laughing at him, not with him. The same scenario was being played out at locations like Rodney's, the Whisky and the Rainbow, where, says Jim Parrett, 'Every time we saw Jim, even though people were deferential to him in some ways, they were laughing about him.'

In October, Nick Kent flew over to see his hero and was shocked to realise that Iggy seemed to have 'the word "Loser" tattooed on his forehead. I'd have to tell people, again and again, "This guy is not a loser. This guy is king of the world. This guy has created a music, you don't even realise it yet, but it's going to change the face of the world!"' As the two sat and talked, Jim was quite often lucid, but revealed to Kent how spooked he had been by the disasters the Stooges had undergone, and how he believed there was a hex on the band. Kent was shocked by Jim's condition, horrified to see him occasionally sleeping rough, or passed out in a parking lot, in a dress, zonked out on who knew how many Quaaludes. Sometimes Jim would cry about the condition in which he found himself. But although existential despair was sometimes the cause, the tears were just as likely to be inspired by his inability to score drugs. Overwhelmed with sadness at the condition in which he found his hero, Kent resolved to help him, and picked up an open-reel tape of the Stooges' disastrous Michigan Palace show in the hope that he might be able to raise some money with it back in Europe.

By now Jim seemed to have made up whatever his last disagreement with Williamson had been. It was impossible to make sense of most of his relationships at the time, says Tony Sales, who had become friendly with James and his girlfriend Evita. 'I know Jim confided in James over that period. And he also told James to fuck off. At times we'd get along, and at other times he'd tell me to piss off. A lot of the time it was the drugs speaking. One's values and intellect and integrity [are] challenged by that shit – it's hard to put a marker on something like that and say that's how someone [really] is.' Jim moved into James's apartment at 306, the Coronet, which gave him some stability, even though most of the building's hookers and Hollywood wannabes who maintained a sideline in selling junk and Quaaludes refused to speak to him, thanks to unpaid drug debts. Earlier in 1974, Jim had been so desperate he'd

even contemplated making a living playing with pick-up bands
for Hollywood's jet-set house parties. He'd also at one point
arranged to audition as the singer for Kiss, but hadn't turned up.
He was, however, mortally offended when Nick Kent asked him if
he'd ever considered putting his impressive penis to work in
Hollywood's thriving porno industry. By the autumn he was
becoming more committed to the idea of reviving the spirit of the
Stooges and reuniting with James – which meant a break with
Manzarek, for the ex-Doors player and James Williamson had little
time for each other musically or personally. However, for the one
show Danny Sugerman had actually booked for the Manzarek and
Iggy supergroup he was attempting to tout, Iggy insisted that
Williamson join the band, despite Ray's misgivings. Iggy sported
pristine new front teeth for the occasion, presumably funded by
Sugerman or Manzarek.

The show Sugerman had booked was a prestigious event that set
Hollywood's rock 'n' roll community abuzz. The Hollywood Street
Revival and Trash Dance, staged at the Hollywood Palladium on 9
October, would be popularly known as the Death of Glitter once
the MC, Kim Fowley, and others got it into their heads that the
event would be a modern-day counterpart to Haight-Ashbury's
symbolic Death of the Hippie ceremony in October 1967. The event
was built around the New York Dolls – the Cockettes were also
booked but were banned by comedian Lawrence Welk, who considered them depraved – and Iggy was determined to show these
upstarts how high-energy rock music should really sound.
Unfortunately, a hurried rehearsal at Wonderland Avenue the day
before meant the band only had time to throw together a set full of
cover versions. The show was competent and aggressive but for
many fans it was a disappointment. As Manzarek, Williamson,
Scott Morgan – ex-singer of the Rationals, who'd ended up in LA
and was called in to guest on harmonica – Nigel Harrison and
drummer Gary Mallaber stormed through rock 'n' roll staples
including 'Route 66', 'Subterranean Homesick Blues' and
'Everybody Needs Somebody To Love', there were flashes of fire

and energy – notably when Iggy kicked a stage-invading female fan in the backside, propelling her back into the audience – and Manzarek was delighted, declaring the band 'rocked like a motherfucker'. But the show represented an end, rather than a beginning. Manzarek declared he couldn't work with Williamson – 'there was no sonic space when you had this guitar turned up to 11, like Spinal Tap' – while Jim responded that without Williamson he would lose his audience. To which Manzarek's response, of course, was, 'What audience?'

Before the show, Iggy had been excited and energised. In the hours before he'd gone on stage, Iggy had discovered that Scott Morgan couldn't get to his harmonicas, which were locked in the room he'd borrowed at the Coronet. As the others discussed breaking in the door, Iggy got into an adjacent third-floor apartment and leapt across an airshaft, over a three-storey drop, to rescue the stranded instruments. After the show, Iggy wandered with Annie Apple, Fred Smith and Johnny Thunders for a bizarre ramble up into the Hollywood Hills, before Iggy and Thunders gave the other two the slip around dawn and hailed a cab to Johnny's room at the Hollywood Inn, undoubtedly to score junk together.

To Danny Sugerman, who'd brokered Jim's collaboration with Ray Manzarek, its termination seemed another example of Iggy snatching defeat from the jaws of victory. But he was running out of ideas, too, struggling to control his own fast-fragmenting life and growing reliance on Quaaludes and heroin. The next time he heard from Iggy was shortly after the Palladium show, when the phone rang at Wonderland Avenue.

'Hello. This is Dr Zucker.'

'I don't think I know a Dr Zucker.'

'I know. I'm sorry. I work at UCLA Neuropsychiatric Hospital, where I'm on call. So far I've admitted two Jesus Christs, a Napoleon Bonaparte, an albino who thinks he's Santa Claus, and now I have this guy the cops brought in who claims he's Iggy Pop, and you're his manager.'

As the conversation continued, it became clear that Jim had

again been picked up by the cops, who'd called following a complaint by a cashier at a Hollywood burger joint and found the singer Luded out and drooling aggressively at the diner's clientele. By now the singer was well known to the LAPD, who'd previously picked him up for impersonating a woman. This time they gave him a simple choice: a prison cell or the psych ward. Iggy was sane enough to elect the latter, and when Sugerman turned up to drop off clothes and other necessities for Jim at the Neuropsychiatric Institute's complex of buildings on Westwood Plaza, he felt a sense of relief. Finally, he could hand the responsibility for his friend over to someone who knew what he was doing. As for Jim, who for so long had rebelled against authority and convention, giving in and finally confronting his mental problems was liberating. It was possible he could have objected to his confinement to a psychiatric ward. Instead, he seized the opportunity.

Jim Osterberg was fortunate to have landed up at one of the world's leading psychiatric facilities. For the next few weeks, his life was conducted according to a rigid but bracing regime. He slept in a simple eight-by-four-foot room, with an unfinished wooden cot, one pillow, one sheet and one blanket. It was bare and clinical, with no running water, and a shared bathroom. Most mornings Jim would get up early and walk into a common room, where he would be allowed to play records; his anthem for the day would usually be James Brown's *Sex Machine* album, which he'd play all the way through. After a breakfast of Cheerios, his day would usually involve group discussions, psychoanalysis, walks in the gardens or games of basketball.

Although Jim avoided most of the shrinks at NPI, he formed a bond with Murray Zucker, the resident who'd been on call when he was first admitted. Zucker was young, smart, open and interested; he liked Jim, respected his intelligence and creativity, and would subsequently keep a close eye on his career. Murray found his patient 'extremely likeable' – not because of the bravado that those who knew his music might expect, but because he was 'very sweet, charming, personable, had a great sense of humour and was very perceptive. There was always this intensity about him. Also there was this little boyish quality, that engendered other people wanting to take care of him.'

It was impossible for any of the NPI psychiatrists to diagnose Jim until he was stabilised and all traces of drugs had disappeared from his system; once that was done, the diagnosis was that his underlying condition was hypomania, a bipolar disorder characterised by episodes of euphoric or overexcited and irrational behaviour, succeeded by depression. Hypomanics are often described as euphoric, charismatic, energetic, prone to grandiosity, hypersexual and unrealistic in their ambitions – all of which sounded like a checklist of Iggy's character traits. Bipolar disorders are genetic, and it has often been suggested that the condition has survived because it confers an evolutionary advantage on the population. Dr Kay Jamison, professor of psychiatry at John Hopkins University, is one of the leading US experts in bipolar disorders; she was also a sufferer from the condition, and indeed was an intern at UCLA during the period Jim was admitted, and later wrote a fascinating memoir of her time at NPI. Dr Jamison has written extensively about the links between creativity and mood disorders, citing the histories of poets from William Blake to Ezra Pound, writers from Tolstoy to Tennessee Williams, and artists from Michelangelo to Van Gogh, all of whom are thought to have suffered from bipolar and other mood disorders. Manic or hypomanic behaviour, with the exalted state it brings, has huge creative upsides – but there are huge numbers of case histories illustrating the downside: depression, confinement to the asylum, and suicide.

Despite Jim's travails, his addiction to a variety of drugs, his wild mood swings and distress that his musical career was washed up, there is little self-pity evident in his own or anyone else's memories of his time at NPI. Instead, even today he demonstrates an affecting empathy with his fellow inmates, who he says included a couple of delusional teens, two full-blown manic depressives, a baseball player who'd thrown himself out of the window while high on LSD and 'saddest of all, lots and lots of those American housewives who just break down. They're the big mental cases in the US, who just break down from loneliness and general mental neglect, they get on pills or alcohol and one day they just lose their orientation.'

Today, Dr Zucker remembers his former patient well; but, intriguingly, he questions the initial diagnosis of hypomania – which normally gets more serious with age – and speculates that Jim's problems were more specifically related to his drugs use, his creative lifestyle and the complexities of the personae he'd chosen to harness. 'At times he seemed to have complete control of turning this persona on and that one on, playing with different personae as a display of the range of his brain,' says Murray. 'But then at other times you get the feeling he wasn't in control, he was just bouncing around with it. It wasn't just lack of discipline, it wasn't necessarily bipolar – it was God knows what!'

Jim was such an intriguing psychological specimen that he was presented at what was known as the Grand Round, when a visiting professor would interview NPI's most interesting or challenging inmates. 'It was fascinating,' remembers Murray, 'you had this world-famous professor, a very small guy, wan and intense, sitting nose to nose with Jim and asking him psychoanalytic-type questions.'

Hugely expert in manipulating his interviewers, Jim was both charming and forthcoming, but Murray looked on in fascination as the professor got down to some 'very hardcore psychoanalytical questions. It was intriguing to watch a showman who's so bright and charming and perceptive that he can parry any situation and put on any persona at will deal with a world-famous psychoanalyst – who wasn't having any of it.'

Unsurprisingly, the psychoanalyis would also cover the subject of narcissism, and one gets the impression from Dr Zucker that what would be excessive for the average individual is unsurprising in a singer. At any rate, Murray's explanation of narcissism – 'this unending emotional neediness for attention, that's never enough' –

would eventually inspire a song, 'I Need More', that was a 'brilliant exploration of the subject,' says Zucker.

While Dr Zucker's psychological counselling and an enforced break from drugs would begin a healing process, it would take years to be completed. Without doubt, Zucker helped banish the sense of failure that haunted Jim, launching an era that would see him harness his exuberance, helping transform him from the man who sang about death trips to one who celebrated his lust for life. But life at NPI could still be boring and frustrating, with few visitors to relieve the tedium. Don Waller, Phast Phreddie and some friends from *Back Door Man* attempted to visit their stricken hero; the door staff decided Jim's well-wishers were drug-dealers and refused them admission – the admirers couldn't even leave the flowers they'd brought, in case they concealed illicit substances. David Bowie was one of the few who gained admittance – according to Jim the doctors were star-struck and admitted Bowie, who was, says Jim, off his face, and clad in a spacesuit – accompanied by the actor Dean Stockwell.

But this was a very different David Bowie from the efficient, almost studious character Jim had known in London. David's opening question was: 'Hey, want some blow?' A later visit was less crazed; this time Bowie brought his new regular companion Ola Hudson – who'd designed his *Man Who Fell To Earth* costumes – and Hudson's nine-year-old son Saul (later better known as Slash, the top-hatted, guitar-slingin' founder of Guns 'N' Roses). By now it was obvious Bowie had problems of his own, but it would turn out that his sympathy, and respect, were valuable assets as Jim attempted to rebuild his battered self-esteem.

Ultimately, the intervention of the LAPD, and Jim's stay at NPI, had probably saved him from a descent into complete mental breakdown, and possibly from death. Yet there was one more, equally crucial therapy, one witnessed by Doug Currie in the autumn of 1974, when Currie sat down in James Williamson's living room at the Coronet and listened as Iggy sang his way through a collection of around eight songs, while Williamson accompanied him on his Gibson Les Paul Custom, plugged into a tiny Pignose amplifier. Even in this raw, unadorned state, the songs had a stark beauty. A few, including 'I Got Nothing' and 'Johanna', were familiar from the old Stooges set, but there was a new simplicity and focus to their delivery. The new songs were mostly affecting but defiant depictions of life on the edge in Los Angeles. 'Beyond The Law', Jim mentioned, described his relationship with Manzarek – 'the straights all hate the sounds we make' – while 'Kill City' was a forensic description of his own predicament, living 'where the debris meets the sea. It's a playground for the rich, it's a loaded gun for me.' These haunting songs exemplified Iggy's predicament. Powerful and uncompromising, they would languish unreleased for many years, yet they illustrated how, even in the absence of any interest from the outside world, Jim Osterberg was compelled to make music – and transform his own life, with all its inspiration, stupidity and suffering, into great art.

Around the same time, the two played these songs for John Cale, who preserved their acoustic performance on his tiny cassette recorder and promised he'd try and find them a deal. Then Cale ran into delays, but Ben Edmonds, a long-term Stooges fan, who'd previously been an editor at *Creem* but had recently moved out to LA, offered to fund some recordings. Edmonds was convinced that Williamson and Pop could make a great record that would embody the legacy of the Stooges 'but show people the Stooges could make something that resembled music'; he was doing some publicity work for songwriter Jimmy Webb, of 'McArthur Park' and 'Wichita Lineman' fame, and managed to hire Webb's home studio in Encino on a costs-only basis, the only fee being for Jimmy's brother, Gary, who would engineer the sessions.

Jim seemed humbled compared to his former self, but was earnest about proving he could be relied upon; he would meet Ben at lunchtime at a café by Edmonds' office at Record World, and they'd work on lyrics and discuss arrangements. There would be lapses, still, where Jim would be beset by doubts; at one point he went into the McDonald's next to the apartment his current girlfriend had rented for him on Pico, and picked up an application form for a Mcjob. He never filled it in, though, presumably deciding that another stint in NPI was more enticing than a job flipping burgers, and he elected to return as a voluntary patient to try to get straight. Hence James would oversee the demo sessions, while Iggy would overdub his vocals on day release from NPI. Fortuitously, Louella Osterberg, who with Jim Senior remained anxious for the welfare of their son, regularly sending him cash, had kept up his Blue Cross health insurance, which covered his attendance at NPI.

Recording was brisk; James and Scott Thurston called in favours from all the musicians they knew, and the band revolved around Williamson and Scottie, who played keyboards and bass on half the tracks, augmented by bassist Steve Tranio and English drummer Brian Glascock, a friend of Scottie's who later joined the Motels. (James's friends Hunt and Tony Sales would also play on a couple of tracks.) All of them played for free. For the two or three days when Iggy added his vocals, James would drive down to collect him in the rickety blue MG Midget he'd just bought – a recent insurance payout meant he was free to devote himself to music – and take him back in the evening. Although Jim was occasionally woozy as the NPI doctors experimented with the dosage of what was probably lithium, his singing in retrospect seems perfect, its slight weariness and air of desperation perfectly suited to the material; and the initial mixes, says Ben Edmonds, were rough, raw and thrilling. One night during a mixing session, Art Garfunkel dropped into the studio on the way to see his friend Jimmy Webb and sat and listened to a couple of songs. For months afterwards, Edmonds found it hard to erase the memory of Garfunkel's frizz-crowned head bopping respectfully up and down to the crazed sound of the Michigan lost souls, whose career seemed the perfect antithesis of his own.

Although there was no immediate reaction from Rocket, whom they regarded as the most promising contender, Edmonds was optimistic about the tapes, particularly when he played them to

Seymour Stein in January 1975. Stein was already a respected industry exec, but he would soon become even more celebrated with his signing of the Ramones, and later discovery of Madonna. Stein loved what he heard. 'These aren't demos – this is an album!' he told Edmonds. But when Edmonds returned to Los Angeles he discovered that, in traditional Stooge style, Williamson and Pop had conspired to sabotage their own career once more, and swiped the master tape from the studio.

Today, Williamson says that he and Jim were advised to take the tapes by Bennett Glotzer, an entertainment attorney who was planning to take over Iggy's management. 'Bennett said to us, "Go up there and get the tapes and I'll do what I can to shop them." So we drove up to Jimmy Webb's house and said, "Hi, can we have our tapes?" and they said, "Sure."' Ultimately, says Williamson, Glotzer despaired of dealing with Iggy, who was 'too frenetic' for him. Meanwhile, Edmonds had shelled out his entire savings from his measly journalist's salary with no return – although, with admirable *sangfroid*, he saves most of his resentment for the limp remix that Williamson would perform on the tapes a couple of years later.

Glotzer's lack of progress in shopping the tapes paled alongside some darker news on 11 February 1975, when Jim received a phone call telling him that Dave Alexander had died in Ann Arbor's St Joseph Mercy hospital the previous day. Jim rushed to Ron's apartment, telling him, 'Zander's dead and I don't care!' Ron was outraged and felt like beating Jim up; James, who was shocked by the news, calmed things down. But Jim's reaction was a kind of denial: he was deeply troubled by Alexander's death. 'He liked to pretend he had no emotions, or only superficial emotions,' says Michael Tipton, who had long conversations with Jim about the dead Stooge, 'but you could tell it really bothered him, and that he was deeply depressed.' Alexander's death was caused by pulmonary oedema, brought on by pancreatis – inflammation of the pancreas – a condition which is often caused by alcohol abuse. Indeed, the autopsy also noted 'severe' alcohol-related damage to the liver.

By the summer of 1975, Williamson had once more drifted apart from Jim, perhaps because of an argument after the guitarist tried to get him to sign a contract covering their work at Webb's studio. James had also concluded that he was never going to make it as a guitarist; he'd cut his hand during a violent argument at an Alice Cooper recording session 'that took a long time to heal, and it was just one more thing in a long sequence of crap'. He spent his time learning audio engineering at Paramount Recorders, by which time Jim's musical ambitions seemed to be once again focused on David Bowie.

By now, David had, as Angie describes it, simply 'gone nuts. And any normal person [would have], when they were working so hard, were so stressed and so pissed.' For the last four years Bowie had been working himself into the ground, but didn't seem to be getting any benefit from the huge sums gushing into and leaking out of the sprawling MainMan operation. As Tony Zanetta describes it, 'David was always in total control. And then he decided not to be.' He seemed to go about acquiring a drug habit with a vengeance. Bowie moved to New York in Christmas 1974, and soon, thanks to Cherry Vanilla, hooked up with one of the city's leading cocaine-dealers. One of the most telling indications of the contrasting characters of Jim Osterberg and David Jones is that, under the influence of cocaine, Iggy Pop usually attained delusions of grandeur, while David Bowie suffered from paranoia and a sense of imminent doom. Around March 1975 Bowie moved out to LA, initially staying at the house of Deep Purple singer Glenn Hughes, and then with Michael Lippman, the lawyer he used to extract himself from his MainMan contract.

It was in the unrelenting sunshine of a Los Angeles afternoon that Bowie was reclining in the back of a stretch limo when he saw a slightly forlorn figure trudging down Sunset Boulevard. He ordered his driver to slow down, wound down the window and shouted, 'Hey, Jim, come here!' Jim thought David looked very pale, thin, 'but essentially happy, at least about his work'. Some of Bowie's happiness was inspired by seeing his old friend, whom he invited back to his house. Jim found David consumed with energy, books scattered all over the floor, including a slim volume about faked landings on Mars which David was discussing making into a movie, while characters like Dennis Hopper dropped in and out and David made final preparations for his role in Nicolas Roeg's movie, *The Man Who Fell To Earth*. Bowie suggested they book into a four-track studio and work on some material.

Rolling Stone writer Cameron Crowe witnessed one of the sessions at Oz Studios in Hollywood in May 1975, over the course of a number of interviews that reveal a manic, driven, fractured Bowie in what would become the definitive portrait of his LA period. Iggy and David had already recorded several tracks, one of which was a song that would later turn up as 'Turn Blue'. Over an intense, instrumental track that David had worked up over nine hours in the studio, Iggy improvised stream-of-consciousness lyrics. Looking on proudly, David pronounced him 'Lenny fucking Bruce and James Dean', before Iggy's current girlfriend dragged him out of the studio. Never to return. A few weeks later, Cameron caught up with Bowie again, and heard how Iggy had overslept the next day, called up drunk a few nights later, and when David told him to 'go away' he did just that. 'I hope he's not dead,' said Bowie, pithily. 'He's got a good act.'

Jim had resumed his wanderings, sleeping rough or with the many LA women who wanted to nurse a down-and-out rock star. One promising venue was the Park Sunset Plaza, just opposite the Coronet, which was a favoured location for Hollywood's wealthy businessmen to install their mistresses. Naturally, the women had a lot of spare time on their hands. Even more incongruously, by now Jim had an established hideaway in the shape of a huge beach-front property in La Jolla, near San Diego. Mike Page, a San Diego musician, had brought his girlfriend Lisa Leggett to LA for some clothes-shopping on Melrose, and a mutual friend offered to introduce them to Iggy, who was crashing on his couch. Within a few minutes of their meeting, as Mike visited the bathroom, Lisa had invited Jim to come and stay at her parents' home in San Diego.

Somehow, Jim sensed that this was no ordinary property, and he was soon a regular visitor to the Leggetts' house, which had been built by hotelier Earl Gagosian, founder of the Royal Inns chain; the place was crass and tasteless, and looked like an overgrown Ramada Inn. Mike Page would have long, earnest discussions about blues music with the impoverished but charming Osterberg; only later did he realise that during her visits to LA, Lisa was inviting Iggy to stay in their suite at the Chateau Marmont, where he would call for Dom Pérignon and order Lisa around imperiously. 'When my friends told me he was getting it on with Lisa, and that he was treating her like shit, it broke my heart,' says Page, although he adds, 'It's possible Jim didn't know we'd been an item for a long time.'

On his stints back in Hollywood, however, Jim was 'floundering'. Towards the end of 1975, he was sleeping in a garage on a lounger mattress he'd stolen from a nearby Thrifty Store. His host was a gay hustler named Bruce, who worked Selma Avenue and whenever he earned a little money would spend it on Quaaludes and share them with Jim. One afternoon Jim downed a couple of Quaaludes, then attempted to steal some cheese and apples from the Mayfair Market on Franklin; once again the LAPD picked him up, and this time he was thrown into jail. By now, the only person willing to bail him out was Freddy Sessler, a well-loved figure on the rock 'n' roll scene, a Holocaust survivor who was friends with Keith Richards and was known, says Jim, 'as the kind of guy who can make the party happen'.

Sessler was horrified at Jim's predicament, and offered him a job. An entertaining raconteur who had the air of Chico Marx about him, Sessler had a finger in a lot of pies, the newest of which was a slightly shady telecommunications venture. Sessler had finagled a list of the Westinghouse phone company's business clients, rented an LA office and put a motley bunch of telemarketers to working the phones, calling motels and mom 'n' pop stores on the East Coast to tell them that Westinghouse were closing down in their area, but that their new company could cut them an exclusive deal.

For a few short days, Jim plied his trade as a telemarketer. Despite his mellifluous voice and convincing manner, Jim was 'a terrible failure', for he was required to start work at five in the morning. Sessler was magnanimous: 'Forget about it, Jim. I tell you what I'm gonna do. I'm gonna call David. You know he likes you. And he wants to work with you.'

Jim was too proud to call Bowie for help, and instead fled to San Diego where Lisa Leggett, keen to help him onto his feet, funded a three-day, $600 'Success and Reinvention' motivational course, while Sessler continued to try to get Bowie and Jim together. (It wasn't a bad course, apparently.) In a lucky twist of fate, especially for anyone embarking on Success and Reinvention, David Bowie happened to be hitting town with his Station To Station tour.

On 13 February, Jim visited David at his hotel. David played him a demo of a new song he and Carlos Alomar, his guitarist, had been working on, called 'Sister Midnight'.

'Would you like to record this?' David asked Jim. 'Then maybe we can record an album around it at the end of my tour?'

'Hell, yeah,' was the reply.

Some time that day, Jim was asked to get a bag and report for duty the next morning at 9am, like 'a rock 'n' roll boot camp', joining Bowie's tour to open what would be one of the most difficult, educational, and ultimately happy and productive periods of his life. The same could be said of David Bowie. Beset by huge pressures, this nervous, jumpy cocaine fiend was, according to so many of those with whom he'd fallen out, selfish and ruthless in his dealings with others. Yet, in his time with Jim, the man who'd called him 'that fuckin' carrot top', David Bowie showed himself a selfless person, one who, says Carlos Alomar, treated his friend with 'understanding, compassion and gentleness'. This friendship would extend over a longer period than most people would ever realise, and would underpin the greatest music that both Iggy and Bowie would ever make.

CHAPTER 11

The Passenger

It was the summer of 1977, and David Bowie and Iggy Pop had just about had enough of each other. For around a year now they'd been living in each other's pockets, going to museums together, reading the same books, riding the same train, getting the same haircut, living in the same house. Now this was war.

This is how a battle might go. David would hear a theme tune from a TV channel and transmute it into a catchy riff, which he'd demonstrate for a few friends on a ukulele. Iggy would top him with an improvised lyric about getting it in the ear, or some other crazed stream-of-consciousness hip poetry, delivering it straight-faced and defying his small audience not to laugh. Meanwhile, the crazed Sales brothers, two manic, impassioned musicians who'd spent much of their time in Berlin paranoid they might be turned into lampshades, would seize control of the song, shooting it in a new direction with a beat that sounded like it came from a drum kit fifty feet high.

Sitting upright behind a mixing desk in a stone-lined studio nestled in a grandiose but war-scarred Berlin masonic hall, David Bowie was in open competition with the man whose career he'd done so much to revive. He was sick of Iggy's rock histrionics, but he was on a roll, the best roll of his life. Jim Osterberg was on a roll too, laughing manically as he wrestled back control of his own music. He had his own apartment, he was living on cocaine, hash, red wine and German sausages, he took a cold shower every morning – or at least thought about taking a shower. He was the happiest he'd ever been in his life.

But at night he'd dream of revenge.

When Jim got on board David's Station To Station tour, he was teaming up with an operation that was far tinier than anyone suspected. Outsiders thought they saw a huge organisation run with fascistic precision, yet in truth this was a family operation, revolving around David, Coco Schwab, Jim, publicist Barbara de Witt and her husband Tim, acting manager Pat Gibbons and photographer Andrew Kent. Each day followed a strict routine; plane flight, soundcheck, short break, show, nice dinner, then sleep. Even with such a tight routine, Bowie found time to check every detail, reviewing the set and looking at slides for release to the press after nearly every show, revelling in running a tight ship rather than the out-of-control leviathan he remembered from MainMan days.

In retrospect, it was obvious that Bowie had made up his mind to rescue Jim Osterberg even before he had set off on the tour, which opened in Vancouver on 2 February 1976. He and Ben Edmonds had discussed the fallen rock star at some length during tour rehearsals, and while Bowie flitted from subject to subject with his characteristic gadfly intensity, there was a fondness in his remarks about Jim, someone who was 'not so hard and knowledgeable and all-knowing and cynical. Someone who hasn't a clue . . . but has insights.'

Comments such as these perhaps gave the impression that Bowie was patronising about the man with whom he'd share most of the next eighteen months. Certainly, many people at the time accused Bowie of being coldheartedly manipulative, co-opting Iggy to gain credibility – indeed, German Stooges fan-club organiser Harald Inhülsen later accused Bowie of kidnapping Iggy as if in

some thrillingly perverse sexual and musically exploitative conspiracy and keeping him 'under his thumb'. Such conspiracy
theorists tended to ignore the depths of Bowie's admiration for
Iggy, a man he knew could achieve feats of which he was incapable.
They also underestimated Jim Osterberg's own resilience and self-
belief. After Jim joined the Station To Station tour in San Diego on
13 February, even close observers such as Andrew Kent and Carlos
Alomar were struck by how unintimidated Jim was by his surroundings, or his so-called rescuer. 'There was no kowtowing,' says
Alomar. 'I saw them simply as real mates. Meeting Jim the first
time [in February] I didn't have a reference for why they were
friends. Nor would I describe them as musical friends – they were
just . . . friends.'

Indeed, while Alomar observed a partnership of equals, his
predecessor, Mick Ronson, thought his old boss was almost besotted with Iggy. I discovered this when the guitarist and I happened
to be discussing Bowie's voice. I had mentioned how David's
singing had changed, as he'd switched to a lower register between
1974 and 1976, when Mick shot me a quizzical look, and in his
beautifully pristine Hull accent interrupted me. 'Well, you know
why that was, don't you?'

'Why his voice changed? [Pause] Er . . . because he was influenced by someone?'

'Exactly!'

'So you think David wanted to sound like Iggy?'

'Sound like Iggy?' Ronson laughed. 'He wanted to *be* Iggy!'

A few years later, asked about Ronson's theory, Iggy leered
cheekily before proclaiming, '*Everyone* wants to be Iggy!' Then he
apologised for being so 'hokey', before pointing out that 'if there
was any wanting going on, it was certainly two-way'. In truth,
while Jim admits that it was pathetic that he'd been reduced to the
condition in which he'd found himself at the end of 1975, he also
points out that even at this low he was 'not without resources'. It's
easy to discern the almost unshakeable confidence – or, in Nick
Kent's words, 'that skyscraper ego' – that drove him, the conviction

that one day his music would be appreciated. By now, with the little knots of fans he knew about in Los Angeles, New York, London, Paris and Germany, Iggy was aware, as he says, that 'my numbers were legion'. Meanwhile, Jim Osterberg, the empathetic, talkative, charming man who liked to nestle up with a good book, had far more in common with David Jones than anyone who took their images at face value could realise: that coy, slightly flirtatious manner, that skilled reading of power structures and social situations, that childlike enthusiasm, that indefatigable energy.

When they'd first met, Jim had been impressed by Bowie's English, vaudevillian aesthetic and his quirky methods of unsettling people – whether it was sporting bizarre haircuts or kissing Ron Asheton full on the lips. Now, as Bowie's tight-knit crew made their way from California through the Midwest into Canada and beyond, all by road or train, there came a more profound respect for Bowie's 'psychic stamina', as Jim watched this notionally effete man play show after show, keep a handle on the business side (which was complicated by a split with new manager Michael Lippman) and still be bursting with creative energy. 'And then he'd go out to a club after almost every show until four in the morning and do all the other things that we were doing. And he never showed bad form, not once.' There were quirks in Bowie's behaviour – 'an odd, theatrical, slightly megalomaniac' way of relating to people – but this hardly perturbed Jim, who knew this was a tendency to which Iggy was prone, too.

In turn, Bowie's crew, notably Carlos Alomar and Andrew Kent, were surprised to see this notorious rock 'n' roll animal join the tour with such civilised self-sufficiency, often engaging their overburdened employer in conversation, or at other times sitting with little glasses over his nose reading the political columns in the morning papers while sipping an espresso. Bowie's quiet mentions that 'we have to do something for Iggy' seemed eminently reasonable, even the fact that Iggy was being given one of Carlos Alomar's best compositions, the brand-new 'Sister Midnight', which the band had introduced to their set during rehearsals in

Vancouver. In its initial form, the song was a taut, tough example of Bowie's new idiom, blue-eyed soul, but even at this stage, there was a new minimalism in the song's mechanistic repetitions. During the long train and car journeys across America, David played Jim Kraftwerk's *Radioactivity* album on cassette (plus Tom Waits, and the Ramones) and they discussed David producing an album for Iggy at Musicland, Giorgio Moroder's studio in Munich. Fatefully, where Jim had rejected the concept of working with Ray Manzarek for fear he would lose his Stooges audience, he grasped the opportunity of working on an experimental, electronic album with both hands, realising instantly that 'there was a power to the music that he seemed willing to provide for me'. David even explained, after playing Jim a rough, raw demo of 'Sister Midnight', probably recorded during the *Man Who Fell To Earth* sessions, that this kind of jagged-edged experimentation was something he might not be allowed to release under his own name; the implication, presumably valuable for Jim's self-esteem, was that in producing an album for Jim, David was not just doing him a favour – Jim would be doing David a favour, too.

This unique partnership would, over a remarkably short period, create four albums that would showcase a radical change in their own music, and just as radical a change in the landscape of popular music over the following decade. Iggy's two albums would prove he could make great music outside of the Stooges; David's two albums would effectively cement his reputation as a world-class artist, one who was happy to exist at the cutting edge of musical trends. Not since Van Gogh and Gauguin spent nine weeks together at the Yellow House in Arles had two artists of such stature, with such distinct styles, cooperated so closely, with such influential and fulfilling results. But where the two painters' creative winning streak had culminated in madness and breakdown, Bowie and Iggy's great, innovative work together would prove a healing process for two severely damaged individuals.

The increasingly obvious personal and musical rapport between the two stars would eventually inspire persistent speculation about whether their bond extended to a sexual relationship, too. Bowie had famously declared himself gay in *Melody Maker* back in January 1972, while Iggy was already celebrated in San Francisco's gay community, just about all of whom claimed to have been the one who treated him to the celebrated blowjob at Bimbo's in 1974. There are plenty of observers who are convinced the two did the dirty deed, and many of them happily share entertaining stories of how it happened. Sadly for those of us who fantasise about such things, the people who were there say otherwise. Jim himself, while agreeing that 'it's good to try new things', unblushingly denies those stories. More tellingly, Angie Bowie – who would regularly vie with her husband for the most outrageous sexual exploits and has treated listeners to stirring accounts of her ex-husband's gay encounters – contends that there was no hanky panky of a sexual nature. 'No. I absolutely doubt it. I would have to ask, who would be on the bottom?'

By the end of March, the Station To Station US tour concluded with a masterful performance at Madison Square Garden, followed by a star-packed party at the Penn Plaza Club, during which David spent most of his time ensconced with Jim, as old acquaintances like John Cale dropped by. Jim looked almost glowing with health, wearing a suit he'd bought for a court appearance with Bowie the previous day in Rochester, New York, to answer charges – later dropped – following a marijuana bust at the Flagship American hotel, four days earlier. Iggy's public appearances represented the first confirmation that he was about to return from oblivion.

When Bowie left New York on an ocean liner bound for Cannes on the 27th, Iggy remained in New York for a couple of days at the Seymour hotel, gaining the first inkling that his life was about to change. For the first time he realised that a new generation of musicians were terming themselves 'punks' and emerging in his image. That weekend he sat down with Pam Brown for the cover story of the fourth issue of *Punk* magazine and, in typical fashion, narrated a crazed, incredible tale of his recent past – most of which, of course, was essentially true. Over the same period he appeared at a reception in his honour at CBGB, the Bowery club run by Hilly Kristal that was the cradle of punk in the US; later he took *Punk* editor John Holscomb and photographer Roberta Bayley out for lobster at Phoebe's. Before catching his plane to Italy, he asked Roberta to post a pair of handcuffs that he'd bought on Times Square to his son Eric. Although he'd hardly seen his child during the preceding year, he was now trying for once to be 'a proper dad', before he embarked on his adventures in Berlin. The final line between his chaotic past and a new beginning had been drawn a couple of days before, when he'd jammed with Johnny Thunders and Syl Sylvain in a New York loft; Johnny asked him if he wanted to get high. For the first time in his life, Iggy said no.

Bowie had been remarkably resilient, considering the stress he'd been under for the last year and the mental torture and paranoia he'd suffered in Los Angeles, a city that he – and ultimately Jim, too – would regard as evil, almost vampiric. He was, Jim noticed at the time, damaged, in need of a soulmate, but wasn't going to show it. That restraint endured until their stopover in Switzerland in April, when he started to open up. Almost certainly, he also discussed the state of his marriage with Angie, a remarkable, unconventional partnership that was showing the strain of their constant separations; it was an open relationship, but Angie was becoming increasingly jealous of anyone who got intellectually close to David. This applied to Jim, about whom Angie was ambivalent, and it particularly applied to Coco Schwab. Coco, or Corinne, Schwab, was an exceptionally able and organised character who'd been hired as a secretary by Hugh Attwooll at MainMan in the summer of 1973. Hugh took a vacation a few weeks later and, he says, returned to find that Coco had learned how to do his job within 36 hours. As a result, Tony Defries decided to dispense with him. Now Coco controlled access to David, relieving the psychically overburdened star of a huge range of responsibilities, but infuriating everyone who felt they'd been frozen out – most notably Angie.

The next, crucial shared experience that would help bond Jim and David was a mysterious train trip to Moscow, arranged on the spur of the moment to fill the gap between stop-offs in Zurich and Helsinki. Andrew Kent, who had the best working knowledge of French, spent a couple of days shuttling between Zurich and Basel to obtain the necessary transit visas for the mammoth rail trip, which was undertaken by him, Jim, David, Coco and Pat Gibbons. As they clattered through Poland, stopping every now and then to take on supplies of soup or bottles of beer, they saw towns still pockmarked with bullet holes and a landscape scarred by unrepaired bomb-craters; drawing alongside a goods train in Warsaw, they witnessed a worker unloading coal piece by piece in the grey, freezing sleet, a dreary, poignant image that would later be commemorated in Bowie's beautifully sombre instrumental, 'Warszawa', on *Low*. Around 700 miles into the journey, the group encountered their first bureaucratic hassles at Brest, the ancient Slav city that now sits in Byelorussia, but which in 1976 straddled the border to the USSR. All the passengers had to disembark as they switched train lines to the broad-gauge Russian system, and as Kent remembers it, they were greeted by a menacing, albino KGB agent with the phrase, 'We weren't expecting you.' Bowie's huge cache of books was searched, and some of them were reportedly confiscated for dubious subject matter which concerned the Third Reich; however, according to other recollections, the party's brush with the KGB was actually inspired by Jim impetuously giving away some of the flowers that filled the group's cabin, an act construed as an attempted bribe.

However intimidating, the hold-up was brief, and any impressions of the KGB's omniscience evaporated when the group arrived in Moscow and found the agent's promise that 'we'll have someone meet you' was an empty one. Finding themselves unmonitored and free to explore the city, they dropped off their luggage at the Metropole hotel, then set off for Red Square, where they posed as troops marched by, soaking in the atmosphere, Jim and David laughing like happy schoolboys. From there followed a trip to the

GUM department store, and a leisurely dinner back at the Metropole – a beautiful Art Nouveau building decorated by Mikhail Vrubel, the site of several crucial Workers' Congress meetings addressed by Lenin, and also a central location in Mikhail Bulgakov's sinister *The Master and Margarita*. Then, seven hours after they'd arrived in the city, the party boarded their train to Helsinki, where they would be greeted with 'Bowie Lost In Russia' headlines.

Bowie's tour resumed in Helsinki, followed by five Scandinavian gigs, travelling thereafter to London – where it's possible that David and Jim did some preparatory recording on 'Sister Midnight' – to face a huge media onslaught concerning Bowie's supposed fascist sympathies, prompted by his remark to a Stockholm reporter that Britain 'could benefit from a fascist leader'. Perhaps it was fortunate no one in the British press had seen photos of Bowie's travelling companion being brutalised by a musician wearing an Afrika Korps uniform and swastika armband. Finally, the tour ended in Paris on 15 May. At the party to celebrate its conclusion, Bowie spent much of the evening canoodling with Romy Haag, the striking, transgendered diva who seemingly embodied all of Berlin's glamour and decadence. Romy reportedly asked David to come up and see her in Berlin.

David and Jim stayed in Paris for a couple of days after the tour, and around 18 May, Laurent Thibault received an anxious phonecall from Coco Schwab, telling him that David needed a refuge from the fans swarming around Paris. Thibault, who'd made his name as bassist with French prog band Magma, had recently taken over management of the Chateau d'Herouville, a luxurious, state-of-the-art residential studio based in a chateau twenty-five miles outside of Paris. It was a huge, rambling, romantic building, famously haunted by the ghosts of its celebrated former residents Frédéric Chopin, and his lover George Sand. That evening David came up with Jim, Coco, his son Zowie and Zowie's two nannies, and they stayed a couple of days. David had brought several flightcases of records and other equipment, and asked for his hi-fi to be set up in a huge room with a wood-beamed ceiling. The first day, David and Jim inspected the studio, which David had used to record *Pin-Ups* in 1973. The second night, he played Thibault records from his flightcases late into the night, including Magma's debut album, which he critiqued, and at around three in the morning he announced he intended to record 'Jimmy's album' at the chateau, and that Thibault would also be playing bass. (There was a secondary benefit to working at the residential chateau, for it meant that RCA would be picking up the living expenses of Bowie and entourage, easing a chronic cash-flow problem that afflicted Bowie after his split with MainMan.)

Around the end of May, Bowie, Jim and Coco arrived as promised, bringing along David's Baldwin electric piano, Dan Armstrong perspex guitar, ARP Axxe synthesiser and Marshall amplifier, and they set to work. David had many of the songs recorded on cassette, and recorded some of his piano parts before asking Thibault if he knew a drummer. 'He wanted a very solid, very rough one,' says Thibault, 'and I said, yes, I know exactly the guy.'

Thibault phoned up Michel Santangeli, who'd played with many French artists, including Alan Stivell and Jacques Higelin; Michel arrived a couple of days later and was initially transfixed with fear, as he'd thought Laurent was joking when he'd mentioned playing with David Bowie. The next day they started working on the backing tracks, with Bowie sitting at the piano and signalling over the sound-screens to Santangeli, who learned the parts as they went along. Meanwhile, Jim sat in the control room, furiously scribbling on piles of paper, crafting impressionistic lyrics that frequently fused his and David's world views; over and over the songs use the first person plural – 'hey baby, we like your lips' – in a kind of collective consciousness.

As they listened back to the first takes, Michel nervously told Thibault, 'OK, I understand what we want now, let's do the proper version.' There was no answer from David, who was listening in rapt attention, kneeling on the control-room chair. Then David announced, '*Suivant!* [Next!]' and it was on with the next song, despite Santangeli's objections that he hadn't even learned the song or tuned his drums. Over that day and the next they recorded the drums and piano on seven songs or so, after which Santangeli was sent back to Brittany, mortified that he hadn't recorded the drums properly or had a chance to chat with Bowie. After a few more days, during which Bowie added electric guitar to the skeletal compositions, he disappeared for a rest and asked Thibault to add some bass guitar. Thibault's instructions were as minimal as were Santangeli's, but he overdubbed around five songs using his Rickenbacker; the results were deemed acceptable, bar one song, called 'Borderline', for which David hummed a new bassline that Thibault duly replicated. And so the recording continued, in an impressionistic, often seemingly random manner, with sounds left rough and accidents incorporated into the final results. Towards the end of the session David called in *Station To Station* bassist George Murray and drummer Dennis Davis to overdub rhythm tracks on some of the songs, including 'Sister Midnight' and 'Mass Production'.

Between takes, David or Jim occasionally wandered around the grounds alone, or explored the huge, rambling building while the other was working. Occasionally one of them would travel into Paris, where Jim went to see his old flame Nico. The chateau often became a sanctuary for friends of the owner, Michel Magne, and that summer the celebrated French left-wing actor and singer Jacques Higelin was staying in Magne's wing. The luxurious apartment was a blissful refuge for Higelin, his girlfriend Kuelan Nguyen and their six-year-old son, Ken, and at the end of August Higelin would record *Alertez Les Bébés*, his commercial breakthrough album, at the chateau.

One afternoon Kuelan was surprised to find an American musician playing piano in the rear living room of the chateau. She was instantly taken with him – he had blond hair, and looked like a Viking – found out via sign language, for he spoke no French and she no English, that his name was Jimmy, and invited him, in gestures, to a birthday party she'd organised for Ken's nanny. That night, Jimmy danced into the room, leaping over chairs and tables, then walked over to Kuelan and simply laid his head on her shoulder. Soon they were sharing a surreal, mystically profound conversation pieced together via gestures, expressions and random words. The evening would be the start of a relationship which, played out against the romantic setting of the chateau, echoed the courtly, doomed love affairs of the eighteenth century. 'It was a complete, real love affair,' says Kuelan, 'but it was not possible.'

Higelin was an advocate of sexual freedom, but found himself becoming increasingly jealous of the *beau*, *blond* interloper. Kuelan hadn't known at first Jimmy was a musician; then one night she heard him shouting 'Iggy Pop, Iggy Pop' out of a window, like a tribal war cry. Meanwhile, Jacques implored her to stay and listen to a song he had written for her. By the time Kuelan managed to see Jimmy he'd become so nervous he was drunk, like a lovelorn schoolboy, blurting out that *he* had written a song for her, before voicing his frustration in pidgin French, 'Je fais abattoir de la terre entière if you leave me.' Kuelan looked into his eyes, put her finger to her lips and told him to 'shhhhh', as if comforting a child. 'I say shush, to calm him. I was half laughing, half afraid he would go to some extreme and hurt himself.' That night she heard a song called 'Borderline' that Jimmy and his friend David had written, while David played with the ambiguity of the situation, as if he were besotted with her, too. By the time Jim recorded the vocals on the song, which was retitled 'China Girl', it incorporated Kuelan's 'Shhh, shut your mouth' response. Its romantic, lovelorn simplicity – 'I'm just a mess without my China Girl' – was engagingly subverted by Jim's acceptance of his own unsuitability, and warning of his own megalomania: 'I'll give you men who want to rule the world.' The song's undercurrent of thwarted love was true to life, for Kuelan ultimately decided she had to stay with her son and family. She would marry Higelin two years later.

After recording for most of July, David, Jimmy, Coco and Laurent had to leave the chateau to make way for a Bad Company session and decamped to Munich to record the vocals and mix the album. Musicland was a panelled basement studio that felt like a bunker; the city itself, the birthplace of the Nazi party, seemed to have a dark resonance too. One evening a couple of studio guests greeted Bowie with a Nazi salute; he ignored them, but muttered an obscenity to Thibault once they were safely past. The quartet stayed on the twenty-first floor of the Sheraton, mostly sleeping during the day; at one point there was a huge summer thunderstorm and they could look down at the lightning below them as their windows shook with each massive peal of thunder.

As the sessions continued, a young British guitarist named Phil Palmer gained an intimate insight into Bowie's working methods. The phone rang at 2am one morning and Phil's mother knocked on his bedroom door to tell him, 'There's a Mr Bowie on the phone for you!' Mr Bowie assured Phil that he was not an impostor, said that Phil had been recommended to him by the producer Tony Visconti, and told him to throw some clothes in a bag and catch a plane to Munich, where he and Iggy Pop were recording.

Palmer turned up for the midnight session and walked into the studio, set in a deserted shopping mall. It felt like the *Mary Celeste*, full of abandoned guitars and drum kits belonging to Thin Lizzy, who were working the day shift. Meanwhile David Bowie and Iggy Pop sat in the control room, chatting affably enough, but the whole atmosphere was spooky and the guitarist was slightly overawed as Bowie rolled the tapes. For five days he experimented with guitar sounds, plugging his Telecaster into a variety of gear, some of it borrowed from Thin Lizzy, and he experienced at first hand Bowie's genius for unlocking musicians' creativity. Iggy and David's manner was 'gentle. But odd.' Sometimes the instructions were cryptic. As Palmer prepared to overdub guitar on 'Nightclubbing', Bowie or Iggy told him: 'You're walking down Wardour Street. Now play the music you hear coming out of the door of each club.' Elsewhere they were more specific. As Palmer replayed Bowie's doomy guitar arpeggios on 'Dum Dum Days', Bowie had him re-record the opening over and over, instructing him: 'Bend that note more.' The order seemed appropriate for the whole session, which felt pretty skewed all round. After a while, Palmer found himself on a thrilling creative roll, but the whole episode was intensely disorientating, whether it was David telling him he was ordering in some sheep brains and would Phil like any, or excitedly flipping through an Erich Heckel monograph and asking Phil's opinion of the paintings. One night he arrived early to witness a member of Thin Lizzy's crew getting a beating for allowing the supply of cocaine to dry up. Bowie and Iggy were obviously slightly 'whacky', although there was no open drug use, and both were intensely focused on the task in hand. The most striking impression came from the fact he never saw Iggy or David outside the hours of darkness. 'Vampiric would be the perfect word.'

Thibault too found the surroundings disorientating. For one song, 'Mass Production', David was frustrated he couldn't get the sound he wanted, and the ex-Magma bassist intervened, making up a huge tape loop of overloaded industrial noises that ran round the entire studio; he remembers Bowie sitting there silently for what seemed like an endless period of time, watching the white editing strip on the tape going round and round the room, like a child transfixed by a train set.

Around the beginning of August Thibault returned to Paris to record with Jacques Higelin, while David and Jim travelled to Berlin, to finish the mixing at Hansa studios on Kurfürstendamm. The studio was located on the fourth floor of an office block and had been recommended to David by Edgar Froese of Tangerine Dream. Bowie called in his old friend Tony Visconti – with whom he'd last worked on *Young Americans* – to mix the bulk of the album and oversee a couple of final overdubs. By now, Bowie and Iggy had moved into an apartment Coco Schwab had found at 155 Hauptstrasse, in Berlin's Schöneberg district, and when Visconti arrived he was struck by Bowie's obvious physical and psychological improvement – he looked radically different from the emaciated creature with whom Visconti had recorded *Young*

Americans – and while Visconti had been told that David was working with the animalistic American Iggy Pop, he was surprised to
meet the polite, cheery and rather civilised Jim Osterberg.

The work was difficult – Visconti got the impression all the
material had been slammed furiously onto tape in a creative rush –
but over a couple of weeks the three of them carved out 'a great,
new sonic landscape,' says Visconti, 'full of angst and torture.' (It's
likely that Thibault's original mixes survived on 'Sister Midnight'
and 'Mass Production'.) The work, which they'd later title *The
Idiot* – derived from Dostoevsky's Prince Myshkin, the wise but
mentally ill subject of a book that each of them had frequently
namechecked to their friends – was a radical departure for both of
its main architects, and it must be pointed out that much of Bowie's
genius lay, as so often, in choosing the perfect collaborator. It could
be guaranteed that the world would be shocked to hear a diehard
rocker, known for cutting himself with broken glass or smearing
himself with peanut butter, front an intense, minimal, electronic
and formidably European opus. But Jim intuitively understood
and in fact relished this experimentation, for his own appreciation
of avant-garde music was as profound as David's. Even though
much of his most recent cultural experience consisted of sleeping
rough in a garage shared with a male hustler, it was Jim who had
emerged from a sophisticated college campus, had performed with
a close associate of Gordon Mumma and Robert Ashley, had seen
Warhol's Exploding Plastic Inevitable on its second outing, back in
March 1966, and even a decade earlier had been cognisant of concerts 'given by a nude woman playing a cello while someone else
beat the strings of a piano with hammers' – experiences which
made Bowie's CV look positively parochial.

Jim was open enough to appreciate Bowie's most left-field ideas,
the quality of which he found staggering. 'He only pitched me
great balls, and I grabbed every one,' he says today, although when
dredging the deeper recesses of his memory, he can remember one
song he rejected, a jaunty little number Bowie played for him on
acoustic guitar, which went 'Iggy Pop, Iggy Pop, when are you

going to stop?' (The song was recorded, however, and remains somewhere in the vaults.) Elsewhere, there was an almost intuitive understanding between the two, with Bowie pushing Iggy to extend the baritone growl that he'd used previously on 'Fun House', or experiment with storytelling lyrics on songs like 'Dum Dum Boys' (which had been called 'Dum Dum Days' back at the chateau). Musically, there are subtle tricks familiar from the Stooges which betray Jim's influence on the songwriting – for instance, the way the strict structure of 'Dum Dum Boys' takes a little detour to follow Iggy as he pensively relives the moment he first saw Scott and Ron Asheton standing outside Marshall's drug store and was 'most impressed . . . no one else was impressed, not at all . . .'

Where some of Bowie's later 'Berlin' trilogy – or triptych, as he termed it – of albums were regarded as cold, even glacial, this prototype demonstrated humanity and even goofy humour amid the hard-edged modernity. 'Nightclubbing' is all Germanic, robotically slow, impossibly imposing until you recognise the musical quote from Bowie's old glam rival Gary Glitter; meanwhile, in a contrasting cultural reference, 'Tiny Girls' evokes Jacques Brel's 'Ne Me Quitte Pas'. 'China Girl' demonstrates Bowie's emerging knack for crafting lofty, inspiring musical bridges – the 'I'll give you television' line prototypes a similar trick used on, for instance, 'feel all the hard time' climax of the 'Absolute Beginners'. Yet Jim's lyrics subvert the simple message, as he tells how he'll ruin it all with his western habits and megalomania. Although there are similarities with the dark, tonal palette of *Fun House*, *The Idiot* would represent a radical departure from the music Iggy had made with the Stooges – which was, of course, the plan. Like *Fun House*, *The Idiot* would remain an album that was more respected than loved, the reviews mostly neutral, at least until it was recognised that the album, released just as the punk wave was about to break, would prefigure the sound of post-punk.

As David and Jim crafted *The Idiot* over the summer of 1976, their personal closeness mirrored their musical relationship. At some point during those first few months in Europe, they had made an informal pact that they would get to grips with their prodigious drug intakes. Perhaps they agreed to cut down on cocaine; almost certainly Jim promised to steer clear of heroin. It was hardly a blanket ban, for they would each manage an occasionally heroic intake of cocaine and alcohol over the coming year, but for both of them, life in Berlin offered the prospect of being more firmly rooted and escaping the flunkies who'd encouraged their excesses. There was the odd lapse; one night, when Bowie took a taxi back to 155 Hauptstrasse, the cabbie recognised him, and as Bowie fumbled for change outside the apartment he informed him: 'By the way you can tell Iggy that the dooj [heroin] he ordered has arrived.' Instantly, Bowie warned that if the cabbie ever obtained heroin for Jim, he would personally make trouble for him. The cabbie fled, duly intimidated, and David never mentioned the conversation to Jim, aware that he shouldn't humiliate him or make himself look controlling.

Bowie in particular relished the anonymity that Berlin seemed to confer, and it was several months before most Berliners noticed that he'd taken up residence in their city. Yet even after they'd realised, they helped maintain the illusion that his presence wasn't registered; often he'd be seen in record shops, such as the Zip stores on Kurfürstendamm or Gedächtniskirche, buying a stack of vinyl with his collar turned up, happy to be ignored, only for the customers to rush to the till after he'd walked out of the door and ask the assistant, *'Was hat Bowie gekauft?'* But the assistants, zealous of his privacy, wouldn't reveal his purchases.

Bowie and Jim both describe their Berlin days as one of the happiest periods of their lives – David remembers being full of 'a joy of life, and a great feeling of release and healing', while Jim describes himself as 'maybe the happiest I was, ever'. For both of them, life was simple and ordered, 'but always,' says Jim, 'with the idea, we're trying to learn something here.' Before his record deal was secured, Jim had the added discipline of living on 10 deutschmarks a day, which David would hand over each morning. Bowie, Jim and Coco's apartment at 155 Hauptstrasse was part of a large block above a car spares showroom, situated over a tree-lined double carriageway. It was fairly elegant with high ceilings, but was generally nondescript, what Berliners would term a typical Altbau, or period, apartment, and while the furniture was tasteful, it was minimal. In Jim's bedroom there was a simple mattress on the floor and not much else. David's main room was full of books, and also a huge roll of paper on which he'd write notes and lyrics; another room housed David's son Zowie, who was enrolled in school in Berlin. The fact that the apartment was nondescript and cheap was part of its appeal, for in the wake of his expensive split with MainMan, with another legal battle on the way, Bowie had to be careful with his cash. Coco kept a close eye on his spending; one night in Munich, Laurent Thibault had been an astonished witness to a scene when Coco interrogated Bowie about a new jumper he'd just bought, as the world-famous rock star assured her, 'Really, it only cost twenty deutschmarks!'

Schöneberg, too, was an attractively anonymous district. There was a sprinkling of bars, bookshops and a market centred round St Matthias Kirche, ten minutes' walk away, with a gay community huddled around Nollendorfplatz just to its north, where Christopher Isherwood lived until 1933; the U-bahn station bore a bronze memorial to Berlin's gay population, murdered in the concentration camps. En route was a sinister, monolithic Nazi air-raid shelter, which had proved impervious to attempted postwar demolition, and was now straddled by a modernist block of flats. In the mornings Jim would take long walks on his own, sometimes wandering for miles, to the point where he eventually claimed he'd covered every inch of the city on foot. One time he came back from exploring the street's Hinterhof workshops – the work premises found at the rear of many apartments – and excitedly told David and Coco that he'd learned how to milk a cow. Compared to David, Jim was confident about venturing into a bar or shop on his own, going up to people he'd never met before, chatting to them in English or his few words of German, and seeing what would transpire. On a typical afternoon Jim and David might stroll around the antique stalls at Winterfeldplatz, or catch the S-bahn to the Wannsee – a beach resort on the Havel river, a seemingly idyllic spot where Himmler had announced the Final Solution – for a leisurely lunch. One day they went out and bought acrylic paints and David showed Jim how to prep a canvas; they both painted all afternoon, and again thereafter. David painted a portrait of Iggy, a convincing work in an Expressionist style influenced by the paintings he'd often contemplated at the Brücke museum.

At night, Jim, David and Coco would often eat at Kreuzberg's Café Exil, overlooking the Landwehr canal, or hang in the smoke-filled back room, which was invariably full, says Bowie, of 'intellectuals and beats'. Other favourite hangouts included the Dschungle 2, the Asibini restaurant and the Paris Bar at Kantstrasse, while the beautiful but decayed Schlosshotel Gerhus, where Bowie and Jim had first stayed in Berlin, was always the favourite choice to house musicians or visitors. Some time after they moved in and added an extra cachet to the street, a gay café, the Anderes Ufer, opened a couple of doors down; Bowie break-fasted there many mornings, and when queer-bashers smashed the plate-glass window one night, David paid for the repairs but insisted they keep his assistance quiet.

If the trio were planning to try a new location, Coco and Jim would venture out on reconnaissance first, to see if it was safe for David. One such evening, they were checking out a fashion party in the Fabrikneu, a loft shared by a bunch of local artistic types, including Tangerine Dream drummer Klaus Kruger and photographer – and later artist – Martin Kippenberger. Kippenberger had created a photocollaged floor with another photographer, Esther Friedmann; together they'd made up over a thousand prints and pasted them all over the improvised catwalk. When Esther and her boyfriend Norbert slid open one of the glass doors that divided up the loft and Esther saw Jim chatting to Kruger it was, she says, 'as if lightning struck'. Jim asked Kruger to introduce him, and a few days later invited Esther over to the Hauptstrasse to listen to the rough mixes of *The Idiot*.

Gamine, vivacious, smart and extremely feisty, Esther was born in Heidelberg but had spent most of her youth in America. Her mother died when she was just ten, and she'd shuttled back to Germany a couple of times to stay with an aunt, finally moving back to attend university, and taking an apprenticeship with photographer Hans Pieler. She would eventually become Jim's first long-term girlfriend, but in those early days she was torn between Jim and Norbert, and encountered initial suspicion from David and Coco, who saw most of Jim's girlfriends as a potential security risk. She'd also seen some of Jim's messy break-up with his previous girlfriend, make-up artist Heidi Morawetz, all of which told her she'd be crazy to mess with him.

Later in August, David returned with Jim to the Chateau d'Herouville, where he worked with Tony Visconti, Brian Eno, and his band – Alomar, George Murray and Dennis Davis – on the album that would become *Low*. The recording sessions sparkled with creativity, but the atmosphere was often desperately unhappy, as David had to travel into Paris for legal meetings to pursue his disentanglement from Michael Lippman. He'd often return on the verge of tears, says Tony Visconti, at which times Jim proved a wise, calming influence – someone who'd been through the mill and survived. The chateau felt gloomy that summer, with most of the staff on holiday, and the evening meals consisted of rabbit, day in, day out, says Tony Visconti. Over this period there was also an argument between Thibault and Bowie; Bowie accused him of leaking Michel Santageli's presence on *The Idiot* to French magazine *Rock & Folk*; there also seems to have been friction between Visconti and Thibault. Although the studio itself was 'a joy', says Bowie, 'ramshackle and comfy', there was an ominous air about the chateau, which the musicians were convinced was haunted by Chopin and George Sand. 'Brian Eno was awakened every morning with a gentle tap on his shoulder around 5am,' shudders Tony Visconti, 'but no one was there.' To lighten the gloom, Jim performed one-man shows a couple of nights, standing in front of a microphone and improvising long, tragicomic monologues about the Stooges, which would leave Bowie, Eno and Visconti aching with laughter at the unbelievable yarns of spectacular van crashes, drum kits being sold piece by piece for heroin or stage invasions by gorillas. Eventually, however, Visconti in particular grew terminally disenchanted with the poor food and the absence of technical staff at the chateau, and around 21 August they decamped to Hansa Tonstudio 2, a larger complex on Köthenerstrasse by the Potsdamer Platz, in search of 'German efficiency', says Visconti.

Hansa 'by the wall' seemed to embody Berlin's ruined grandeur, and its spirit would imbue Jim and David's recordings over the next year. Its imposing classical façade was designed to showcase the skills of the Berlin stonemasons' guild, for whom it was built in 1912. The building, known as the Meistersaal, had been bought by the Meisel publishing dynasty in 1973 and they'd been rebuilding it and repairing wartime damage ever since, building two studios within it to augment their existing Tonstudio 1 on Kurfürstendamm. But in 1976 it still looked semi-derelict: the triangular pediment that topped it had been blown off, the fluted Ionic pillars were chipped and scarred, many of the windows were bricked up with pigeons roosting within, and one quarter of the square courtyarded block to which it was attached was in total ruins.

Köthenerstrasse faced Potsdamer Platz, a bleak no-man's land adjoining the Berlin Wall. From the control room of Studio 2 there was a clear view, via a demolished house, of the wall itself. Behind the wall, on the East German side, was a tall building, on top of which a hut housed a couple of DDR border guards armed with machine guns and binoculars. Edu Meyer, the engineer who worked on *Low*, *Lust For Life* and "*Heroes*", was blasé about their presence. One evening at dusk he pointed out to Bowie and Visconti that the guards were watching them through their binoculars, grabbed an anglepoise lamp and shone it at the guard post – Bowie and Visconti both leapt from their seats to seek cover behind the console. Yet the wall's presence was, in some ways, romantic and optimistic – it emphasised that this city, marooned on the edge of the West, allowed both Jim and David peaceful anonymity. 'The wall was beautiful,' says Jim. 'It created a wonderful island, the same way that volcanos create islands in the sea. The opposing pressures created this place that they all studiously [ignored] and nobody bugged you. It was wonderful.'

Every now and then they'd drive out to East Berlin, which still possessed most of the city's most beautiful and historic houses and museums; Tony Visconti cropped both David and Jim's hair in a military crew cut, and on one trip through Checkpoint Charlie the normally surly border guards doubled up laughing, once they compared the two studious-looking gents in macintoshes with their passport photos, which showed them both with flowing, rock-star locks. Occasionally, David, Jim and Coco would get in David's Mercedes and drive into the East for days at a time, or head towards the Black Forest, stopping off at any village that took their fancy.

It was at some point after the conclusion of the *Low* recordings that Angie Bowie came to visit her husband, who obviously had no intention of moving into the house that she had found for the family in Corsier-sur-Vevey, near Montreux. Angie wasn't impressed with the 'boring' music they were creating; she was even more riled by what she saw as their cultural colonialism: 'Two big-ass girls' blouses thinking they were discovering something. It was cultural sluttery.' On one of her visits David told Angie he planned to divorce her; shortly afterwards Angie went up to Coco's room, took all the clothes she'd ever bought Coco and threw them out into the street. And then left. 'That was what I thought of Berlin.' With that long-dreaded confrontation out of the way, David's demeanour markedly improved, and life at the Hauptstrasse seemed blissful, almost domestic. Jim called round to see Esther regularly, and sometimes would croon Sinatra tunes, like 'My Funny Valentine', while Norbert, a vascular surgeon who also happened to be a skilled pianist, accompanied him. When the time came to shoot the cover photo for *The Idiot*, Jim borrowed Esther's jacket for the session. David had bought the reproduction rights to Erich Heckel's 'Roquairol' – a haunting portrait of the mentally disturbed Ernst Kirchner – but at the last moment they decided that Jim would echo his pose in a photo by Andrew Kent. With his hair dyed black for the shoot, Esther's double-breasted jacket and his angular pose, Jim's severe, European look signalled a radical departure from the music of the old Iggy.

David had masterminded his friend's first solo album. He found him a record company, helping broker a deal with RCA. Finally, he arranged his first solo tour and found him a band: perhaps the only band in the world that could out-play the Stooges, formed round the nucleus of two crazy brothers, whom Jim had met back in his lost LA years.

Hunt and Tony Sales had grown up hanging with Frank Sinatra and other hep-cats. They had played professionally for mobster-connected Maurice Levy's Roulette label while in their early teens, and recorded their first album, with Todd Rundgren, when drummer Hunt was sixteen and bassist Tony was nineteen, before they made their way to Los Angeles. David had met the brothers in New York in 1972, after which they'd sent him some demo tapes, and it was his idea to give them a call. They flew into Berlin in February 1977 to start rehearsals for a live tour to promote *The Idiot*.

Over the end of 1976 and beginning of 1977, the atmosphere around the Hauptstrasse had been, by most accounts, calm and optimistic, with a sense of damaged psyches being healed. In the wake of Hunt and Tony Sales, however, the adjectives being thrown around seem to change: 'manic' and 'crazed' are two that pop up regularly. From the moment the brothers checked into the Schlosshotel Gerhus, the intensity levels shot up into the red, and stayed there. Hunt Sales remembers staying up for days on end: rehearsing late into the nights, returning to his hotel to sleep for twenty minutes, then staying up drinking and drugging all night before going straight on to the next rehearsal. 'The atmosphere was like the cover of that Doors record, *Strange Days*, full of these bohemian bums. I remember sitting at, I think, the Tribe Bar one particular night, and there was a midget on top of the bar, dancing with a girl.'

With Bowie playing piano and the quietly expert *Low* guitarist Ricky Gardiner on guitar, the quintet rehearsed at UFA studios, the giant, semi-abandoned movie lot that still contained filing cabinets packed with Nazi-era paperwork, starting at around 11pm or midnight, and continuing till five in the morning. After hours, one favoured haunt was a dark club named the Café Kees, its dance floor enclosed by panelled booths equipped with phones, which had, according to Tony Sales, been used by SS officers to arrange assignations with their mistresses back in the 1930s. Tony and Hunt, despite their Jewish heritage and jokes about being turned into lampshades, shared Bowie's fascination with Berlin's rich, seamy atmosphere, and the small team gelled instantly. Of the band's two creative leaders, it seemed that David was the more effusive, the one who revelled in being part of a family. Jim, in contrast, was philosophical, content to ride the momentum of what was happening, even if he wasn't in control, says Tony: 'He was just like, Whatever. He doesn't put up too much resistance to the improv of it all. It was sort of like jazz.'

After the unrelenting emotional traumas of the previous four years, it was hardly surprising that Jim was beginning to regard the prospects of success and failure with equal indifference. Every album he'd made previously had been conceived in a spirit of near-euphoric megalomania, only to disappear into oblivion with soul-crushing inevitability. Appropriately, now Jim Osterberg had attained his own sangfroid, it transpired that those long-neglected albums had inspired a new generation of musicians – musicians who, it turned out, regarded Iggy's music as being as iconoclastic as did its creator.

CHAPTER 12

Here Comes My Chinese Rug

Little by little, Stooges disciples scattered along the length and breadth of the planet had been spreading the message. In New York, Lenny Kaye, a guitarist and writer who had written one of the first positive reviews of the Stooges' debut album back in 1969, had formed a band with poet Patti Smith – the two of them had gone to visit Iggy and James in the Coronet back in 1974, and the next year had released their stunning debut album as the Patti Smith Group, *Horses*. The Ramones, most of whom had also bought the Stooges' debut and seen them at the Electric Circus in May 1971, had recorded their own debut album, under the auspices of Danny Fields, in February 1976. In Germany and Paris, prominent fans included Harald Inhülsen – whose fanzine *Honey That Ain't No Romance* published numerous photos of his girlfriend Mechthild Hoppe naked but for strategically placed Stooges literature – Marc Zermati, owner of the record store Open Market in Paris, and photographer and writer Philippe Mogane, who launched the Stooges fan club in France. In London, the influence of the Stooges was even more profound. Brian James had first heard *Fun House* in 1971 and had subsequently embarked on a long quest. Early in 1976, he met a singer named Dave Vanian and wrote to a friend that his quest had been fulfilled: 'I've finally found my own Iggy!' Together they would form the Damned, include the Stooges' '1970' in their set, and release the UK's first homegrown punk single, 'New Rose', in October 1976. Mick Jones, a member of the audience at King's Cross, and briefly a member of the band London SS with Brian James, would form the Clash with Joe Strummer, ex-singer of pub rock band the 101ers, in the summer of 1976. John Lydon was another member of the King's Cross audience. In the summer of 1975 he started hanging out at the King's Road clothes shop Sex, run by Malcolm McLaren, where *Raw Power* was a staple of the in-house record collection. Lydon joined up with the Swankers, the band that McLaren was masterminding, who were renamed the Sex Pistols, and christened himself Johnny Rotten. The Stooges' 'No Fun' would become a cornerstone of their live set, and the B-side of their third single, 'Pretty Vacant'.

It was during his visit to CBGB back in April 1976 that Jim had first become aware of what would be termed the punk movement (he himself ascribes the first use of the term to Lenny Kaye, via his description of the Stooges' debut as 'the music of punks cruising for burgers'). That first encounter with the CBGB regulars gave him a sense that 'something was about to break', which was heightened as he heard tapes of the Sex Pistols and the Damned later in 1976.

But even as the first punk singles trickled onto the market, Iggy would release an album that showed his acolytes how it was done. *Metallic KO* was a live recording of the band's final, painful show at the Michigan Palace, and was midwifed by Nick Kent and Marc Zermati. Nick had obtained the tape of the show, which was recorded by Michael Tipton, in late 1974 from James Williamson. Zermati – who had launched his own Skydog label with an EP by the Flaming Groovies in May 1973 – later got hold of the tape of the Stooges' earlier Michigan Palace show, and edited the two tapes to make up a 39-minute album that was released in September 1976. It remains for many the ultimate punk album: flawed, like so many contemporaries, pathetic in its proud inarticulacy ('One, two, fuck you pricks'), yet unutterably majestic when the band was in full flight, on 'Raw Power' or 'Louie Louie'. For Peter Hook, bassist in a Manchester band who'd later rename themselves Joy Division, *Metallic KO* would be both a huge influence, and a signpost to where he himself was heading. 'It just sounds like the sort of gig that we used to have in the early days – on a knife edge. That was why it was so fucking exciting, the best live album ever made, far more so than most bloody live CDs where everyone's clapping.' Without a doubt, *Metallic KO*'s negativity and violence influenced the emerging UK punk movement, encouraging bottle-throwing and spitting, and for Jim himself, says Nick Kent, 'It [was] a dark record. I know that Iggy was spooked by it.'

Dark as it was, *Metallic KO* would be the first Stooges album released into a world that was finally ready for it. In the UK, both leading music weeklies, *NME* and *Sounds*, had reinvented themselves on the back of the emerging punk movement, and both the *NME*'s Nick Kent and *Sounds*' Giovanni Dadomo championed the album and its singer consistently and devotedly. Despite legal threats from Tony Defries, who sent cease-and-desist letters to Zermati, stating the Stooges were still under contract to MainMan, the three-year-old recording became one of the key releases of the UK punk scene in particular, and would sell over 100,000 copies. It would soon be followed by a Stooges single, 'I Got a Right', mastered from a MainMan-era demo supplied by James Williamson. Released by Philippe Mogane's Siamese Dog label in March, this lost, once-rejected piledriving track was greeted with extravagant praise right across Europe.

As England embraced his past, Jim flew over to showcase his present, opening a tour to promote *The Idiot* on 1 March 1977 at Aylesbury Friars – a small club an hour out of London that David Bowie favoured for low-key launches before the higher-profile London shows. The tour was organised by Bowie's MAM agency, run by John Giddings and Ian Wright, who told Friars promoter David Stopps that Bowie would be guesting on keyboards, but swore him to secrecy. That afternoon, the band were tense, with

Iggy quite obviously nervous; instead it was David Bowie, in brown cords, chequered shirt and flat cap, who was the epitome of low-key affability, greeting Stopps like an old chum – 'What's a smart young guy like you still doing in a place like this?' – remaining calm when the band's equipment was delayed in customs, and instructing the promoter to open the doors and let the fans in, even though they'd had time for only the most cursory soundcheck. 'David was definitely playing second fiddle to Iggy – and enjoying it,' remembers Stopps, 'revelling in the lack of pressure.'

The show was packed with London's punk aristocracy: the Damned's Brian James, the Heartbreakers' Johnny Thunders and Billy Rath, the Sex Pistols' Glen Matlock and Iggy's long-time supporter Nick Kent were all present, as were members of Generation X and the Adverts, who watched a slick show, drawn from all three Stooges albums plus *The Idiot*; as the audience realised who was playing keyboards, the crowd grew deeper at Bowie's side of the stage. Faced with the legendary singer who, for many of them, was a icon of aggression and excess, the crowd were mostly ecstatic at seeing him alive and well – albeit disappointed to see him dispensing with the practices that had nearly rendered him dead or damaged. '[Iggy] was mesmerising,' says Brian James, who was slightly disturbed by the presence of David Bowie on keyboards, while Kris Needs, who reviewed the show for *Roxette* magazine, pronounced Iggy 'captivating – but not the Detroit Demon we'd hoped for'. After the show, Brian James got into an argument with Johnny Thunders, who complained that the Bowie-backed Iggy had 'gone cabaret'.

Much the same positive but restrained reaction attended subsequent live dates, as well as *The Idiot* itself which was released later that month and was promoted in tandem with Bowie's own *Low*, released in January. Some fans expected Iggy's new album to sound like the last one and regretted the loss of James Williamson's high-octane guitar assault, although there were enough adherents to ensure that, at last, Iggy made the upper reaches of the album charts: *The Idiot* appeared at a respectable number 30 in the UK (it would later chart at number 72 in the US). Only in retrospect would most people realise the dark power of songs like 'Nightclubbing' and 'Dum Dum Boys', which prefigured the sound of 1980s pop. Those juicy synthesisers, doom-laden vocals and dark, gothic guitar work would establish the tonal palette for bands like Siouxsie and the Banshees, Magazine, the Birthday Party and Bauhaus. More poignantly, *The Idiot* would be the favourite album of Joy Division's inspirational, emotionally disturbed singer Ian Curtis; the album was still spinning on Curtis's turntable when the singer hanged himself in May 1980. 'Although,' says Curtis's friend and bassist Peter Hook, with a mixture of sadness, sympathy and trademark black humour, 'I don't think Iggy can take the rap for it.'

As the tour progressed, Iggy's antics became wilder, and the band's performance at London's Rainbow, propelled by the Sales brothers' unstoppable momentum, was viciously efficient (Johnny Rotten turned up after the show to pay tribute). Ironically, they would still fall foul of a newly emerging punk conservatism in the pages of *Melody Maker*, where Mark P, of punk fanzine *Sniffin Glue*, complained that Iggy didn't 'get in the audience and break some seats'. Ricky Gardiner in particular was regularly criticised in print for his lack of aggression, but in fact that was part of the plan: Gardiner's clangy Stratocaster sound and Bowie's electric piano had both been chosen to add a new clarity to the mix and give Iggy's voice more prominence. But if the band ignored punk convention for those early dates, as they tore through twenty-six shows in six weeks there was plenty of backstage carnage to complement the onstage professionalism. Tony Sales would regularly find himself 'walking through the hallways of hotels naked and stoned. It wasn't a party. It was strange. It was over-the-top exhaustion and to cover the exhaustion you'd do more cocaine and after a while it doesn't do anything.' Hunt and Tony Sales calculate they each lost around twenty-five pounds in weight over the six weeks; as the tour went on, Tony remembers Iggy climbing a monitor stack before falling backwards and smashing onto the stage. 'He didn't feel anything when it happened, because he was so out of it.' Bowie reckoned, 'The drug use was *unbelievable* and I knew it was killing me, so that was a difficult side of it.' By the time the band reached America, says Hunt Sales, they were 'pretty burnt', while their singer was becoming 'very erratic, very obsessive, and you don't know from one moment who you're dealing with'. But for all his infuriating, confusing manias and obsessions, Hunt points out, Iggy was 'a trooper. He did a great job every gig.'

Jim Osterberg, too, would turn in some fabulous performances, most notably on Dinah Shore's afternoon talk show, where he incongruously guested alongside Bowie on 15 April. The show was filmed at the CBS studios off Beverly Boulevard, and Iggy is introduced as the 'originator of punk rock', performing elegantly on the two songs, 'Sister Midnight' and 'Funtime' – a taut bundle of callisthenic energy, kept firmly under control until the thrilling climax of each song. But it is Jim Osterberg, doe-eyed, boyish and coy, who wins over Dinah Shore, who sighs in horror at the prospect of what Iggy was doing to himself physically, before Jim cheekily interrupts, 'and to other people too', fluttering his mascara'd eyelashes, charming with his Jimmy Stewart voice and his naughty Donald Sutherland smile. The same cheeky charm was evident in the many press interviews Jim participated in on what was his first proper, professionally organised world tour. Throughout all of these encounters there were two common threads: first, the open acknowledgement of his many faults, and his readiness to denigrate or mock himself. Second, the almost scarily consistent belief in his music, the sense that he has a manifest destiny to make it, and the conviction that his music will change the world.

Perhaps this sense of destiny was what drove Iggy's next creative act. Possibly it was augmented by the unique, intense artistic environment of Berlin, by the supreme musicianship of his band, or by a newly emerging creative rivalry with David Bowie. In truth, all of those involved in the recording of *Lust For Life* share the same feeling, that it was impossible to analyse what lay behind the sensation of being carried along in something that was bigger than all of them: 'It was like a dream,' says Tony Sales. 'We were sleepwalking.'

A necessary rite of passage before Iggy's recording of *Lust For Life* was Jim's renting of a flat of his own. It came shortly after a last fling in LA at the end of *The Idiot* tour, when he sunbathed on the beach, enjoyed a brief romantic idyll with writer Pleasant Gehman, and hung out at the Whisky, just as he turned thirty. On his return to Berlin, Jim signed the contract for his new flat with landlady Rosa Morath, who also owned Bowie's apartment; incredibly, it was the first time Jim had had a long-term lease in his own name, paid for with his own money, thanks to a new contract and a $25,000 advance from RCA, negotiated back in January. The flat was at the rear of the 155 Hauptstrasse building, in the Hinterhof – the more modest, lower-ceilinged mews apartments that would once have served as servants' quarters or work premises. The rent was just 184 DM per month – cheap, because the flat had no hot water, which suited his new no-frills, hard-working ethic. It was a new start and Jim Osterberg 'felt real good'.

For *The Idiot*, David Bowie had contracted the studio time and owned the master tapes, according to Jim, and had been in the stronger position. By now, Jim believed, Bowie was pretty sick of Iggy's rock histrionics, and Jim was 'pretty sick of where Bowie was coming from – so there was a lot of friction'. But both were fired up by the project, and the irritation each felt with the other was laced with respect: 'It was an ideas friction, not a personal one,' says Jim.

From the moment the project was mooted, there was intense competition between the two, both of them vying to contribute more songs. Bowie called Carlos Alomar to ask him to take charge of the band – which in the case of the Sales brothers, and quite possibly Bowie and Iggy too, was like being asked to tame a particularly nervy purebred stallion. Alomar loved the challenge of harnessing what he called their 'wanton abandonment', realising he could channel the Saleses' rambunctiousness, even if he couldn't hope to turn it on and off like a light switch.

For both Bowie and Iggy, the *Lust For Life* sessions were the first project conceived and completed in Berlin, and the city's ambience would be firmly imprinted in the grooves of the record. The two main protagonists, as well as the Sales brothers, had immersed themselves in the decadence of Los Angeles, but Berlin offered them the chance to turn their excess into art, rather than the rootless confusion they'd all suffered in California; the city offered a better class of decadence, one that focused their energies rather than sapping them. And throughout there was the vision of the Berlin Wall, which was still visible from Tonstudio 3, says Carlos Alomar, with the gunners and their elevated hut now at eye level, 'and beyond that the desolate nothingness of possible minefields and then in the background the silhouetted skyline of some buildings. Pretty dark, dismal and depressing.' That image would impose its foreboding presence on David's next project, *"Heroes"*, giving it a taut, wired edge, but on *Lust For Life* the spectre of the wall would inspire a glorious carnality and celebration, like the explosion of sexuality that had engulfed both London and Berlin in wartime. And in this isolated outpost of the West, Jim in particular found his own, curiously warped peace: 'I was living on coke, hash, red wine, beer and German sausages, had my own little place and I was sleeping on a cot with cold-water showers.' Iggy was also, as Tony Sales puts it, 'on fire'.

By the time the sessions began in June, David had already crafted the bulk of the music, some of it recorded on cassette, some of it played out on electric piano to the band, but every song was radically reworked in the studio, with others assembled from scratch. The album's title track was one that defined the session; the opening chords of 'Lust For Life' were inspired by the staccato parping of a German brass-band theme from the Armed Forces TV network, and, says Jim, written on the ukulele in David's apartment. The song was instantly seized upon by Hunt Sales, who slammed out the distinctive, exuberant rhythm, pulling the rest of the band in his wake. 'You can't play a counter rhythm to that,' says Alomar. 'You just had to follow.' The drum beat sounded like the rhythms that newly freed African Americans had been playing back in the Mississippi hill country since the 1880s, advertising to listeners for miles around that a party was about to start.

For Iggy, the sessions fast became a high-wire act, a test of his ability to improvise lyrics and vocal melodies as quickly as the musicians nailed the backing tracks. And, as Tony Sales observed, he was on fire. The lyrics to 'Lust For Life' were, according to most recollections, snatched out of the ether. The narrator is recognisably Iggy, but is namechecked as Johnny Yen, a William Burroughs character from *The Ticket That Exploded*; then a succession of arresting images follows, most of it off the cuff: 'Who the hell but Iggy would dare say, "I've had it in the ear before"?' asked Alomar. 'What the hell does he mean? Is he reluctant to say it? No. Is David reluctant to put it on the album? Hell, no.'

Plenty of songs were composed on the spot. Earlier in the year, Ricky Gardiner had enjoyed a moment of Wordsworthian inspiration when he was wandering in the countryside, 'in the field beside an orchard, on one of those glorious spring days with the trees in full blossom'. A distinctive, circular chord sequence had popped into his mind. When David Bowie asked if Ricky had any song ideas, he remembered the riff, and Iggy seized on it, much as he had the first time he heard Ron Asheton play the 'I Wanna Be Your Dog' chord sequence. The lyrics were, like practically every other song on the album, written in the studio, or overnight, celebrating his journeys on the Berlin buses and U-bahn, where he'd ride and ride, contemplating the stars and the ripped-back signs (the song's mood and title, he later mentioned, were inspired by a Jim Morrison poem). Like 'Lust For Life', 'The Passenger' was a simple celebration of life, of the long walks he'd taken soaking in his surroundings ever since he'd grown up in Ypsilanti; a reconciliation with the wide-eyed child Jim Osterberg, and the repudiation of Iggy Pop, the creature who'd sung about a 'Death Trip'.

The atmosphere between David and Iggy at the sessions was competitive, slightly manic at least on Iggy's side; it was also 'very loving', according to Alomar and the Sales brothers. David drove

Iggy hard, but understood implicitly how to channel the creative flow, ready to drop any other part of the recording whenever Iggy had a vocal idea he wanted to get down on tape. At some points, Iggy insisted on getting his own way; dissatisfied with David's original melody on 'Success' – as heard on the finished version's guitar counter-melody – which he thought sounded like 'a damn crooning thing', he arrived early at Hansa with the Sales brothers to egg him on and reworked the song, adding an optimistic six-note tune, and engagingly simple lyrics: 'Here comes success . . . here comes my Chinese rug.' The sentiment was semi-ironic, but it was semi-sincere, too, for Jim had just bought Chinese rugs for his simple cold-water apartment, and was relishing the prospect of, as Jim describes it, being 'dragged kicking and screaming to a good outcome'. On 'Success', and other songs, there is the near-palpable presence of Esther Friedmann – whom Jim had been calling regularly for the last six months, despite the fact she was still living with surgeon boyfriend Norbert. She was the ideal woman and muse: 'In the last ditch . . . I think of you.' The infectious enthusiasm was highlighted by Hunt and Tony's joyous backing vocals, recorded live in one take later that day, and the first time most of them had heard Iggy's lyrics properly – you can still hear their giddy amusement at repeating lyrics like 'Here comes my face . . . it's plain bizarre'. (Bowie would mention later how he would emulate Iggy's spontaneous approach to lyric writing, noting down a couple of words and improvising the rest, on "Heroes".) The electrifying atmosphere was emphasised by Edu Meyer's idea of plugging Iggy's vocal mike into a Music Man guitar amplifier that was sitting outside the control room, which added a glassy, overdriven edge to his voice.

The skeetering, exuberant energy hardly let up throughout the sessions. 'Some Weird Sin' and 'Tonight', both with music by Bowie and worked up during The Idiot tour, and 'Sixteen', with music by Iggy, maintained the opener's confident swagger, but in retrospect, 'Turn Blue', the song that Iggy and Bowie had worked up in May 1975, assisted by Warren Peace, was an unformed mess, the sessions' only uninspired moment. 'Fall In Love With Me', the album's closer, was again written on the spot, with Hunt picking up a bass, Tony a guitar and Ricky Gardiner on drums. A subdued meditation reflecting the exhaustion each member of the band had reached by the end of the recording, it sounds slight in such over-bearing company, but its poignant charm came to the fore later, when it was featured in the 1989 movie *Slaves Of New York*. Again, its loving fascination – 'the way your eyes are black, the way your hair is black' – evokes the image of Esther Friedmann, as well as Jim's excitement that love, as well as success, is just around the corner.

As the sessions rushed to their conclusion, there was an almost religious conviction shared by all its makers that they had achieved something special. For Carlos Alomar, seeing Bowie and Iggy working together was also a unique privilege. 'Seeing the two of them in partnership, just like when you split an atom and you get a pair of twins.' David seemed to have unlocked something new in Iggy – his intelligence, his civilised, intellectual, cosmopolitan side. Namely, he'd manage to free Jim Osterberg and bring him to share the limelight with Iggy. The point was underlined with *Lust For Life*'s cover photo, shot by Andrew Kent in a dressing room as Jim waited to work his charm on a BBC interviewer during his UK tour in March. 'It was a lucky great shot,' says Kent. 'This was Jimmy. The nice guy, a guy you'd like to hang out with.'

But Iggy would wreak his revenge.

There are both complex and simple explanations for why Iggy Pop would repeatedly sabotage his own career, for this is what Iggy would go on to do around the end of 1977. The complex explana-tions are psychological – to do with insecurity, fear of success, or the depression that often afflicts creative individuals just as they've completed their best work. But the simple explanation is cocaine. Shortly after receiving a finished copy of *Lust For Life*, Iggy Pop locked himself in a room at the Schlosshotel Gerhus, the fairytale palace built by art collector Walther von Pannwitz, now filled with a motley collection of 1960s furniture and still surrounded by bombed-out houses. He stared and stared at the sleeve, all the while hoovering up a small mountain of cocaine, waiting to see if he'd like the cover photo. Eventually he decided he hated it. He listened over and over to 'The Passenger', waiting for it to be faster. It didn't, and he decided he hated that, too. The whole process was torture, unbearable torture, and he continued to torture himself. Finally there was an intervention: David heard what was happening, and asked Barbara and Tim de Witt to whisk Jim away on holiday to Capri. But Iggy had been unleashed, and it seemed there was no way to put him back in his box and rescue Jim Osterberg.

CHAPTER 13

Missing in Action

'We just need David Bowie.' It was a phrase that had popped up many times over the marketing and A&R meetings where Arista boss Charles Levison had discussed Jim's recording career. Charles liked Jim, even enjoyed the 3am phone conversations when the bored or worried singer would call up to discuss some minor point, but unflappable as he was, the pressure was mounting. Clive Davis, Charles's boss, creative powerhouse, disco freak and tough motherfucker – his nickname at the record company was 'the Godfather' – was breathing down his neck, and although Charles had kept his cool, near-panic was starting to spread around the office. Davis was convinced that the singer was a loser, a deadbeat who'd had several shots at the bigtime and pissed all of them away. Charles and his team had set out to prove him wrong. So far they'd failed. Now the endless stories and rumours that snaked back to Arista's headquarters near Grosvenor Square were mostly negative. There were interminable technical problems, tales of guns being brandished in the studio and, worst of all, Iggy seemed to have lost his nerve. He was scared to sing. If anyone could coax him out of this funk, Charles was convinced, it was David.

The call, when it came, was not at three in the morning. It was a sensible hour, maybe lunchtime, when Charles got the news that David Bowie had dropped by at the isolated farm in Wales in response to a call for help. But as Julie Hooker, who'd been sent down to oversee the sessions, ran through what had happened, a cold realisation began to dawn. There had obviously been a disaster. Yet however often Julie ran over the story, Charles could not work out what the hell had gone on. The tales of cocaine abuse and paranoia were familiar in the record industry. Likewise the account of how all the musicians were at one another's throats was hardly a new one. Even the stories of musicians being threatened with a gun he'd heard before. But how in the hell could these sessions, the ones that were to make or break Jim's career, have been derailed by David Bowie in a Scarlet Pimpernel outfit, Princess Margaret, and an East End gangster with a huge cock?

It's hard to disentangle the reasons why Iggy Pop's promising career at RCA ended in disenchantment. Many of the label's staff were truly enthused by Jim Osterberg; he seemed the perfect artist, obliging, ebullient, perhaps even more charming than his friend David. Few of them, however, understood his music, while Iggy's own erratic behaviour exacerbated the mutual incomprehension between artist and label. Yet it seems that the ultimate responsibility lies with Iggy's fellow RCA artist: Elvis Presley.

Ironically, David Bowie had been signed by RCA so that the company could banish the spectre of Elvis Presley, the musician who ensured that for RCA, the 1960s never happened. For nearly two decades, Elvis had made the label uncool – so uncool, Tony Defries liked to joke, that it was better known for its washing machines than its records. But on 16 August 1977, Elvis passed away, his great heart finally succumbing to the twin depradations of cheeseburgers and codeine, atop his toilet at Graceland. Suddenly, the King once again became RCA's most important artist, and the company's pressing plants started to work overtime meeting demand for his back catalogue. And somewhere in the rush, *Lust For Life* disappeared. The album had been pressed up in respectable quantities well before its release on 7 September, and reached number 28 in the UK charts, a decent-sized hit. But once the first pressing had sold out, there were no stocks to replace it: '*Lust For Life* just disappeared from the shelves,' remembers Tony Sales, 'and that was it.'

Whereas *The Idiot* had received generous coverage in the press, *Lust For Life*, the most overtly commercial album of Iggy Pop's career, and his joyous return to health and happiness, was relatively starved of column inches. And then during one press day for the album there was a rumpus when Iggy, in a fit of megalomania, told one journalist, 'That's too bad [that Elvis died], I'm the new Elvis!' before pissing in the wastebasket under the desk of the office he'd borrowed for the interview.

With a general lack of press reaction, there was only one way to promote the album: the road. The Sales brothers once again made up the nucleus of the band, with Stacey Heydon joining on guitar, and one-time Stooge Scottie Thurston drafted in on keyboards to replace David, who spent most of the autumn promoting "*Heroes*"; Esther came too, persuaded to join up in a professional role as the tour photographer, and the shows, which came at a gruelling pace – forty dates in just over eight weeks – were generally regarded as terrific.

Backstage, things seemed very different. Now thirty, Jim appeared a sensible, almost collegiate-looking character, with black hair in a side parting, and he wore glasses for reading. It was a good 'look'; it seemed to symbolise the long-subdued intelligence and wit that his schoolfriends could remember. Esther liked it a lot. Iggy Pop, too, looked terrific, wearing white face for some shows, which gave him the air of an evil European mime artist, together with leather pants and a horse's tail attached by a wide leather belt. This was the first time he'd toured Europe, and there was an obvious pent-up demand from the kids who'd discovered his music via fanzines, the conventional music press, or even via David Bowie. Most of the performances were fiercely tough and professional, the band finely honed, even if their obvious musicianship and skewed cowboy cool didn't conform to the regulation punk aesthetic.

It was all a long way from the *Metallic KO* days, one would have thought. But to Scottie Thurston – whose last shows with Iggy were during one of the most legendarily disastrous tours of all time – it appeared that things hadn't changed that much. The organisation was more professional than in the Stooges days, the shows were consistently good and Iggy always made it on stage. The Sales brothers struck him as 'real talented. And pretty mad. Especially together.' This time around there was no smack, no Quaaludes, no singer passing out. But 'it was the age of cocaine,' says Thurston, 'which is not a very together drug for a singer.' Scottie had a deep affection for Jim; he was 'very charming, a sweet guy – a pleasure to be around'. He'd seen Iggy suffer, and there was a profound pleasure in seeing him achieve some success. But during much of the next year, Thurston observed, Jim was 'kind of boorish and childlike. Not a lot of fun.' Back in the days of the Stooges, Jim had shown no self-pity, no bitterness about his lack of success. Now that Jim had hit his thirties, that resilience seemed to have diminished and he often, thought Scottie – who is a fair, non-judgemental man – seemed 'needy and wanty. And when he was like that, you avoided him.'

It was a cruel irony. For years, Iggy had suffered a harsh fate – being too original, too ahead of his time, and being mocked for it. Yet he'd emerged unbowed. Now just at the point when success beckoned, when his influence was finally being acknowledged – indeed, over that autumn, the honorific 'the godfather of punk' started being regularly attached to his name – he seemed to succumb to the bitterness he'd avoided for so long. Esther Friedmann finally moved out of Norbert's apartment early in 1978 – she'd packed her stuff for the tour, told Norbert she'd be back in two weeks and returned seven years later. Esther loved Jim; 'Thinking back, I wonder whether he was the love of my life,' she says. He was sensitive, funny, intelligent – 'a thinker'. But often, says Esther, 'he drove himself nuts, just thinking.'

The two would enjoy many insane, good times together, as well as quiet evenings in their Hinterhof apartment, which Esther moved into later in the year. But for much of the time Jim seemed, quite simply, sad. It was a big deal to make him laugh, 'and that's what I tried to do,' says Esther. 'I tried to amuse him and put on little skits for him to make him laugh. Because he did seem a little sad.' Much of this was down to drugs, as alcohol followed cocaine, and lows followed the highs. Much of it was due to money, too, or rather lack of it. Jim was never good with cash, but even as larger amounts flowed in, larger amounts flowed out, most of it on professional expenses. Over the first quarter of 1978, he earned £71,436 in record-company advances and live receipts, his English accountant informed him. His expenses, mostly for musicians' salaries and studio bills, were £75,892.

To make things worse, there was David's conspicuous success to deal with. Jim was happy for David; David was consistently kind and considerate, but sometimes that kindness made Jim feel like even more of a failure. 'I don't think David was ever any more famous than at that period and he was still a sweet, regular guy to Jim,' says Esther, 'but sometimes when people are good to you it's worse.' Jim would be invited along for holidays, and David would pay; and for a singer with a skyscraper ego, this generosity was difficult to accept. Mixed into this complex cocktail of emotions was Jim's conviction that his music was simply better than David's.

Undoubtedly, underneath the mutual respect between Jim and David lay a streak of mutual envy; David admired Iggy's intuition, his electricity and lack of self-consciousness; Jim realised David had a whole raft of professional abilities which he himself needed to master. Yet while David incorporated some of Iggy's skills to magnificent effect, most notably on the gloriously untrammelled singing on 'Heroes' – six inspiring minutes which finally banished the notion that David's music was clever, rather than deep – Iggy still seemed a hopeless novice at acquiring David's prime skill, that of self-sufficiency, let alone another crucial ability – that of making money. The two would remain very close over the subsequent years, although an idyllic Christmas dinner, with a huge goose baked by Coco, at David's apartment, where many Berlin acquaintances, including Edu Meyer, were invited, was the last big get-together in the city, for Bowie was on tour throughout nearly all of 1978, and finally left the Hauptstrasse in the spring of 1979 to base himself in Switzerland, New York and London.

All the way through the recording of *The Idiot* and *Lust For Life*, says Jim, he had been troubled by fantasies of 'revenge. Every night I would go to bed dreaming: as soon as I get a chance I'm gonna take some of this, take some of that, do this to her, do that to him.' And it was probably fantasies of revenge that inspired a cheap, counterproductive shot that lost him all of the career momentum he'd worked so hard to generate: namely a live album, recorded for a pittance, which would get him out of his deal with RCA and net him a quick influx of cash.

From the moment he'd been signed by RCA, Iggy had been regarded as something of a curiosity. RCA treated David Bowie with respect, because he was a proven money-earner, and because Bowie's formidable organisation intimidated the company. But RCA regarded the punk explosion as an aberration, ignoring it completely in favour of AOR bands like Sad Café, the label's major signing for 1977. *The Idiot* had been treated to a certain amount of support, but when Iggy's press officer Robin Eggar first heard a white label of *Lust For Life* and pushed the company to release 'The Passenger' as a single, guaranteeing it would be a hit, he was ignored. 'I think Iggy knew RCA didn't have a clue,' he remembers, 'and I suspect he had a lot of fun torturing them.' A live album, which would fulfil his contract and net him a full album advance, seemed like the perfect way of getting revenge. Assembled from soundboard tapes of *The Idiot* and *Lust For Life* tours, which were given a sonic brush-up by Edu Meyer at Hansa, *TV Eye Live* was released in May 1978, and was Iggy's swansong for RCA; shortly after, he'd brag in print how the album had cost him $5,000 to make, but had netted him $90,000 (the figure sounds like an exaggeration). The previous November, Iggy had publicly complained about the 'sub-standard' *Kill City* album, released by Bomp Records in the US and Radar in the UK from tapes sold to them by James Williamson. Yet it was *TV Eye Live* that looked like a cheap rip-off; although the performances were good, the obvious contract-filler seemed to signal Iggy had run out of creative steam.

Earlier in 1978, Jim had decided to fire the Sales brothers; they were aggressively assertive, and although they were inspirational musicians they were 'trouble on a stick,' says Esther Friedmann. According to Tony, Iggy broke the news in a wantonly brutal fashion. 'Iggy called me at the end of the tour. This is after hundreds of shows, all kinds of shit, after we had been together for two years. He said, "I don't need you!" I said, "I hope you're kidding, man!" He said, "You Sales brothers are like heroin, and I don't need you."'

Hunt, too, was traumatised. 'He fucked over everybody. I was walking down Sunset Strip and saw a record in the window, *TV Eye*. I hadn't been told anything about it and I hadn't been paid for it. It's quite surprising for somebody who has had it really rough like Iggy to turn round and not consider other people.'

Esther Friedmann, in particular, points out that Jim was generous to a fault with his money during his Berlin period and always seemed scrupulous about paying his musicians; in fact, he'd seized on the idea of *TV Eye Live* to get out of a hopeless predicament. Yet it seems some of the spite directed at the Sales brothers was motivated by what seemed a typical act of self-sabotage. If so, his masochism was rewarded with the treatment he'd receive at the hands of his next musicians, the Sonic's Rendezvous Band, or SRB. Formed by MC5 guitarist Fred Smith with Rationals singer Scott Morgan, Dum Dum Boy Scotty Asheton on drums and Gary Rasmussen – who'd played with the Up – on bass, the SRB would become Detroit's lost supergroup, issuing just one legendary single, 'City Slang', in their lifetime. Iggy had jammed with the band in Detroit during his 1977 tour, and later asked them to come over to Europe to help promote *TV Eye Live*; they agreed, leaving Scott Morgan to kick his heels in Ann Arbor for the summer. Hiring SRB seemed a perfect way of revisiting Iggy's guitar-heavy Detroit rock;

but Fred Smith – a fiendishly talented guitarist, but a proud, taciturn character – refused to listen to any of Iggy's records, insisting on working the songs out again from scratch. 'There was a stand-off,' says Scottie Thurston, who was supposedly directing the rehearsals in a freezing-cold studio in Battersea, South London. 'With a proper meeting it could have been a viable band . . . but it wasn't set up that way.'

During a gruelling string of dates across Europe, the band developed a heads-down post-Stooges set that trampled roughshod over Iggy's RCA material, transforming 'Lust For Life' and even 'I Wanna Be Your Dog' into dull generic rockers, but performing fiery, aggressive versions of 'Kill City' and a new song called 'Five Foot One'. There was continuous, niggling friction between Iggy and Fred Smith, and when Jim asked the SRB to work with him in the US, the band turned him down – to Scott Asheton's chagrin: 'We had a holiday coming up, I hadn't been home in a while. But if I've had known it meant so much I swear to God I would have stayed.' It would be twenty years before Iggy would again play with the man he'd frequently namechecked as his favourite drummer, while his rivalry with Smith turned particularly nasty once he'd heard that Fred had gone over to Esther's flat to listen to some records with her. Shortly afterwards Iggy managed to get into the apartment when Esther was out and, says Esther, trashed it: 'He took razor blades and put them in everything, in the lampshades, behind the mirrors, everywhere.'

Over the next few years, Esther learned to accept such paranoia and insecurity, as well as Iggy's rampant behaviour with groupies on tour: 'After a while you realise that it's all part of the Iggy persona,' she points out, while stressing that Jim Osterberg – the character she spent most of her time with – was sweet and considerate. If he had money, he'd share it; he was intelligent, romantic, always buying impulsive presents or flowers. He was also lovably humble when necessary. For instance, after one particularly bad quarrel, Esther heard the front door open and looked up to see a ludicrously kitsch clockwork doll waddling its way down the hall, chanting, 'Baby come back, baby come back.' 'How could you say no to that?' Esther laughs. 'So we had a reconciliation. I couldn't believe he actually went to the trouble to find this silly doll.'

By the autumn of 1978, there was a comfortable domesticity at the Hinterhof apartment, which Esther decorated with tasteful pillows and artworks. This was Jim's first regular experience of living with a woman, shopping, cooking, spending time together, or going round to friends', like Martin Kippenberger, for Sunday brunch. David's portrait of Iggy took pride of place in the living room alongside a hi-fi, tape recorder, TV and a shiny new Fender Telecaster with the price-tag still attached. Iggy would spend hours working up riffs, using a copy of the Stones' *Some Girls* for inspiration, and 'Stern' pills – a mild, legal upper favoured by German schoolkids cramming for exams – for stimulation. With the advance from *TV Eye Live* banked, there were no financial pressures, and Jim had a new manager negotiating a new record deal. Peter Davies, who left his position as a senior executive in RCA London's international department to take on Iggy's business affairs, was a well liked, rather public-school character who was devoted to Iggy's music; and Davies soon found a welcoming audience in the guise of Ben Edmonds – the *Creem* writer and editor who had recently joined Arista UK as head of A&R – and Charles Levison, the company's managing director. They were both eager to sign Iggy. Edmonds was as convinced that Iggy could make a great commercial but aggressive album as he had been back in *Kill City* days, while Levison thought Iggy was 'terrifically credible, wonderfully charismatic, an intriguing, complex character, and one of the brightest, most intelligent artists I'd ever met'.

There was only one problem: the founder of Arista, Clive Davis, the man who'd been persuaded to sign Iggy Pop to Columbia back in 1971, who wasn't about to repeat the mistake. According to Levison, Davis's objections were not to do with Iggy's personal habits: 'Clive was used to rock 'n' roll behaviour. His objections were purely commercial.' Davis had hired Levison in January 1978 to oversee all of Arista's business outside the US, and after fierce discussions, he allowed Levison to have his own way. But Davis's repeatedly and forcefully stated objections increased the pressure on both Levison and Iggy.

Clive Davis's lack of enthusiasm presented a potential problem for Iggy's records in the US, but with Arista's advance cheque in the bank and a small selection of songs written, Jim was happy, and worked hard, overjoyed to have secured a deal under his own auspices. In the autumn, Scott Thurston flew over to Berlin to work on more material; the partners were productive, composing three songs that would make the final record, reviving two others that they'd worked on back in Iggy's down-and-out Kill City era – 'Angel' and 'Curiosity' – and at least four or five more. Some of the new material fell through the cracks; one of the best lost songs, according to Thurston, was called 'Hey Coco', presumably dedicated to Coco Schwab. Only years later, says Scott, who went on to work with Jackson Browne and Tom Petty, would he realise what a creative musician Iggy was. 'I would say he was pretty fabulous. Pretty fantastic. But I don't think I appreciated it back then like I would now.' Today, Thurston reflects that he simply 'didn't quite have the writing chops' to do justice to Iggy's work, describing the results as 'not totally unsuccessful. And not totally successful.' His opinion would be shared by most of those involved on what became the *New Values* album.

It was David Bowie who found Jim a drummer; he called up Klaus Kruger, a friend of Martin Kippenberger who'd hung out in the Berlin clubs with David and Jim, and had just played drums on Tangerine Dream's *Force Majeure* album at Hansa. Peter Davies and Jim had called up James Williamson out of the blue, and Ben Edmonds was enthusiastic about hiring him as the producer – even though he blamed James for running off with the *Kill City* masters that Ben had funded back in 1974. 'I didn't ever bring up the subject,' says Ben. 'What a chump!' (He does point out that at the time James took them, the tapes had no commercial value.) Scottie Thurston brought bassist Jackie Clark, who'd played with him on his last gig, Ike and Tina Turner.

The band and producer assembled in Los Angeles, and they bonded well during their rehearsals at SIR and in Scottie Thurston's basement rehearsal studio. They were a hilariously disparate crew: Klaus was all earnest, his playing tight and crisp, and spent much of rehearsals with headphones on listening to a click track; Jackie Clark had been strictly an R&B musician, but 'got it' straight away, and started dressing for the part in a country-and-western Nudie suit and Stetson. Scottie, as ever, was cute, amenable and enthusiastic. Williamson, too, was hard-working; he was wearing slick suits, and showed a new focus on being organised and professional. Williamson's new image was something of a front for his own insecurity; his musical self-confidence had been irreparably damaged by his disastrous career with the Stooges, and he had more or less given up the guitar. 'I used to have fun playing the guitar, but it was always an emotional outlet for me,' he says today, adding with understatement that 'there was some baggage associated with that'. Williamson, understandably given their history, was cynical about Jim's motives. At the end of 1978 his only contact with Jim was via Peter Davies, who called regularly to complain about his involvement in releasing *Kill City*. Then when the album, which was credited to 'Iggy Pop and James Williamson', became a critical success, it seemed Williamson's name had a commercial cachet once more and Davies' phonecalls suddenly got friendly. 'Jim was hoping I would come back and get the rock dream again,' says Williamson. 'But by that time I had changed my views.' Williamson was determined to avoid personal involvement with his one-time friend. 'This was strictly a professional effort.'

With three-fifths of the old Stooges finally assembled in one place, there were many mementoes of their old lifestyle, too. The band got kicked out of the Tropicana for attracting too many groupies and making too much noise – Iggy would sit in his room naked but for his Telecaster, which he played at staggering volume at three in the morning. Peter Davies arrived with his girlfriend Clare, who became Esther's friend and companion when Iggy disappeared to find groupies. Davies had organised the trip impeccably, but his professional manner didn't last, according to Esther: 'Peter was very, very together in the beginning, but unfortunately the guy developed a taste for cocaine and just became hopeless – but that was definitely a result of hanging out with us. He hadn't gone near the stuff before.'

As the small party of musicians were thrown out of one hotel after another, their surroundings became progressively seedier, concluding with the Wigwam Hotel, a kitsch 1930s hotel complex with individual chalets fashioned as brightly coloured concrete tepees, which was dilapidated and crumbling; its clientele was now mainly hookers and their johns, who'd rent a chalet by the hour.

Although the amounts of cocaine consumed during the recording of *New Values* at Paramount Studios – which was where James had trained as a recording engineer – were prodigious, the sessions were efficient, with Thurston directing the band, and James working closely with Iggy on the lyrics and vocals. On the best songs, 'Five Foot One' and 'I'm Bored', the sound was taut and stripped down, obviously influenced by the Stones' *Some Girls*, but tougher and more malevolent: there was a new restraint in Iggy's singing that only emphasised the power he had in reserve, and there were new, intriguingly minimal experiments like 'The Endless Sea'. Other promising songs, though, were lost under a bland mix and swamped by corny overdubbed horns and backing vocals, leading Ben Edmonds to conclude that: 'James was a good producer, but he was so concerned with pushing his professional credentials, he mixed the songs like he was mixing cardboard.' For all that, *New Values*, released in April 1979, was a modestly impressive album and became a modest success, reaching number 60 in the UK album charts, while 'I'm Bored' became a staple of rock radio across Europe, and also in the US, especially on East Coast stations like Boston's WBCN. But Clive Davis, preferring to concentrate on his own artists, like Whitney Houston and Barry Manilow, refused to release *New Values* until the autumn, by which time it had become old news, and the album peaked at number 180 in the US.

Once again, it seemed that the best way to promote the album was with live dates, and Iggy hit the road once more. Sometimes it felt, over the next four years, that he never left it.

Ex-Sex Pistol Glen Matlock – whose own band, the Rich Kids, had just split – was sitting in his Maida Vale flat one day wondering what to do next when the phone rang, and Peter Davies asked if he would like to speak to Iggy Pop. A few days later, he was lunching with Jim Osterberg at Mayfair's Athenaeum Hotel, and he agreed to join Iggy's band on bass, with Jackie Clark switching to guitar. He spent the next two months on the road, bringing his friend Henry McGroggan – who'd been road manager for the Rich Kids and, before that, Scottish glam band Slik – along too; McGroggan would become the longest-serving accomplice of Iggy's career. As an ex-Sex Pistol, who'd written most of the music to hits like 'Anarchy In The UK', 'No Future' and 'Pretty Vacant', Matlock looked to be a useful signing, given that Iggy had not so far set the world alight with his solo songwriting. Perhaps for that reason, Scott Thurston, who'd been Iggy's main musical partner over the last year, decided to bail out, taking his friend Jackie Clark with him. (Jackie Clark would die a few years later.) The last straw for Scottie was hearing the band was due to record another album straight after the tour, in Wales. 'Finally I blew up. I was like, why the fuck have we got to work with Glen Matlock? Why do you want to record in Wales? Why have Peter Davies as manager? Why the bullshit? Why don't we just do something *good*?!'

By the summer of 1979, Iggy Pop was an artist who commanded almost universal respect. He was widely acknowledged as the architect of much of the musical landscape of the late 1970s; and, more than many, he seemed, in the form of *Lust For Life* and *New Values*, to have progressed from the simple punk blueprint that so many of his acolytes were still following. It was this reasonable assessment of his career that seemed to inform the strategy of 'one last push', which inspired the recording of Iggy's next album,

Soldier. 'One last push', everyone agreed, might finally help Iggy achieve mainstream success – to 'cross over', in the industry parlance. But as any military historian would confirm, the strategy of 'one last push' invariably precedes a disaster.

Early in 1979, Ben Edmonds had left Arista for EMI, leaving Arista's new head of A&R, Tarquin Gotch, to manage the career of Edmonds' major signings, Iggy Pop and Simple Minds. There was little rapport or understanding between Gotch and Iggy. 'We simply never had a proper conversation, or a proper relationship,' says Gotch, who did, perhaps, make the suggestion of teaming Iggy with a British 'New Wave' band and having him record out in Wales at Rockfield, a residential studio based in an old farm near Monmouth. Once again, Williamson was engaged as producer. Williamson had been fairly happy with *New Values* – 'Jim came in with a bunch of crap to record and we had turned it into something half decent' – but felt he'd expended a huge amount of his personal capital and energy on the work. The second time around, he found it impossible to muster the same commitment, and he was particularly unhappy about having to record in Wales, without Scott Thurston. 'With *New Values* I'd been able to exert a lot of control,' he remembers. 'This time around, Iggy and Peter Davies were trying to get that control back.' Despite his reservations, Williamson agreed to take the job, for one last time.

As far as Glen Matlock and Klaus Kruger were concerned, the preparations for *Soldier* started promisingly. Klaus had driven over from Berlin to London, met up with Jim and James Williamson, who were both renting apartments in Mayfair, and was impressed to see Williamson playing guitar at rehearsals: 'He had his Les Paul cranked up through a fifty-watt Marshall amplifier, and it sounded fantastic.' Yet, for all the bravado and aggression of his Stooges days, Williamson was still unhappy about playing guitar, and once Matlock brought in his ex-Rich Kids bandmate, Steve New, Williamson withdrew, leaving New to play all the guitar parts. Matlock, however, noticed the pressure on Jim, who'd been called on to write a new album immediately after coming off the road, whether inspiration struck or not, and without a band with whom he knew he could gel.

Keyboard player Barry Andrews, a founder member of quirky Swindon popsters XTC, was another new recruit brought in to add some New Wave credibility. Since leaving XTC, Andrews had dropped out, living in a squat and, he says, practising 'extreme sex'. For a while he'd worked part-time at London Zoo, so it soon became a standing joke with the musicians that Andrews was there to add a certain English weirdness. 'Whaddya expect, he came from a zoo!' At his first lunch with Jim and James, Andrews thought Williamson seemed exceptionally straight – almost excessively concerned with being the efficient, radio-friendly producer. Jim was charming and bizarrely flirty, 'as he seemed to be with all the young boys,' says Andrews. But once he joined the rehearsals at a studio near Borough Market, he was bemused to discover how casual it all seemed. Glen Matlock was the closest thing to a bandleader, the one who told everyone the chord changes, but overall there seemed more interest in the large bins stocked with cold beers than in honing the material. It all seemed thin, ill-prepared and worst of all, says Andrews, 'No one was flying the plane.'

At this point, although it had been a struggle casting around for inspiration for lyrics, Jim seemed unconcerned. So far, all of his albums had come together at the last moment, and there seemed no reason why this time should be different. But as the tapes rolled at Rockfield Studios, and the band and Peter Davies settled into their quarters, scattered round the farmhouse just outside Monmouth in the rolling hills of the Wye valley, the atmosphere started to become increasingly tense.

James Williamson was proud of his recording prowess, and chatted proudly to Klaus Kruger about the subtleties of microphone placement that he'd learned at Paramount, but as far as the musicians were concerned, his idea of being professional was to order retake after pointless retake. 'James would go, Let's do it again and do it again as though this was some test of his production rigour,' remembers Barry Andrews. 'Which it wasn't, of course; instead everyone was getting tireder and tireder and it was sounding worse and worse.' As the musicians became increasingly fatigued, Matlock's bass and Kruger's drumming became more and more leaden. Williamson, who had never wanted to record out in Wales, realised the project was spinning out of control, and, according to Glen and Klaus, who called him 'Straight James', he started to brandish a bottle of vodka and a revolver around the studio. 'The word was it was loaded – but I didn't ask,' says Matlock, who unsurprisingly didn't complain about the repeated requests for one more take. As Williamson started knocking back more and more vodka, he also started to fixate on how to synchronise two tape machines to allow 48-track recording, which caused endless technical delays.

Julie Hooker was the A&R at Arista who was directly overseeing *Soldier*, as well as Simple Minds, who were recording at Rockfield's other studio. She also had to field Clive Davis's calls, as he monitored the tiniest details. Julie liked and respected Williamson, with whom she agreed deadlines and budgets. Like Charles Levison, Hooker was optimistic about the project; she'd heard the rehearsal tapes and they sounded great, but as the recordings dragged on, frustratingly slowly, she increasingly found herself walking in on confrontations between singer and producer. On some of those occasions, she'd catch Williamson blinking back tears.

Marooned in what seemed like the middle of nowhere, the participants had little distraction from the tension that was obviously building. Only Barry Andrews, who was essentially a visitor to the mad musical world of Iggy, seemed immune, wandering off into the countryside with the attractive young tape operator whose name was Mariella Frostrup, with Andrews keeping an eye out for magic mushrooms. The others found Andrews enigmatic, but they were amazed, when the tapes rolled, by the way he instantly conjured up a variety of dazzlingly inventive keyboard parts. There were some moments of light relief, notably a drunken party for Julie Hooker's birthday on 13 September at which each musician performed skits, but Williamson seemed constantly concerned by distractions that threatened to make the recordings overrun. Each evening, the band would play back rough mixes of the day's work on a ghetto blaster in the dining room; every now and then, Barry or Glen might record something peculiar or ridiculous as an experiment or a laugh. Whenever that happened, or someone was taking too long to work up an idea, Williamson developed the habit of telling them, 'Save that for the dining room.' When Iggy attempted to sing anything too out there, he would get the same comment. 'Dining-room music meant music you play for your own pleasure, which is ultimately wanking,' says Andrews, who noticed Iggy getting increasingly irritated whenever the phrase was uttered in his direction.

The recordings were running well behind schedule when three guests showed up at the studio. One of them came to play guitar. Two arrived for moral support. Ivan Kral had received a phone call from a friend at Arista who told him that Iggy was looking for a guitarist. David Bowie and Coco Schwab had simply come to help their friend.

According to Jim Osterberg's account, David Bowie breezed into the isolated studio looking like the Scarlet Pimpernel, complete with cape. Not everyone else remembers the theatrical garb, but all of them remember a drama in which, when the curtain whisked away for the final denouement, several of the key actors had met their end.

It seems that David's original plan was simply to dispel the air of gloom surrounding the recording. To do so, he seemed to take as a model Iggy's hilarious monologues that had so captivated the musicians working on *Low*. After a few scattered conversations, which charmed most of those present – Steve New was particularly starstruck, gazing at David like an adoring puppy, while a couple of members of Simple Minds had also dropped by to share the excitement – he gathered a small audience round him in the control room after dinner. Everyone listened in rapt attention as David chatted and joked, sipping from a glass of red wine, before embarking on a long, enthralling yarn about a character named Johnny Bindon.

Bindon was a one-time gangster who'd made his living as an actor and at one point worked as a bodyguard for Led Zeppelin. David recounted event after event of his shocking, bizarre life, such as the time he worked as an enforcer for the Kray Twins and cut a gangster's head off in a pub, or the story of how he won a police bravery medal for rescuing a drowning man when it was he who'd thrown the victim into the Thames in the first place. The best part was how Bindon had the biggest cock in London – an attribute that was particularly appreciated by Princess Margaret, who'd invite him to stay over with her on the island of Mustique, or call him over for 'love trysts' at Kensington Palace.

All of the musicians sat around laughing at the incredible tale – all of them, that is, apart from James Williamson, who sat there glowering. They started chatting about how being a criminal could be cool, better than being a musician, particularly if you had royal connections. Soon ideas were being scattered around as Iggy picked up the story, improvising a rap about Bindon and Princess Margaret. Fired up with enthusiasm, they trooped into the studio.

Suddenly, the sessions were coming alive. James Williamson had kept invoking all these rules about how you make a hit record, but now Bowie was showing how it really should be done: throwing out the rule book and creating a stimulating environment. He was a creative playmaster, taking charge in an unassuming 'Mind if I have a go?' manner. It was touching to watch; David and Jim had obviously been through a lot together, and here David was, revelling in Iggy's creativity 'in that way that properly creative people do – where somebody's talent isn't a threat to you, it's something to be delighted in,' says Andrews. James Williamson, meanwhile, seethed at what he saw as the intruder's pretentious posturing, and retaliated for having his session hijacked by flicking a switch on the control board that sent piercing howls of feedback through David's headphones. Despite Williamson's efforts, they soon crafted a song, with a stripped-down synthesiser backing, chugging drums, an 'I wanna be a criminal' chorus and lyrics based on a hilarious spiel from Iggy, along the lines of 'I wish I was Johnny

Bindon with the biggest fuckin' dick in London and a private income . . .' Sadly, that line never made it into the final version of 'Play It Safe'.

For the first time, thought Andrews, it felt like they were making a record to be proud of, and he was privately speculating about how cool it would be to have Bowie stay on and produce the album, when a loud argument broke out between Iggy and James. James was trying to explain how his job was to produce an album that would get on the radio, and that rude lyrics about Princess Margaret were guaranteed to get the record banned. And at some point, he uttered the phrase, 'Save it for the dining room, Jim!'

'Fuck you about the dining room, James,' was the reply. 'And I don't think you belong on this project.'

Bowie, meanwhile, looked into the distance in a 'This is all nothing to do with me' manner, before everyone shuffled away, embarrassed, and then went to bed. By lunchtime the next day, James Williamson, David Bowie and the enigmatic Coco Schwab were all gone. 'It was like a stage play where all the lights go dark,' says Andrews, 'and when the lights come up again there are three fewer people left around the table. And the feeling is, what's gonna happen now?'

What happened now is termed 'a salvage job'. Charles Levison arrived in Wales to counsel his troubled artist. Tarquin Gotch drove down in his company Ford Granada and also called in to see Simple Minds, whose sessions too had hit problems. Simple Minds insulted him to his face, as was customary etiquette with one's A&R man in that era, broke into the Granada and splattered farm-fresh eggs and cowpats all over the seats. (Ironically, Gotch would later nursemaid Simple Minds' first worldwide hit, when he included 'Don't You Forget About Me' in the music for John Hughes' hit movie *The Breakfast Club*.) Meanwhile, Peter Davies rushed around with an 'I'm the next guy to be sacked' look on his face. Rockfield engineer Pat Moran helped finish the recording; Iggy seemed to suffer a loss of confidence, repeatedly failing to nail the vocals, even attempting takes in the farmyard in search of

the right vibe. Ivan Kral added some searing guitar solos, augmenting Steve New's effects-laden New Wave guitars. There were
odd moments of inspiration, when Iggy threw out existing vocal
melodies and reworked the songs from scratch, but the sessions
dragged on and on, the tedium relieved only by an argument
between Iggy and Steve New, who'd declined the invitation to join
his live band. Barry Andrews was so bored that he would drive
down to the local girls' school and stand outside, desperate to see
some young, happy faces. Finally, the recordings were deemed
complete, although the mix was postponed until later. Julie Hooker
was so fraught with worry about the project that she didn't even
consider whether the album was any good. 'Just the fact it was finished was a relief.'

There were a couple more minor twists in the troubled saga of
Soldier, an album that, like a classic Hollywood turkey, was
crammed with collaborators and co-writers, none of whom would
take responsibility for the awful mess. The first twist came in New
York a few months later, when Ivan Kral was hanging with Iggy at
the Mudd Club. A serious-looking David Bowie came up to him
and chatted about how it was all going before saying, 'Ivan, you
know there is great respect among the British people for royalty
and the British crown. Even though that was a great take, can you
do me a favour and not release "Play It Safe"?'

When the album was mixed by Thom Panunzio over the
Christmas holiday, the mentions of Johnny Bindon and Princess
Margaret that had provoked the final split between Jim Osterberg
and his friend James Williamson were completely excised. Even
more bizarrely, the rousing guitar parts played by Steve New disappeared too, making the album sound lumpy and disjointed. Glen
Matlock had contributed his favourite recent composition,
'Ambition', to the album, and as far as he was concerned the
bizarre mix was an act of sabotage by Iggy, performed in revenge
for New's refusal to tour with him. 'I was really annoyed about
"Ambition",' declares Matlock: '[Iggy] mixed out Steve's part
'cause he bore a grudge. But he mixed out the hook to my song.

And that's why I didn't want to bother with him any more.'

It's hard to know how much difference a better mix could have made, for *Soldier* was Iggy's first truly uninspired studio album. There were some intriguing, quirky lyrics and a ragbag of interesting ideas, none of which threatened to gel into a coherent whole. Nakedly exposed in the absence of New's electric guitar, Kruger's drums and Matlock's plodding bass seem to be playing different songs; there are tom-tom fills on songs like 'Ambition' that sound like an irate child tossing a drum kit down a stairwell. The wit and intelligence of Jim Osterberg is gone, to be replaced by empty manic babbling, in a kind of 'Don't like this idea? Here's another crazy one!' desperation. Worst of all, the magnificent, proud voice of Iggy Pop seems to have completely disappeared, to be replaced by either a thin yelp, as on 'Loco Mosquito' or 'Dog Food', or else, as on 'I'm A Conservative', an exaggerated warble that sounds like the mooing of a cow. Only Barry Andrews' cheeky, chirruping keyboards betray any semblance of musical invention, scattered all over the record like chocolate chips on a cowpat.

The reviews were kind, as befitted an artist of Iggy's status, bandying around words like 'quirky' and 'interesting'. Radio play was, naturally, notable by its absence, while the album struggled to number 62 in the UK charts (in the typically perverse manner of the music business, Clive Davis elected to release *Soldier* immediately in the US, where it briefly appeared at number 125). But the most telling assessment of *Soldier* came from Barry Andrews who, again in typical music-business fashion, had to buy his own copy of the album that spring. 'I was flattered, there were so many of my keyboards on it,' he says. 'Then, quite quickly, I realised it had none of the virtues of a good Iggy Pop record.' For years afterwards, when friends discovered he'd played on an Iggy album and excitedly asked him which one, he would reply, 'The one that came *after* the good ones.'

For a moment I don't recognise James Williamson, the famed and feared Dark Lord of the Stooges. It's not the grey hair, or the sport jacket over a blue shirt, or his low-key demeanour, it's more a general sense that this organised, efficient-looking businessman could surely not be the person responsible for the ruthlessly aggressive guitar riffs or the revolver-waving antics that so many people remember.

We had been warned, though, for this is the Dum Dum Boy who, Iggy told us, 'has gone straight', as if it's the ultimate indictment. Yet, as we sit in a San Jose hotel in February 2006, in the heart of Silicon Valley, where he now works, incongruously discussing the horrendous, relentless train of disasters that assailed his band, James Williamson's career move seems like an eminently sensible act of self-preservation. For all his legendary ruthlessness, it became obvious that Williamson, a smart and ambitious kid whom his bandmates described as 'a wild, on the street speed-shooting guitar-playing maniac', was nowhere near as cutthroat as the business, or the singer, that employed him. For all the toughness he put on from the moment his illiberal stepfather sent him to a juvenile home, James always judged himself by results. Which, in his terms, seemed to be a failed band, and a best friend who betrayed him. 'Maybe the Ashetons already knew it, but I found out that Jim was very ambitious – that he didn't care how he had to do it. And when he threw me under the bus for the sake of his career at MainMan, I guess it showed me I had to develop my own independence.'

It seems to be the consciousness of his own vulnerability that contributed to James's intimidating demeanour. Called back in by his friend Jim for one last production job, James knew it was 'a terrible idea'. But when he's asked about his antics in the studio, waving around a revolver, he winces, looking terribly hurt that anyone would have felt threatened by what they surely knew was only a replica air pistol, before observing, 'I guess I have a very different internal view of myself than apparently my external effect is.'

Of all the ironies in the Stooges' history, perhaps the most supreme one is that James Williamson, a man whose work was revered by generations of guitar players, simply didn't believe he was that good. It's somehow sad when you realise this; then, as you have a reassuringly normal conversation with James, talking about family, Japanese food or the buildings in the area, you realise how liberating it can be, turning your back on the narcissism, selfishness and childish behaviour of the music business. And how, of all the masks we can wear, that of being normal and efficient can be the best protection of all.

CHAPTER 14

The Long, Long Road

The first trial of Iggy Pop had been the last stand of the Stooges: nine months of disasters interspersed with the odd inspiring performance, followed by humiliation, oblivion and then a year of sleeping rough. But even in those dark times, the music had been something he could cling to.

The second trial of Iggy Pop would last a full four years. Over this period there was a certain amount of love and support to nurture him, there was just enough money to survive, and there was always the prospect of respect or acclaim, somewhere like Paris, or Helsinki, or Sydney. But none of these luxuries could quite erase the consciousness that, this time around, the music was simply Not Very Good. Only one thing numbed that consciousness: alcohol, but the alcohol made the music worse still. This simple equation defined a downward spiral, suffused with a new emotion, fear. And again, madness awaited.

Almost immediately after Jim returned from his long, tortuous sessions in Wales, he drove to London with his band to rehearse for an American tour to promote *New Values*, which was finally being released in the US. It seemed a ludicrous predicament, being rushed into recording a new album before its predecessor was even released in its biggest market, but if it bothered him he didn't show it. Meeting his latest guitarist, Brian James, the formidable British player, who was an adherent of James Williamson's tough guitar style, Jim seemed the epitome of professionalism: conscientious, abstaining from alcohol or cigarettes in order to get his voice in trim, polite but always specific about what he wanted. The only surprise about meeting Jim was the subtle, Bowie-esque Cockney accent he seemed to have picked up in London. Fortunately, Brian James had been schooled in what to expect by his friend Nick Kent, who told him about how to deal with Jim, and how to deal with Iggy. 'He told me, Jim is like a scholar, he's the one talks about interesting things. Then, at the drop of a hat, he's Iggy, and he's an animal.' Brian soon realised Iggy had always had a close relationship with his guitar players, and had developed a range of techniques to handle them, sometimes treating them with intimate affection, at other times catching them off their guard to generate aggression that he could tap into.

For the first few days of rehearsal, Jim drank only water. Around five days in, he had a large mirror placed in the rehearsal studio near London Bridge, to practise his moves. On the last couple of days he started drinking Brian James's Scotch whisky and walking around stark naked. And then they were off.

Brian James had played with the Damned for two frenetic years, but his three months with Iggy would be among the most gruelling experiences he'd ever encounter. 'A total blur, fly into town, check in the hotel, soundcheck, play, back to the hotel, wake up, fly. It was like being in a bubble, every hotel a Holiday Inn, and you never know where you are, or even what time it is.' This was the bubble that would envelop Iggy for the next four years.

Ivan Kral, the tour's other new recruit, would share that bubble for two of those years. After arriving at Rockfield Studios for the closing days of the *Soldier* sessions, he'd spent an evening being interrogated by David and Coco, who asked about every aspect of his life. This was one of David's classic gambits; he liked to find how people ticked, and of course if he got to ask the questions he could maintain his own privacy. But Ivan thought there was a specific motive to David's questioning. 'I felt that David wanted to dump Jim on me. It was like, "I'm trying to help him, but he always screws up, so maybe, Ivan, you could be his buddy and spend time with him."'

A talented musician with European good looks, Kral had been a key member of the Patti Smith Group but had ultimately become frustrated by Patti's lack of hunger for the big time. He would become Iggy's key musical collaborator over this period, playing both keyboards and guitar, becoming so close that Kral's own mother would describe him and Jim as being like brothers. Yet while Ivan remembers that he and Jim had 'great times' together, like all of Iggy's future collaborators he knew he was strictly an employee. 'I knew how far I could go . . . I knew there were certain discussions where I would have to let him win. You just kind of smile and let them be the centre of attention.' This would be the crucial difference between Iggy and the musician with whom he did his best post-Stooges work, namely David Bowie – a man who could truly charm his musicians, and hence get the most out of them. Brian James, too, liked Jim and enjoyed their chats, but was also conscious of that hierarchy. After a year of dealing with the Sales brothers, Iggy never seemed to want to get close to his fellow musicians again. It was consequently that much easier for them to look on, believing the tales of his invincibility, as Jim's life began to spin out of control once more.

Meanwhile, on the periphery now that he'd moved out of Berlin, David Bowie seemed to keep a kindly eye on what was going on, sending his driver, Stuey – famous among Bowie fans for his role in *The Man Who Fell To Earth* movie – to ferry the band around, and apparently turning up to counsel Jim whenever possible.

The *New Values* US tour, much like Iggy's last outing with the Sonic's Rendezvous Band, mostly relied on superior meat-and-two-veg rock 'n' roll, veering from crazed, *Raw Power* material like 'Your Pretty Face Is Going to Hell', to messy, enthusiastic versions of some of the songs from the as-yet unreleased *Soldier*. More unexpected was a very nearly transcendent version of Sinatra's quintessential torch song, 'One For My Baby'. The song's loneliness, bar-room setting, and consciousness that there was a long, long road stretching ahead was scarily appropriate, even if the audience didn't always appreciate it. Glen Matlock had engineered the introduction of one of his favourite songs, 'China Girl', into the set, the first time Iggy had played it since sacking Hunt and Tony Sales. The more sophisticated air these songs added was somewhat undercut, though, by Iggy's use of a loose cap on one of his front teeth as part of his stage act. At key points in the action he'd pull off the cap and leer at the audience with the malevolent gap-toothed grin of a pantomime villain, the perfect accompaniment to the piratical assault of the music.

For both Brian James and Glen Matlock, who'd spearheaded Britain's punk revolution, this two-month series of high-energy performances, night after night, was far more intense than anything they'd experienced. Their leader's energy levels seemed almost superhuman, although Brian in particular was occasionally shocked by the levels of aggression, as Iggy bounced up to adoring kids crushed into the front row of the audience and slapped them on their faces, enjoying the shock and chaos he generated. Backstage, the atmosphere could be just as crazed. In the mornings, Glen or Brian would have conversations about books or history with Jim, who seemed like a studious young uncle. Then in the evenings, Iggy Pop would delight in stealing groupies from under their noses.

By the time the *New Values* tour came to an end with a show at Hurrah's in New York City on 9 December 1979, both English musicians had had enough. Brian James wanted to return to his own band, a decision that meant he was cold-shouldered on his last evening at the Mudd Club after the show. Matlock phoned Peter Davies over the New Year's break to tell him he was quitting soon after he'd heard the finished mix of *Soldier*, which he considered an act of sonic sabotage that amounted to Iggy 'cutting off his nose to spite his face'. To be fair, *Soldier*'s mix was as likely to be an attempt at damage-limitation as revenge on Steve New, but the outcome illustrated Jim's inability to keep his musicians – in particular the talented songwriters with whom he needed to collaborate. Over the same period, manager Peter Davies disappeared from the picture. A sweet, considerate man who bought tasteful presents for his friends – Charles Levison treasured a first edition of an Arthur Rackham-illustrated *Sleeping Beauty* that he'd given him – Davies had been engulfed by the chaos that seemed to surround Iggy, had already been cut out of the loop with Arista, and finally had a falling-out with Jim over money.

There was barely time to rehearse Matlock and James's replacements – guitarist Rob Duprey and ex-Heartbreakers bassist Billy Rath – before yet another tour started in February 1980 to promote *Soldier*. The run of dates apparently started well, with an ambitious set packed with new songs, including 'Hassles', 'Sacred Cow', 'Joe And Billy' and 'The Winter Of My Discontent', but after two weeks of European shows, the band ground to a halt in New Orleans during the first two nights of a string of American dates. Iggy, according to Kral, decided to sack his rhythm section, explaining, 'Klaus never smiles, he's boring – and Billy is a junkie.' Kral flew to New York to audition more cannon fodder, and found Mike Page – blues fan, ex-Chubby Checker bassist, and, by coincidence, an acquaintance of Jim's from San Diego – and drummer Doug Bowne. Together, this small crew would play month in, month out over the coming year, crisscrossing America and Europe. And it was two-thirds of the way through those 100-odd dates, most of them agree, that things got 'dark'.

Mike Page and Rob Duprey were both young musicians who were ecstatic to get the gig with Iggy, and lapped up the high-energy experience of live shows night after night, groupies lined up in the dressing room after the show, and drinking until the early hours. 'It wasn't until later that I realised what a skanky existence he was living,' says Duprey, 'that he was just surviving. And how towards the end it got pretty grim.' That year there was a show every day or two throughout February, March, April and May 1980, with another string of dates, the *Nightclubbing* tour, arranged at smaller venues from September, which according to Mike Page were arranged so that Jim could pay off a huge IRS tax bill. 'That was the point when it really got gruelling, when he had to muster up all that energy into playing the same places, night after night. Then it became a grind.'

In retrospect, there was a single upside to the relentless touring that Jim embarked on over the late 1970s and early 1980s. 'I did invest a lot of time in the people, touring Europe over and over to no avail,' he remembers. 'They threw fish in Scandinavia, beers in Belgium, stones in Germany. And they set fire to my drum kit once.' Little by little he was building up a new, grassroots following, who appreciated that very rarely, as Mike Page points out, did Iggy give a show that was anything but totally committed: 'For live shows you'd see him get himself into the head space where the past, the present or the future didn't exist. He'd work himself into being pure unadulterated rock 'n' roll.'

It was once he was offstage that Jim Osterberg would become truly disorientated; for one thing, having worked himself up to a frenzy, there was only alcohol or sex to help bring him back down. Many nights he suffered from insomnia. After months on the road, during which Mike Page became his most consistent drinking companion, he would call Page's room in the middle of the morning if he couldn't sleep, and ask him, 'Are you with a girl? Would you send her over?' According to Page, he always obliged. 'I didn't care. I never figured out their names usually until the next day anyway.'

In time, Page would become numbed by the 'absolutely staggering' number of groupies the band went through, and he decided to get married a year later. But for Jim, alcohol and groupies seemed an addiction. And where, in his youth, there was a certain innocence – according to those who were there – in his predilection for young or underage girls, now he was in his mid-thirties that innocence was gone. One girl, who encountered Iggy when she was fifteen, describes how intelligent he was, how he 'taught me a lot of things' – and it emerges that the main part of her education at the hands of this rock 'n' roll Henry Higgins was being tutored in deep-throat techniques.

By 1980, Esther had learned not to come on tour with Jim. She hadn't had a rock 'n' roll background, and hadn't even heard of Iggy before they met; it was Jim Osterberg she'd fallen in love with, not Iggy Pop. 'I think I was a good influence on Jim for a long time because I was coming from a different environment. I was a little Jewish princess.' When she saw Iggy walk into the dressing room after a show, point imperiously at the young girls waiting for him and tell them, 'You, you and you,' sending the rest away, she understood that this was Iggy and not Jim talking and learned not to resent it.

One time Esther organised a swap with an ex-boyfriend, whose new girlfriend she knew Jim fancied. Jim liked the idea of being a decadent European; they did the swap and all had a great time, but when the other couple left, Iggy turned on Esther, telling her, 'Don't get me into this fucking European ménage-à-trois shit. You might like it, you're some European slut, but that's not happening here and if you ever do it again I'll kill you!' It was a demonstration that Iggy was a good old Midwestern traditionalist at heart.

Esther's other tactic was to make friends with Iggy's latest fling; that was guaranteed to make him jealous. In a couple of cases, though, she accepts he occasionally had good taste in girls who in Europe, she says, 'were more pleasant. You could have a conversation with them.' Brian James was a bemused witness to Iggy's cavortings with one woman Esther had allowed backstage, brandishing a bottle of champagne. Brian had popped over for a reunion with his former employer after Iggy's show at London's Rainbow Theatre. James was introduced to the new band (he was slightly nonplussed to discover that a Bowie-style full kiss on the lips was the greeting *du jour* for the new line-up) and Jim asked him to come along to a party in Knightsbridge the following evening. It was a sophisticated affair, attended by Marianne Faithfull and husband Ben Brierly, actress Eva Ferret, Weimar-style singing duo Billy and Eve, ex-Sex Pistol Paul Cook and other aristo-punk celebrities; the party's host was Francesca Thyssen-Bornemisza, later known as Francesca, Duchess von Habsburg – the woman who, had the Habsburgs not renounced their claim to the monarchy in 1919, would ultimately have taken the title of Empress of the Austro-Hungarian Empire. After the party, Brian took Jim and Francesca to a late-night drinking den he knew on the Fulham Road, where they sipped wine from coffee cups and Jim charmed the baroness. 'He was very charismatic, but relaxed. He didn't have to put on a show because he knew he'd pulled,' says Brian James. Esther, in this instance, liked having an aristocrat around: 'She was good for the entourage. And she gave great dinner parties.'

By early 1980, the demands on Jim Osterberg were becoming immense. So far in his career he had recorded eight albums, most of which had required a huge emotional commitment, but the stock of ideas that sustained him was being diminished just at the point when the pressure from his record company was being increased. Charles Levison had been understanding about the *Soldier* debacle – he felt it was an 'interesting' album and believed that Iggy's presence gave Arista UK a certain cachet – but the *Soldier* sessions had gone over budget and Levison was under growing pressure from Clive Davis to justify his investment. Jim and Charles had an unusually close relationship, characterised by long, late-night phone calls, and Levison made it plain that, for the next album, the company needed a commercial breakthrough.

Understandably, Iggy chose to pretend this pressure didn't exist, and, he says, decided instead to spend his time thinking, 'Where can I get fucked, where can I get stoned, where can I have a good time?' Yet, however hard he tried to ignore the problem, Jim would also be troubled by the question of 'Where can I make music that's gonna go *Pow*?' In retrospect it would be obvious to Jim that 'Pow' – the simple power and energy that had always characterised his music – could never be unlocked in his then mental state, with his inexorable live schedule, and with musical collaborators who could not make him focus his energies. And while Jim's musicians were inclined to overlook their singer's troubles as they expended most of their energies in pursuit of good times, it was increasingly obvious to a few of those close to him that Jim Osterberg's mental condition was becoming increasingly desperate.

Dayna Louise was a 14-year-old music fan who lived in Austin, Texas and became Iggy's regular companion on his visits to the state. When they had first met in early 1980, he was protective and caring: 'He made me feel really smart and beautiful at a time I was younger than everybody else and felt a little inadequate.' Dayna seemed to epitomise Iggy's growing need for 'adoration'; something he'd often complained wasn't forthcoming from Esther, and that he could command more easily from younger girls. But during his subsequent visits to Texas, Dayna observed that Jim's mental state seemed increasingly parlous. One moment he would be charming, considerate, 'real loving', and then all of a sudden he would be on the verge of tears: 'Everything is shit, this all sucks, I hate my life.' There was no purposeful nastiness, but it seemed to Dayna that Jim had never learned to be pleasant to other people if his own mood was low. 'He's absolutely sincere when he's kind. But he's never nice when [he doesn't feel good] and his lows were pretty low. He was pretty hardcore.'

Dayna describes Jim's mental state as 'poster boy bipolar'; often he'd wake in the morning sober, energised and optimistic, in an 'everything is beautiful and good' mood. On such days he would enjoy scribbling lyrics while Dayna did girly things, took a bubble bath or painted her nails, enjoying the Humbert-and-Lolita vibe. Sometimes they maintained that blissful atmosphere for three or four days, 'and then everything would fall to hell. It was very, very extreme. I really think he was cracking up.'

For once, Jim's manic energy – what Vincent Van Gogh used to describe as the 'electricity' that underlay the artist's periods of intense creativity – seemed to turn in on him, rather than powering his music or his showmanship. Whereas in Stooges or *Kill City* days he had been compelled to create even in the depth of his mental torment, over this period his own music was becoming stunted. Meanwhile, the force of his personality convinced the musicians around him that all was well. 'I would never have seen [Jim's predicament] for one microsecond,' says Rob Duprey. 'That his situation was for whatever reason declining.'

It was in this enervated mental state that Iggy was scheduled to make what had to be his breakthrough Arista album. Over the summer of 1980, Esther was staying in Port Washington, New York, with her friend Anita Pallenberg, who was undergoing a painful break-up from Keith Richards. Meanwhile, Jim spent a reasonably calm week in Haiti with Ivan Kral at the chic Hotel Oloffson, a favourite of Jackie Onassis and other jetsetters, before the two of them booked into the Iroquois Hotel in New York to work up material.

Ivan Kral remembers the genesis of what would become the *Party* album as being almost idyllic. Ivan would work out songs on his Prophet 5 synthesiser, then take cassettes over to Iggy who would work up lyrics: 'really good lyrics'. This, thought Kral, was the opportunity and this was the material that would make Iggy 'bigger than this punk who is left-field, only for a certain kind of people'. Ivan remembers the pair writing a huge number of new songs, and was driven by a belief that this was finally the opportunity for Jim, as Charles Levison used to put it, to 'cross over'.

Sessions were booked at New York's Record Plant in the late summer of 1980, with Thom Panunzio engaged as producer. Panunzio had worked with Jimmy Iovine to help Patti Smith score her first mainstream hit with 1978's 'Because The Night' for Arista, and the intention was that *Party* would do the same for Iggy. Perhaps the idea was his music just needed to be shorn of its rough edges; perhaps it was that typical 1980s record company belief that an expensive studio, a glamorous photo session and an impressive drum sound was all that was needed to score a hit. But the sketchiness of the plan was evident from the moment the sessions started; even Iggy's band felt like passengers on the venture, reduced to plonking away like automatons on horribly predictable chord sequences.

During the first sessions for *Party* there was some pleasant material recorded, notably 'Pumping For Jill', based on a chugging guitar sound reminiscent of the Cars' 'My Best Friend's Girl', the archetypal New Wave crossover hit. 'My Best Friend's Girl', however, had a chorus, a necessity conspicuous for its absence on *Party*'s supposedly 'commercial' material. Most of the other songs were competent and eminently forgettable. 'Happy Man', however, wasn't, however hard you tried: a cringingly simplistic ditty with risible lyrics, in which the singer who once crafted taut poetry of streetwalking cheetahs yelps 'I'm a happy man and she's my only romance', against an oompah Eurovision brass band backing, in an attempted ska genre. A truly pitiful moment, it even made those present on the recording wince; Mike Page reckoned, 'He was really bending over and taking it in the butt.' Page speculated that the mostly pitiful lyrics represented Iggy's attempt to 'screw up' this shot at commerciality. Kral, too, believes that Iggy set out to 'destroy the project' himself, although in fairness Kral's own bland and dated music must take at least some of the blame.

Although Iggy must shoulder the ultimate responsibility for this distressingly dull album, there is something ineffably sad about the story of *Party*. One is reminded of a toothless old lion, once the proud king of the jungle, now a sad flea-bitten relic shuffling round a circus ring to the crack of a whip. *Party* stands to this day as a warning against the dire effects on the brain of cocaine and alcohol (if one conveniently forgets that *Lust For Life* was fuelled by the same chemicals).

Nonetheless, there were more indignities to come. Having heard the original recordings, Charles Levison decided that 'we had lost the plot'. Somehow, after casting around for a name producer who could rescue the project, Arista settled on Tommy Boyce, who, with Bobby Hart, was best known for writing 'Last Train To Clarksville' and other Monkees hits. Boyce had found a profitable niche in the UK music business working with 1950s revivalist bands like

Showaddywaddy and Darts, both of whom notched up bestselling singles in the supposed heyday of punk. Levison knew Boyce via his work with Showaddywaddy and Beatles pasticheurs the Pleasers for Arista, and in desperation, for the label had now spent heavily on Iggy and Clive Davis was 'breathing down my neck,' says Levison, he and Tarquin Gotch decided that Boyce was the man to salvage Iggy's album.

Boyce's arrival at the studio, says Mike Page, was 'a horrible joke'. The producer arrived with 'an LA haircut, and clichéd LA garb right down to the gold cocaine spoon round his neck'. According to Kral, Boyce's main obsession was scoring cocaine with Iggy, and the two locked Kral in a cupboard to prevent him interfering. Boyce picked on Ivan Kral's song 'Bang Bang', another tune with Cars-style throbbing guitars, adding strings and shuffling disco drums. The song was inoffensive, if blatantly derivative of Blondie's New Wave dance songs, which is more than can be said for two ghastly, syrupy cover versions, of Phil Phillips' 'Sea Of Love' and the Outsiders' 'Time Won't Let Me'. 'I was forced, I had no choice,' says Jim today, of recording the songs. 'And boy, did I butcher them.'

Mike Page, a positive, generous man who treasures his work with Iggy, describes *Party* as well as anybody when he says 'it stood for everything Iggy tore down'. Charles Levison readily admits the album 'didn't work. And it broke the confidence that Jim had had in me.' The album's reception, when it was finally released in August 1981, confirmed their misgivings. One review speculated that Iggy had spent more time phoning the Uptown Horns to book the studio session than he had writing the lyrics for the entire album. It was the first Iggy Pop album to be universally panned, and reached just number 166 in the US album charts.

As the *Party* tapes sat around, awaiting release, the band resumed their incessant touring, again to approving and often ecstatic audiences. The shows were ramshackle, but still powerful, and Iggy still seemed a potent force while, in his 'up' moments, his mental powers seemed undimmed. That February, there was a hilarious appearance on Tom Snyder's chat show in New York; breathless after playing a raucous version of 'Dog Food', Jim mumbles while regaining his energies, and then, in response to the usual predictable questions about being a cartoon punk, delivers a brilliantly lucid explanation of the difference between Dionysian and Apollonian art as Snyder looks on in open-mouthed incomprehension. The interview was illustrative of a wider lack of understanding of Iggy's own art: how he was celebrated for the broken glass and blood rather than the music. One night around this time, Jim broke down in tears, telling Mike Page how he was fed up of becoming 'the Don Rickles of rock 'n' roll', known only for insulting his audience. Yet mostly, he drowned his feelings in alcohol. 'I had to get drunk onstage to make it sound good and that was the worst part. I feared playing without being drunk. Because it didn't sound good enough.' Sadly, with most of Arista's advances swallowed up in recording expenses, he had no choice but to continue.

For Ivan Kral, the hit record that he hoped to make for Iggy had become a travesty, and there were stories within the band that he had been accosted by Bowie in the streets of New York, who asked him, 'What the fuck were you thinking?' A sincere, passionate man, when he had joined Iggy he had somehow thought, 'I would always look after him,' but on the first night of the tour to promote *Party*, he'd finally had enough. Kral was disgusted by the rock 'n' roll lifestyle, of 'using women as receptacles', and had himself been riding an emotional rollercoaster which he could endure no longer. He had hired the Uptown Horns, for the opening dates at New York's Ritz Club on 31 July 1981, and arrived for the soundcheck, he says, to find that Jim had dropped a tab of acid and was crying like a baby. He made his decision then to quit, phoning road manager Henry McGroggan after the third performance.

More replacements were called in to fill the breach. Gary Valentine had been Blondie's bassist – he'd written their hit '(I'm Always Touched By Your) Presence Dear' – and stepped in on guitar for Iggy's tour, while Patti Smith keyboardist Richard Sohl joined up too; he lasted until 3 September. Like his predecessors, Valentine found touring with Iggy 'a blur', full of relentless dates, many of them 'tiny, hole-in-the-wall dumps', fuelled on alcohol and, in the main, inspiring performances by Iggy, who still seemed in full possession of a Nijinsky-like grace and was, even in this reduced setting, 'unequivocally one of the best performers I've ever seen. I can't think of a time when I came away from a show thinking he wasn't on it tonight or he didn't really nail it. There were a couple of times when we didn't – and he would give us a strong talking to.'

Even Carlos Alomar, who joined the tour along with Blondie drummer Clem Burke in October 1981, thought Iggy was 'very controlled' – although it was all a far cry from the refined atmosphere of a Bowie tour. Carlos learned to dress in black leather, which offered more protection against the beer with which the band were constantly splattered, and particularly remembers one performance on a New Orleans riverboat, from which, once it had left the pier, there was no escape. 'Iggy came out in a little T-shirt, fishnet stockings, and he's hung like a horse so with not even a third of the song finished he would always rise up and there he was totally exposed and singing his ass off. At one point I think he took a shit on stage right behind the speakers. It was, what the hell is that smell? It was outrageous.' Carlos loved the experience, and Clem Burke later told the band his three months with Iggy were the most enjoyable tour of his life. 'It was certainly the most debauched,' he says today, while Gary Valentine in particular remembers the 'rough customers', who would be lined up in the dressing room after the show. 'They weren't very attractive. Maybe they could cater to his needs, I don't know. I do remember this one woman in a dressing room telling [Iggy], "Your cock never tasted as good until it was in my cunt." Or something like that. It was pretty rough language. I remember this one girl there and she was pretty new to this and she was like "Oh my God!" She'd never heard anything like this before.'

Even in his reduced state, forced to tour to pay the bills, aware by now his record contract was in jeopardy, and reliant on alcohol – 'Is Mr Daniels here yet?' was his customary query before a show – both Jim Osterberg and Iggy seemed reliably intact. Backstage, Jim's thick glasses and unkempt hair were a vital camouflage. But when Iggy was on, there was still a sharpness about his thinking – just like the behaviour of *Kill City* days, which prompted one observer to liken him to Rommel positioning his forces ready for an assault. Valentine noticed how adept Iggy was at playing a back-stage crowd, the promoters and hipsters who turned up with their little offerings of drugs or gifts. 'He would just eat them up. He'd just take and keep on taking whatever they had and they'd get maybe three minutes of conversation. Then they were standing there empty-handed and looking like, what was that all about?'

They'd been Iggy'd.

In most cases, there was no harm done, but over this period Iggy displayed an increasingly childlike selfishness and ignorance of the consequences of his actions. Which was why, suggests Dayna Louise, he seemed intuitively to search out people who'd tolerate his behaviour. 'As an adult, I can see that a grown woman would probably see through his manic depression and say, dude, you're pretty fucked up. Whereas children, young girls, would just be so starry-eyed and enamoured of him that they wouldn't care.'

Iggy had taken Dayna, who was now sixteen, to Houston in the autumn of 1981, but after an argument had abandoned her in the hotel, leaving a couple of hundred dollars on the mantelpiece for her to get home. Dayna returned to her parents in New Orleans and enrolled at high school. Iggy later tracked her down, sent flow-ers and begged forgiveness before, bizarrely, moving in with Dayna and parents; her mom put him to work on jobs around the house before he disappeared to a hotel. For a short time they shared romantic walks around the French Quarter, as Dayna returned to Iggy's hotel on the way back from school each day, but Iggy was fascinated with the quarter's gris-gris ladies, and also recruited a pair of dilaudid and heroin dealers as friends. Soon the atmos-phere turned nasty; Dayna's mother ascribed it to the gris-gris ladies, Dayna blamed it on the dealers. 'They were a pretty rough crowd that did a lot of skank,' says Dayna. 'I kinda toyed with it, and I think he was getting into it honestly, 'cause he started getting very mean and very abusive again. And at that point I came home to the hotel from school and there was this woman in bed with him. I'm like, What the fuck's this? And he goes, Well, baby, you've been replaced. He was fucking her as I packed my stuff up and left. And that's the last I saw him.' Some time later, Iggy apparently regretted his impulsive rejection of Dayna and started phoning her house. But Dayna's mom, who had kept a watchful eye on how the singer treated her daughter in New Orleans, told him to stay away: 'You hurt her, cheri. And you're done.'

Contemplating her time with Iggy, Dayna describes him as 'talented . . . but tormented', and then 'primal', before, on reflection, she summarises his actions as 'vampiric. Like a succubus.' Now in his mid-thirties, he seemed irrevocably committed to repeat the destructive behaviour of his youth, seemingly without any clue how to extract himself. And while the live shows were consistently exciting, there was the odd echo of former humiliations, most notably when Iggy was booked at the behest of Keith Richards to support the Rolling Stones for two nights at Detroit's 80,000-capacity Pontiac Silverdome, from 31 November 1981. On the second night Iggy appeared on stage in a ballerina dress, with what looked like a semi-erection clearly visible through his brown and cream stockings. Seemingly within moments, a hail of bottles, Bic lighters and shoes started spinning to the stage. This time around, Iggy told his band that such a reception was a sign of affection in Detroit, and at the end of their set the promoter, Bill Graham, read out an itemised list of the objects, in lieu of an encore. Graham would note in his memoirs that Iggy had attracted the most projectiles of any act he'd ever worked with. This was tragedy rewritten as farce.

Iggy's recording contract had obviously been in serious jeopardy by the summer of 1981; Charles Levison, his champion at Arista, had been the victim of political manoeuvrings at the company throughout the year, and eventually jumped ship to WEA, at which point Jim was officially informed his Arista contract would not be renewed. Eventually, it transpired Blondie founder Chris Stein was starting his own record label, Animal, and was willing to fund a new album; early in 1982 Iggy and his guitarist Rob Duprey started working on material, mostly at Rob's home studio set-up in his apartment on 6th Avenue. By now, Jim had moved to a new apartment in Bensonhurst, Brooklyn, an area he'd acquired a taste for since seeing John Travolta in *Saturday Night Fever*, and there were occasional scenes of near-domesticity. Eric's mother, Paulette Benson, had decided that he needed to spend more time with his father, and the 12-year-old started visiting Jim and Esther more regularly. The couple did their best to look after his son, and they responsibly concealed their spliffs and cocaine – although Eric, who'd been brought up in California, almost certainly knew what was going on. James Senior and Louella, too, kept a close eye on Eric, delighted in their role as grandparents.

In the run-up to the recording of their album, Jim spent six weeks in Duprey's apartment as they experimented with new material. As was his wont, Jim was a generous boss – he had received a $50,000 advance from Animal, but split the $10,000 he'd received for his own living expenses equally with Duprey – but he still lived 'like a cat,' says Rob. Each week he'd receive a stipend from his agency, FBI, and would disappear for a couple of days, although every now and then Duprey might see him taking 'some big blonde' into his room, blasting out his own single, 'Bang Bang', at staggering volume while he was doing 'who knows what'. After three or four days his money would be exhausted, so Jim would instead skulk around the apartment, raiding the refrigerator for food, 'being really friendly. Like a cat. Then as soon as the money came in the next Wednesday, he'd be gone again.' When he was based in Brooklyn, life was more organised; Esther put Jim on a budget of $20 a day, handing over his spending money each morning, just like David used to back in Berlin. He'd keep a record of his expenditure, carefully noting his consumption of Big Macs (one for him, one for Rob Duprey), Cokes and other junk food, 85 cents for smokes, $4 for a cab and $4 for a nickel bag of grass.

For all that Duprey knew he didn't have a close friendship with Jim – 'he really associates with who he needs to associate with, I wouldn't call him a particularly friendly-type person' – he felt privileged to work with him. 'I was just a bratty kid, and got treated really well . . . even if *Zombie Birdhouse* turned out to be his most pretentious record.'

In fact, pieced together for less than $50,000 at Blank Tapes, a budget 16-track studio in New York, with Chris Stein on bass and Clem Burke on drums, *Zombie Birdhouse* was a flawed but grown-up album, studded with odd moments of quiet, slightly weary beauty. Although the album was dominated by declamatory self-conscious exercises, such as 'Bulldozer', the Weill-esque 'Life Of Work' and the painfully arty 'Watching The News', there were intriguing experiments, such as 'The Ballad Of Cookie McBride', a skewed, catchy tale delivered in a yee-haw Southern yodel, and the stark, vulnerable 'Ordinary Bummer' – one of the finest songs Jim had written since *Lust For Life* days. Ultimately, the album would be regarded as a failure – not unreasonably, as its opening quartet of songs are strident and unlistenable – but it showed at least a desire to experiment and defy expectations, perhaps as David Bowie had done with ventures such as *Baal* earlier in the year. It was certainly a desire to 'diversify like David' that inspired work on an autobiography, tentatively entitled *Run Like A Villain*, at the suggestion of Jim's old Ann Arbor friend Anne Wehrer – the woman who, with then-husband Joe, had first sheltered Andy Warhol and his Exploding Plastic Inevitable in Ann Arbor back in March 1966. According to Wehrer, the book was instigated with Bowie's encouragement; Esther Friedmann, however, remembers Bowie counselling Jim that 'you can only write your autobiography once', perhaps sensing, as had happened so often recently, that this was yet another project that would go off half-cocked.

Wehrer had started her work as ghostwriter during the autumn 1981 tour, although unsurprisingly she'd found it difficult to make substantial progress thanks to the various distractions on offer. Occasionally she'd manage quiet conversations in Jim's hotel – she remembers how he would personalise his soulless room by placing tapestries over the lamp and bed – and eventually she built up a close rapport with this one-time schoolfriend of her son, Tom. Anne, a rather patrician woman, had lost a leg to cancer and over the course of the tour grew to believe that Jim, like her, was damaged and vulnerable; that belief, she says, drew them together and they became lovers. Back in New York, though, progress was slow. Jim would take the subway to Anne and designer Wyn Loving's loft, and sit in the huge clawfoot bath and dictate to them, but his anecdotes, hilarious as they were, were disjointed and hard to turn into a coherent story. Often, on quiet afternoons, Jim would take his newly purchased typewriter down to the street corner or local park and fashion stream-of-consciousness stories or reportage. They were hugely imaginative, intense and slightly scary, suggestive of mania. On one typewritten manuscript he mentions how he's feeling good and is managing without the Valium, which was presumably prescribed to calm him down – the note is a poignant sign of a damaged psyche, and perhaps a portent of a coming crisis.

CHAPTER 15

Night of the Zombies

With recording of *Zombie Birdhouse* complete, Jim flew to Haiti around April 1982 to finish up his autobiography with Anne Wehrer, and then to holiday and shoot cover photos for *Zombie Birdhouse* with Esther.

Wehrer thought Jim was a mess – 'really drugged out, all of the time' – but she did what she could and disappeared back to New York, happy to have seen Baby Doc Duvalier, who moored his boat by the local bar, the owner of which bought everyone drinks and told them – especially Jim – to not even glance at the notorious dictator. Esther, who stayed on, had a worse time. The couple were in Haiti for three months and, as far as Esther was concerned, what was meant as a holiday turned into a scary downward spiral, a nightmare of voodoo, zombies and murderous Tontons Macoute. 'We went to hell and back. And it was all because Jim antagonised a voodoo priest. It was a voodoo curse. I never would have believed it if I hadn't seen it with my own eyes.'

Over their first few weeks, the holiday seemed blissful, Esther recounts, as they cocooned themselves in the luxurious surroundings of the Habitation LeClerc and got blasted on the cornucopia of delights available at the unregulated Port-Au-Prince pharmacies. In particular, you could take in empty 1.5-litre Coke bottles and get them filled with paregoric – camphorated tincture of opium – for two dollars, then use it to top up your piña coladas throughout the day and night. As was their wont, Jim and Esther also managed to line up suppliers of alternative substances within their first few days in Haiti.

As they sprawled around the beautiful but slightly decayed hotel, which had been owned in colonial times by Napoleon Bonaparte's sister Pauline and was purchased in the 1930s by dancer and anthropologist Katherine Denham, who later became a voodoo princess, the surreal nature of their surroundings, in the middle of a huge botanical garden, was highlighted by the constant presence of a Christian group, preaching the gospel and distributing condoms. For their first couple of weeks, wherever Jim and Esther wandered, the Christians seemed to be there too, looking well scrubbed and scarily righteous.

It was a simple urge to dance that seemed to launch the harrowing series of events. After Anne Wehrer's departure, Jim and Esther moved out of Habitation LeClerc to stay in Jacmel, a small town filled with French colonial-style nineteenth-century mansions; it was an isolated coastal town, and the local police checked their passports on the way in, keeping track of all visitors. After a few days, the couple managed to find an insider who offered to take them to a voodoo session. It was held in secret – practising voodoo had been forbidden by the Baby Doc regime – but Jim and Esther sat down in the darkness under the eyes of the locals, sipping some unknown but potent brew, believing they were about to witness nothing more than a colourful Saturday-night dance. Then the musicians started a drum roll and launched into a hypnotic rhythm. When Jim heard the drums start he leapt up, ignoring Esther's pleas to keep quiet, ripped off his shirt, jumped into the middle of the ring of revellers and started dancing; soon he'd attracted a gaggle of Haitian girls to dance alongside him, but as Esther glanced around, she saw the priest who was directing the ceremony glaring at Jim. He was muttering, outraged at the disruption of his ceremony.

Esther ran to Jim, shouted, 'Let's get out of here,' and pulled him away. 'It was creepy,' she remembers, 'and then . . . for the next three months everything started to get out of hand.'

Initially a sceptic, Esther started to get increasingly spooked by her surroundings. At night there were always mysterious figures around, only their eyes visible in the darkness, who she became convinced were zombies. One afternoon she was sipping a drink when a rat ran across the floor in front of her – a local leapt out from nowhere and crushed it under his foot, all the while staring right in her face. And then she noticed Jim had started to give away his possessions. First his guitar disappeared. Then he had given much of his money and most of his clothes away. Soon they were down to their last two hundred dollars.

One night Esther woke up and saw Jim was gone. So was the local they'd hired to watch the room. She grabbed her clothes and ran out, found their guide and drove off into the night; they finally located Jim in a hole-in-the-wall bar, dancing with the local hookers. Esther ran in, shouting at him, 'Where's our money?' As she'd dreaded, he'd given it away, and despite Esther's pleas to the women – 'I know you think we're rich, stupid Americans, but that was our last two hundred dollars. Please keep half, but please give me half back' – they were left penniless.

Finally Esther and her helper bundled Jim into their rented VW Beetle and they started off home, their guide at the wheel. The couple fell asleep; then Esther awoke and realised they were on a tiny dirt road, glanced out of the window and saw faces staring in. 'I screamed! I yelled, They're going to kill us!' Their driver was so alarmed by the bloodcurdling scream that he wrenched at the wheel, crunching the Beetle into a stone wall. As it skidded along, Jim jumped out, hitting the wall and, it later transpired, breaking three ribs. While the driver cradled his head, which he'd hurt in the crash, Esther screamed at him to get out; she took the wheel with Jim beside her, leaving the driver, turned the badly damaged but still driveable Beetle round and drove back along the dirt track until finally she reached the hotel.

The next day Esther decided she needed to obtain a police report to explain the damage to the rental company. Accosting her guide, who'd turned up at the hotel, she marched him down to the police station, leaving Jim back in their room. The commissioner at the desk was a portly, intimidating figure who reminded Esther of Idi Amin, and at one end of the police station was, Esther remembers, 'a cage, with a guy hanging in it. I swear to God; it was like a bad movie.' Esther realised her guide was transfixed with fear; she looked down and saw he'd wet himself and quickly mentioned it was she who'd been driving the car when they crashed. Finally they managed to get the requisite report and left; the guide was so grateful not to have been left in the clutches of the police, and their feared secret service counterparts the Tontons Macoute, that he found an uncle or cousin who repaired the Beetle.

Over subsequent weeks Esther found a job to raise some cash, assisting a Belgian dentist named Pierre, who specialised in bargain-basement extractions. 'It cost one dollar with nothing, two dollars with procaine, and three dollars for a tooth out with a shot of anaesthetic.' While Esther was away, Jim would stay with a local woman, her numerous offspring and her one-legged dad, all of them crammed into a tiny hut. The woman was just a friend – 'I don't think anything unseemly was going on' – but he'd sit there all day while she braided his hair. The skewed domesticity lasted until Esther's dentist friend was murdered – 'the Tontons Macoute slaughtered him – it turned out because he was competition for the local dentist' – and again they moved on, fleeing Jacmel in the middle of the night after being warned that someone would be lying in wait for them on the single road out.

It was at this point that Esther became convinced that the voodoo priest had put a curse on them. She began attempting to get the two away, but whenever they tried to get to the airport, something would stop them, and all the while Jim was becoming more and more mentally disturbed, says Esther: 'He was ill. I mean really ill.' They made it to the airport and even had their luggage on the plane for Los Angeles one time when Jim disappeared. Frantic,

Esther searched the airport. 'Then finally this dude comes up to me and says, if you're looking for your boyfriend, he's gone off in a car to do something. So it was bam, luggage off the plane. And this happened at least three more times.' From Jacmel they moved to a bungalow on the beach, rented from an American expat who gave them credit; she seemed to rent out most of her rooms to CIA agents or other people with something to hide. They remained there for a month or so before renting another house. Jim would bring kids back so they could get to try sleeping on a bed; Esther would wander around and chat with the landlord as the man took his cow for a walk. By now, Esther was calling her friends all over the world, her father, ex-boyfriend Norbert, and Jim's agents, FBI, to raise enough money to pay off their debts and get another flight home. Meanwhile, Jim was either flying away on some doomed manic escapade or slumped like a morose drunk, incapable of the most basic functions. She started hiding his clothes, just like Ron used to in the Stooges days, to ensure he wouldn't wander off at night, but that didn't necessarily stop him. One night he disappeared, naked but for one of her skirts, took the rental car, even though he couldn't drive, crashed it and then hitched a lift to the Hotel Oloffson, from which someone called Esther, begging her to take him home.

Within a few days, Esther had phoned around to raise more money, and this time managed to get Jim home to Brooklyn. Still he seemed deranged. Unable to endure any more, Esther took the advice of a friend back in Haiti, who told her the couple were undoubtedly the victims of a voodoo curse. Following their instructions, she took a pair of scissors, bent over Jim when he was asleep and snipped through the yellow T-shirt that he'd been wearing since the start of their holiday and gently pulled it off his back. Taking the remaining clothes he'd been wearing throughout their time in Haiti, she set fire to all of them, banishing the spell.

She also had to find medical care for Jim. Danny Sugerman managed to track down Dr Zucker, who was now working at Northridge Hospital in Los Angeles; Eric's mother, Paulette

Benson, agreed to meet Jim off the plane and take him to the hospital. Esther's main worry was that Jim wouldn't be allowed on the plane, because he was literally raving; but she knew that his chances were infinitely better in first class. Finally she managed to buy the ticket using a borrowed credit card, put Jim on the plane to LA, and told him to sleep and not say a word. She watched the plane take off, and waited for him back in Brooklyn.

Jim spent a few weeks in Northridge. It was like going back in time to 1974, and again he had to spend a week or so cleansing his body of its cocktail of drugs before he could sit down and talk with Murray Zucker, who admired Jim but also worked hard on the underlying issues that caused the singer's predilection to crash and burn. Just as last time around, once Jim was settled and out of his rock 'n' roll habits, Murray found him a vulnerable, sensitive and empathetic character. There was a disturbed teenager in the same unit who suffered from Duchenne's disease, which meant he was somewhat malformed, could only walk with difficulty and whose life expectancy was severely shortened. The boy was deeply depressed; Jim gave him his jacket and transformed his condition. It was a wonderful thing to behold, Zucker thought; far more effective than any treatment he could have prescribed; Jim's spontaneous act of sympathy turned round what remained of the youngster's life. At another point during his hospitalisation, a psychotic inmate attacked a nurse; Jim spontaneously leapt up and wrestled the patient to the ground, saving the nurse from possible serious injury.

It was probably during his stay at Northridge that Jim made the decision to quit his destructive lifestyle. But still there was the omnipresent problem of money, or lack of it. For the only way to generate cash was live work: 'What else could I do? I didn't even think about it.'

In October, he hit the road again, promoting *Zombie Birdhouse* and his autobiography, *I Need More*. The book was a hilarious read, but showed only occasional glimpses of Jim's intelligence and insight, handicapped by the circumstances in which it was written. Esther contributed dozens of photos, Anne Wehrer and designer Wyn Loving spent weeks finding rare shots, but the costs of putting it together were perilously close to the advance from the small New York publisher, Karz-Cohl, while the text itself was riddled with mistakes, occasional grandiose fantasies and gratuitous insults aimed at most of those with whom Iggy had worked. Back in Ann Arbor the word was that Scott Asheton, Jim's closest friend in the Stooges, arranged a barbecue and invited his friends around to watch his copy burn on a bonfire in the garden.

Unsurprisingly, *Zombie Birdhouse* sold poorly, and by the end of the tour to promote it which opened on 13 October, Jim was, say the rest of the band, more crazed than ever. New drummer Larry Mysliewicz was apparently freaked out; Frank Infante, yet another recruit from Blondie, lapped up the experience, which reminded him of the *Last Days Of Pompeii*. One night Iggy was smashed full-on in the head with a Heineken bottle. He kept singing. The band was hassled by Hells Angels in London, and then, on a quick flight to Newcastle to film the TV show *The Tube*, Iggy turned up at the end of the soundcheck and fell backwards into the drums, destroying the carefully-placed array of microphones. Iggy returned to the hotel before the show; the house security guard heard suspicious noises in his room and decided to investigate. As he opened the door with his pass key, he was treated to the entertaining spectacle of a stark naked Iggy with his foot braced against the wall, attempting to pull out a live power outlet socket, which he'd apparently decided would make an attractive belt. The long-suffering Henry McGroggan managed to persuade the hotel management to let the rest of the band remain at the hotel, as long as Iggy flew back to London straight after the show. After a short break for January 1983 the live shows resumed again, this time presciently titled *The Breaking Point*.

In May 1983 there was a brief respite. Jim and Esther had moved to a new apartment in Columbus Avenue, New York, and he continued tapping away on his typewriter. 'Decided not to bother with hospital this year,' he wrote. 'Too much monkey business, rather take my chances.' He continued a few lines later: 'I believe I am a farmer of sound. I treat my crops with infinite devotion and tenderness.'

Despite his unquenchable enthusiasm for music, there seemed little chance of a new record deal, even with the assistance a few weeks earlier of Cars founder Ric Ocasek, who'd produced some studio sessions for him in Boston, with Ministry guitarist Al Jourgensen. There was some good news from the UK, where David Bowie's *Let's Dance* album, which featured David's version of 'China Girl', hit number one, dangling the prospect of songwriting royalties to come. But in the meantime Jim's energies were directed at a tour of Hawaii, Japan and Australia.

On the plane over to Hawaii, Jim had a word with Mike Page, telling him he was worried about Mike's drinking. Mike assured him he had it under control. Jim gave him a steady stare. 'Don't bullshit a bullshitter,' he warned him. A couple of weeks later, on 20 June at the Sun Plaza in Tokyo, Iggy spotted an attractive 22-year-old in the audience and employed his usual gambit of singing to the girl next to her, tantalising her. At the end of the show he sent Henry McGroggan out to find the girl, but she was not in the auditorium. But it happened to be raining outside, and the girl, whose name was Suchi, walked back in to collect her umbrella from the coat-check stand. That night she joined him on the tour. One week later, David Bowie's version of 'China Girl' hit the Top Ten in both the UK and the US. Three weeks later, Jim had abandoned the tour and was on a plane to Los Angeles with his future wife.

The sun is beating down relentlessly in San Diego, the neatly maintained city that has always seemed a refuge for those with nowhere else to go, voyagers who've run out of friends in San Francisco and then LA, and eventually find themselves stranded in this last stop before Mexico. I'd been calling Mike Page, an enthusiastic, energetic man, for a few weeks before I made the trip from San Francisco in the summer of 1995, and he promised me a great time:

he'd get us the best room at the city's finest hotel, as he was friends with the manager. We'd get complimentary food and drink at the Hard Rock Café, which had one of his basses hanging on the wall. Then he would introduce me to some of the city's young musicians.

I liked Mike; a big, solid-looking, funny guy who reminded me of New Order's celebrated bassist, Peter Hook, and I could see why he'd been Iggy's closest companion on those gruelling tours, night after night, when the singer was getting smashed in the head by Heineken bottles, dodging collapsing PA stacks, or rushing out of hotels. It was seeing Iggy shrug off all those assaults, Mike told me, that convinced him his ex-employer was indestructible. 'Iggy is not a normal human being,' he told me. 'I've got proof of it. I've got pictures of him where he'd jumped in the crowd, when he's been scratched from his shoulder to the bottom of his waist and you can see the marks. I took a photograph of it in the tour bus, when he was asleep. If it was you or I, a fingernail cut, which can be real dirty, those scratches would be there for a week. They'd broken right through the skin. But with him, within two days it was gone.'

As we chatted over successive rounds of Becks at the Hard Rock Café, the conversation was riveting, but like the stories Mike related, the evening was punctuated by misfortune. Mike called his hotel-manager friend who said he was sorry, but the place was fully booked. There was a new manager at the Hard Rock who'd never heard of him; I stumped up for their overpriced factory food despite his objections. Later in the evening Mike's plans of being the perfect host took another turn for the worse as we sat, morosely, in a local 'alterna-rock' club, whose pale, listless patrons were not impressed by the English writer Mike had brought along. Then suddenly Mike disappeared. His friend Steve, a lawyer currently going through a divorce, asked me to help look for him in the toilets – Mike had blacked out there the previous week, Steve told me, and he was really worried about Mike's drinking. Mike turned up eventually, without mentioning where he'd been, and rather than checking into the city's best hotel, we went off to sleep on the floor of Steve's one-bedroom flat.

But we didn't sleep at all. Instead, we spent the night singing Rolling Stones songs, taking turns on a plastic Maccaferri guitar Steve had just bought, until dawn, when I left to catch my plane. I fended off the inevitable hangover by drinking throughout the next day, too.

Over succeeding months I called Mike again and again, but he'd apparently walked out of the guitar shop where he worked. Months turned to years, and I often wondered what had become of him, reflecting on the grim toll Iggy's lifestyle had taken – particularly on those who, like Dave Alexander, Zeke Zettner and Jackie Clark, played bass guitar. It was nearly ten years later when the phone rang in my LA motel room, and I recognised Mike's voice. We laughed about our hilariously disastrous night in San Diego, and as our chatter continued Mike described how his life had since followed a familiar, but happy, pattern. He'd quit drinking, turned to soundtrack work, and his career was on the up. And in a typical California parable, he'd found the best place to network for new business contacts was in his local AA meetings.

CHAPTER 16

Hideaway

> I found by having a fixed address I can actually roam far-
> ther afield. Because I have somewhere to come back and
> crash at.
>
> Jim Osterberg

In the end, it all came down to money. It took five years for the farmer of sound to reap his harvest, but around the middle of 1983 the cash started flowing. There were royalties from the Sex Pistols' version of 'No Fun', which had taken several years to arrive, then came income from Grace Jones, who had a Top Ten dance hit with her 1981 *Nightclubbing* album, featuring Iggy and David's song; around this time Dan Bourgoise from Bug Music had been putting Jim's publishing in order, and the Grace Jones song was the first from which the royalties started to arrive without delay. Soon there was the cash from David's hit version of 'China Girl', which started to trickle in quickly from radio and TV airplay.

On the plane back to Los Angeles, Jim walked back from the first-class section to talk to Mike Page. Jim was trashed, but not too trashed to tell Mike that he was thinking about taking a break for a while. Then he said, 'She thinks I drink too much. Do you think I drink too much?' The rest of the band were still in a state of shock – they had expected the tour to continue to New Zealand – but they had noticed Jim withdraw from them over the last few weeks and were reasonably resigned to their fate. Esther Friedmann, too, gradually realised Jim wasn't coming back, despite Louella and James Sr's protestations that the split was surely only temporary. 'When he looked at her he didn't think of blow; when he looked at me he probably did,' says Esther, philosophically. 'That's what happens when you do drugs with people. So I knew it was time to get my shit together.' Jim told her to keep whatever possessions she wanted, including David's painting of him; but David arrived at Esther's Kreuzberg apartment a few months later and asked for it back.

Back in LA, Jim hooked up with two of his confidants from *Kill City* days, Murray Zucker and Danny Sugerman, and decided he needed to stay in California for a while before he could brave New York again. Zucker counselled him through his stay on a chemical-dependency ward, and Sugerman sent an intriguing commission his way in the form of the title song for Alex Cox's upcoming movie, *Repo Man*, for which Sugerman had wangled a role as music consultant. But perhaps the most crucial therapy was Suchi; for the first time in his life, Jim Osterberg had to take responsibility for another human being.

Suchi Asano was a music fan, stylist and occasional model whose father worked in the police department in Tokyo. She'd learned to speak English at school, and once the couple arrived in LA she enrolled in a Berlitz course. But it was Jim Osterberg who took on the responsibility of coaching her in the language. As the son of an English teacher, he'd been waiting to tell someone else how to speak properly for thirty years or so. 'I've given her a good accent,' he would proudly proclaim after a year's tuition. 'She doesn't swallow her consonants like a lot of Japanese do.' For the first six months their communication was pretty basic; Jim found it impossible to explain some of the dilemmas and issues that troubled him, which brought him to a crucial realisation: 'OK, there's not so much need to make a big flap over every little thing that happens every day.' Conquering his need for chaos and drama would represent a crucial breakthrough.

During his stay in Los Angeles, Jim had introduced Suchi to most of his musical circle at a party at the China Club, an upscale restaurant in Hollywood; the couple seemed joyful and optimistic, while Jim looked markedly different from the rather raddled figure he'd cut of late: sparkly-eyed and boyish with short hair and a side parting, dressed with classic elegance in a red cardigan and banded white golf straw hat (some of his friends started calling him Bing behind his back, because his casual attire reminded them of Bing Crosby). Danny Sugerman seemed to be his constant guide around Los Angeles society and displayed a puppydog enthusiasm about being reunited with the singer who seemed like his surrogate elder brother. Sugerman, too, was supposedly drug-free; this was the new ethos in Los Angeles, which had belatedly wised up to the deleterious effects of cocaine – although quite often, as photographer Robert Matheu points out, 'drugs-free' simply meant that it was not cool to share your cocaine any more; instead, everyone snorted in private.

Sugerman had the idea of teaming Iggy for the title song with Chequered Past, the short-lived LA supergroup comprising Blondie's Clem Burke, Silverhead's Michael Des Barres, Silverhead and Blondie bassist Nigel Harrison and ex-Sex Pistol Steve Jones; Jones had recently kicked heroin with the aid of Sugerman and Harrison. It was an inspired pairing, and singer Michael Des Barres stepped back with good grace, although Chequered Past's fifth member, Tony Sales, was understandably upset at not being included, given his previous relationship with Jim; the insult was compounded by the fact Jim seemed to be avoiding him.

With a clean-cut, organised Iggy singing and directing rehearsals, the quartet, all efficient and drugs-free, spent a couple of days working up the song at EMI America's rehearsal studio on the Sunset Strip; Jim was focused, and showed his familiar, hard-working, creative side, working up perhaps seven or eight sets of lyrics, remembers Nigel Harrison, for the intricate song arrangement.

Despite his clean-cut, reformed image, it turned out that Iggy
was still in love with the idea of chaos and drama and the conflicts
that often made music – and life – exciting. There was one last
escapade, which started when he sent Robert Matheu and Steve
Jones off to borrow a Les Paul guitar from David Bowie. The two
were delighted with their errand and the sight of David's abode
just behind Sunset, which was furnished in a tasteful East Indies
style; David was in town to play the Los Angeles Forum, and Jones
chatted with him for ten or fifteen minutes. But when Matheu
brought the guitarist back to the studio, he realised the stunt was at
least partly a ruse to keep Jones – who was under heavy orders to
stay drug-free – away from Danny and Iggy, who were 'definitely
up to something'.

Once the session started, says Nigel Harrison, 'Iggy was
buzzing!' The singer had 'scabs of cocaine and a cold sweat, and
everything we'd rehearsed went right out the window'. They
started taping at Cherokee studios at four in the afternoon, and at
four in the morning the band had run through perhaps thirty different versions of the song; for the final version, Iggy made
Harrison play two bass parts, then came up with yet another set of
lyrics and contributed a crazed vocal performance. The recording
sounded all the more thrilling for the fact you could hear the musicians tracking Iggy, locked onto him like guided missiles on the
trail of a fighter jet. Although, as with all of Iggy's music, this song
had little connection with blues, its very mutability recalls the way
John Lee Hooker's musicians would swerve to follow their singer.
'There is an analogy between Iggy's music and someone like
Hooker,' says Clem Burke, 'in the way it doesn't have to be completely in time and meter – he leads the band with his movement
and expression and being primitive. It's a jazz ethic. And to work
with the energy he exudes was amazing.' With its claustrophobic
semitonal riffs, vaguely reminiscent of the *Batman* theme, Jones's
roaring guitars and galloping, muscular bass and drums from
Harrison and Burke, 'Repo Man' was undeniably the best rock
song Iggy had recorded since *New Values* days – it was also scarily

appropriate for a skewed LA movie whose script was inspired by the Liverpool-born Cox's time spent studying at UCLA, during which he lived next to an auto repossession specialist. The song was the highlight of a raucous, rowdy soundtrack that leant heavily on LA punk bands including Black Flag and the Circle Jerks; it was significant, too, in that it illustrated how Iggy's music sounded as contemporary against a backdrop of 1980s hardcore as it had against 1970s punk.

'Repo Man' provided a fitting coda to Jim's Los Angeles experiences, which had inspired both the wired optimism of *Fun House* and the washed-up rootlessness of *Kill City*. But where both of those albums had embodied a current or imminent crisis, 'Repo Man' commemorated one; in the following years Iggy Pop would generally only get loaded, he says, at 'weekends and special occasions'. There were several strands to this profound turnaround in Jim's life: as well as the crucial new element of financial security, the encouragement of Murray Zucker and other professionals and the influence of Suchi, Jim's own intelligence and even his narcissism all unmistakeably told him, 'It never looks good to be forty and failed.'

As much as he had deluded himself, says Jim, there was a point at which he was forced to realise that 'there was a line I was crossing into picaresque behaviour. I was becoming Don Quixote. There's a fine line between entertaining flamboyance and being a prat – I had known I was becoming one [earlier], but that realisation would last for about thirty seconds.'

Tellingly, Jim describes how in life, little by little, 'you change as much as you have to'. By the autumn of 1983 he finally had no choice. The example of 'Repo Man' notwithstanding, he had been forced to recognise that the habits that had once powered his music were now handicapping it. In place of drugs, success and normality would be the experiences Jim would now experiment with, and savour. Without the aid of conventional therapy, or rehab, he simply decided to give up drink and cocaine relying solely on his willpower. While there were occasional relapses, and even a couple of frenzied spending sprees, this was pretty much how it would stay.

After three months in Los Angeles, it was time for a more traditional therapy in the form of a vacation at the invitation of David Bowie, whose Serious Moonlight tour had concluded in Bangkok on 12 December. Jim and Suchi flew over to meet with David and Coco for their trip to Bali and Java after the tour finished. The quartet spent New Year's Eve together, and over the vacation David and Jim came up with a new song, 'Tumble And Twirl', their first real collaboration in seven years and the beginning of a renewed songwriting partnership that would underpin both of their next albums, albeit one that was radically different in mood from the manic creative energy of *Lust For Life* and *"Heroes"*.

For Jim and Suchi, there was a quick trip to Manhattan in February 1984 looking for a new apartment; like many, they found the rounds of real-estate agents and overpriced property a drag, so they flew down to Myrtle Beach, South Carolina, where James Sr and Louella had retired in the autumn of 1982, to relax; Jim spent much of his time playing golf with his dad. Back in New York a couple of weeks later, they found a rental in the Gramercy Park area, and Suchi and Jim spent much of the time exploring the neighbourhood together, like wide-eyed tourists, before heading for Canada in May, where David Bowie was recording what would become *Tonight*, the follow-up to his multi-million-selling *Let's Dance*.

For perhaps the first time, David Bowie was about to deliver a train-wreck of an album. Again, for the first time, David Bowie – a personality who, like Jim, was so often animated with an infectious, boyish enthusiasm – seemed bored. And according to Hugh Padgham, who would be credited as producer on this problematic, but ironically bestselling album, the one change that would have made the work better would have been more input from Jim Osterberg: 'I think Jim was there for around five days, he was an inspirational influence. If he had been around for longer, we might actually have had a great album.'

Tonight, it turns out, was rather like Iggy's own *Soldier*, meandering through two producers, with no guiding ethos and generally indifferent material. Bowie had recruited a new producer, Derek

Bramble, who soon proved inadequate for the task. Padgham, who'd already produced huge hits for the Police, had taken the gig as engineer because he was eager to work with David, so was the perfect person to step in when Bramble left the session after a couple of weeks. Yet Padgham ultimately found the experience frustrating. David was energetic, chain-smoking with that slightly jittery intensity, but most of his energies seemed focused on outside distractions, rather than the songs. They were recording in a residential studio, Le Studio, in the rather boring provincial ski resort of Morin Heights, Quebec, and David seemed more preoccupied with picking up a local girl, who invariably had a friend in tow. Jim, in comparison, was a calming influence. 'He was laid-back . . . *very* laid-back, I did wonder if he might be on tranquillisers,' says Padgham, and the two had experimented on more inventive, left-field material that, if included, would have hugely improved the final results, Padgham believes.

There was still plenty of David's craftsmanship on view – the album's major hit, 'Blue Jean', was neatly constructed, with a luxurious sheen that concealed the absence of an inspiring chorus – but for once, he seemed to have run out of creative ideas. In Berlin, in Jim's company, he had fused a kind of European expressionism and intensity with jagged electronic instrumentation and R&B rhythms, making music that was uniquely emotive and original. This time around, the guiding principle seemed to be that of recording an assortment of cover versions in a bland, airbrushed reggae style. Yet there must surely have been another motive at play when one considers that five of the nine songs included on the album feature Iggy Pop's name on the credits: the newly written 'Tumble And Twirl' and 'Dancing With The Big Boys', plus 'Tonight' (in a dreadful reggaefied version, with Tina Turner duetting on over-emotive, strangulated vocals) and 'Neighborhood Threat' from *Lust For Life*, and finally 'Don't Look Down', one of Iggy and James Williamson's last collaborations, from *New Values*.

David Bowie had been commendably just in his dealings with Jim back in the Berlin era, careful to point out that they were equals and avoid any patronising implications that he had rescued his friend. And although David's recording of 'China Girl' brought huge financial benefits for Jim, the song was undoubtedly included on *Let's Dance* because of its obvious commercial potential. Yet it's hard to see the recording of 'Neighborhood Threat' and 'Don't Look Down', both fine but hardly commercial songs, as anything other than an act of charity, an impression deepened by Padgham's memories of David, during the quieter moments in Morin Heights, proudly telling him, 'You know, I rescued Iggy.' Padgham was treated to a long yarn depicting Iggy's craziness, as David described how Iggy's tour of Australia and New Zealand was cancelled because of legal threats from a woman in the audience whom Iggy had accidentally injured, kicking her in the chin and in the process making her bite off a chunk of her tongue. (The story, says then road manager Henry McGroggan, was apocryphal.) The implication seemed to be that Iggy was every bit as unreliable as his public image suggested, although it's possible that this was behaviour as much to be admired as sniggered over. Certainly, if Bowie thought of this period as one characterised by his own largesse, rather than a partnership of equals, there was some truth in it: despite its generally insipid quality, *Tonight* became Bowie's fastest-selling album to date, reaching platinum status in just six weeks and promising Jim a substantial income over the following year. In the mid-1980s, mechanical royalties on a full-price album were approximately 5 cents per track, per copy sold, which would mean earnings of over $100,000 from those six weeks alone; that sum would probably have been equalled by air-play royalties over the same period.

That autumn, Iggy's new-found celebrity as collaborator with Bowie on the latter's glossiest, blandest album to date led to him being featured in *People* magazine, with colour photos that depicted the Godfather of Punk shopping for fabrics with Suchi in Manhattan, or vacuuming in his new, top-floor Greenwich Village apartment. There was something touching about seeing Iggy and Suchi as a celebrity couple, as well as the notion of this alien, who'd fallen to earth from Planet Rock, becoming gradually familiar with everyday traditions. 'My hand still shakes when I make out a cheque,' he told writer David Fricke, 'or my eyes get fussy and I can't see. It's because a cheque always was something that was used by people I didn't like.'

In most respects, the image of Jim and Suchi at home in Manhattan was one of an innocent domesticity. Jim would get up 5 or 6am and potter around, enjoying his thoughts in the stillness of the early morning. As had become his habit since moving to Brooklyn, he'd type perhaps a couple of pages of poetry, prose or odd ideas; often he'd read through the papers and clip out stories, underlining resonant or quirky phrases which he'd work up into random collages. Usually he'd tidy up some of the debris from the previous night and clear up the papers and magazines; then he'd fetch a take-out breakfast for the two of them when Suchi woke up, vacuum the apartment and sometimes make hamburgers for lunch. 'I'm basically garbage, vacuuming and bits and pieces patrol and she's got the washing, cooking's half and half and I help with shopping,' was how he described the allocation of domestic chores. In the afternoons he might take long walks on the way home with his shopping; Suchi might get to work on either of the two sewing machines she'd set up in the apartment, using fabric chosen on their jaunts around the city. The days of jumping in a cab to see friends, as he'd done in Brooklyn, were over; instead he and Suchi would take the subway around Manhattan, careful lest their outgoings exceed their income.

Many hours, in late 1984, were occupied in filling out the interminable immigration forms for Suchi; it was to clarify her residency status, Jim would explain later, that the two would get married the following year – one senses that Midwest embarrassment at expressing personal feelings in the practical, businesslike rationale Jim espoused for his second marriage. They made a sweet, almost childlike couple, those around them thought; charming, not particularly lovey-dovey – but attentive to each other, in a caring, innocent kind of way.

At other times there would be odd little conversations with other residents in the same block, including photographer Robert Mapplethorpe, or visits to a local health club, followed by TV in the evenings, or perhaps relaxing with a novel by V.S. Naipaul or Paul Theroux. On quiet afternoons or mornings Jim would take his tiny Brother EP20 typewriter to the park and work on more ideas, sometimes for three or four hours a day. Around the end of 1984, he enrolled in an acting class. Such was the routine, typical of perhaps thousands of New Yorkers lucky enough to have a small private income, that defined Jim Osterberg's peaceful new life, which was punctuated only by the occasional vacation in Mexico.

Some time in 1984, Jim and David had discussed making an album together; indeed, in September, Bowie told the NME that recording an album with Iggy was his main ambition for the following year, alongside writing something 'extraordinary and adventurous' for himself. But apparently he was in no particular hurry: the creative blitz of 1976 and 1977 seemed a thing of the past, and for most of 1985 Bowie busied himself with two movie projects, Absolute Beginners and Labyrinth. Bowie's musical efforts were mainly confined to recording the B-side of Band Aid's charity single 'Do They Know It's Christmas', together with a magisterial, grandstanding performance at Live Aid that July.

By the spring of 1985, however, Jim had pieced together eight or nine songs, and intent on getting things going on his own called up Steve Jones, who was at a loose end now that Chequered Past had splintered in the wake of their poorly received debut album. The last time Jim and Steve worked together, eighteen months before, they'd both been struggling with going straight. This time around, once Jim flew to LA where they rented a house and worked on songs throughout June, they revelled in the new-found experience of being sober, organised and professional. Each time the inspiration faltered, rather than 'taking some drug or getting drunk' they would head for the beach. Within the month they worked up twenty songs, and went on to record nine of them in September and early October at a home studio in Hancock Park owned by fashion and glamour photographer Olivier Ferrand. The songs were simple and strong; Jones's sparkly, multilayered guitars and the simple drum-machine rhythm tracks left plenty of room for Iggy's voice, which sounded warm, clear and almost affable. Jim started shopping the tapes around New York and they were already generating interest, he says, when he got a call from David early in November, saying, 'I want to play you some demos.' Jim's reply was, 'Great, I'll play you some of mine, too.'

David loved the songs, which included 'Cry For Love', 'Winners And Losers' and 'Fire Girl', but eminently practical as ever, told Jim, 'They're all mid-tempo, so you'll need some fast ones and some slow ones,' and volunteered to fill the gaps. In December, David, Jim, Suchi (and, probably, Coco) decamped to Bowie's holiday home in Mustique, taking along David's custom-built portable studio, then moved on to another of his houses in Gstaad. In between skiing, enjoying dinner parties and relaxing, David and Jim worked inter-mittently on writing more songs at a gentle, civilised pace, taking three months to build up enough material for an album. After a short break in March and April, David booked recording time at Mountain Studios in Montreux, an upscale, high-tech studio owned by the rock band Queen, which David had first used to record *Lodger* early in 1979; it was handy for David's Lausanne home, and he'd started to use it more often for soundtrack and demo work. The plan was that Steve Jones would play on the album, but according to Jim there was a last-minute glitch: 'He didn't understand about visas, and couldn't get out of America.' David, he says, 'wasn't too upset, as they didn't have a huge common vocabulary', and instead called up Kevin Armstrong – who'd been musical director for both Bowie's Live Aid appearance and his 'Dancing In The Street' duet with Mick Jagger – and Erdal Kizilcay, a classically trained multi-instrumentalist who'd worked with Bowie on demos for *Let's Dance* and co-written 'When The Wind Blows'.

It was a peaceful, civilised time, and together David and Jim crafted a peaceful, civilised album. Erdal Kizilcay and his wife had met Jim and Suchi a couple of months before at a dinner with

David and Coco, where David had mentioned that he wanted
Erdal to oversee most of the music. Erdal liked Jim and his jokes:
for instance, his wacky boasts about how many bags of potatoes he
could carry. Kevin Armstrong got to know Jim during a rowing
excursion on Lake Geneva; Jim was wearing glasses, had a short,
college-boy haircut, said 'cool' a lot, and pointed out the Villa
Diodati, where Lord Byron had entertained Percy and Mary
Shelley, and where Mary had written *Frankenstein* in a storytelling
competition. The air of European, jet-set sophistication was not
what Armstrong, who'd bought most of Iggy's albums as a
teenager, expected; his slight disorientation was increased by Jim's
manner: obviously cultured and intelligent, with an elegant, almost
military bearing. It was a big change from Alien Sex Fiend, the last
act that Armstrong had worked with, but it was somehow refreshing to watch Jim and David in the process of growing up, sorting
their lives out and relishing their status as survivors.

David seemed heart-warmingly devoted to the welfare of his
friend, and ran the sessions armed with a clipboard, ticking off a to-
do list of items to be recorded each day, dedicated to the task in
hand and imbued with his customary jittery intensity. In turn, Jim
seemed calm, focused, happy to be immersed in this little creative
bubble. By now, David too had apparently banished even occasional use of cocaine, but as Kevin Armstrong points out, this
didn't make him any more laid-back, for he was chain-smoking
sixty to eighty cigarettes a day and would bring his own espresso
machine and supply of Java coffee wherever he happened to be
working. 'He'd be chucking down the coffee and fags, and seriously it would be pretty neurotic and manic around him. Also,
being in the orbit of someone who's so hugely famous, there's a
kind of electrical crackle around them, because those people
behave differently, don't they?'

Kevin Armstrong would go on to work with Iggy for the next
eighteen months, and would later play in Tin Machine alongside
Bowie and the Sales brothers. He is well aware of the selfish, neurotic, narcissistic nature of the entertainment industry; still, having

seen Bowie working with Iggy at close quarters, he believed that he was seeing a real selflessness being played out. 'I really think it *was* selfless. His association with Iggy always reflected well on him, sure, but I think he was quite simply helping his friend. He was genuinely saying, hang on, Iggy needs a hand here – I'm the guy that can do it, I've done it before and I'll do it again.'

That selflessness was epitomised by the song 'Shades', which David had written after seeing Jim give Suchi a present. 'He turned it around,' says Jim, 'made it into one of those "reformed guy" kinda songs.' The lyric unwraps an image of the narrator's surprise at receiving a present – 'I never thought I was worth much, or that anyone would treat me this way' – while the tune itself was based around the same five notes of 'Cry For Love', in a kind of tonal empathy. The song seemed the perfect metaphor for David's sonic rehabilitation of his friend, who for years now had been regarded as a pariah by the record industry. Alongside 'Absolute Beginners', 'Shades' was the best ballad that Bowie would write during the 1980s, a period in which his fortunes as a singles artist seemed on the wane. Now he simply gave away one of his best efforts to his friend.

Even David's more workmanlike songs, such as 'Hideaway', with its simple three-chord structure and crisp Linn Drum beat, displayed an effervescence and deftness that seemed sorely lacking on Bowie's own overblown *Tonight*. Iggy, too, seemed to pull something unique out of the bag in the form of 'Cry For Love', a conventional, confessional, almost slick ballad that marked a new Bowie-esque craftsmanship in his songwriting. For all its professionalism, the song was nonetheless affecting and sincere – it even featured the LA-bound Steve Jones, whose guitar solo from the September demo was edited into the finished take. Even old friends like Jim McLaughlin from the Iguanas would recognise 'Cry For Love' as a new departure, an admission that this ambitious, confident man was vulnerable: 'He's saying he's got a soul and a heart that is easily bruised, and that he lets himself be used because he needs somebody so bad. That's revealing him in a way I never knew, and I became a complete believer in his music after that.'

The album that would eventually be titled *Blah Blah Blah* was undoubtedly a work characterised by professionalism rather than excess and by order rather than chaos, and for that reason it would be described by Iggy supporters as an 'Iggy-flavoured Bowie album'. Yet if it's classified as a Bowie album, it definitely qualifies as Bowie's finest work of the era, with better songwriting and more energy than Bowie's own *Tonight* and its successor, *Never Let Me Down*. The only serious questionmark attaching to *Blah Blah Blah*, however, was whether it would succeed in its primary aim: to establish the label-less Iggy Pop as a viable commercial artist.

The answer came in within weeks of tapes being distributed to record companies in New York. Richard Branson, who was planning to set up the Virgin label in the United States, made a personal call to Iggy to get him to sign to his label. Nancy Jeffries, of A&M records, was another enthusiast: 'I loved the record. It came in pretty much finished, and was almost like a David Bowie record that as a record company you wished you'd had, but never got.'

Jeffries, one of New York's most-respected A&Rs – she'd made her name by discovering Suzanne Vega – was more than just a Bowie fan. She was also the ex-singer of cult 1960s band the Insect Trust, and was intimately aware of Iggy Pop's history, for her quirky, eclectic band had once opened for the Stooges in Ann Arbor. She was surprised and enthused by the fact that the album revealed a new facet of Iggy. 'For my money, and perhaps this is speaking as a woman, the fact the man can write these beautiful songs that are very moving, and display this intelligence, was a wonder.' Jeffries was also confident that the album could get played on the radio, but the price tag was large – probably $500,000, which included a production fee for Bowie – and she had to clear the deal with A&M's founder Jerry Moss. In the end, A&M made the successful bid over Virgin, for Jim was keen to sign with a company that was established in the US. 'The money was big,' says Jeffries, 'but with David Bowie's name attached it wasn't as difficult as it might have been. Everybody came in with their assets – it was like, "Here we are, we've done this, we're the coolest people who ever lived. Here's something you can sell and you can use our name."'

Everything that had gone so wrong on *Party* seemed to go right on *Blah Blah Blah*, aided by Jim's undoubted charm, which impressed all of A&M's staff; Suchi, who was supportive and particularly good at remembering people's names, and Jim's efficient, likeable new manager, Art Collins, added to the air of professionalism. But a key component of the success of *Blah Blah Blah* was an avowed Iggy fan in A&M's London office, marketing manager Jason Guy. Guy was one of the generation of English kids who had auditioned for teenage bands by playing 'Search And Destroy', and as he listened to the pre-release tape of *Blah Blah Blah* he started pondering about the album's opening song: a straightforward, throbbing version of 'Real Wild Child (Wild One)', the sole worldwide hit of 1950s Australian rock 'n' roller Johnny O'Keefe (the song had also been covered by American rockers Jerry Allison and Jerry Lee Lewis). 'I had a hunch that "Real Wild Child" was a good Christmas party single,' says Guy. 'Everybody thinks pop and R&B are the big party singles, but if you sit and watch accountants, they like that rock 'n' roll stuff. If you want to see them lurching around drunk on the floor, that's what they do it to.' A small gang of Iggy fans in the London office, including art director Jez Pearce, press officer Chris Poole and radio plugger Alan Jones, shared his hunch. 'This could be a surprise hit, is how we presented it to the media and radio. We just knew it could be a dark horse at Christmas and we were kind of right. It just exploded and we cobbled together a video, made it a priority record and hammered it through. It was just one of those moments when the stars align.'

It is one of the traditions of rock 'n' roll that pioneering American acts, like Jimi Hendrix or Nirvana, notch up their first hits in the unregimented, non-conformist UK market. In the most delicious of ironies, Iggy Pop, the punk rock pariah, enjoyed his first hit single, reaching number ten in the UK charts, by being marketed to drunken accountants and other salary slaves enjoying their moment of token rebellion in the intoxicated run-up to Christmas.

An extra piquance was added when A&M's Alan Jones arranged an in-person appearance on the Saturday morning *No. 73* kids' TV show. Skipping and bouncing around ludicrously in front of the pre-teen studio audience, Iggy was the last act, and as the credits rolled at the end of the show he seized a large teddy bear and started copulating with it. 'The credits were coming up and the host was sort of dancing along, as they do, and their faces were aghast, grinning and trying to clap while he was shagging this giant teddy bear. It was a great TV moment,' remembers Jason Guy fondly. For many years afterwards, the tape of Iggy simulating anal sex with a huge teddy bear was a staple of A&M's Christmas parties.

Although 'Real Wild Child' had been picked out as a single by A&M in the UK, in New York the staff had fallen for 'Cry For Love', says Nancy Jeffries: 'I see record companies do that, where they ignore an obvious single because they fall in love with something more soulful – then at the end of the day they can't really sell that to the radio people.' 'Cry For Love' received minimal airplay, and consequently sold poorly as a single, and the sales of *Blah Blah Blah* were generally respectable, if not dazzling, reaching number 43 in the UK, 74 in the US, as well as making the Top Twenty in several European markets, where Iggy had built up a strong fanbase with his incessant touring. 'It did pretty well, but not amazingly well,' was the verdict of Jeff Gold, Vice President of Creative Services at A&M in New York; yet Iggy's charm and patience, during the inevitable endless conferences and meet 'n' greets, made the A&M staff feel good about having him on their roster.

Once again, Iggy Pop would hit the road to promote his new record. Instructed to assemble a band of English musicians, Kevin Armstrong selected keyboard player and guitarist Seamus Beaghen, who'd previously played with Madness, plus drummer Gavin Harrison and bassist Phil Butcher. In October, they launched into a daunting schedule that would run for almost ten months, with a short break that Christmas. These were the longest shows Iggy had ever played, many of them ninety minutes a night, plus there was the added burden of endless meetings with local promotions people and press. For the first time in his life he would play night after night without the aid of drugs or alcohol. 'And he was taking to it like a duck to water,' says Kevin Armstrong. 'And I never felt like this was a real effort or really stressful, he was exuding good energy all the time.' For Seamus Beaghen, like Jim, learning to play sober was a totally new experience. 'I found it quite scary at first, but really got into it, you're totally aware of what's going on – and you suddenly seem to have loads more time.'

As the band travelled across North America in their tour bus, Jim conserved his energies, relaxing on the bus, always focusing on the evening's performance, but invariably ready to chat volubly after the performance with visiting fans and celebrities, such as Elmore Leonard, who turned up for the Detroit show. After the first two-month stint across North America and Europe, there was a three-month run of stadium dates supporting the Pretenders, starting in January 1987; at practically every show Chrissie Hynde would kiss the stage where Iggy had performed ('despite the fact it was covered with mucus and other bodily fluids,' says Armstrong), as if she were not worthy to follow her hero. Gradually, the band had introduced more Stooges songs into their set, which was growing more intense by the day, and by April, when they played Fender's Ballroom in Long Island without the Pretenders, there was mayhem; with too many people crammed into the club, and most of them seemingly on angel dust or worse, one PA stack toppled over. And, for the first time, Armstrong saw Iggy revelling in the chaos. 'He was really enjoying it. And it was the one little flashback where I thought, God, there is a demon in there.'

There were other, odd little flashbacks: moments outside hotels, when groupies who'd entertained Iggy on his previous tours showed up. He would tantalise them, joking to his band about how they wanted what was inside his pants, while still dancing around in his coquettish manner, almost as he had back in Prime

Movers days, seemingly immune to temptation. Although twenty years older than most of his band, he had a physical and mental stamina they all envied, with an endurance and presence they couldn't quite fathom. In particular, he had an almost mystical ability to calm crazed fans who managed to evade the minimal backstage security. 'He seemed to be able to communicate something to them on a deep level,' remembers Armstrong, 'as if saying, I have been as crazy as you and even crazier and I understand what you're going through. He would deal with them really calmly, he'd say calm down, and touch them, take time to diffuse the situation – and these people would go limp immediately. It was like a benediction.'

Although Jim exuded calm and a sense of control, by six months into the tour there was a brutal, testosterone-laden atmosphere backstage, and Armstrong in particular was starting to fall apart; bassist Phil Butcher bailed out just before a short run of Japanese dates in April 1987 and was replaced by Barry Adamson, who had just left Nick Cave's Bad Seeds. At one point Armstrong confided in his employer, telling him his marriage was cracking under the strain of his insatiable cavorting with groupies. 'I was telling him about my wife, my kids, so he turned around and snapped at me, You're better off without 'em!' Iggy's opinion, it seemed, was 'That's what guitarists are about. Go out and conquer.' Even Seamus Beaghen, who'd kept things cheerful with his skits and jokes, was 'frazzled' by the end of a second and final European tour in July 1987, while Kevin Armstrong was well on the way to being another victim of the Iggy Pop demolition derby. 'In the end, frankly, I was a bit of a wreck. A mess. I had to do a lot of hard thinking about myself. And then I had to put my life back together, brick by brick.'

Exhausted, but still slightly exhilarated by their experience, most of the band members returned to London, while Jim and Suchi flew back to New York. Iggy's tour had drawn many near-ecstatic reviews; he'd proven himself focused and hard-working and had finally racked up his first hit single. At last, it seemed, he could enjoy a measure of security. As usual, events would intervene.

With a full fourteen months of recording and gruelling touring behind him, Jim Osterberg returned from the Blah Blah Blah tour and, for the first time, could truly enjoy the fruits of a certain kind of respectability. An awareness that popular culture had finally caught up with him was heightened by the impressive start he'd made with his acting career, which included a brief cameo role alongside Suchi in Alex Cox's *Sid And Nancy* movie and an appearance as a pool-hustling wannabe in Martin Scorsese's *The Color Of Money*. The sense that his time had arrived was deepened by the dominance in the arts of all those left-field people who admired him, from Andy Warhol to John Waters, Jim Jarmusch to avantgarde composer Robert Ashley, who tried to persuade Iggy to sing in his opera *Atalanta*. For a man with a skyscraper ego, the feeling that he'd finally been vindicated was powerful and liberating, although he underlined his avoidance of the mainstream by moving from Greenwich Village – which seemed full of people touting movie scripts or arts projects – to the Christadora apartment building on Avenue B in the Lower East Side, which seemed, like Jim Osterberg, to be a little more unpredictable and on the edge.

For the many people involved with Jim over the end of 1987 and the beginning of 1988, their dealings were characterised by an impressive professionalism. Working steadily towards his next release, Jim decided right from the start he wanted to make a rock album dominated by guitars, which would feature Steve Jones. The crucial choice of producer seemed straightforward, too. Both Jim and David Bowie had admired Bill Laswell's production of PiL's *Album* – a controversial work, during the recording of which the hip, in-demand producer and John Lydon had sacked all of PiL's existing line-up and replaced them with session musicians – and it turned out that Laswell had hung out in Ann Arbor and had even seen the Stooges' performance at the post-apocalyptic Goose

Lake festival. The two got on well during Laswell's production of Ryuichi Sakamoto's *Neo Geo* – Iggy had contributed a warm, crooning vocal on the song 'Risky' – and Laswell soon became a regular visitor to Jim's Avenue B apartment to lay plans. For musicians, Jim retained Seamus Beaghen from his live band, and recruited bassist Leigh Foxx to replace Barry Adamson, who was embarking on a new solo career with UK record label Mute, and hired ex-Psychedelic Furs' drummer Paul Garisto. Jim seemed to have a plan for seemingly every aspect of the projected album, right down to the sleeve design, which would be the responsibility of Grande Ballroom poster designer Gary Grimshaw, and the video, for which he picked out Sam Raimi, the *Evil Dead* director whose warped but hard-hitting aesthetic seemed perfect for the raw, back-to-basics rock album that Jim had in mind. Every prospective collaborator was impressed by Jim's clear direction, as well as by the way, like Bowie, he was happy to delegate to people he trusted. 'He had a vision but he didn't micro-manage, he was perfect to work for,' remembers Grimshaw. Even minor details, such as booking the musicians' plane tickets and finding them nice apartments near Avenue B, were taken care of by Art Collins and Suchi. Nothing had been left to chance. Apart from the songs.

All of those who worked on the recording of *Instinct* remember the most minute attention being paid to the sound, with loving care lavished on Iggy's vocals, which were recorded in a Brooklyn basement studio for the requisite warm but edgy resonance. The band had experimented with the arrangements of each song before entering the studio, and Steve Jones had apparently worked out a comprehensive plan for each of his guitar overdubs. Each guitar part was tracked several times, to combine a solid bottom end, a muscular middle and a jagged treble edge, a high-tech approach to recording heavy rock that had been more or less invented by producer Mutt Lange via his mega-selling albums with AC/DC. Yet throughout all this painstaking work, no one seems to have been concerned by the stultifyingly predictable material. There was perhaps the faintest reminder of Iggy and Jones's thrilling teamwork on

'Repo Man' on the album's standout track, 'Cold Metal', with its 'I play tag in the auto graveyard' vocal hook, but otherwise song followed turgid song at the same plodding pace.

Before the recordings began, Laswell had considered whether to take the aggressive approach he had with PiL: 'I probably would have done what I had been doing in the eighties, which is band comes in, fire the band and do all the music yourself. Initially, I was probably thinking about making a much different record, but I realised to do that I'd really have to pull a number on him and actually it's a risk. There was no guarantee. It could have been a disaster.' There seemed instead to be far more sense in using the skills of Steve Jones and following Jim's vision of returning to the rock sound he felt he'd abandoned on *Blah Blah Blah*. Yet the results of this sensible, logical approach were nonetheless a disaster: a mind-numbingly dull exercise in corporate rock. Iggy had made bad albums before, but this was the first time he'd been boring. And even the corporation that was contracted to release the album lost much of its enthusiasm when faced with its dull, dated riffing. Despite the usual heavy touring – this time with a 'hair' band featuring Hanoi Rocks' Andy McCoy on guitar, while our hero sported an ill-advised sleeveless denim jacket and poodle-rock teased, gelled hair – *Instinct* sank without trace, missing the US Top 100 entirely. Unimpressed by *Instinct*, A&M had spent significantly less on promoting it than it had on its predecessor, and when it came time for a follow-up, the company offered half the recording budget for that of *Instinct*. By now Jim had a new A&R to deal with, and as they discussed the album it became clear that: 'I didn't like him and he didn't like me – and in the end it was a way for me to walk.' Iggy's contract was dropped by mutual agreement, and what had looked like a promising career revival was at an end.

CHAPTER 17

Undefeated

By the end of 1987, Iggy Pop's career seemed to demonstrate that simple professionalism could make the difference between success and failure. With the right skills, the right voice, an engaging reformed rebel image and efficient marketing, comfortable prosperity seemed inevitable. But real life turned out to be not so simple. The years that looked so comfortable and safe from the outside turned out to be full of unrelenting work and the knowledge that, at any moment, it could all fall apart.

The commercial failure of *Instinct* sealed what had been a dreadful decade in terms of Iggy Pop recordings. One album, *Blah Blah Blah*, could be regarded as a qualified success, but most of the credit for that rested with David Bowie. Besides, David and Iggy's artistic relationship promised diminishing creative returns compared to the heady, chaotic days of *Lust For Life*, while Iggy's other creative partnerships throughout the decade had ultimately proved artistic and commercial failures. Even the title 'Godfather of Punk' was an honorific that had diminished in value, as the New Wave finally receded in favour of sleek, airbrushed rock 'n' roll manufactured by slick platinum-selling bands like Van Halen and Bon Jovi.

There was one bright spot. Having spent much of the last decade on the road, investing so much of his time in intense, gruelling touring, Iggy could at least claim a devoted fan base. Yet even the new reformed Iggy found it impossible to totally erase the record industry's conviction that he was, at heart, a misguided, deranged loser, someone who'd always threatened to crossover, but who would never quite cut it as a major artist. Ian Hunter, Iggy's fellow MainMan artist, had proclaimed in the mid-1970s that 'Iggy's the all-time should-have-but-didn't – and it's because he's not quite good enough'. Well over a decade later, that opinion was widely shared; as Jim remembers, 'I had a terrible rep in the USA; terrible. Somewhere between Andy Kaufman and a serial killer.'

If that were not enough, Jim was now entering his forties, a tough age for a man who'd always revelled in his own beauty and boasted of his indestructibility.

If Jim Osterberg's confidence did flag in the late 1980s, though, there were few outward signs. Even without a record label, he was fortunate enough to have a persistent but likeable manager who never seemed to give up on his charge. Nancy Jeffries, the A&R who had signed Iggy to A&M back in 1986, had been impressed with Art Collins, who had first made his name working for Atlantic and later became president of Rolling Stones Records. 'He was always lovely,' says Jeffries. 'Very persistent, but at the same time very friendly.' A few months after signing Iggy to A&M, Jeffries had followed her old boss Jordan Harris to take a dream job building up the artist roster from scratch at the newly established Virgin America. Eventually, Jeffries took a call from Art Collins, telling her, 'We're free. Do you want to do anything?'

One of Nancy Jeffries' first signings at Virgin had been Keith Richards, as a solo artist. This would prove a prescient move, helping the aggressive new label headed by Jordan Harris and Jeff Ayeroff eventually to net the Rolling Stones and facilitate its sale to EMI at a humongous price, but at the time, says Jeffries, the deal provoked criticism: 'People felt that once you got past a certain age you weren't allowed to breathe any more, you weren't allowed to make music any more – and you should just go home.' Jeffries wanted to sign Iggy for much the same reason she had signed Keith Richards; but this would not be a big money signing. A deal was made on what were, thought Jim, 'very very good terms – for them. Low royalty, low budget, a no-security contract with all the options on their side.'

In Iggy Pop's long and colourful recording career, every record contract he'd ever signed had been launched in a blaze of optimism. This time around, he was joining a label launched by 'a couple of California hard-heads who weren't gonna fuck around', and there was a consciousness that if this new album failed 'they would have dropped me there and then'. For the first time, if he wanted to continue making music for a living, Iggy would make his next album believing that 'if it wasn't a hit . . . it was all over'.

Fortunately, also for the first time in Jim's life, his record company suggested a producer who was 'nice! Who I can talk to!'

Don Was and Jim Osterberg had gravitated towards each other at a record-industry dinner, when it turned out that the Stooges were one of the first bands who had 'corrupted' the young Donald Fagenson, as he was christened, when he was at Oak Park high school in Detroit. The two collaborated on 'Livin' On The Edge Of The Night' for Ridley Scott's *Black Rain* (the song ultimately didn't make its intended slot), but Don Was remained in awe both of Jim Osterberg's startling intelligence and articulacy, and Iggy Pop's music.

By now, Was qualified as one of America's hottest producers, having worked with the then down-and-out Bonnie Raitt on what turned out to be her bestselling album ever, *Nick of Time*. Yet Was had no complex masterplan of how to produce Iggy beyond concentrating on good songs that would demonstrate the intellect of Jim Osterberg, as well as the primal power of Iggy Pop. 'I always viewed it as me taking a black and white photo of Iggy; capturing how complex he was, what a unique character he was, what a deep guy he was.'

Was had decided right from the off to use the team of session musicians he'd called on for many recent projects, most notably the terrifyingly proficient drummer Kenny Aronoff (who'd made his name with Tony Defries' other big discovery, John Cougar Mellencamp). The main recordings were at LA's state-of-the-art Ocean Way studios, a place where, says Jim, 'these really expensive, muscular American rock stars make fantastically boring records'. The combination of classy studio and sophisticated musicians such as Aronoff, bassist Charlie Drayton and guitarists David Lindlay and Waddy Wachtel was a scary one; while he trusted Don Was, Jim was beset by doubts. But as the recordings commenced, the two evolved a new working technique, of Jim playing his electric guitar in the studio and teaching the musicians each song, then recording a take before they'd started to get comfortable. Jim's nerves eased when two other guest musicians who'd asked to play on the album, Slash and Duff of Guns N' Roses, arrived at the studio dressed in chain mail and studs, complaining that they'd set off all the metal-detectors in the airport, in true Spinal Tap style.

Just as the recording of Brick By Brick seemed to embrace convention, so did the songs: reflective adult ballads like 'Main Street Eyes', or bluesy rockers, like 'Home'. This was Iggy Pop the grown-up but still quirky rebel, in a safe package that was nonetheless refreshingly no-frills and almost minimal compared to the overblown rock fare of the late 1980s, with its booming drums and shrieking guitar solos. For the first time, Iggy sounded of his time; not ahead of his time, as on Fun House or The Idiot, nor behind it, like Instinct, and while there was undoubtedly a sense that this was a more acceptable Iggy, it was obvious that he was trying something new, rather than simply repeating himself. Much of the time, it seems, Iggy was still struggling to work out what his place in the world was. 'I Won't Crap Out' is the narrative of a man who made music as an outcast and now searches for new values in a corporate world; 'Candy', a duet with Cindy Pierson of the B-52s, is a poignant lament for Betsy Mickelsen, the 'beautiful, beautiful girl from the North' who, he says, haunts him still. For 'The

Undefeated', Iggy called in his son Eric Benson and a bunch of Eric's LA friends, including guitarist Whitey Kirst and bassist Craig Pike, whom he nicknamed 'the Leeching Delinquents', to hang out and sing in the studio. With the song done, and the session almost over, Iggy allowed himself a brief return to his old ways, hoovering up a huge line of cocaine off the mixing desk before taking Whitey and friends off to Club Vertigo, where Debbie Harry was playing that night. As Iggy and the young guitarist walked into the club the crowd parted to let Iggy and entourage through, and Debbie's band started up 'I Wanna Be Your Dog' in preparation for a duet. That night Iggy and Debbie dry-humped on stage, and a great evening was of course had by all.

Released as a single early in 1991, 'Candy' would be Iggy's first ever US hit single, scraping into the Top Thirty. *Brick By Brick* would become a gold album, shifting decent numbers in seemingly every overseas territory, staying in the US album charts for thirty-seven weeks and becoming Iggy Pop's bestselling album by far. The sense of a well-earned comeback was heightened by the success of 'Did You Evah', a kooky duet with Debbie Harry from *Red Hot + Blue*, the Cole Porter tribute album that benefited AIDS research.

There was, of course, a supreme irony in the fact that *Brick By Brick* would outsell the incandescent albums that had helped make Iggy a legend. The album was filled with occasionally subtle craftsmanship and intelligent lyrics and even today sounds far more arresting than contemporary albums by, say, Robert Plant or Mick Jagger. Yet the fact that *Brick By Brick* would go on to outsell the far more creative and tuneful *Lust For Life* is, in retrospect, ludicrous. But only about as ludicrous as the way in which *Lust For Life* had been scuppered by Elvis's seizure atop his throne.

As Jim Osterberg travelled around the world for the string of press and broadcast interviews to promote *Brick By Brick*, there was a sense that this final historical revenge was sweet. The scary manic fervour of his Berlin days was gone, as was the slightly sad grandiosity of the early 1980s. Instead, he would confess his

worries about working with Don Was and weave a fascinating narrative from the picaresque events of his life, mocking his own
ludicrous behaviour, yet remaining fiercely proud of the music he
had made, all the while commendably modest when discussing
the many musicians who now paid tribute to his music. The
impression was of a man who had lost most of his battles, yet after
twenty-one years had just heard he'd won the war.

Just as significant a sign that the world was turning Iggy Pop's
way came with his first big show that summer, the Gathering of the
Tribes at Shoreline Amphitheatre, which featured Seattle band
Soundgarden, who'd released their first EPs on Sub Pop and
recently signed to A&M. By the next summer, the same venue
would host the first Lollapalooza tour, signalling the death of the
hair metal bands who had suppurated the airwaves over the last
five years, and the rise of a new generation of bands headed by
Jane's Addiction, LA's Red Hot Chili Peppers and Nirvana, whose
breakthrough *Nevermind* would hit the UK Top Ten late in 1991,
and the US Top Ten the following January, going on to sell over
seven million copies.

The rise of these bands marked the point at which the values of
punk finally percolated into the American mainstream, and all of
the scene's key architects seemed to namecheck Iggy Pop. Jane's
Addiction and the Chili Peppers emerged from an LA music scene
in which Stooges covers like 'Search And Destroy' or 'I Got A Right'
had become staples, where Perry Farrell would play 'Fun House'
backstage and Chili's guitarist John Frusciante would say of the
Stooges that 'everything they did blows me away. They can't make
music with that attitude now.'

In June 1987, Iggy had joined Sonic Youth on stage at London's
Town and Country Club to perform 'I Wanna Be Your Dog'. 'This
was a crucial endorsement of Iggy as iconic American punk god-
head by a new generation,' says Keith Cameron, who would
become one of the key writers documenting Nirvana and other
Sub Pop bands for the *NME*. 'Prior to this, I think Iggy was someone respected for his past work but whose contemporary relevance

was minimal.' Two years later, the Stooges' influence on the emerging mainstream was signalled when Nirvana jammed the same song with Tad and Mudhoney at London's tiny Astoria club; Kurt Cobain would confide to his journals that *Raw Power* was his all-time favourite album and write a song, 'Talk To Me', for Iggy, while Sonic Youth's Thurston Moore would fantasise, 'I'd really like to see Nirvana as Iggy's backing band, that would be way cool.'

Undoubtedly, Iggy's had become a hip name to drop, but the Stooges' influence went far beyond mere lip-service: the guitar drone of 'I Wanna Be Your Dog' was easily discernible in Sonic Youth and Dinosaur Jr's ringing guitar sounds, while James Williamson's aggressive but concise guitar attack was most obviously recognisable in John Frusciante's playing. Iggy's lyrical and visual imagery was just as pervasive, whether it was in songs steeped in boredom and alienation ('oh well, whatever, never-mind'), Anthony Kiedis's appropriation of Iggy's shirtless *Fun House* look (together with lyrics proclaiming 'we can dance like Iggy Pop'), the ripped jeans sported by most of the Seattle bands, or the way in which crowd surfing and the breakdown of barriers between performer and audience that Iggy had invented became an integral part of rock performances. By the mid-1990s, almost every key stylistic element of Iggy and the Stooges had been absorbed into the American mainstream.

Crucially, most of the bands who would dominate the American 'alternative' and grunge scene of the 1990s would see Iggy as a still-vital force and an inspiring live performer, rather than a mere nostalgia act. Iggy's only rival as the spiritual father of this new movement was Lou Reed; yet by now Lou had become notorious for delivering limp, tedious live shows, and as Black Francis of Pixies, those vital precursors of grunge, puts it: 'I want to find the most true, pure rock and roll available from this time period of, say 1968 to 1977, and Iggy is it. I love Lou Reed, but who is more rocking? It's him. It's way more pure.' Like John Frusciante or Thurston Moore, Francis had studied the most obscure Stooges out-takes and bootlegs; at last, those lost works the Stooges had been compelled to make even when there was no prospect they would ever be heard had found an audience. After discovering *Lust For Life* and *The Idiot*, Francis had been the most moved by a collection of demos, including 'I Got A Right' and 'Johanna', released on Bomp: 'For me personally this is the most ice-hot, adrenalised, just full-on album . . . because there's no one there. There's no one there except them. Haunting is the right word for those demos.'

From being a kind of totem of old-school punk on the Virgin label, which was bought by EMI in 1992, Iggy Pop was becoming one of its hippest acts, sharing top billing at international festivals with the likes of Sonic Youth and Nick Cave; when Virgin came to release his next album, 1993's *American Caesar*, there was a new swagger in their pitch for the artist: 'Born in a log cabin by the Detroit river in 1862, Iggy Pop the punk pioneer cleared the land, killed the sharks and bears, and changed the sound of American music with his mighty axe and his band of Stooges.'

American Caesar was recorded with a largely new band (*Brick By Brick* tour bassist Craig Pike had been killed in a car accident in 1993), that included guitarist Eric Schermerhorn – who lived down the road from Jim in the West Village and had previously played in Tin Machine – and Eric's room-mate from college, curly-haired bassist Hal Cragin, plus drummer Larry Mullins, a longtime Iggy fan who'd 'stalked' him in the late 1980s and finally joined his band in 1990. Jim would approach writing sessions with an unrelenting work ethic, obviously in love with the stimulants that had fuelled his glory days but exhibiting impressive self-control. 'He'd drink half a glass of wine, go, man, that's good, and leave the rest undrunk,' says Schermerhorn. 'The same with a cigarette – he'd inhale deeply maybe twice, and you could tell it had a real effect on him, then he'd stub it out.'

Jim would get up early each morning each day and spend half an hour or so working on qigong, a form of t'ai chi that helped him keep his skinny body in trim, before walking over to Schermerhorn's apartment, often buoyed up with childlike glee by the odd sights he'd noticed en route, and then they'd work on material. The songs they developed showed Iggy liberated, confident and ready to experiment, and reflected his current reading matter, including Edward Gibbon's *Decline and Fall of the Roman Empire* ('It wasn't the condensed version, either,' says Schermerhorn).

Over the next couple of years Jim's hard core of friends included Johnny Depp, whose first encounter with Iggy had been at a show in Florida, back in 1980; Depp had made a nuisance of himself screaming obscenities after the gig and was rewarded with a close encounter with his hero, who walked right up to him and shouted, 'You little scumbag!' Thereafter Depp was a regular sight at Iggy shows in the early 1980s – Esther Friedmann certainly noticed him – and finally got to know Jim during the filming of John Waters' *Cry-Baby* in 1989. Two other regular friends included tattoo artist Jonathan Shaw, son of bandleader Artie Shaw, and Jim Jarmusch, who'd filmed Iggy with Tom Waits for his *Coffee And Cigarettes* project in 1992. But bit by bit, the friendship with David Bowie seemed to have receded into the background. There have been suggestions that there was a falling out over money when Jim bought back the masters of *The Idiot* and *Lust For Life* for reissue on Virgin, but Bowie himself offered the most perceptive explanation later in the decade, when he mentioned, candidly, 'I think there was a moment where Jim decided that he couldn't do a fucking article without my name being mentioned – and I don't think that's a very comfortable feeling.' There was a poignancy to Bowie's belief that Jim had taken umbrage at incessantly being linked to his so-called mentor: 'That's a shame, because I would have liked to remain closer to him.'

Jim and David's friendship had been a unique one in popular music, but perhaps, as in so many relationships, their egos couldn't be held in check for ever. 'I think in any close friendship you can use the word love,' says one observer who was close to both of them, 'and in many close friendships you'll see that one person loves the other more than the other loves him or her. And I believe David loved Jim more than Jim loved David. And, in the end, I think Jim found he could manage without him.' The complex interaction of two egotistical men had been characterised by mutual admiration and rivalry – 'They each have what the other guy wants,' says Eric Schermerhorn – yet, ultimately, it seems Bowie's respect for Iggy ran deeper than Iggy's respect for Bowie. Furthermore, by the mid-1990s, Bowie's cerebral, intellectual take on music was, Nirvana cover versions apart, out of favour compared to Iggy's visceral, intuitive approach, and there were other friends to be made.

As Bowie receded from Iggy's public circle of admirers, newer replacements emerged, most notably Henry Rollins, the one-time singer of Black Flag whose diverse output stretched to spoken-word performances and poetry (and who would later oversee a reprint of Iggy's *I Need More* at his own 2.13.61 publishing house). Rollins would be a key advocate for Iggy in the 1990s, extolling both his dumb punk onslaught and his eloquence.

It was in the glow of both general acclaim and financial security that Iggy went to New Orleans in September 1992 to record *American Caesar* with producer Malcolm Burn and the new band, whom he termed 'similar to what I started with, three lost souls who didn't fit anywhere'. The plan was that, as with the Stooges, the recording would stimulate a sense of crisis and push the whole outfit to the limit – a plan that worked, for there were many disagreements behind the scenes that somehow made for the edgiest most adventurous album Iggy had recorded in a decade or more. 'Wild America' was a tough, half-spoken meditation underpinned by a nasty, repetitive guitar riff that documents Iggy being thrilled by his country's edginess and repelled by its complacence; it is at once original and also evocative of the intensity and claustrophobia of *Fun House*. 'Hate' sets revenge fantasies to an unpredictable gothic rolling chord sequence, while 'It's Our Love' is an ethereal ballad with echoed drums and strings shimmering in the distance. Elsewhere, off-kilter but catchy songs utilise fairground drumbeats ('Highway Song') or set stream-of-consciousness imagery against a jug-band backing ('Fuckin' Alone'). It was with a sense of accomplishment that Iggy handed the tapes in to Virgin, only for them to say, according to Jim, 'We love the album – but where are the hits?' There followed, he says, the requisite artistic tantrum before he acceded to their suggestion that he record a version of 'Louie Louie', and then looked back through his old tapes to find the demo of 'Beside You', a ballad that he'd recorded with Steve Jones in the run-up to *Blah Blah Blah*.

If there was something depressing about acceding to his type-casting and recording 'Louie Louie', then Iggy didn't admit it, says bassist Hal Cragin. 'I thought it was a great decision. That was a very near and dear song for him because it was so raw and loose – the magic of it was a real template for his career.' In truth, the commitment with which Iggy and band revisit the hoary garage classic that launched Iggy the singing drummer is both scary and touching (even if, post 1978, it's difficult to dissociate the song from John Travolta and Olivia Newton John's disturbingly similar 'Summer Nights'). 'Beside You', a 1980s-style power ballad reminiscent of U2's 'With Or Without You', is similarly formulaic and affecting in equal measure, and went some way towards fulfilling Virgin's desires by scraping into the UK Top 50. However, *American Caesar*, which despite a couple of filler tracks was Iggy's most creative album of the 1990s, sold in barely respectable quantities, reaching number 43 in the UK, but missing the US Top 100.

The lacklustre sales of *American Caesar* were not a terminal problem, for as Hal Cragin points out, Iggy's live shows were making 'a ton of money', while his back catalogue was also generating a good income. But for the rest of the 1990s, Jim's life would settle into a calm routine where the next album would be made in ten days or so with a modest budget and ambitions, and where in general the surprises and the thrills were modest too. For all that, his influence would continue to percolate into new corners of the world's culture, as Iggy Pop began to be regarded as a more left-field and even more gnarled Keith Richards-style totem of rock 'n' roll cool. His image as a subversive mainstream personality spread wider via his guest appearances on Nickelodeon's hip kids' show *The Adventures of Pete and Pete*, plus roles in *Tank Girl*, *The Crow: City of*

Angels and a hilarious sequence in the *Rugrats* movie, where he voiced a newborn baby alongside Patti Smith, Beck and Laurie Anderson.

Appropriately enough, as Iggy Pop started to become a mainstream personality, Jim learned to take on serious responsibilities as a father. He and Esther had started looking after Eric for the odd week here and there in the early 1980s. Eric had later trained as an accountant and worked to get himself through college, but by 1990 had grown his hair and was planning a career as a rock singer, hanging out with bands in LA; his father arranged vocal lessons and, he says, did 'all the wrong things'. Eventually, Eric battled his own substance-abuse problems; Jim paid for his therapy, not, he says, 'out of any warm, fatherly concern. I dealt with it because I had to.'

Murray Zucker, who remained friends with the family, maintains that Jim's relationship with Eric demonstrated 'a loyalty, obligation and [a] sense of connection which sustained through the years'. Dr Zucker is surely the most objective of observers, but it's hard to square his observations with Iggy's own pronouncements on his son, which have at times been disturbingly cold-blooded: 'When he was in rehab they'd all blame me, and that's the sort of American thing I won't accept. That kind of "let's study your family" bullshit.' Jim would later employ his son as a personal assistant, but Eric never seemed able to earn his father's praise. Eric Schermerhorn, like many musicians who worked with Jim, remembers his generosity in, for instance, sharing songwriting royalties, but was unimpressed by his complaints about Eric: 'He was grumbling about dumping money on the kid. It was so selfish – what if he'd wanted to go to Harvard? And when you think about how his parents spoiled him.' Undoubtedly, Jim did try hard to be a good father; he simply didn't have the requisite abilities to be one, and would never acquire them.

Jim himself was solicitous about acknowledging the influence of his parents. ('One thing I should say is how supportive they've been of me,' he told me in 1993, 'that's why I've purposely used the name Osterberg more in recent years, in honour of their name.')

When Louella fell gravely ill before her death in March 1996, Jim was devastated and would break down sobbing at some points, channelling his grief into songs he poured onto tape. Jim Osterberg Sr was overwhelmed, says Nick Kent, who consoled Jim Jr on the phone. 'I spoke to Jim about his father because his mother had just died and his father had almost gone completely crazy with the grief – but his dad had been able to pull himself back.' Jim talked at length about his father, remembers Kent. 'His dad is a loner, an intellectual – someone who pulled himself up through singular odds and didn't have an easy time. At the same time his father found solace and peace in his relationship with his wife because they really were one of those inseparable couples. Jim was always in awe of that.'

As Jim approached fifty, like many of his generation a youthful rebelliousness was augmented with a respect for what his parents had achieved. It seemed more apparent now that he'd inherited his father's dedicated work ethic, for even over a period when the income from live performances was no longer vital, he continued to work the road year after year, evangelistic about the Stooges' music, and still shot-through with the competitiveness he'd exhibited back in Detroit.

Schermerhorn, Cragin and Mullins were a dedicated little band of brothers, assisted by a tiny crew headed by Henry McGroggan and Iggy's personal roadie, Jos Grain, and although their leader might often disappear into the dressing room after the show, paranoid that the audience's response had not been sufficiently ecstatic, he was still a focused, inspirational force. Often he'd counsel his musicians like a bizarre father figure, warning them against drinking beers given to them by rival bands at festivals in case they were spiked, still imbued with a Detroit 'Battle of the Bands' aggression. On live tours, he'd fuel his body with red meat, and would never watch TV the day of a show, for fear it would sap his energy. Although, in their latter days, Schermerhorn and Cragin would engage Jim in constant arguments over money and retainers, there was still an incredible emotional bond between singer and band:

during one show in Warsaw that was being filmed by the Lodz film school, Schermerhorn was standing over a sweat-splattered Iggy when the singer took a full-voltage electric shock from a metal guard-rail. Eric stared into his eyes wondering what the hell was happening until Jos pulled Iggy out. Later, Jim told him, for all the much-touted encounters with broken glass and Detroit bikers, this was the closest he'd ever been to death. He seemed matter-of-fact about it.

Night after night, Iggy would deliver on a level that arguably no singer before or since has achieved. Whatever drama was going on in his personal life would always fuel his performance; during the *American Caesar* tour, he and Suchi were having rows, and when he hit the stage, says Larry Mullins, 'It was like war.' One night Hal Cragin was nearly speared by a mike stand that Iggy launched at his chest; a few nights later Eric Schermerhorn announced he was leaving after being the victim of a similar assault. Jim was apologetic and puzzled after the show, hardly remembering what he'd done onstage.

Photographer Bob Gruen was a friend of Jim and Suchi's in the early 1990s; they'd occasionally go out for a meal or to a club together and Gruen enjoyed Jim's wit and repartee. In June 1996 Gruen flew over to London for the much-fêted show which saw Iggy share a bill with the newly reunited Sex Pistols, whose rise Gruen had documented twenty years before. Gruen and Jim had exchanged a few words that afternoon, and a couple of minutes before Jim was due to go on stage, Gruen spotted the singer walk over to a quiet corner. The photographer was about to go up and offer some words of encouragement, when Art Collins motioned him aside and warned him, 'I wouldn't do that now.' As Gruen looked on, he saw Jim immersed in some kind of deep breathing exercise, 'And then, suddenly, it was like watching the Hulk, when some normal person, the secret identity, turns into this incredible creature.' Gruen watched wave after wave of an almost inhuman energy surge through him. 'You could almost see him become larger and more powerful. Jim had become Iggy and taken on all this mass, this power. And you just knew it was time to stay out of the way and not get anywhere near where he'd be.'

That afternoon's show was crazed, as Iggy writhed around and humped the Marshall back-line, determined to steal the limelight from the Sex Pistols' return to the stage. Finally, spent, Iggy walked off the stage and into the backstage area, right by Glen Matlock, with whom he hadn't talked in fifteen years or so. Jim Osterberg shot Glen his trademark, slightly goofy grin before asking, 'Hey? What you all been doing back there? Puking up?'

'You could tell he understood implicitly how we felt,' says Glen Matlock, 'that we were all shitting ourselves about to go on stage in front of 30,000 people. That it was a big deal for us.' Jim had also, says Matlock, dropped 'No Fun' from his set list so the Pistols could save the song for their encore.

By 1996, Iggy was fronting a mostly new band, with Eric Schermerhorn replaced on guitar by Whitey Kirst, who'd played briefly with him for the *Brick By Brick* tour – and, it's said, turned road manager Henry McGroggan's hair white in the process – and Pete Marshall joining on second guitar. The sound was thrashier and trashier, with a set-list drawing on the high-energy but woefully predictable new album *Naughty Little Doggie*. Iggy's new A&R apparently had the bright idea of teaming Iggy with Thom Wilson, who'd produced that year's big punk band, Offspring. 'Every record every year Virgin would say, "Oh, we'll set Iggy up with the latest guy,"' says Hal Cragin. 'Thom Wilson knows how to do a meat and potatoes rock production . . . and that's exactly what we ended up doing.'

Predictably, the eight million purchasers of the last Offspring album remained blissfully ignorant of Iggy's existence; less predictably, a new generation of fans were instead turned onto his music via the hit movie *Trainspotting*, which was released that July. Based on the debut novel by fervent Iggy fan Irvine Welsh, the film's exuberant opening sees junkies Ewan McGregor and Ewen Bremner fleeing the cops to the hedonistic swaggering drums of 'Lust For Life'. Iggy is omnipresent throughout the film, his music a leitmotif for Renton, McGregor's smackhead antihero, while another key character splits with his girlfriend and becomes a junkie after she tells him, 'It's me or Iggy Pop'; the song 'Lust For Life' would become a cornerstone of the film's heavily marketed and hugely successful soundtrack album. Reissued as a single in the UK, 'Lust For Life' reached number 28 in the singles charts and inspired a Virgin Best Of compilation, *Nude And Rude*, that featured Gerard Malanga's 1971 nude, junkie Iggy, judiciously cropped on the sleeve.

The surprise chart status of 'Lust For Life' illustrated one benefit of never having achieved long-term mainstream success; it meant there was always an audience for whom Iggy's music was undiscovered, unmapped territory. And over the next decade, the media that disseminated his music included dozens of movies, from *Basquiat* to *Great Expectations*, *A Life Aquatic* to *School of Rock*, and an increasingly wide variety of TV commercials, most notably Nike's 1996 'Search And Destroy' commercial, and Caribbean Royal Cruise's use of 'Lust For Life' – voted the most inappropriate use of a rock song in a commercial by NPR listeners in 2005. Many fans savoured the irony of a song written on Chinese rocks being screened in the middle of the Olympics, or of a paean to schnapps and cocaine touting family cruises; blog commentators around the world proclaimed it a sell-out. Iggy justified the licensing on the basis that these were songs that the world had never had a chance to hear.

When one considers the almost unprecedented, almost unbearable ordeals Iggy had survived in pursuit of his music, which had remained ignored in America for decades, it was a plausible defence. Yet not even the most silver-tongued snake-oil salesman could have concocted a reasonable explanation for the ROAR tour, which Iggy and band embarked on in the summer of 1997, bankrolled by US Tobacco, who were hoping to sell Skoal chewing tobacco to disenchanted youth all across the USA. Iggy at one point claimed that the tour offered the opportunity of playing to bigger crowds, rather than the same old mid-sized clubs, but as the tour continued, that justification crumbled into dust. Even if one were not shocked by Iggy's cynicism in helping hawk nicotine to teenagers, one remains astounded by his naivety in signing up for a venture that was so obviously doomed.

The atmosphere that gathered around the tour was darkened by the increasingly obvious problems afflicting Jim's marriage. He loved Suchi, profoundly, but over the years had got into the habit of treating her like a flunkey, sauntering around airports with his hands in his pockets while she struggled with the bags, his musicians observed; when they had arguments he'd often respond like a teenager, humiliating her by flirting with the women who inevitably congregated backstage. By 1996, Jim was surreptitiously inviting other girlfriends onto his tours – guitarist Pete Marshall was given the task of babysitting both Suchi and her new Argentinian love-rival Alejandra that year – and around 1997 Suchi announced she'd finally had enough and moved into an apartment Jim had purchased near 7th Street for a trial separation. Some clues to Suchi's emotional state can be inferred from her debut novel, *In Broken Wigwag*, which was published that autumn by United Press. It told of the melancholy of Japanese émigrés in New York, fleeing the repression of Tokyo yet achingly vulnerable in their new habitat. At one point her narrator explains how a couple: 'Never possess equal power. There is the one who tells stories and the one who listens.' Suchi would no longer play Jim's adoring audience, and his grief was so obvious that drummer Larry Mullins moved into an apartment nearer to him to try and keep an eye on his friend. 'He was spiralling into this very negative, very depressed state. And it started getting a little bit scary.'

The Revelations Of Alternative Rhythms, or ROAR, tour featured a motley line-up of bands which included the Reverend Horton Heat, Bloodhound Gang, Tonic, 60 Ft. Dolls, Sponge and future Pink and Christina Aguilera songwriter Linda Perry, as well as a 'Lifestyle Entertainment Village' where kids could challenge their friends to a game of virtual sumo wrestling or bouncy boxing. As soon as the tour was announced in April 1997, anti-tobacco pressure groups started issuing press releases denouncing the conglomerate's evil efforts. Having initially pumped a huge amount of money into the tour, US Tobacco started to pull back on advertising and before long the bands were playing in huge arenas at which the security personnel outnumbered the crowd; in panic, the organisers switched some venues, thus producing the ludicrous sight of twelve huge tour buses lined up outside a tiny club like the Stone Pony in New Jersey.

As date followed ill-attended date across the USA, Iggy started to become obsessed with the singer of Sponge, a dreadful Detroit covers band who'd belatedly hopped on the grunge bandwagon and lucked into a gold album. Before long, the venerable Godfather of Punk was engaged in a game of oneupmanship with the grunge-by-numbers upstarts. 'Whatever Jim did one night, the singer from Sponge would do the next night,' laughs Hal Cragin. 'One night he climbs up the PA side-fills, so the next night this kid climbs the PA side-fills. And instead of saying, Fucking kid, it just cranks him up.' Drummer Larry Mullins started to worry that there was something more serious at work: 'He was really creeping me out. He was doing this increasingly bizarre behaviour every night . . . it felt like he really wanted to kill himself on stage, to do something really crazy, or really violent.'

The duel with Sponge's singer became an obsession, probably in an attempt to blot out the problems with his marriage and with the obviously doomed tour, in which audiences of one or two hundred turned up at 15,000-seater amphitheatres. Despite his band's attempts to calm down the feud – 'We're saying, just relax, they're only a fuckin' covers band!' says Pete Marshall – Iggy was determined to 'push the envelope', until one night he was faced with a tiny crowd at the huge Polaris Amphitheatre in Columbus, Ohio. The band launched into 'Down On The Street' to a gaggle of bemused kids who were trying to work out who he was. 'They look as if they've come to see Britney Spears or something, but here's this little guy with that maniacal look on his face and muscles bulging out everywhere, and he scared the hell out of them,' says Whitey. Both Whitey and Cragin were studying the tiny crowd, who seemed transfixed with confusion and fear by this bizarre apparition, as Iggy ran straight to the edge of the stage, and launched himself out into space. 'I was watching their shocked faces as he flew towards them,' says Cragin, 'and they just scattered.'

Iggy hit a bank of chairs, face first, with a sickening impact. 'It was ugly,' remembers Whitey. As the musicians kept playing, wondering what had happened, Jos Grain bundled the singer back onto the stage. Blood streamed from his face, and one shoulder hung at a bizarre angle, a few inches below his collarbone. For a few minutes he knelt on the stage, clinging to the mike-stand, 'His eyes all weird, in some weird place,' says Whitey. For a while he seemed to be singing some bizarre, unknown song. Hal thought it was maybe Spanish. 'Whatever it was sounded real cool,' says Whitey, 'but it definitely wasn't "Down On The Street".' Finally Jos decided Iggy had sustained serious damage, hoisted him over his shoulder and carted him into the wings. The band played out the song before leaving the stage to a few half-hearted boos.

Eric Benson had joined the tour as his dad's assistant, and drove Jim back from the doctor's as Henry McGroggan explained the situation to the band. Jim had suffered a split head and badly dislocated shoulder – there had apparently been some problem with the anaesthetic required to reset it, such was his still-heroic tolerance to opiates – and he would have to wear a sling for the rest of the tour. For his next performance Iggy skipped on stage wearing the sling, which worked loose within seconds, leaving his arm flapping around. Jos the aspiring paramedic appeared with a roll of electrical tape, securing the injured limb to Iggy's body so he could finish the set.

The tour limped on for another nine performances, half of them in tiny venues like the House of Blues. On 5 July, the tour was finally cancelled, with Iggy's dislocated shoulder cited as the reason for why the planned forty dates had been cut back to half that number. Although Henry McGroggan managed to negotiate a substantial pay-off from US Tobacco, it was obvious that Iggy Pop's attempted sell-out had met its usual fate.

Some time after the initial injury, Jim had consulted a doctor who told him, 'Because your arm was all wrapped up, you've got a lot of nerve damage and the circulation cut off . . . I don't know if that arm will ever work again.' Once the tour was over Jim returned to the Christadora, still without use of the afflicted limb. It was not until several weeks later, when he was reading a newspaper, instinctively reached out and picked up a coffee with the damaged arm, that he could be sure there was no lasting damage.

However cynical Iggy's acceptance of US Tobacco's dollar had appeared to the American media, the fact that his dedication to duty had resulted in serious injury seemed to help him emerge with credibility intact. That credibility was enhanced by his only album release of 1997, a remixed version of *Raw Power*. The master tapes had apparently surfaced in Europe, where a fan had given them to the Henry Rollins Band – Rollins apparently wanted to collaborate on the new version, but Iggy elected to remix the album solo. This time around, Iggy was polite about Bowie's mix, with no mentions of sabotage by 'that fuckin' carrot-top'; instead, he claimed the new version unleashed the sound of 'a rip-snortin' super-heavy nitro-burnin' fuel-injected rock band that nobody in this world could touch'. The new mix was more coherent, if more one-dimensional, with a cranked-up sound that often bleeds into distortion, its original glammy edge totally excised. Once Columbia released the remixed version, they deleted the original Bowie mix, meaning that the version of *Raw Power* that had inspired a generation of punk bands was unobtainable, an act of historical revisionism that prompted Ron Asheton to observe, 'Now, when everyone hears [the remix] they say the same thing – I really love that original David Bowie mix!'

There was a further flurry of interest in the *Raw Power* era in the run-up to the launch of Todd Haynes' *Velvet Goldmine* movie, which was based loosely on the relationship between Bowie and Iggy; despite a media onslaught, the movie disappeared without making much of an impact and was mocked by most of those who were there, with the exception of Angie Bowie, who pronounced it an accurate portrayal of the era. The movie marked the public return of Ron Asheton, who'd recently occupied most of his time acting in B-movies; joined by Mudhoney's Mark Arm, Sonic Youth's Thurston Moore and Minutemen bassist Mike Watt, he recorded 'TV Eye' and other songs for the soundtrack, playing back-up band for Ewan McGregor's Iggy Pop–Lou Reed composite, Curt Wild. With Ron playing Stooges material once more, there were rumours he and Iggy might finally settle their differences, which became more persistent once it transpired that the über-producer Rick Rubin had discussed producing the reformed band. But when the subject was mentioned, Iggy would make the same old jibes about Ron still living with his mom and tell interviewers he had no interest in playing the old hits: 'And, furthermore, I don't have to.'

Rather than reunite with the Stooges, Iggy's new musical project was, he told everyone, to cover 'some standards'. It was nearly thirty years since he'd first sung 'Shadow Of Your Smile' to unappreciative live audiences, and he'd introduced Sinatra's classic Johnny Mercer torch song, 'One For My Baby', to his set back in 1978. Furthermore, he was now going steady with a new girlfriend, who had a taste for bossa nova. Jim had first noticed Alejandra when she'd met his son, Eric, during the *American Caesar* tour in Buenos Aires, and looked her up during a subsequent visit. She taught him Spanish – he was a quick learner – and he'd croon versions of Antonio Carlos Jobim's 'How Insensitive', or the Mercer/Kosma classic 'Autumn Leaves', to an acoustic backing at Hal Cragin's home studio. The kind of songs that the broken-hearted Frank Sinatra would intone as he was in the process of splitting from Ava Gardner seemed appropriate for a period in which Jim was negotiating a divorce settlement with Suchi. The split 'really, really hurt him,' says Larry Mullins. 'Although much of it was his own fault, it was very hard on him, one of the most dedicated long-term things he'd ever been involved in. It represented a huge loss.' Ultimately, it seems, the divorce from Suchi was reasonably amicable, for she visited him on tour later, but Suchi's well-documented role in Jim's professional rehabilitation meant that she was entitled to a hefty divorce settlement.

As he had done so often before, Iggy turned his predicament into music, calling in Don Was, who had long wanted to collaborate on a largely acoustic album that showcased Jim's voice. In the months before the recording started in May 1998, Jim worked hard, rehearsing standards with Cragin, to the stark backing of a string bass and acoustic guitar: 'It really was cool . . .' says Cragin, 'but in the end he got paranoid about it.'

For those who'd followed Iggy's career, the idea of a collection of dark torch ballads was an enticing one; there were precedents in his own work, notably his sombre, European-sounding *The Idiot*. More recently Nick Cave, who'd started out playing Stooges-influenced rock with the Birthday Party, had attained a career summit with *The Boatman's Call*, a dark collection of minimalist acoustic ballads; later Johnny Cash would maintain his own career comeback with the stripped-down, spooky *Solitary Man*. Yet when Iggy started work on *Avenue B*, the album that would document the emotional ruins of his own life, he seemed simply to lose his nerve, tidying up the wreckage with a muso sheen courtesy of the super-competent Blue Note jazz trio, Martin Medeski and Wood. Behind the sonic airbrushing and the tasteful middle-class bongos, however, was a world of imposing darkness. 'Nazi Girlfriend', the album's most fully realised song, sees the narrator intimidated by a woman with four-inch heels and a desert in her stare, set against crystalline broken chords. 'I Felt The Luxury' features diamond-hard lyrics in which the hero coldly speculates about his leopardskin-clad lover's next suicide attempt: 'If cold's what I am, I'm cold to the end.' (The song seemed both a warning to future lovers, and a threat to Eric lest he run up any more bills at his therapist.) Elsewhere, a workmanlike cover of Johnny Kidd's 'Shaking All Over' exemplifies a crucial predicament: that with old age comes competence, but a certain dumb eloquence is lost.

By the time *Avenue B* was released in September 1999,

Alejandra – the subject of many of the songs – was gone after another messy split-up, the dust had settled on his divorce and Jim had left New York for Miami – 'I don't mind being a millionaire, but I don't want to live next to millionaires,' was how he justified it to those around him, typically trumpeting his own wealth and the enduring belief that he was an outcast in one sentence. Predictably, *Avenue B* was marketed as a 'divorce album', and predictably, it was released to mixed reviews. Some proclaimed it an exercise in self-pity, failing to recognise its emotional brutality; and while most people assumed Iggy Pop had constructed a new warm and cosy retreat for himself in Miami's North Beach, life was not quite as tidy. For the *Avenue B* tour that autumn – which effectively combined existential acoustic musings with meathead versions of Stooges classics – Jim was stealing women off his musicians like the old days; an 'unprotected sexual predator,' says Hal Cragin. There were minor emotional crises, though, such as the time he picked up a girl in Sweden and it turned out her dad was a huge fan of Iggy's music, a generational juxtaposition that he didn't appreciate. The encounter illustrated how Jim's first career revival, back in the mid-1970s, was already a quarter-century away. But in a sense, the fact he was well into his fifties changed little about him: that childlike innocence had always been combined with a kooky eccentricity, the way he'd talk to odd-looking strangers in the street, or call people 'sir'.

In the early days at the Christadora, Jim appreciated the eccentric mix of boutiques on one side, with crack dealers a couple of blocks in the other direction; once the whole area was cleaned up, the East Side lost its attraction for him. Miami offered a more exotic version of that eccentric mix, where he would spend afternoons on the more far-flung, seedier beaches, or drive around in his 1969 Cadillac convertible, checking out the little old WASP ladies, three decades retired, rubbing shoulders with heavy types who'd made their money from intriguingly vague, doubtless illegal pursuits. And, of course, the Miami chicks. It was on one such cruise around the city that he noticed two striking, Latina-looking women in a pizza parlour. He stopped, got out, walked towards them to say hello, thought better of it, then got back in his Cadillac – and finally offered them a lift. Nina Alu was half Irish, half Nigerian, a statuesque airline stewardess half a head taller than Jim. She was, as one friend puts it, 'very va va voom' and soon became his regular companion. They made a sweet couple, often talking quietly or sharing an expensive bottle of red wine together in the evenings.

Iggy and his band had a quiet year in 2000, restricting their shows to the usual huge, lucrative European festival dates. Hal Cragin had left after the *Avenue B* tour and was replaced by Body Count bassist Lloyd 'Mooseman' Roberts, who joined Whitey and Pete Marshall on guitars. Whitey's brother, Alex, had joined as drummer for the *Avenue B* tour; Jim enjoyed the vibe of once again having a pair of brothers in the band and decided to name the resultant outfit 'the Trolls'; that's when he didn't call them 'my little band', as if they were domestic servants. By now, he had forgone the routine of auditioning players; normally Art Collins would simply ask them to turn up, for Jim was more bothered about attitude than skills. After all, Whitey had been famously bad on his first tour with Iggy (Henry McGroggan said he thought the band was doing all new material, as he couldn't recognise a single song), but little by little had started making a vital contribution to songs like *Avenue B*'s 'Corruption'. By the winter of 2000, Whitey was cranking out most of the key riffs, which Jim would arrange and order, and the small band arranged and recorded a new album in less than two weeks, with Iggy producing. *Beat 'Em Up* was not remotely groundbreaking, but it was effective lamebrained metal, with Iggy's maniacal diatribes attacking music-biz weasels, fakers and creeps with the temerity to chat up his girlfriend, and for the most part the stream of riffs and rants obscured the lack of original ideas. The most memorable track, 'VIP', was a quintessential example of Iggy mocking the hand that feeds him, a seven-minute attack on celebrity culture inspired by the band's performance, at the personal invitation of Donatella Versace, at a Versace launch in January 1999.

By the time *Beat 'Em Up* was released in July 2001, its bassist had become a victim of the aggression that seemed to pervade it. Mooseman had returned to Los Angeles after the recording, and was apparently working on a car in his South Central driveway when he was killed in a drive-by shooting on 22 February.

Mooseman's death filled out a grim roll call: Dave Alexander, Zeke Zettner, Jackie Clark and Craig Pike had all played bass for Iggy and died, while Tony Sales, too, had been found near-dead after a car crash in 1979, a gear stick in his chest, and was in Cedars Sinai Hospital in a coma for ten weeks before recovering (Bowie came to visit him; Jim never called). The number of musicians who had been damaged or drained to a husk by their career with Iggy was almost beyond number; but it was a matter of pride now that he keep going. It was simultaneously impressive and inexplicable – David Bowie used the word 'obsessive' about Iggy's compulsion to tour – but there was an internal logic. Jim knew he'd made his best music in the first ten years of his career, and he also believed he'd blown it. He often blamed the Ashetons – even in 2000 or 2001 he'd still often bring up the subject of Ron's laziness or predilection for dope – but he knew his own excesses or simple lack of psychic stamina were a key reason why the Stooges had crashed and burned. Now he still had to prove his stamina, to make up for those weaknesses of three decades ago. In interviews Jim was unfailingly charming, but there was a rare moment of testiness when one interviewer implied he was a flaky rock 'n' roller: 'Listen, dude,' he retorted. 'I've done this for thirty years. The first fifteen years were highly creative and featured a low discipline level. The second half has been a reverse. There was overall less striking creativity but more discipline.'

It was a classic control-freak situation. Iggy Pop had won the war, but he was still fighting to erase the memory of the battle he'd lost, twenty-five years before. And he continued that fight throughout most of 2001, battling against every band with whom he shared a bill throughout April, May, June, July, October and November. Although the shows were, by all accounts, generally superb, these were not easy months. There were the same old fights between brothers, the same escapades of musicians crazed on drink or drugs – which, in fact, were even worse when confined to a tiny private jet – as well as entirely new hassles, such as a falling-out with his son Eric, newly promoted to road manager for that tour, but who disappeared following an argument after the David Letterman show in New York and subsequently became estranged from his father. By the end of the tour, most of the band were in a state of paranoia that one or all of them would be sacked.

It wasn't only Iggy's band who were worried about their employment prospects. In March 2002, EMI announced it had been underperforming in the US market and that it was planning thousands of redundancies from its worldwide staff, accompanied by a drastic culling of its artist roster. It was inevitable that the company would be looking closely at how much Iggy was contributing to the corporate coffers.

Around the same time, Jim got into the habit of piling up his own CDs at home. They made a large stack. In the fickle, transient world of the entertainment business, the fact that he'd been adding to that stack every couple of years had been a source of pride. Now he started to think about how it would look if he were to divide the CDs into two stacks, one for the great albums and one for the mediocre ones. He was smart enough to realise that the latter stack would be much taller than it should be. And at some point he started to say to himself: If I'm going to add to the stack, it had better be for a good reason.

CHAPTER 18

The Reptile House

Jim Osterberg pads around his modest, single-storey Miami retreat with a puppy-like bounce and enthusiasm, attending to visitors with old-fashioned courtesy – fussing over you, asking if you need a cold drink, checking if the unrelenting Florida sun's in your eyes.

Before we sit down, with Southern politesse he takes us on a tour of his tiny one-bedroomed house. A long lawn with wiry Florida grass, a couple of palms and four or five rhododendron bushes shelter the wooden-fronted bungalow from the street. A black Rolls Royce Corniche shelters from the sun in the lean-to garage adjoining the house. The house itself is tiny, toy-like, and although there are a good number of artworks – naive Haitian paintings, Russian icons, a Brion Gysin drawing, his own painting of the Stooges based on a photo a fan sent him, a Norman throne – the overall effect is spare, like a monk's retreat. There are just a few boxes of CDs visible, piled up in a tiny room where Iggy writes lyrics at a toy piano. In a glass-fronted cupboard nearby sits a bright red toy Woodstock drum kit, about eighteen inches tall. It's at this drum kit that the looming, six-feet-tall Scott Asheton – 'Rock Action', the hoodlum Dum Dum Boy – sits, when the reformed Stooges rehearse at Iggy's bungalow, in a Latino district on the edge of the city. I can think of few things more ludicrous than this vision of three sixty-year-old men, childhood friends who've reunited over thirty years on, rehearsing and exchanging reminiscences in this tiny room, crouched over toy instruments.

On a table near the back door, there's an affectingly conventional display of family photographs: a photo of Louella sits next to one of James Sr – a semi-formal black and white photo with an engaging smile, in his Air Force uniform. Jim is still in regular touch with his father, who's now in an assisted-living facility in Myrtle Beach, although any photos of Eric, or Jim's new granddaughter, whom he apparently has never met, are nowhere to be seen. Next to the photo of his dad is a fuzzy, amateurish kitsch snapshot of an elderly gentleman with a beatific grin embracing an Amazonian girlfriend whose torpedo breasts are on a level with his head. It takes a couple of seconds until I realise it's a terrifically bad photo of Iggy, who, in what could be a snapshot of any Florida millionaire, looks like an old man next to Nina. There's something touching about its lack of self-consciousness. Nearby, there's the celebrated Gerard Malanga photo of a naked Iggy in his prime – another frame is strategically positioned to obscure his impressive penis. For a few seconds we discuss the photo, as I mention how featuring it on the cover of a particularly depraved issue of *MOJO* magazine, which I'd edited, was one of my proudest moments. He looks at me, seemingly in horror, and says, 'I know, I can't believe you did that.' I examine his expression, hard, to see if he's winding me up, but there's no sign. This sets the tone for our afternoon: discussing depravity, betrayal, revenge and life in a mental institution, with a mature, well-bred innocent who speaks as if all of this happened to somebody else, or as if he were Candide, simply carried along on the mad tide of history.

This is not Jim's only house – there's a bigger apartment he shares with Nina in Miami proper, as well as a holiday home in Mexico and another property recently purchased in the Cayman Islands – but this is his retreat, where he works and sits alone contemplating nature, and he frequently displays a childlike wonder at the beauty of the calm but slightly grungy surroundings. Occasionally manatees swim slowly down the creek at the back of his house, and he jumps up in pure, simple excitement as he spots a turtle or a crane – 'Look at that little fella, there!' At the back of the garden there's a Tiki Hut – a palm-topped gazebo built in one day by a sturdy crew from El Salvador – where he often sits at three in the morning, listening to Dean, a Hell's Angel who lives on the other side of the creek, working on his cars. Sometimes trains pass by on the other side of the road early in the morning 'and you hear a blues whistle', like the noises he remembers from the trains behind the Leveretts' fields in Ypsilanti. This place gives him the kind of tranquillity he'd enjoy walking in the wilderness around Coachville, he says, before they built a four-lane highway through it.

He tells me a five-foot-long iguana lives in a tree at the edge of Dean's plot – he often sees it basking in the sun. I wonder if his metabolism, too, slows down in this idyllic spot, how much time is spent in contemplation and how much in reflection on events past. But it's apparent that, like a reptile's, Jim's is a pragmatic view of life. There's no energy expended on regret, either for his own sufferings or for those casualties trailed in his wake.

Jim talks with an earnest simplicity and enthusiasm, his conversation full of joke voices, deep laughs and moments of silence as he stares in rapt attention, listening to a question or pondering a response. The five-year-old Jim Osterberg described by his friends – coy, funny, adept at incorporating his questioner's thoughts and expanding on them to build up rapport – is instantly recognisable. The Iggy Pop I've seen before – all staring eyes, muscular springiness, as magnificent and scary as a wild horse – is only occasionally with us today, but Jim mentions at one point how perhaps he really is Iggy, now that he's inhabited that persona for most of his life. Occasionally he'll encourage this duality, this idea of an alter ego; at other times he'll mock it. Overall, you get the sense that Iggy Pop was a place he had to go to make his art; a place from which in the past he couldn't always return, but which is now safer, because it's been mapped. He knows where the edges of this world are now, and is in less danger of falling off.

Later I'll discuss this issue with Murray Zucker, who back at NPI in 1975 diagnosed Jim Osterberg with a bipolar disorder but who now wonders, given Jim's present-day stability, whether the talent, intensity, perceptiveness and behavioural extremes were who he truly is, not a disease: that Jim's behaviour was simply him enjoying the range of his brain, playing with it, exploring different personae, until it got to the point of 'not knowing what was up and what was down'. With illness eliminated as a cause, we are therefore left with someone who went to the brink of madness simply to see what it was like, in the cause of his art or for the joy of exploration. And someone who returned from the brink simply because the time seemed right – someone who simply, his friends recall, decided to give up drink and cocaine with an almost superhuman strength of will.

In some recent interviews, I'd heard Jim – or was it Iggy? – revel in a sense of triumph. His schoolfriends tell me of an interview broadcast recently on PBS, in which he described how casually nasty they'd been, and boasted how Iggy had made him a rich man, a comment surely aimed at the architects' and realtors' sons he believed looked down on him at school. Today, in contrast, he revels in a sense of calm; that his reputation is assured, that a restful retirement awaits, and that he has made some kind of peace with the world, and with the Asheton brothers, those strange, lost boys who helped Jim Osterberg create Iggy, forty years ago.

He's engagingly honest about the Ashetons, in that Darwinian way of his, describing how commercial reasoning rather than mere camaraderie got them together. It turns out that his record contract at Virgin was under review, and when he suggested including the Stooges on *Skull Ring*, his 2003 album full of guest stars, his A&R belatedly got excited. The Ashetons, meanwhile, had been touring successfully with J. Mascis and Mike Watt, which meant that Iggy stopped thinking of Ron as someone who lived with his mom, but instead as someone with a following in his own right. As he discusses working with them again, he starts to analyse it in almost businesslike terms, how in America particularly 'people love to see reunification, they like to see you haven't forgotten your friends, and there's something very basic about that'. It's intriguing how he ascribes such warm fuzzy sentimentality to others, rather than himself, but it's nonetheless obvious that, behind that reptilian exterior, there is a deep fellow feeling with two men who are in many respects his own crazy, lost brothers.

Belatedly, this ambitious man, who was always driven by a need for more love, more affection and more respect, is finally satisfied with the reception he's receiving. 'I do feel that affection. I've been getting more appreciation than anyone deserves. Sometimes people write something kind about what we did and I think why not the Seeds, why not the Thirteenth Floor Elevators? And of course the answer is what's happening now turns people's attention towards what you did then. So for me it's been really, really, really good. It's a nice circle.'

Throughout the baking hot afternoon, we disinter the remotest events of his past, mostly with a rare openness, although he's adept at changing the subject when necessary: ask him about his abilities in the school debating team and he shifts the discussion to how it prepared him for being a rock singer. When we briefly allude to Bob Koester, the man who sheltered him in Chicago and was rewarded with a glass full of piss, his face goes dark: 'What did he say about me?' he glowers. I answer vaguely, saying Bob told me they had not parted as friends; he ponders for a moment, wondering whether to go into a detailed backstory, before telling me, regretfully, that there's a 'gang mentality' prevalent in rock 'n' roll, and then blames Scott Richardson for leading the escapade. 'Scott represents a certain kind of musical expediency . . . he made fun of Bob, they weren't nice to him, and I didn't stop them.' He looks sad, and it occurs to me that perhaps this is how he really remembers the encounter, the way all of us erase unpleasant family squabbles from our memories. For at other moments he's disarmingly honest. When we discuss the latter-day Stooges, when James Williamson had supplanted Ron Asheton as his musical foil, I ask whether he ever noticed Ron's grief at being demoted to playing bass guitar, relegated to a mere sideman in the band he'd co-founded. He pauses for a long time, before responding, without evasion: 'No. I never noticed. I was too busy trying to do what I was trying to do. So I just never noticed.'

He seems entirely without paranoia, open to intrusive questioning, perhaps even revelling in it – he knows he can tell a great yarn, and relishes the opportunity to dust down a new one – so it's easy to forget that this is so often a tragic tale, full of failure and the prospect of oblivion. At one point I mention Michael Tipton's remark that those later days of the Stooges were actually comedic, and I see a flicker of hurt register in his eyes. 'There must have been some humour . . . to the audience . . . at least we were alive.' Then I think of all the people laughing at his depression and misery, Flo and Eddie mocking him on their radio show, Hollywood types pointing him out as a loser backstage at the Whisky, and I feel briefly guilty, as if I've mentioned enjoying a snuff movie, before pressing on with the story of the Stooges' dark days. And again I'm struck, as people so often are, by his lack of self-pity and his obvious sense that there was always some historical destiny at work. For, as he says of Slade, or Peter Frampton, or Blue Öyster Cult, or any other band that was triumphant when the Stooges were floundering, 'Where are they now?' Even as he confesses to the Stooges' present-day quarrels, problems that 'surface and resurface', he calmly pronounces himself blessed that this kind of peace took so long to arrive: 'I feel lucky, I really do. Who else, at my point, my age, whatever you call it, can say there's that kind of ascension?'

Comebacks are never cosy. In fact, comebacks in pop music are usually simply not very good. Perhaps the closest counterparts to the Stooges were the Velvet Underground, who reassembled for an uninspired reunion tour in 1992, all their aggression and frustration replaced by a dull professionalism, tarnishing their reputation in the process. The same was arguably true of the Stooges' first reunion on record, four noisy but unfocused songs on *Skull Ring*, the generally underwhelming Iggy album released in November 2003. But by the time the album appeared, the real story was the Stooges' appearance at the Coachella festival on Sunday 27 April, sandwiched between the White Stripes and the Red Hot Chili Peppers.

There was a certain matter-of-factness about the performance. On a clear, dry evening in the California desert, the Stooges hit the stage in a workmanlike, Detroit kind of way, as if topping a bill in front of 33,000 people thirty years after they crashed and burned were no big deal. The one concession to nostalgia was bassist Mike Watt's T-shirt, given to him by Scott Asheton, which bore the image of Dave Alexander ('So we were all there,' says Ron). Yet the true marvel of the Stooges at Coachella was not that they acquitted themselves well with their fire largely undiminished, nor that sax player Steve Mackay made a surprise appearance, it was simply that in this setting, the 30-year-old music sounded every bit as contemporary as that of the other bands topping the bill. There was no fanfare, no allusion to the fact this moment had taken thirty years to arrive – here was simply another rock 'n' roll band, but one who happened to be, *Billboard* would report later, 'the dirtiest, sexiest, rawest' band of the festival. Their performance was proclaimed a 'miracle in the desert' by Jay Babcock, reviewing the show for the *Los Angeles Times*. 'Even today, I remember the enthusiasm in which I wrote that review, and I feel it now,' says Babcock. 'It was astonishing. I still think it's a miracle.'

There had, in fact, been a little last-minute argy-bargy behind the scenes. Pete Marshall had been expecting to play bass with the new Stooges ever since Ron had started sending Iggy tapes in the late 1990s; Iggy had pushed for him too, on the basis he wanted someone familiar standing beside him, but finally backed down and agreed to Watt taking the job, on condition that there was 'no slapping, no triads . . . and no Flea-ing around on stage', alluding to his friendship with Chili Peppers' funky bassist, Flea. In retrospect the decision was the right one, for Watt brought a new propulsiveness to the sound, as well as his own following from the LA punk SST-label scene, and proved utterly dedicated to building on the Stooges' legacy. Called in to play at short notice in the middle of a tour with the Secondmen during which he'd been beset by ill-health, Watt had been doubled up in agony in the lead-up to Coachella, hiding his predicament from Iggy in case it sapped his confidence. Iggy had seemed almost scarily on the ball during rehearsals, specific about what he needed, assertive yet diplomatic. When the show actually started, Watt was transfixed with fear, feeling 'real pale, whiter than a winding sheet'; yet as the band hit Ron's guitar solo on 'Down On The Street' and he saw Iggy leap on top of his amplifier and start humping it, the adrenalin pumped in, and he was able to hold on.

By the following year, the Stooges topped the bill at Coachella, which as they prepared to take the stage seemed a terrible mistake – for most of the crowd had elected to avoid the traffic jams and leave immediately after the White Stripes' set, which had been dogged by technical problems. As the Stooges launched the three-chord assault of 'Loose', thousands of weary fans were walking back to the parking lot . . . 'Then you visibly saw everyone stop. Pause. Listen,' says audience member Andrew Male, 'and then they turned back. It had started off with you thinking they've screwed up, the audience is wondering who's this old guy on stage. Then there was a total sea change. You felt a rush, like the wind behind you, with thousands of people running towards the stage. All around were these obviously euphoric experiences, kids turning to each other with huge smiles, looking into each other's eyes.' After the show, Iggy remained for a magazine cover shoot with Jack White, the new standard bearer of Detroit rock. White held Iggy in his arms in a quasi-religious pose, like Mary Magdalene contemplating Jesus in the Deposition from the cross (photographer Mick Hutson reflected afterwards, 'There was love in that look – and not normal man-love!'). Speaking to the Christ-like figure a few weeks later, White told him, 'I have always felt that the blood that runs in your veins is so much thicker than normal people that nothing can pollute it. That's the vibe I've gotten from you.' An unabashed fan, White had picked up on a perception shared by many, that despite the chaos that had so often engulfed him, Iggy Pop's devotion to his music, which had resulted in all those still visible nicks and scars, endowed him with a strange kind of purity.

And so it went on, 'like a dream or something,' says Ron Asheton, a stream of validation that seemed 'so special that it seems almost too good to be true. You're gonna go whoop, I'm gonna wake up now and be back in the bar playing for ten dollars a night.' For both Ron and Scott Asheton this was an unparalleled, almost mystical experience, that after thirty years in which their music gestated, finally to percolate into every corner of the contemporary rock scene, they had their moment in the limelight. Yet this could be no easy ride, for with every show came the nervousness before, and anxious post-mortems, as the Stooges gradually made their way to the top of bills across Europe and the USA. For the three founder Stooges, one crucial rite of passage was their headlining show at London's Hammersmith Apollo in August 2005, the first time they'd topped a bill in the city since July 1972. In a highlight of London's All Tomorrow's Parties season, the band would play their *Fun House* album in its entirety. *Fun House* producer Don Gallucci took a few days off from his real-estate business to attend the event, for which, despite all those years of experience, both Iggy and Mike Watt were beset with nerves.

In the event, the dream continued. Iggy skipped onto the stripped-down stage of the Apollo with the bounce and energy of a spring lamb, yelling a terse welcome before leaping onto bassist Mike Watt's Marshall stack and dry-humping it as the Stooges launched into 'Down On The Street'. And all those years, all those injuries, all those humiliations simply melted away, as Iggy danced, lithe, beautiful, untroubled and untainted by history. The band seemed almost unbelievably confident: Rock Action's drumming supple, playing the song rather than the beat, and Ron Asheton's guitar style, while frenetic, seemed intelligent and refined.

Iggy and his various backing bands, particularly the Trolls, had always been a superior rock act, but the Stooges seemed to represent something far more unconventional: experimental, on the edge, like an art happening, but one propelled by a barrage of guitars. Iggy, too, seemed less a rock singer, more a dancer: lithe, balletic, fluid. As Iggy conducted the sturm und drang, commanding his comrades – 'Wait a minute!' 'Take it down!' – or imperiously ordering another violent surge of noise, it was like watching a magician conducting a thunderstorm or parting the seas. After playing *Fun House* in its entirety, they hit the stage again for a run of songs from *The Stooges*: '1969', 'I Wanna Be Your Dog', 'Real Cool Time', and then carnage ensued, as a planned stage invasion got out of control with fractured limbs and broken teeth, Ron Asheton standing to the rear and quizzically observing the madness surrounding his singer, who eventually sat down calmly in the middle of the chaos, like a king surrounded by his motley retinue. For the encore, they hit the brakes for a mid-paced, menacing 'Little Doll', Ron coaxing the bendy, minimal riff out of his Reverend guitar, Mackay shaking maracas, and up on the balcony boys were kissing girls romantically, joyously, in a way that never could have happened thirty-five years ago. As they walked off the stage, Don Gallucci shouted at me, 'I think they nailed it.'

After Iggy had limped, painfully, backstage into the dressing room, as was his habit he interrogated those around him: 'How was it? What did people think?' Detroit photographer Robert Matheu was there, as for so many of the Stooges' performances first time around, and told him: 'This is the Stooges in their prime.' Today, he cites that performance as superior to the Ford Auditorium shows, 'where they were awesome in their power'. This time around, in an unbearably hot auditorium, the music 'physically drove into the crowd's bodies'; this was the place and the audience that the music was made for. Don Gallucci, too, was as astonished by the performance as he had been by the Stooges' show at Ungano's in February 1970: 'Amazingly, it didn't feel like a nostalgia event. It felt like it did at the time – fresh. And I looked around and there were these kids, two generations younger, experiencing it as if for the first time too.'

After the show, Gallucci was reunited with Ron Asheton. It was a surreal sight, Ron more portly than in his prime but still with a certain presence, chatting with his ex-producer about their last encounter, when the Stooges were being dropped by Elektra. 'So, Ron . . .' says Gallucci, 'do you remember our going in your room? With all those German uniforms?' Jim has disappeared for a quiet glass of wine with Nina, as he does most nights. Instead, Gallucci has to content himself with a warm hug from Steve Mackay and a quick photo with Rock Action, who as ever seems the most unpredictable Stooge. He's the only one who thanks Gallucci for his work on *Fun House*, the album they were showcasing this evening – 'Without you, Don, this wouldn't have happened' – but when Don asks him how the tour's going, Rock starts thanking his sponsors, as if he's being interviewed on the red carpet for MTV. One senses why there was always this widespread perception of the Ashetons as loveable but unworldly – for that's exactly what they are: innocents.

Over the autumn of 2006, the Asheton brothers and Iggy spent weeks huddled over toy drum kits and tiny amplifiers at Iggy's monastic retreat, before moving to Chicago to work up an album. Rick Rubin, the man who had helmed so many hit productions, couldn't make the Stooges' schedule, while Jack White, who had lovingly tended Loretta Lynn's *Van Lear Rose*, was rejected, for reasons unexplained, in favour of Steve Albini, whose own stellar CV includes the Pixies and Nirvana.

When *The Weirdness* was released in March 2007 its reception was every bit as confused as that of its predecessors. But this time around the music was confused, too. On its pedestrian opening tracks the monumental simplicity of the Stooges' heyday was absent, the instrumental tracks crowded, Iggy's voice occasionally weak and wavery. Yet, despite the poor song choice and murky sound, songs like the title track and the magnificently nihilistic 'Idea of Fun' were heroic, untamed, in their own way miraculous despite the album's obvious failings. So clever, so stupid.

In truth, it was impossible for any one album to make sense of the crazed, picaresque events of the forty years since Iggy and his Stooges first huddled together in Chicago and decided to make music. Although the Asheton brothers pronounced it merely a start, *The Weirdness* must surely represent a comfortable closure, the prelude to a peaceful retirement for all concerned, most likely punctuated by the odd speaking engagement where Jim Osterberg can demonstrate his talent for rollicking yarns. And for all the adoration the Stooges receive from a new generation of fans, it seems they will always be outsiders. In 2007, the Stooges were shortlisted for the sixth time, again without success, for induction into the Rock and Roll Hall of Fame, an institution that has already embraced the likes of Bill Haley, the Four Seasons and Lynyrd Skynyrd: perfectly acceptable acts all, but none of whose music resounds to the present day. Instead, Iggy and his Stooges must simply look on as disciples such as the Ramones and the Sex Pistols gain the accolades that continue to elude them. Yet, as their story shows, the sheer genius of Iggy and his Stooges lies in how they were always compelled to make their music, whether or not anybody cared.

And in the end, for all the blood, drugs and pain, a simple miracle makes it all seem worthwhile: the moment when a pleasant, well-spoken, elderly-looking gentleman with a noticeable limp taps into something primal and primitive that emanates from a drum kit and a stack of Marshall amplifiers. Then this gentleman skips onto the stage with the carefree joy of a child, borne on the incessant waves of the music.

Suddenly this devotion to the music, which so often looked like stupidity, looks like greatness. Then we all take a ride on the pretty music, the past is another place, and there is only the glorious now.

NOTES AND SOURCES

PROLOGUE
This material is based on author interviews with Jim Osterberg, James Williamson, Ron Asheton, Scott Asheton, Scottie Thurston, Michael Tipton, Don Was, Peter Hook, Brian James, Nick Kent and other sources also listed against Chapter 9, Beating a Dead Horse. The description of Jim Osterberg's demeanour refers to my 1990 interview with him.

CHAPTER 1: MOST LIKELY TO
The sources are author interviews with Jim Osterberg (JO) plus the following. The opening car-crash scene is as told to me by Lynn Klavitter. Early days (trailer park, elementary school) sources: Duane Brown, Sharon Ralph, Brad Jones, Patricia Carson Celusta, Mary Booth, Mrs Rachel Schreiber, Michael Bartus, Irvin Wisniewski and Mike Royston. Background sources for James Osterberg Senior as a teacher: Randy Poole, Robert Stotts, Sherry and Bob Johnson, and Joan Raphael. Tappan Junior High sources: Jim McLaughlin (JMcL), Mim Streiff, Denny Olmsted, Arjay Miller, John Mann, Sally Larcom, Cindy Payne, Don Collier, Dana Whipple and Ted Fosdick. Ann Arbor High sources: Mike Wall, Ricky Hodges, Ron Ideson, Jannie Densmore, Clarence Eldridge, John Baird, Scott Morgan and Jimmy Wade. Unquoted sources for background information include Joan Raphael, Connie Miller, Mike Andrews, Glenn Ziegler, Dennis Dieckmann, Janie Allen, Francie King, Pat Huetter, Nancy McArtor, Bobbie Goddard Lam, Bill Kurtz, Joan Campbell, Jim Carpenter, Ron Ideson, Dan Kett, Ted Fosdick, Pete Fink, Bob Carow and Carol Martin. Background Ann Arbor and University of Michigan information is taken from www.umich.edu. Some details (the Atomic Brain, the Bishops) are taken from Iggy Pop's I Need More.

James Newell Osterberg Senior. The account of James's adoption was told by James Senior to Esther Friedmann. Background information on James Senior was obtained by historical researcher Alfred Hahn.

Committed, capable and fair. Joan Raphael was one of Mr Osterberg's English students, and managed to talk him into allowing her performance of English madrigals on clarinet to count towards her credits. Osterberg complied, but only after she'd submitted to the class a rigorous, detailed verbal justification, researched at Wayne State University library, of the cultural background of her project. 'He was a very creative individual, and one of my favourite teachers also,' says Joan today.

Louella Osterberg, née Kristensen. According to an interview conducted for Per Nilsen's book *The Wild One*, Louella's father was Danish and her mother was half-Swedish, half-Norwegian. Strangely, Louella Osterberg insisted that James Senior's adoptive parents were not Jewish, but James Senior informed Esther Friedmann that the two sisters who adopted him were Jewish, of Swedish ancestry.

Parents could leave their children to play around the [trailer] park. Sharon Ralph Gingras: 'My feeling one reason the Osterbergs stayed in the trailer was because it was a secure place. Other people were always looking out for all the children.'

Jim was regarded with some indulgence and fondness by the [elementary school] teaching staff. 'He was bright-eyed and alert. Responsive, with a quick sense of humour,' says Mrs Rachel Schreiber, who retains a good recollection of Jim and his father.

Jim absorbed stories of frontier culture. The 'Daniel Boone and Jim Bowie' quote is from David Fricke's 1984 interview with JO.

Arjay Miller . . . shouldered the burden of . . . [Ford's] severe financial straits. According to *Wheels for the World*, Douglas Brinkey's excellent history of the Ford company, when Arjay arrived at Ford, company lore had it that the automobile giant assessed its debts by weighing the piles of invoices.

Kenny Miller's 'schoolboy crush'. Most of Miller's fellow pupils remember the Ford boss's son particularly fondly, pointing out that, unlike some of the middle class kids, he was not a snob. He seemed even more charmed by Jim than any of his contemporaries, says Denny Olmsted: 'Kenny went off to boarding school from tenth grade on, but in junior high he had almost a crush on Osterberg.' Perhaps it's necessary to point out that 'schoolboy crush', in the 50s, merely meant admiration.

Teacher's pet. 'I remember Mrs Powrie's English class, where she expressed enthusiasm for Jim's use of idiom,' recalls Mike Andrews. 'He had written a short story, mentioned "the men of the cloth", and he had used the phrase correctly. She expressed her pleasure very publicly . . . I think he might have been her pet.'

Jim seemed excessively ashamed of his background. 'Jim had a real inferiority complex,' says Bob Hallock. 'He did make comments that he was embarrassed that he lived in a trailer. He never talked favourably about his parents and he never invited us to his home.' Many classmates, like John Baird, knew other people who lived in trailer parks: 'Artsy crafty people, some were professors, educators, it didn't seem too odd.'

'I had a couple of friends lived in another trailer park on Packard [Street],' says John Mann, 'so I don't remember being shocked.'

Even fairly casual acquaintances would hear Jim griping about his trailer home. 'It was an issue he had more than we had,' says Denny Olmsted, whose dad, an engineer, earned the same or less than Jim's high-school-teacher father.

An impressive figure who was undeniably part of the classy set. Bill Kurtz, like many, considered Jim 'a notch above me on the economic scale. He was certainly with the in-crowd, a clean-cut kid in a seersucker sports coat.'

'I particularly remember his sweater with baby alligators!' laughs Francie King.

No longer seemed so painfully reliant on the approval of his peers. The dividing line between childhood confidence and arrogance is a tough one to define, but Jim teetered very close to it. Nancy McArtor sat next to Jim in Humanities, and spent much time chatting with him, enjoying his funny, quirky take on life. Nancy was on the student council, a home-coming queen, one of the most popular girls in the class. Sometimes they would have long, lively phone conversations in the evenings. And then 'abruptly, with absolutely no niceties or wind-down, he would say, "Okay, goodbye." Either he didn't like where the conversation was headed or he'd gotten bored – probably the latter. And he was gone.'

CHAPTER 2: NIGHT OF THE IGUANA

The main sources are author interviews with JO, JMcL, Don Swickerath, Nick Kolokithas, Brad Jones, Lynn Klavitter, Michael Erlewine, Dan Erlewine, Bob Sheff ('Blue' Gene Tyranny), Ron Asheton (RA), Kathy Asheton (KA), Pete Andrews, Cub Koda (CK), Jeep Holland, Lynn Goldsmith, Scott Richardson, John Sinclair (JS), Vivian Shevitz, Barbara Kramer, Charlotte Wolter, Joan Boyle, Lauri Ingber, Bill Kirchen (BK), Dale Withers, Janet Withers, Dave Leone, Sam Lay, Al Blixt.

The opening Bob Koester story is based on accounts by Koester, Ron and Scott Asheton, and Scott Richardson, all of which are consistent. Jim Osterberg today says, 'I wasn't [horrible to Koester] but they were, particularly Scott Richardson. They weren't nice to Bob and I didn't stop them . . . there is an element of gang-ism to all rock bands . . . and, er, sometimes I dropped my hands and laissez-faired . . .'

[The Iguanas] booked into United sound recorders in Detroit. The Iguanas' recordings have now been released by Norton Records as *Jumpin' With The Iguanas*, and feature demos of most of their set, recorded at Jim McLaughlin's house, plus the 'Mona' single.

The spectre of military service in the Vietnam war. Jeep Holland's account of Iggy's appearance at the draft board differs from that in *I Need More*, where Iggy claims he paraded with a hard-on. I've used Jeep's account because it's less well known and more convincing. Iggy's version, like many stories in *I Need More*, is at odds with the facts in that it contains a fictitious account of the death of the Rationals' drummer, Bill Figg, in Vietnam. To add insult to injury, Iggy blames Bill for his 'death' by claiming he was too afraid of the disapproval of others to evade the draft.

Iggy and Big Walter Horton. The 'Look old man, give me a break' quote is from a Weasel interview with Iggy Pop: WHFS, Bethesda, MD, 1980.

'It was like a horrible nightmare.' Today, Koester says he was not gay and had no sexual designs on Iggy. 'But even if I had been gay, why would that be an excuse for those guys behaving like they did?'

CHAPTER 3: THE DUM DUM BOYS

Sources: author interviews with JO, JMcL, RA, KA, Scott Asheton (SA), Bill Cheatham (BC), Jeep Holland, Ron Richardson, Jimmy Silver (JS), Wayne Kramer (WK), BK, JS and Russ Gibb. The Jeep Holland interview was conducted in 1996. The 20 January 1968 date for the Stooges' professional debut comes from a newspaper cutting kindly supplied by Ben Edmonds; other useful Grande dates were listed at www.motorcitymusicarchives.com. Ben also uncovered the genesis of the Byrds' inspiration of the Stooges' '1969', via a *MOJO* interview with Ron Asheton about his first acid trip. Scott Morgan first pointed out to me the resemblance between 'I Wanna Be Your Dog' and Yusuf Lateef's 'Eastern Market'. The opening description of the Stooges in July 1969 is based on an account by Cub Koda.

The [Stooges'] professional debut was on 20 January 1968. The Stooges invariably cite Blood Sweat & Tears (3 March 1968) as their first show. However, they played with SRC and Apple Pie Motherhood Band on Saturday 20 January, and were reviewed by Steve Silverman in an article called 'The Grande: Fun, Phantasmagoria' the following week.

The band were supporting the James Gang, on a bill that had originally featured Cream [21 April 1968]. Jim Osterberg distinctly remembers his disastrous birthday performance as the Stooges' support slot to Cream. In fact, Cream didn't play that evening – their gig was postponed to mid-June and the event was instead headlined by the James Gang. The fact Jim didn't notice Cream hadn't played is perhaps explained by the two hits of Owsley Orange Sunshine.

'The Pharaohs never wore a shirt'. Jim's Osterberg's description of how his stage garb was inspired by the Ancient Egyptians comes from his interview with Terry Gross, 'All Things Considered', *NPR*, July 2004.

Iggy's arrest in Romeo, Michigan. The story of this infamous performance is based mainly on the detailed account sent to me by Luke Engel – for whom the show represented the end of a promising career as a promoter.

White Panther Party's claimed exploits. The White Panther Party claimed to have blown up a CIA building. However, research has shown the damage was limited to one broken window.

CHAPTER 4: OH MY, BOO HOO

Sources are as for previous chapter plus Danny Fields (DF), Jac Holzman (JH), John Cale, Richard Bosworth, Lewis Merenstein, Joel Brodsky, Ben Edmonds (BE), Steve Harris (SH), Natalie Schlossman (NS) and Hiawatha Bailey (HB). In addition, I should note that Per Nilsen's research on the dates of Stooges' gigs was invaluable for the following Stooges chapters, particularly in 1971. Together with other paperwork, including the *Popped* newsletter and items from Jeff Gold's collection, I believe this has allowed me to present all the Stooges' triumphs and disasters in the correct sequence for the first time.

22 September 1968. Fields says he saw the band at the University of Michigan's union ballroom in Ann Arbor on the afternoon of Sunday 22 September – the band also played at the Grande that evening. This is consistent with dates at motorcity.com. Per Nilsen and Loren Dobson believe Fields actually saw the Stooges at a show on Monday 23rd; the Stooges did play the Union on that date.

Elektra's deal with the band was concluded on 4 October 1968. John Sinclair wrote in *5th Estate* that Elektra signed both the MC5 and the Stooges on 26 September 1968. Surviving Elektra paperwork owned by Jeff Gold reveals the Stooges actually signed on 4 October; it's likely the MC5 signed on this date, too, and that, as Jimmy Silver agrees, Sinclair 'jumped the gun'. There are no records of when Holzman and Harvey saw the Stooges at the Fifth Dimension, but given that it was a Saturday night, the only plausible date is 28 September.

Jimmy Silver wrote updates to Danny Fields, delaying the album sessions until [Iggy] returned to health. Details of Jim's bouts of asthma are taken from Jimmy Silver's letters to Danny Fields, now in the collection of Jeff Gold: 'He's much healthier than when I left him but still very flippy from being so sick and it's going to be a while before he's in top shape. He says he can put out a good performance [at the sessions] next week, though, and I have faith in him.'

The Fun House. Exact details of what posters were on the wall of the Fun House come from Natalie Schlossman's Stooges newsletter, *Popped*. Details of the house's internal geography come from Jimmy Silver and Bill Cheatham.

Fields was investigating a producer for the Stooges' first album. Jim Peterman has been cited as a suggested producer for *Fun House*; Jimmy Silver maintains he was actually suggested for the first album. This makes sense; Peterman also worked in promotion for Elektra, and the review copy of the album he gave to *Rolling Stone* magazine's Ed Ward was 'defaced', says Ward, 'because [Peterman] hated the record so much.' It's doubtful he would have entertained producing *Fun House* when Peterman had by now apparently decided he hated the Stooges.

Danny Fields introduced [the Stooges] to the city's cornucopia of delights. It was Per Nilsen who first discovered the Stooges visited New York in mid-November 1968; and in fact this is the only plausible sequence of events, as Nico filmed the 'Frozen Warnings' promo in Ann Arbor in the winter of 1968.

The gossip was that [the song 'Ann'] was inspired by Anne Opie Wehrer. Anne Wehrer was the wife of the University of Michigan's Joe Wehrer and was the subject of a memorable Once group performance, which was simply entitled *Anne Opie Wehrer* and featured multimedia re-enactments of various aspects of her fascinating life, according to Bob Sheff.

Silver and Bomser went to see Holzman [to renegotiate the Stooges' contract]. This story totally contradicts Iggy Pop's accounts, including a 1982 interview with Scott Isler, in which he claimed, 'I charmed Holzman into giving us $25,000 by making a list . . . he saw the logic.' Iggy's meeting might have softened Holzman up; however, I have discounted his version, which is consistent with much of Iggy's megalomania in that period; at a time when his life was out of control, he clung to the illusion that he was *always* in control.

The recording session started on April Fool's Day. Most Stooges stories date the recording sessions as having happened in June 1969, but Natalie Schlossman's contemporaneous *Popped* newsletter dates the sessions as starting on 1 April. The original booking was at the Record Plant, 17–21 March, from 1pm to 7pm, and was probably cancelled either because of Jim's ill health or because of the contract renegotiations.

The band returned to the Chelsea Hotel and wrote 'Little Doll', 'Not Right' and 'Real Cool Time'. Ron Asheton: 'We went with "I Wanna Be

Your Dog", "1969", "No Fun", so I'm going, oh yeah, we got songs. That was the magic Stooge time, when I could just sit down and come up with the shit. So we went there and we did what we had, along with "We Will Fall" which was Dave's chant. At the Chelsea I sat down for one hour and came up with "Little Doll", "Real Cool Time" and "Not Right", it had to be simple, and Iggy came down [and said], "Okay, yeah," and we rehearsed it one time and did it the next day, one take for each tune.'

Iggy would claim, 'John Cale had little or nothing to do with the sound. He shouldn't have been there.' Iggy's rivalry with Cale has been mapped by his pronouncements: '[He was] someone more adult, more worldly, from a band I respected . . . Someone with weight and sensitivity that would tolerate us! And therefore it helped give me confidence.' (To the author, 1992.) Or, ' John Cale had little or nothing to do with the sound. He shouldn't have been there!' (To Scott Isler, 1982.) But he has always maintained he performed the remix with Jac Holzman, an account that must surely be confused by the fog of war – or hashish, in this instance. To be fair, Jac Holzman remembers few details of the Stooges' time on Elektra, so his lack of memory of a remix is not conclusive. But as Lewis Merenstein points out, 'Cale's version is correct. I don't know why [it should hurt Iggy to admit that], he was an amazing performer and led the band throughout.' And when Fields described Iggy's dismissal of Cale as 'unworthy' he goes on to point out, 'Look, mister, in the fall of 1968 who on earth would have touched you? Much less one of the most distinguished avant-garde and far-seeing people in the musical universe!'

'[Wendy] was a virgin. I just had to have her.' This quote is from *I Need More*. I've trusted Jim's account of meeting Wendy in *I Need More*, although as elsewhere his recollections are suspect. For instance, he suggests she fell in love with him because she'd been impressed by hearing his debut album, despite the fact they married a month before it was released. He also claims Wendy turned him on to the Velvet Underground, when he'd actually seen the band back in 1966. Louis Weisberg biographical details taken from Louis's 2004 obituary in *Cleveland Jewish News*. Iggy writes in *I Need More* that he left Wendy for Betsy Mickelsen; in fact, he embarked on a brief affair with Kathy Asheton before he got together with Betsy.

Louis Weisberg pressured for annulment . . . 'It was all done on the pretext that [Jim] was a homosexual.' Although papers were filed at Washtenau County for Jim and Wendy's wedding, which gave details used here, I haven't been able to locate the paperwork for the annulment to confirm Ron's memories.

The *Rolling Stone* review. For years, *Rolling Stone*'s review of the Stooges' debut has been cited as 'stoned sloths making music for boring, repressed people', thanks to Lester Bangs quoting this phrase in *Creem*'s epic review of *Fun House*. However, the original *Rolling Stone* album review, written by Ed Ward, was supportive. The *Rolling Stone* review has often been credited to one Chris Hodenfield – who, however, reviewed it for *Go*, and did describe it as a dud, except for one standout track – 'We Will Fall!'

The album sold a just about respectable 32,000 copies. Sales figure mentioned by JO to *Zig Zag*, 1983.

Ron Asheton's guitar playing . . . was unique. Jim Osterberg once claimed, 'If someone told us we had to play Chuck Berry or die, we would have to die.' Ron Asheton's guitar style, unlike that of successor and nemesis, James Williamson, is indeed devoid of conventional blues stylings, although there are corners of northern Mississippi where his 'modal' approach might sound familiar. Most blues styles revolve around the I, IV and V chords (the three chords used in 'Louie Louie'); 'I Wanna Be Your Dog', 'Real Cool Time', 'Not Right', 'Dance of Romance' and even '1970' from *Fun House*, all revolve round an entirely different structure of the I and flattened III – nowadays, a classic stoner rock change.

CHAPTER 5: FUN HOUSE PART I: I FEEL ALRIGHT
The sources are as for the preceding chapter, plus Leo Beattie, Dave Dunlap, Steve Mackay, Esther Korinsky (EK), Don Gallucci, Leee 'Black' Childers, CK, Dave Marsh, Rumi Missabu, Tina Fantusi and Ed Caraeff. Many crucial dates, for instance when the band flew to LA, are taken from *Popped*.

Iggy was the most beautiful thing many women had seen. Tina Fantusi saw Iggy play at the Fillmore in May. 'He was the first guy I had ever been attracted to, a guy with a beautiful body. It was the first time a man's appearance hit me on a physical level. I definitely found myself appreciating the male form, that beautiful muscle definition.'

'I know I'm at the beginning . . .' From John Mendelssohn's interview in *Entertainment World*, May 1970.

It would be six years or more before he stopped falling. The Stooges' zenith was at Cincinnati Summer Pop Festival, 13 June 1970. On 8 August, Iggy sacked Dave Alexander, and around 18 August he set out to score heroin in New York. This marked the beginning of a slide in his fortunes that continued until at least 1976 and the recording of *The Idiot*.

Preparatory rehearsals at SIR. Few of my interviewees remembered that the Stooges had rehearsed with Gallucci before the Elektra sessions. However, Ben Edmonds established that they worked there, for his superlative sleeve notes to the Rhino Handmade *Fun House* box set.

Gallucci dictated the band should record one song per day, in the order of the band's live set. It's likely there were a couple of adjustments from the band's normal set list, notably 'Down On The Street' – the most 'commercial' song was recorded first, rather than the normal set-opener, 'Loose'. The band also attempted one take of 'Lost In The Future', which had appeared in their live set, but they rejected it. A version appears on the Rhino *Fun House* 2-CD reissue.

'We all took a whole bunch of cocaine.' Ed Caraeff: 'I think that was someone else [who gave the band cocaine]. I am 99 per cent sure I had never done cocaine at that point, it was later.' Although no blame can attach to Ed, for the Stooges would surely have sampled cocaine a week or so later and Jim was also turned on to the drug by Danny Fields, both Jim Osterberg and Steve Mackay specifically remember sampling cocaine in the *Fun House* sleeve photo session.

On 13 June in Cincinnati. Most fan sites and books name the televised show as being from Cincinnati Pop, which actually took place at Cincinnati Garden on 26 March. Summer Pop took place at Crosley Field on Saturday 13 June. Dead Boys singer Stiv Bators claimed to have been the fan who gave Iggy the jar of peanut butter, but there's no supporting evidence, and when I contacted fans who claimed to have been with him for the show, they all became remarkably evasive. It was Cub Koda who witnessed Iggy being lifted by the crowd in the March Cincinnati performance.

CHAPTER 6: FUN HOUSE PART II: THIS PROPERTY IS CONDEMNED
Sources: as for the preceding chapter plus Bill Williams, Nick Kent, Dan Carlisle, Wayne Kramer, James Williamson (JW), Michael Tipton,

Hiawatha Bailey, Steve Paul, Rick Derringer, Liz Derringer, Gerard Malanga, John Mendelssohn and Lisa Robinson.

Iggy was a guest on Dan Carlisle's WKNR radio show. Carlisle's interview with Iggy can be found at http://www.keener13.com/wknrfm1970.htm.

In the grim heroin roll call, Adams and Mackay went first. Most of the finer details of the band's involvement with heroin come from Steve Mackay and Bill Cheatham.

Doc, the incontinent parakeet. Doc's name first emerged in Brian J. Bowe's interview with Iggy, printed in the excellent *Heavy Liquid* box set.

Jim Osterberg: I really have to talk to you. Transcript courtesy of Danny Fields.

By now they had developed a set of all-new material. At this time, the Stooges' set included the songs 'I Got A Right', 'You Don't Want My Name', 'Fresh Rag', 'Do You Want My Love' and 'Big Time Bum'. In late 1970 the band announced in *Motor City Rock and Roll News* that 'Big Time Bum' would be their next single. It's possible their set list included the song 'Dog Food', too. There is an unimpressive bootleg CD of the band's performance at the Factory, St Charles on 27 May 1971; however, I have heard an as-yet-unreleased tape of their Chicago show that is far more brutal and impressive.

Jac Holzman wrote to Danny Fields recommending a rehab clinic . . . Elektra demanded the return of $10,825. My special thanks go to Jeff Gold of Record Mecca, who gave me access to Danny Fields' files. These contain much intriguing information, including Jac Holzman's suggestion of rehab for Iggy, and Elektra's demands that the Stooges' performance income should go directly to the label. Also intriguing is a letter dated 29 September 1971 from Bill Harvey to Jim Osterberg, care of Danny Fields, which informed him: 'We are pleased to advise you that . . . pursuant to our agreement with you of 4 October 1968 we are exercising our option to enter into a contract with you for your individual services as a recording artist.' By late September 1971 this letter was irrelevant, as Iggy had already committed himself to MainMan, but the singer was unaware that Elektra had tried to retain him until Jeff informed him of this letter in 2005. The news, I am told, 'blew his mind!'

Jac Holzman was apologetic . . . and gave Jim a Nikon camera. This was mentioned in Iggy's 1982 interview with *Trouser Press*. By now, although Jac Holzman still presided over Elektra, he had sold the company to what became the Warner Communications Group for a reported $10 million.

Ron, Scott and Jimmy Recca played one last show with Steve Richards in place of Iggy. 'I taped the show,' says Michael Tipton, who also taped *Metallic KO*. 'It was Jimmy Recca on bass, Ron on guitar and Scott on drums, of course. And a guy named Steve Richards, from River View, Michigan, hopped up and did about six or seven songs.' It is Tipton's tape of this three-piece band, without Iggy, which I believe is featured on various bootlegs, playing the songs 'Ron's Jam' and 'What's You Gonna Do'.

Iggy was making plans with a junkie's deviousness. This might sound ungenerous, but Iggy was behaving as all junkies do. As Wayne Kramer points out, 'All dope fiends betray one another all the time. In the rock world it might sound exciting or romantic. But it's not. This stuff is utterly mundane, deadly boring and completely predictable.'

David wanted to meet Iggy. Recollections of that evening, where Bowie went with the Robinsons to Max's Kansas City and the Ginger Man are, Lisa Robinson told me, 'like Rashomon. All seven different people remember it seven different ways.' Lisa believes that Jim had turned up at the Ginger Man dinner earlier in the evening. However Danny, Jim and Tony Zanetta all agree that David met Jim at Max's and, as Fields points out, 'We were too lazy to walk all the way to the Ginger Man.' Although in the end I didn't follow Lisa's sequence of events, I would like to thank her for her patience in discussing that evening, a long conversation that also involved husband Richard and Danny Fields.

CHAPTER 7: STREET-WALKING CHEETAH
Sources: Tony Zanetta, Lisa Robinson, JO, RA, SA, JW, Hugh Attwooll, Nick Kent, Michael Des Barres, John Newey, John 'Twink' Alder, Mick Farren, Dave Marsh, Richard Ogden, Wayne County, Angie Bowie, Cherry Vanilla and Leee 'Black' Childers.

There was an innocence about the encounter between the two 24-year-olds [Iggy and Bowie]. Tony Zanetta: 'David was very passionate about music and also the theater. He was excited about his career. But he was more innocent than portrayed these days.'

[Iggy's] performance was as classic in its way as anything seen at Ungano's or the Electric Circus. 'It was like a lightbulb went on and Jim could see that [Bowie and Defries] were good for him,' says Zanetta. 'He was American and they were English and fascinated by everything American. That morning, about living in the trailer, he played that up pretty big.'

The notion that Clive Davis could succeed where Jac Holzman had failed appealed to the Columbia boss's ego. Steve Harris [head of marketing at Columbia]: 'I tried to explain [to Clive Davis] that you have to market this guy very differently. He didn't understand. He just saw the chance of taking an act that didn't make it and after it went on CBS and made a hit he would say, "See what I could do and they couldn't!"'

Will you do Simon and Garfunkel? Taken from Iggy's 1974 interview with Lester Bangs for *Creem* magazine.

The Columbia advance was widely touted as being $100,000 but this was typical Defries grandstanding. I am hoping that more details will surface on this deal in the near future. Zanetta believes the advance was either $25,000 or $37,500 for one album. Peter and Leni Gilman, who apparently had access to Gem paperwork, put the figure at $25,000.

No English rhythm section was aggressive enough. David Bowie did call Twink, of the Pink Fairies, to ask him to audition with Iggy and James. Twink called, and they told him they were going back to America and didn't need a drummer. Bowie had also suggested calling the Pink Fairies' other drummer, Russell Hunter, who tells me, 'I can say with absolute confidence neither Sandy nor I were ever contacted about doing anything with him or his prospective band.' (Russell did, by coincidence, audition for Johnny Thunders a few years later.) Jim Avery, World War Three's bassist, also confirms that neither he nor drummer Paul Olsen auditioned for the Stooges.

'The full-on quality of the Stooges was great, like flame-throwers.' Quote from John Robb's *Punk Rock: An Oral History*.

'My insanity bar was raised so high . . . nothing sounded bent enough – ever.' Taken from Jim's comments to Brian J. Bowe, for the sleeve notes to the *Easy Action* box set, which contains the Olympic versions of 'I Got A Right'.

A *Time* magazine feature headlined 'Search and Destroy'. The relevant issue was dated 4 September 1972. Iggy has remembered its subject as the Vietnam war, which was of course featured most weeks, most notably via Nick Ut's famous photo of Kim Phuc after a napalm attack at the end of June.

Williamson used to punctuate the riff with the exclamation 'Kill it, gooks'. From Arthur Levy's interview with Jim, *Raw Power* remix reissue notes.

The sessions started on 10 September. The recording dates come from a MainMan schedule, which was fortuitously retained by writer Kris Needs, who at one time ran the Mott the Hoople fan club. The sessions were complete by 6 October. This means that, for instance, songs like 'Search And Destroy', which was inspired by the *Time* article, were written and recorded within a couple of weeks of Iggy's walk in Hyde Park.

CHAPTER 8: SHE CREATURES OF THE HOLLYWOOD HILLS
Major sources include JO, RA, JW, SA, Leee 'Black' Childers, Angie Bowie, Rodney Bingenheimer, Evita Ardura, Lori Maddox, Lonnie, Annie Apple, Kathy Heller, Cherry Vanilla, Tony Zanetta, Jayne County, Nick Kent, Bob Sheff, Mark Parenteau, Ricky Frystack and Kim Fowley.

'That fucking carrot-top.' This quote about Bowie comes from Lester Bangs' April 1974 *Creem* interview with Iggy and James. In the interview, James also suggests that 'David waited five months to go in and mix *in three and a half days* an album that was so fuckin' complicated' – a time frame that, as so often, doesn't fit the confirmed facts. In 2006, Williamson confirmed that his recollection was that the album was mixed in late October 1972, just after it was recorded. In 1991, Bowie told *International Musician* that 'He had the band on one track, lead guitar on another and him on a third. Out of twenty-four tracks there were just three tracks that were used. He said, "See what you can do with this." I said, "Jim, there's nothing to mix."'

Iggy . . . adrift on planet heroin. Main interviews for where Iggy's head was at include Nick Kent, Bob Sheff, Kathy Heller, Leee Childers, Nancy McCrado, Kathy Heller, Evita, James Williamson and Lonnie. Obviously, I also interviewed James, Scott and Ron about this period, but their memories don't feature heavily here because by now they tended to ignore their singer's erratic behaviour.

Ford Auditorium show. Based on accounts by Robert Matheu, Ben Edmonds, Bob Baker and Skip Gildersleeve. Ben Edmonds recalls the performance as being comparatively restrained, the Stooges on their best behaviour, only enlivened by the crazed piano of Bob Sheff. Robert and Skip both remember James Osterberg Senior and Louella, in their best clothes, in the audience to hear Iggy introduce 'Cock In My Pocket' as a song 'co-written by my mother'.

Warren Klein. Although I traced him, Klein never returned my calls, and presumably wants to forget his momentary career as a Stooge. He has since gone on to contribute his tasteful, rootsy work to records by Marshall Crenshaw, Peter Case and, most notably, Beck's album *Mutations*.

CHAPTER 9: BEATING A DEAD HORSE
Sources as for preceding chapters, plus Doug Currie, Scott Thurston, Jeff Wald, BE, Don Waller, Steve Harris, Michael Tipton, Natalie Schlossman, EK, Lenny Kaye, Bob Czaykowski (Nite Bob), Bebe Buell, Dave Marsh, Phast Phreddie Patterson, Robert Matheu, Joel Selvin, Bob Baker, Skip Gildersleeve and Hiawatha Bailey.
    Opening quotes: all author interviews.

'Don't fuck with me or I will hurt you.' Jeff Wald: 'I was very intimidating. I would fight at the drop of a hat anybody, a cop or whoever. It was insanity, my behaviour, getting arrested for doing various assaults on a continual basis. I didn't take any shit from anybody.'

'You should count yourself lucky . . .' This account is second-hand, but was described by Danny Sugerman to many friends, including Ben Edmonds, at the time.

Manager with a gun. Bob Sheff: 'This kid actually went into the bank with a gun to cash this cheque 'cause he was afraid somebody was gonna steal the money from him. I don't know if this was Danny Sugerman but it was . . . dumb.'

Max's rehearsals. Both Ron Asheton and Michael Tipton mentioned how Iggy missed three consecutive flights from Los Angeles to Max's, and arrived late for the first shows. But most other witnesses seem to remember the Columbia rehearsals being before that show, so this is how I've constructed the chain of events.

Ashley Pandel. Pandel's name was detailed in Iggy's interview with Henry Edwards for *After Dark*, November 1973.

Watergate story. Main sources are Bebe Buell, Scott Thurston and JW.

New York Dolls arrived in LA on 29 August. Thanks to Kris Needs for the New York Dolls information and Syl Sylvain quotes; outtakes from *Trash*, Kris's New York Dolls book on Plexus.

Whisky-a-Go-Go shows. Interviews and information, Don Waller, Phast Phreddie Patterson, Tom Gardner and Jeff Gold.

Michigan Palace, October. Thanks to Michael Tipton and Natalie Schlossman for their detailed accounts of this chaotic night. For the sake of accuracy, I should also acknowledge that Natalie points out that 'Most of the time it was not as crazy as that – usually I would just see Jim with one woman,' although she went on to mention that 'I do remember three girls all trying to have a go at Jim at the same time.' It was Michael Tipton who mentioned that the band reintroduced 'Louie Louie' to their set at the Michigan Palace: Michael taped 'Raw Power', 'Head On', 'Gimme Danger', 'Search And Destroy', 'Heavy Liquid' and 'Open Up And Bleed' from the second night's performance, which have since turned up on several CDs; the first three songs were included on the original vinyl release of *Metallic KO*, and the entire recording was issued on the later *Metallic KO* × 2.

Iggy was asking a promoter for a one-million dollar fee to commit suicide. The rumour going around Rodney's, according to Kim Fowley, was that Iggy had told one promoter, who was associated with publicist Gary Stromberg, that if he could guarantee him $1 million to play Madison Square Garden, then he would commit suicide on stage. I contacted Stromberg, who said no such conversation took place.

News of the death of Zeke Zettner. Zeke, who played bass with the Stooges for just a few months, died on 10 November, 1973 in the Bi-County Community Hospital, Michigan. The cause of death was recorded as perforated peptic ulcer and cerebral oedema caused by a heroin overdose. Zeke was twenty-five and had returned to East Detroit, working in the automotive industry and living with his parents.

Rock and Roll Farm, Wayne, Michigan. Ken Settle was a photographer who frequented several shows at the Rock and Roll Farm including Bob Seger the same week. 'The Scorpions were a rough biker club from Detroit's West Side. They seemed to hang out at the R and R Farm; I think the guy that ran it liked them hanging out there because they were like free bouncers if anyone got too rowdy.' The farm was at 34828 Michigan Avenue.

'That's it, we're gone.' Ron Asheton: 'The leather-studded big dude blasts Jim, Jim fell down, then got up and goes to me, "We're gone, that's it, unplug, we're getting out of here." We go back to the dressing room and all of a sudden these biker dudes are coming in . . .' In *I Need More*, Iggy remembers playing 'Louie Louie' at the end; Ron believes they didn't.

That didn't stop them from appearing on Detroit's WABX radio station and challenging the Scorpions. Unfortunately, despite my interviewing WABX DJs, including Mark Parenteau and Dennis Frawley, no one is certain whose show the Stooges' challenge was broadcast on.

Dirty and a little threadbare. Ben Edmonds: 'The costumes looked impressive from a long way away. Close up it was obvious they'd seen better days, and that the band needed someone to do their laundry.'

The Stooges had enlisted the help of God's Children, a biker gang based in Ypsilanti. Hiawatha Bailey (www.thecultheroes.com): 'God's Children were based in Ypsilanti and were like the police force for the revolution. John Cole was the coolest guy. In order to join you had to have the Kiss of Fellowship. All the bikers would all get drunk, then puke, then French-kiss you. Then they'd shake your hand and you were one of the guys.'

'He had fun with it.' It was Michael Tipton's tape that was used for the *Metallic KO* album. 'There [was] so much more antagonisation of the audience than you hear on the record – there's a lot of dead time between songs where he's rambling on about shit, which I edited.'

CHAPTER 10: KILL CITY

Main sources for this chapter include JO, JW, RA, BE, Philippe Mogane, Ray Manzarek, Danny Sugerman, Jim Parrett, Thom Gardner, Michael Tipton, Annie Klenman (aka Apple), Doug Currie, Harvey Kubernick, Pamela Des Barres, Don Waller, Nigel Harrison, Rodney Bingenheimer, Michael Des Barres, Tony Sales, Brian Glascock, Dr Murray Zucker, Nick Kent and Mike Page. The Danny Sugerman information and quotes come mainly from an interview conducted by Chris Carter and George Hickenlooper, in an out-take for the movie *The Mayor of the Sunset Strip*, for which I must offer my grateful thanks. I have also selectively used information from Danny's book *Wonderland Avenue*. Thanks to all these sources, I believe I have for the first time mapped out Jim's movements over this period. In particular, the story of his mysterious trips to San Diego has never been told. However, the hand-to-mouth nature of Jim's existence means it's difficult to be confident that all the events are always in the correct order.

[Iggy] was convinced there was a hex on [him and the Stooges]. Nick Kent: 'I had a number of conversations in 1975 where he felt like the Stooges were hexed. There was a curse on them. He became superstitious and he felt that there was no way out.'

New Order. The main New Order musicians included one-time Stooges bassist Jimmy Recca, the MC5's Dennis Thompson on drums and Dave Gilbert, who'd previously sung with Ted Nugent.

Danny Sugerman [took over Jim's] management. In *Wonderland Avenue*, Sugerman describes Iggy as suggesting that he become his manager and team him up with Ray. Ray remembers that it was Danny who talked both Ray and Iggy into the scheme.

'Do you want to see blood?' Details of this exchange come from Ron Asheton.

Attacking the Maserati with a hatchet. Danny cited this as happening the morning after Rodney's in his interview with Carter and Hickenlooper. However, it could well have happened at some other point and, as with some of the stories in *Wonderland Avenue*, it's possible that he reworked some for dramatic affect, or else confused them. In fact, over a period in which most of the participants were heavy users of heroin or Quaaludes, time frames can often seem elastic, to say the least . . .

Scott Morgan was called in to guest on harmonica. I interviewed Scott twice without him mentioning that he'd played harmonica at the Hollywood Trash show. I was inspired to interview him once again by the excellent story on Sonics Rendezvous Band, formed with Morgan and the MC5's Fred Smith, at http://www.i94bar.com/ints/srb1.html.

The [Hollywood Trash] show was competent. Most fans, including Jim Parrett, Don Waller and Greg Shaw, thought the outfit looked like a competent bar band; a couple thought they sounded like a semi-competent bar band. Nick Kent says, '[They] decided, let's kick the New York Dolls' arse, [and] that's what they did. It was good. It was the Stooges with Manzarek on keyboards, basically, and it was fantastic.'

Danny's growing reliance on quaaludes and heroin. Several people maintain Sugerman's heroin addiction was never as serious as portrayed in his uproarious memoir, *Wonderland Avenue*. But Ray Manzarek, while acknowledging the book's dramatic licence, agrees that Sugerman was indeed 'fucking stoned' all the time . . .

Shortly after the Palladium show. The only independent evidence I have for this is Danny's *Wonderland Avenue*, which is elsewhere inconsistent on timing, but this sequence fits with all the surrounding events.

'Hello. This is Dr Zucker.' This exchange is based on that remembered by Danny in *Wonderland Avenue*. Dr Zucker: 'I don't know whether [the first visit] was involuntary or not but he certainly had no problem in staying until stabilised; it wasn't under contest that he was there.'

Jim Osterberg was fortunate to have landed up at one of the world's leading psychiatric facilities. Dr Kay Jamison wrote an enthralling memoir, *An Unquiet Mind* (Picador 1996), about her struggles with manic depression, which encompassed her time at NPI and makes illuminating background reading. A second book, *Touched with Fire* (Free Press 1993), analyses the links between manic-depressive illness and the artistic temperament. She cites, for example, more than eighty poets thought to have suffered from mood disorders, including Baudelaire, John Berryman, Blake, Burns, Chatterton, John Clare, Coleridge, T.S. Eliot, Thomas Gray, Victor Hugo, Keats, Robert Lowell, Vladimir Mayakovsky, Pasternak, Plath, Edgar Allen Poe, Pushkin, Delmore Schwartz, Shelley, Tennyson, Dylan Thomas and Walt Whitman; the list of novelists and musicians is just as comprehensive. Recently Vincent van Gogh, a celebrated bipolar, has been claimed by the temporal-lobe-disorder crowd.

The diagnosis was that his underlying condition was hypomania, a bipolar disorder. In 2005, John Gartner's *The Hypomanic Edge* theorised that hypomania drives many of the USA's entrepreneurs; Gartner suggests that hypomania and manic depression are more common in immigrant societies, which are less risk-averse, and that there is an evolutionary advantage to this behaviour.

Bowie was one of the few who gained admittance . . . accompanied by the actor Dean Stockwell. Jim Osterberg: '[Bowie] came up one day, stoned out of his brain in his little spacesuit, with Dean Stockwell the actor. They were like, "We want to see Jimmy. Let us in." Now the strict rule was to never let outsiders in: it was an insane asylum. But the doctors were star-struck, so they let them in. And the first thing they said was, "Hey, want some blow?" I think I took a little, which is really unpleasant in there. And that's how we got back in touch.' (1996, quoted in *MOJO*'s Bowie special edition, 2003.) Kevin Cann places Bowie's first visit at around June 1975, but it must have been several months earlier, predating their studio work together in May, which followed the chance meeting on Sunset Boulevard. In my interview with Jim Osterberg in 2005, he mentioned that Bowie was about to work on *The Man Who Fell To Earth*, and played him recordings from *Station To Station*. According to most Bowie chronologies, of which Kevin Cann's is the most informed, this too seems impossible, so it's likely that Jim conflated two periods, or that the recordings were demos. Although most magazine features and stories date the recording of *Kill City* to mid-1975, the sessions were definitely complete before Edmonds played the first mixes to Seymour Stein in late January 1975.

By the summer of 1975, Williamson had once more drifted apart from Jim. This information comes from Ken Shimamoto's interview with James. Ron Asheton has repeatedly mentioned that the original Stooges split after James attempted to get Jim to sign this contract, but I believe he's confused the chain of events. There are plenty of witnesses, including James and Doug Currie, who confirm that all the Stooges had decided to quit before they returned to LA after the *Metallic KO* performance; the contract dispute was therefore almost certainly after *Kill City* was recorded.

Bowie moved to New York in Christmas 1974. Date taken from Gilman, p. 493.

Fred Sessler and Lisa Leggett. This element of Jim's life has never been mentioned elsewhere; it derives from an interview with Jim I conducted around 1993, in which he mentioned his stint in San Diego and a 'shady' businessman whom he didn't name. By coincidence, I discovered the complete Lisa Leggett story during a long, crazed evening with Mike Page a few years later. Jim then filled in the blanks during my interview with him in 2005, as well as including tasty details, such as the fact that Lisa paid for him to go on a motivational speakers' course. Fred Sessler was a well-loved figure; he died in 2001. Lisa Leggett, according to Mike Page, subsequently married Willy DeVille, of Mink DeVille, and recently passed away.

CHAPTER 11: THE PASSENGER
Main sources include JO, Andrew Kent, Carlos Alomar, Roberta Bayley, Laurent Thibault, Kuelan Nguyen, Phil Palmer, Tony Visconti, Edu Meyer, Esther Friedmann (EF), Klaus Kruger, Angie Bowie, Tony Sales and Hunt Sales. The opening scene is based on a description by Jim Osterberg.

[Iggy is] 'Not so hard and knowledgeable and all-knowing and cynical. Someone who hasn't a clue . . . but has insights.' Taken from Edmonds' interview with Bowie for *Circus*, cover date April 1976, and conducted during rehearsals for the Station To Station tour.

Bowie . . . keeping Iggy 'under his thumb'. This is from Harald's letter to Ben Edmonds, 17 May 1976.

Mick Ronson thought his old boss was almost besotted with Iggy. Author's interview at the Dominion Theatre, London, February 1989. I'm not suggesting that Ronson was a disinterested commentator, but his view seemed to be that Iggy had railroaded Bowie as much as vice versa.

They discussed David producing an album for Iggy at Musicland . . . in Munich. Iggy mentioned the possibility of recording in Munich to *Punk* magazine in April 1976. All other details drawn from my 2005 interview with JO.

For a court appearance with Bowie the previous day. Dates taken from Kevin Cann's Bowie chronology and newspaper reports collected on the Bowie Golden Years website.

For the first time in his life, Iggy said no. Jim: 'And if I'd gotten high with him that week, we wouldn't be here talking. And that was the first time I was beginning to turn a corner and acquire some powers of resistance. And it was something . . . that lightbulb that went on and off with me for quite a few years after that.'

[The] mysterious train trip to Moscow. Most books on Bowie place his trip to Moscow as being right at the start of his European trip. It seems more logical to me that this journey took place a few weeks into it, between his shows on 17 and 24 April in Bern and Helsinki respectively. Although stories about Bowie having books confiscated have been repeated often, along with a quote from Bowie that he'd bought the book as reference material for a movie on Goebbels, they seem full of factual inaccuracies, with an impossible date and an inaccurate route. I haven't found any contemporary reports detailing this affair and my suspicion is that the story has been exaggerated in the retelling. There's no doubt that David and Jim had some interest in Nazism but – disappointingly for a good yarn, I know – it's clear, from speaking to third parties, including Jim's (Jewish) girlfriend Esther Friedmann, that Bowie's interest in Hitler was mostly confined to an interest in his mythology, his graphic and stage design and generally to wind up his interviewers. Bowie's most specific statement about Hitler was made to Cameron Crowe, around May 1975, and wasn't mentioned in Crowe's February 1976 *Rolling Stone* story but was included in his longer *Playboy* profile of September 1976. In it, Bowie says, 'Hitler was the first rock star,' a quote I suggest was plagiarised from Ron Asheton.

The Idiot **rhythm tracks.** The final version of *The Idiot* incorporates parts from Davis, Murray, Santageli and Thibault. They can be distinguished, with some difficulty, according to the sound. Dennis Davis's snare drum was smaller and tuned higher; George Murray uses a bass guitar with a rounder sound than Thibault's Rickenbacker. Davis and Murray seem audible on 'Sister Midnight' and 'Mass Production'; Santageli and Thibault seem to have made the final mix on, for instance, 'China Girl' (with its superb Joy Division-esque bass part) and 'Baby', although in every case the effects-laden mix makes it harder to work out who is who – and on several songs you can hear two snare drums at once.

'Nightclubbing' features a Roland drum machine and a bass part played on Bowie's ARP Axxe synthesiser.

As Palmer prepared to overdub guitar. It has been reported that the recorded version of 'Sister Midnight' is played by Carlos Alomar, probably from an initial recording made during the *Man Who Fell To Earth* soundtrack sessions at Cherokee in Los Angeles. Palmer was certain he recognised his own work on the album, while Carlos Alomar regards it as perfectly plausible his own guitar parts were replayed by another musician: '[David's] done this to me a million times. I'll put down three or four guitars and then he'll hire another guitar player and then one of those parts that I did he just goes to another guitar player and there's another little difference in it.'

Hansa studios on Kurfürstendamm. This is sometimes misidentified as Hansa by the Wall. There were two Hansa studio buildings; that on Kurfürstendamm contained a single studio on the fourth floor and opened in 1971. The Köthenerstrasse studio, in the much grander Meistersaal building, was purchased by the Meisel family in 1973 and overlooked the Berlin Wall. It initially contained two studios; Tonstudios 2 and 3, another was added later.

Thibault's original mixes. Laurent believes his original mixes were used on at least two songs. 'Sister Midnight' contains a squelch of feedback from the Musicland mixing desk that can be clearly heard [at 1.05] on the album version; while 'Mass Production', according to Laurent, uses his tape loop, and sounds like it was mixed using his trademark method, which involved mixing a section at a time, then splicing the final version together with a series of tape edits.

Musical quote from Gary Glitter. 'Rock And Roll Part One' features an identical drum beat and funereal tempo.

Favourite [Berlin] hangouts. The information is mainly from JO, Esther Friedmann, Wolfgang Doebeling (who had an office at Hansa and often saw Bowie in the local record shops), Edu Meyer, Klaus Kruger and Tony Visconti. Bowie's take on the Exil and his later quotes on Berlin come from an interview with *Uncut* magazine. Thanks also to Ed Ward, who helped me orientate myself in Berlin. The Schlosshotel Gerhus, for prospective sightseers, is now a Karl Lagerfeld boutique hotel named Schlosshotel

Vier Jahreszeiten, and has apparently scrubbed up nicely. The Café Exil is now the Horvath bar.

Later in August 1976. Kevin Cann's Bowie chronology states that Bowie and crew started work on *Low* on 1 September; however, according to Edu Meyer's records from Hansa, the sessions moved to Hansa 2 on 21 August, so my assumption is that they must have started work at the chateau in August, a dating confirmed by Visconti's memory that all the French chateau staff were on summer holiday, which would have finished by the end of August.

'A joy, ramshackle and comfy'. Bowie in *Uncut*.

Hansa seemed to embody Berlin's ruined grandeur. The Hansa information is from Edu Meyer and from the booklet that celebrated the restoration of studio 2 as a concert hall in 1994. The building is now used mainly as a venue for classical performances, but there remains a later-built Hansa studio on the fourth floor. Thanks to Alex Wende for giving me a tour of the studio and building.

The Sales brothers had played professionally for mobster-connected Maurice Levy's Roulette label. Maurice Levy was an intriguing, slightly scary figure, of the type who built the early rock 'n' roll business. He was Chuck Berry's publisher, was the inspiration for mobster/music mogul Hesh in *The Sopranos*, and was also involved in the bizarre saga of John Lennon's *Rock And Roll* album, in which Lennon covered several songs by Levy artists to avoid a lawsuit over his 'borrowing' a melody and some lyrics from Chuck Berry's 'You Can't Catch Me' for *Abbey Road*'s 'Come Together'.

It was [David's] idea to give the Sales brothers a call. Jim: 'Hunt and Tony had always been his boys. They got his gig with me because they'd submitted tapes to him.'

CHAPTER 12: HERE COMES MY CHINESE RUG
The sources are as for preceding chapter, plus Ricky Gardiner, Marc Zermati, Nick Kent, Kris Needs, David Stopps, Brian James and Glen Matlock (GM).

'Punks cruising for burgers'. This would have been in Lenny Kaye's review of *The Stooges*; apart from his obviously crucial roles as guitarist and song-writer in the Patti Smith Group, Lenny was also responsible for the superb *Nuggets*, a groundbreaking compilation that gathered together many garage classics that had influenced the Stooges, the Ramones and others.

Both leading music weeklies. The third UK music weekly was *Melody Maker*, which was owned, like the *NME*, by IPC. The *NME* set out to differentiate itself from its sister publication by its focus on punk; their contrasting reactions to the Stooges are exemplified by Nick Kent's masterfully researched and written May 1975 *NME* feature 'The Mighty Pop versus The Hand Of Blight', and Chris Charlesworth's 1973 *Melody Maker* review, in which the outraged writer asks, 'How low can rock and roll sink?' 'I don't know what the songs were called,' Charlesworth harrumphed (obviously having done his pre-show research), 'but they all seemed to contain more than a smattering of strong language intended, it seems, to insult the audience.' On the same page, the venerable journal saves its praise for Stackridge, and the cutting-edge saxophone skills of Tommy Whittle, Kathy Stobart and Jimmy Skidmore.

Bowie reckoned, 'The drug use was *unbelievable'*. Interview in *Q* magazine, 1993.

Jim Osterberg would turn in some fabulous [TV] performances. There's also a hilarious interview with Peter Gzowski in the Canadian Broadcasting Company archives, http://archives.cbc.ca/IDC-1-68-102-761/arts_entertainment/punk/.

A romantic idyll with Pleasant Gehman. Pleasant had met Iggy back in 1975 when he was a classic fallen rock star, living in a decayed apartment on Flores and asking visitors, 'You got any drugs?' the moment they walked through the door. She met him again in 1977, a couple of days after she'd fallen down some steps; she had a cast on her wrist and a bruised, swollen face. Jim recognised her and whisked her away from her friends, and they spent an idyllic couple of weeks in a beachfront house in Malibu. 'We were smoking pot and drinking red wine and went out onto the jetty. We were talking about everything; about the Romanovs and the Russian Revolution, we were talking about painting and abstract stuff, we were talking about communism, we were talking about life. Then we had sex a lot, more than I'd ever had. He was amazingly considerate. He had a great body and then the next morning he asked if I wanted to move in with him . . . I was treated like royalty.' Over the same period, Jim also hung out with the Germs and others, and he posed for some excellent photos by Jenny Lens.

New flat and contract details. These are from paperwork in the possession of Esther Friedmann, which she kindly allowed me to examine to help identify some of the crucial dates.

The irritation each felt. This is according to Jim's recollection. It could be that David Bowie felt no irritation whatsoever with Jim; unfortunately, he declined to speak to me to tell me himself.

By the time the sessions began in June. Edu Meyer's partial records of the Hansa sessions detail the recording session as being on 8 to 12 and 14 June, with mastering in July. This contrasts with most other chronologies, which date the sessions in late April. Most of the musicians remember the recording sessions as lasting about ten days.

Ukulele. This story has been told by Jim many times; asked by *Uncut* if this account was correct, David replied, 'Absolutely.'

'Kicking and screaming.' JO: 'Yes, ["Success" was written] in an ironic manner. And to me, just to have a little Chinese rug. But also the unironic manner . . . this happens to me, sometimes when my back is against the wall I'll sorta kick the floor a little bit, enter a successful zone or situation and then proceed to bitch! And kinda have to be dragged kicking and screaming to the good outcome. But I kinda just felt, in that particular song . . . we had a good friction in the studio . . . and came up with that slightly demented vocal, which you hear a big difference in the vocals between [*The Idiot* and *Lust For Life*], rockism was starting to set in, and I was starting to revert, but there was a nice balance. And he [Bowie] was sick of the whole thing at that point and just wanted to get the damn thing over with. But he did well.'

Warren Peace. Warren Peace, aka Geoffrey MacCormack, was Bowie's backing singer and later travelling companion. He was supplanted in the latter role by Iggy. JO: 'David was looking for a [new] sidekick [in 1976], he likes to do things that way, and Warren Peace had become more Hollywood than was great for their relationship.'

CHAPTER 13: MISSING IN ACTION
Main sources: JO, Charles Levison, Julie Hooker, Tarquin Gotch, Tony Sales, Scott Thurston, EF, Robin Eggar, Edu Meyer, Hunt Sales, Gary Rasmussen, SA, BE, Klaus Kruger, JW, GM, Kingsley Ward, Barry Andrews and Ivan Kral (IK).

Opening based on accounts by Charles Levison, Tarquin Gotch and Julie Hooker, all of Arista Records. Hooker points out that although many staff called Davis 'the Godfather', this wasn't a comment on his business practices, but a reflection of how intimately he oversaw the business.

Lust For Life **disappeared.** Robin Eggar, RCA press: 'The RCA pressing plant was, I think, in Hayes, and they didn't just turn 90 per cent of their production to Elvis – it was more like 95 per cent, which was incredibly short-sighted.'

Pissing in the wastebasket. JO: 'I think I said something terrible up at RCA after [Elvis] died, saying, OK, that's too bad, I'm the new Elvis, and I think I peed in the wastebasket under the guy's desk whose office I was using during the interview and it became ta ta . . . it became psst psst pss.' [i.e. Iggy started getting the reputation of being 'difficult'.] I contacted some members of RCA's A&R department in the late 1970s, and they couldn't remember this incident, although as one of them succinctly puts it, 'I was so stoned I don't remember diddly. We were all out of it, all the time, back then.' Iggy's cocaine paranoia episode at the Gerhus occurred shortly before, or shortly after, this incident.

'Needy and wanty.' Scottie Thurston, when asked if Jim was more together in 1977 than in 1973: 'Well . . . I don't know. I really don't know. You see . . . it was the age of cocaine, which is not a very together drug for a singer. He could have done a lot better job. So could have we all. I don't look back on it as a regretful period, I just think . . . we honestly all could've done a lot better.'

Kill City **[was] released by Bomp.** The *Kill City* album augmented the tracks recorded at Jimmy Webb's studio with two songs, 'Lucky Monkey' and 'Mastercharge', recorded on a four-track at Scottie Thurston's house, during the period when Scottie had found Jim an apartment near him in Venice Beach, probably in the spring of 1974. All the tracks were remixed by James Williamson – according to Ben Edmonds, the original version was much tougher and more like the Stooges.

The Sonic's Rendezvous Band issued just one legendary single, 'City Slang'. This historical oversight was corrected in late 2006 with a lavish box set of SRB material issued by the Easy Action label (www.easyaction.co.uk). There is an excellent retrospective of the SRB by Ken Shimamoto at http://www.i94bar.com/ints/srb1.html, with a hilarious story of the time an unruly Scandinavian crowd threw fish at the band. Many Iggy fans cite SRB as one of his best backing bands, but some of their performances and song arrangements must stand as the absolute antithesis of Iggy's original musical manifesto; their versions of 'Lust For Life' and 'Little Doll' in particular sound like dreadful Yardbirds ripoffs – this from a man who criticised Bowie for copying the same band.

Charles Levison, [Arista's] managing director. Levison was given the job of managing director of Arista Worldwide, overseeing the entire company outside the USA. His main task, along with Edmonds, was to establish the company as a major force in the UK, bringing in new, hipper talent, trying to break artists signed by Arista's head office in New York – in particular, Barry Manilow – as well as trying to eke out the careers of two artists the UK company had inherited, namely retro-glamsters Showaddywaddy and one-time bopper idols the Bay City Rollers. Levison was a charming, well-loved man; he died on 7 July 2006, of complications following a heart attack.

'Peter was very together in the beginning.' I have spent many days trying to track down Peter through ex-colleagues at RCA, friends and other acquaintances, to hear his own recollection of events, without success. He was universally respected by those who dealt with him in the early days, but unfortunately, as Barry Andrews and others remember, he was engulfed by the chaos that started to envelop Iggy over this period.

Bindon was a one-time gangster who'd made his living as an actor. Barry Andrews: 'Bowie was holding court really and talking about Princess Margaret being shagged by Johnny Bindon, who has the biggest dick in London, and cut a guy's head off in a bar, and all those Johnny Bindon stories which we now know. And it grew out of the conversation, "What's the safest thing you can be? A criminal."' The account of 'Play It Safe' here is based on the recollections of Andrews, who was there throughout the session, seems to have been more sober than most of the other musicians and has no axe to grind. James Williamson, however, while acknowledging that he detested Bowie's intrusion, remembers the final row being about Iggy's vocals. From this period, Glen Matlock has also told in print an enthralling story of how Steve New encountered David Bowie talking to his girlfriend, Patti Palladin, and punched Bowie out in the belief he was chatting her up – only to find that Bowie was merely cadging some cigarettes. However, Glen was in London during Bowie's visit to the studio, and New was reportedly overawed with Bowie, so I have regretfully been forced to omit this story from the main narrative.

CHAPTER 14: THE LONG, LONG ROAD
Main interviews: JO, EF, IK, Brian James, GM, Charles Levison, Tarquin Gotch, Mike Page, Rob Duprey, Carlos Alomar, Frank Infante, Dayna Louise, Margaret Moser, Anne Wehrer (interviewed in 1996) and Gary Valentine. Thanks also to Dr Murray Zucker for background information. Tour dates courtesy of Per Nilsen.

'I felt that David wanted to dump Jim on me. It was like, "I'm trying to help him, but he always screws up."' Note that this is what Ivan *thought* Bowie meant, not necessarily what Bowie actually meant. Ivan certainly thought that Iggy didn't appreciate, or perhaps deserve, Bowie's help, but this isn't necessarily David's perception.

'One For My Baby'. This song had first appeared in the set with SRB, but became a fixture over the *New Values* tour. It was later recorded, with a rather staid arrangement, during the *Party* sessions.

Iggy Pop would delight in stealing groupies from under their noses. Glen Matlock: 'There was these three good-looking birds [in Toronto]. And the guys in the band were sitting round having a drink and we're kinda trying to chat 'em up. Didn't really get anywhere. And then it kinda dawned on us that at certain times there was always a different one missing. And they'd all been up to Iggy's room and come back. But we had the last laugh, 'cause the next morning he was in a foul mood. What happened was one of them had the coil fitted wrong, and it cut his dick up really bad. And when we got to do the gig that night, not only did he get his dick out, which he normally does, but he'd got it wrapped up in Kleenex. And he's pulling bits of Kleenex off his dick and throwing it into the audience. You know they say the band behind the stripper gets the best view? Well, it was 'orrible.'

'**Cutting off his nose to spite his face**'. It is of course possible that the *Soldier* mixes were a mess for other reasons.

Boyce was the man to salvage Iggy's album. Charles Levison has been blamed for recruiting Tommy Boyce, but his memory was that 'that was probably Tarquin's suggestion, although I [would] have been involved in the decision'. Tarquin, meanwhile, although he doesn't remember specifically, says, 'I'm happy to take the blame if nobody else will, but I thought it was Charles's suggestion, because it's that sort of American older connection.'

CHAPTER 15: NIGHT OF THE ZOMBIES
This chapter is mainly based around Esther's account of her and Jim's disastrous holiday in Haiti. It is the first time this story has come out in print, and I'm extremely grateful to Esther for sharing it. She tells me she has also performed a full, two-hour version containing other bizarre episodes not mentioned here, which is guaranteed to leave an audience frazzled and emotionally exhausted. I can't wait to hear it. While it is of course amusing, like so many stories pertaining to Jim Osterberg it is also tragic, and ends in our hero succumbing to madness, and one bystander dead. At the close, I have written that Jim descended into madness, which is not the word that Esther used; she said 'illness'. I don't mean to be fanciful. It is the word, however, used by psychiatric experts such as Kate Jamison to describe the kind of behaviour Jim exhibited in Haiti. Other sources include Mike Page, Rob Duprey, Anne Wehrer, Murray Zucker, Ric Ocasek, and the JO interview with David Fricke also cited in Chapter 16.

Collapsing PA stacks. Frank Infante remembers this show as being in Portland, Mike Page remembers it as being at the Santa Monica Pacific Auditorium. Unless the tour information I have is incorrect, Infante's line-up didn't play Santa Monica.

CHAPTER 16: HIDEAWAY
Main sources: JO, Nigel Harrison, Robert Matheu, Clem Burke, Dr Murray Zucker, EF, Kevin Armstrong, Erdal Kizilcay, Seamus Beaghen, Nancy Jeffries, Jeff Gold, Olivier Ferrand, Dan Bourgoise and Bill Laswell. For Jim's years out of the limelight, one priceless source was an interview conducted in October 1984 for *People* magazine by David Fricke of *Rolling Stone*. David demonstrated an unrivalled combination of generosity and

organisation – keeping an interview tape and then locating it twenty years on. Huge thanks also to Kris Needs for supplying a copy of his *Creem* interview from 1986, which filled in more gaps over this period.

Iggy's tour was cancelled because of legal threats. According to road manager Henry McGroggan, this tale is incorrect, and the tour of the Far East was cut short simply due to Iggy's exhaustion.

Olivier Ferrand. According to Ferrand, Iggy and Jones recorded eight songs: a mellow version of 'Purple Haze', 'Get To The Point', 'Fire Girl', 'Warm Female', a rather bland take on 'Family Affair', 'Cry For Love', 'Beside You' and 'Winners And Losers'. It's possible the songs also included 'When Dreaming Fails' and a messy cover of the Animals' 'It's My Life'.

Iggy-flavoured Bowie album. This was mentioned in a generally supportive review by Richard Riegel in *Creem*, February 1987.

New manager Art Collins. Art was part of a management duo with Barry Taylor, but Art was the one that most A&M staff remember; he went on to manage Iggy solo, and was much loved. Art died in July 2005; Iggy's long-term road manager, Henry McGroggan – also known for his work with the Corrs – took over his management.

Iggy seized a large teddy bear and started copulating with it. In polls of greatest TV moments, this appearance has been listed as being on *Motormouth*, but it was actually the ITV kids' *No. 73*. Hopefully the video will eventually surface on youtube.com.

A three-month run of shows supporting the Pretenders. For the Pretenders shows, Andy Anderson replaced Gavin Harrison on drums.

Iggy had made bad albums before, but *Instinct* was the first time he'd been boring. Nick Kent, whose critical opinions I naturally respect, chooses *Blah Blah Blah* for his personal disdain: 'I actually fell asleep the first time I heard it I was so underwhelmed.' However, I would choose *Instinct* as the most soporific of Iggy's albums, with its endless mid-paced chugging guitars, mind-numbingly predictable riffs, sterile solos and forgettable lyrics. However hard I try to concentrate on this album, I find myself diverted to some more stimulating activity, like filing press cuttings or tidying the cutlery drawer.

CHAPTER 17: UNDEFEATED

Main sources: JO, Nancy Jeffries, Don Was, Whitey Kirst, Charles Francis aka Black Francis, Eric Schermerhorn, Hal Cragin, Larry Mullins, Bob Gruen, Glen Matlock, Pete Marshall.

'Livin' On The Edge Of The Night' . . . **didn't make its intended slot on** *Black Rain.* Although the song appears on the OST compilation, both Don Was and Iggy mentioned that their original song wasn't used.

'Did You Evah'. Helped by a snazzy Alex Cox video, the single reached number 42 in the UK.

'Everything they did blows me away.' Taken from 'Heroes', *Guitar* magazine 1992, interview by Cliff Jones, as is the Thurston Moore 'I'd really like to see Nirvana as Iggy's backing band' quote.

The American 'alternative' and grunge scene of the 1990s. Thanks to *MOJO*'s Jenny Bulley – who was at the 1989 Nirvana Astoria show – Keith Cameron and Andrew Perry for discussing Iggy and the Stooges' influence on grunge.

'You little scumbag!' Johnny Depp: 'We actually met in 1989, on the set of John Waters' *Cry-Baby*. But I had already met him long before. We were in a bar in 1980. At this time, I was part of a band who played first part of his show. I was seventeen. It was in Gainesville in Florida. After the concert, we all gathered in a bar and I absolutely wanted to draw his attention to me. When they closed the bar, I was totally drunk and I started yelling obscenities at him. He didn't react at first, after a while Iggy came close to me, looked me straight in the eyes and said, "You little scumbag!" Then he left. I felt at the top of the world – at least he finally knew I was existing. That was great.' (Interview by Christophe d'Yvoire.)

'I think there was a moment where Jim decided that he couldn't do a fucking article without my name being mentioned – and I don't think that's a very comfortable feeling.' Bowie went on to say, 'I completely understand – I really, really do. Unfortunately, I think Jim took it personally, and that's a shame because I would have liked to remain closer to him.' To Robert Phoenix, gettingit.com, October 1999.

Henry Rollins. Rollins has a hilarious monologue of his admiration for and rivalry with Iggy, based around his attempt to blow him off stage at successive performances; it's included as an extra on the *Live At Luna Park* DVD.

'Beside You'. Of course, the original 'Beside You' recorded at Olivier Ferrand's would have predated U2's 'With Or Without You'. The original demo made by the Godfather of Punk and his English lieutenant was apparently strongly reminiscent of a Police song – possibly 'Every Breath You Take'.

'[I did] all the wrong things [with Eric]'. Most of Jim's quotes here, and other vital information on Jim's relationship with Eric, come from Garth Cartwright's excellent interview for the *Times* Saturday magazine in September 1999. Although, to be fair, Eric's was not a conception planned by his father, Iggy is disturbingly brutal about his son when one considers the devoted support he received from his own parents. Meeting Iggy in 1999, says Garth, 'What struck me most about him was a certain reptilian quality – he was absolutely cold-blooded when talking about his son, ex-wife or old Stooges.'

The woefully predictable *Naughty Little Doggie*. According to Hal Cragin, Iggy had worked on more adventurous material before retreating into 'bonehead rock' in the studio. The songs on the album, while competent enough punk-by-numbers, mostly repeat earlier themes: 'I Wanna Live' fuses the chord sequence of 'Real Cool Time' with the Kinks' 'You Really Got Me'; 'Innocent World' evokes 'Gimme Danger'; the opening of 'Knucklehead' sounds like 'Your Pretty Face Is Going To Hell' spliced with the Monkees' 'Stepping Stone'; 'Pussy Walk' returns to the subject of *Brick By Brick*'s 'Pussy Power'. 'It's about going to high schools, seeing young girls and thinking about what kind of pussies they have under their skirts,' says Cragin. 'He thought it would make a good single.' The final song, 'Look Away', recalling the story of Johnny Thunders and Sable Starr, is one of the album's more intriguing moments, but as so often on this album, sounds half finished, breaking into a drearily predictable Ramones three-chord sequence. Given the album's overall sparkling digital clarity, one also wonders why producer Thom Wilson didn't edit out Iggy's nervous, out-of-tune vocal takes.

[Iggy's] music was included in dozens of movies. There's a good summary of Iggy and the Stooges' presence on movie soundtracks at www.imdb.com/name/nm0006563/.

Iggy claimed [the ROAR] tour offered the opportunity of playing to bigger crowds. Iggy justified the ROAR tour by telling Colin McDonald: 'It has always been to my regret that I've never had the opportunity to play places like Pittsburgh, Davenport, Milwaukee, Huntsville on a good stage with good sound. I've never had that chance and I wanted to show people what I do before I can't do it any more.' Considering the conviction with which Iggy Pop can propound the most outrageous arguments, one suspects our hero already realised the game was up.

ROAR tour. Skoal originally announced that the ROAR tour would reach forty cities across the USA. The actual number of dates played, recorded at drummer Larry Mullins' www.tobydammit.com, is twenty. ROAR information here comes from Pete Marshall, Hal Cragin, Whitey and Larry Mullins; the information about Jim's suspected nerve damage comes from Ron Asheton. For another band's recollections of the doomed ROAR tour go to http://www.baboonland.com/sstories_iggy1.htm

Jos Grain. Grain now has his own following on the web, thanks to the hilarious eighteen-page rider he wrote for the Stooges, which you can find at www.thesmokinggun.com/archive/1004061iggypop1.html.

'Furthermore, I don't have to.' From the interview with Colin McDonald, 1997.

Iggy . . . seemed simply to lose his nerve. I've dealt with *Avenue B* briefly here, as it's an album that seemed to sink without trace, although to me the work seems one of the biggest missed opportunities of Iggy's later career. Coincidentally, during a few recent interviews with Jim we had discussed Nick Cave, Tom Waits, Kurt Weill and Sinatra's *Only The Lonely*, debating how an intense, stripped-down, piano-led album could pack as much emotional muscle as an electric recording. In this instance, I do believe Don Was's attempts to make the album more tasteful diluted the appeal it might have had.

For the *Avenue B* tour that autumn. From this tour, Whitey's brother, Alex Kirst, took over on drums from Larry Mullins, who was now playing for a variety of people, including the Residents.

David Bowie used the word 'obsessive' about Iggy's compulsion to tour. 'I think he does far, far more touring than I do. I like touring, but I don't like it quite so obsessively as [he does].' Bowie to Robert Phoenix, gettingit.com, December 1999.

'Listen, dude,' he retorted. The quote is from the San Francisco *Chronicle*, April 2001.

The same old fights . . . were even worse when confined to a tiny private jet. Whitey: 'We were playing in the Pyrenees mountains so Jim rented a helicopter. We looked down over these mountains and saw wild horses and chased the wild horses. That was super cool. Then for a while he wanted to fly in private jets, which seems like a cool idea, but when you take four sweaty guys half out of their minds, Jim's got his head cut from God knows, and stick them in a box together and keep feeding them all wine it gets pretty nutty.'

CHAPTER 18: THE REPTILE HOUSE

Main sources. The interview described at Jim's house took place on 26 April 2005, just as I started work on this book, and was commissioned by *MOJO* magazine. Sad to say, the Tiki Hut was demolished by Hurricane Katrina.

Murray Zucker diagnosed Jim Osterberg with a bipolar disorder, but now wonders . . . 'I always got the feeling he enjoyed his brain so much he would play with it to the point of himself not knowing what was up and what was down. At times he seemed to have complete control of turning this on and that on, playing with different personas, out Bowie-ing David Bowie, as a display of the range of his brain. But then at other times you get the feeling he wasn't in control – he was just bouncing around with it. It wasn't just lack of discipline, it wasn't necessarily bipolar, it was God knows what.' Jim Osterberg since confirmed that his apparent bipolarity was a product of his lifestyle, and that the condition seems to have disappeared.

Superhuman strength of will. Eric Schermerhorn was one of many who observed, 'This guy cleaned up on his own, he had this inner strength, and bam, simply stops drinking . . . it was incredible.' Schermerhorn went on to discuss more about Jim, including his superhuman metabolism, before simply concluding, 'He's a freak!'

His record contract at Virgin was under review. I didn't want to include the full story of *Skull Ring* here, as in my view it's a fairly disposable guest-led album. His songs with the Stooges, I would suggest, are messy and unfocused; for how they really can sound, the listener should check out the two versions of 'You Better Run', their superb contribution to *Sunday Nights*, the Jr Kimbrough tribute album. Jim explains their reunion thus: 'Virgin also had gone through a restructuring and parted ways with a lot of artists and that time I didn't want to leave there . . . so I proposed that I do a guest ménage! You should have seen their faces when I said, I want Justin Timberlake, I want Puff Daddy! But I was serious! They never pursued those. So the Stooges looked better and better to me. And I didn't anticipate the reaction, nobody did, the A&R was sort of allowing it to happen grudgingly and was only gonna give us a tiny budget for one song, then he got a call in his A&R office from *Rolling Stone* . . . everything changed! Suddenly back-slapping cos he was getting attention and he realised there was interest here . . . and before we were done mixing we had a gig offer. I kept turning them down . . . but they wouldn't go away so I gave up and we did the [Coachella] gig.'

Watt had been doubled up in agony in the lead-up to Coachella. There is an enthralling diary, which covers Watts's shows with the Stooges, at www.hootpage.com. For Watts's own fascinating recollections of the first Coachella performance, including Iggy's suggestions on how to play and instructions what to wear, go to www.hootpage.com/hoot_thecordthat-tourdiary4.html.

Speaking to the Christ-like figure a few weeks later. Jack White was interviewing Iggy for *MOJO* magazine in May. Thanks to Andrew Male for providing the full transcript of their conversation.

DISCOGRAPHY

1. THE STOOGES ★★★★★

Recorded: Hit Factory & Mastertone studios, NYC, 1–10 April* 1969; **Released:** Elektra, August 1969 (US), September 1969 (UK); **Chart Peak:** – (UK), 106 (US); **Personnel:** Iggy Stooge (v), Ron Asheton (gtr), Dave Alexander (bass), Scott Asheton (drums); **Producer:** John Cale; **Engineer:** (Mastertone) Lewis Merenstein.

Rock music stripped down to its most vital essentials, this album still sounds fresher and more extreme than most of the punk and alternative material it has inspired over the decades. The lyrics reject intellectualism for a documentary depiction of boredom and anomie, delivered deadpan over an imposing, monumental backing. It sounds simple, but each element of this monolithic structure has been hoisted into place with painstaking care, most notably Ron Asheton's precise, memorable riffs on songs like 'No Fun', '1969', 'I Wanna Be Your Dog' and 'Not Right'.

2. FUN HOUSE. ★★★★★

Recorded: Elektra Sound Recorders, La Cienega, LA, 10–25 May 1970; **Released:** Elektra, August 1970 (US), December 1970 (UK); **Chart Peak:** – (UK), – (US); **Personnel:** as *The Stooges*, plus Steve Mackay (tenor sax); **Producer:** Don Gallucci; **Engineer:** Brian Ross-Myring.

For their album debut, the Stooges felt they'd been railroaded by Elektra and restricted by their own inexperience into recording 'drippy, drippy little songs', says Scott Asheton. For their second release, Ron Asheton's guitar playing progressed from charming primitivism to something much more powerful and concise. Thanks to an inspired production from one-time 'Louie Louie' organist Don Gallucci, who decreed the band would perform their customary set as if playing live, Iggy working the floor with a hand-held microphone, *Fun House* captured all the elemental power of the Stooges in full flow. Yet while the album revels in exquisitely dumb riffs – 'Loose', '1970' – there's a confident, sophisticated swagger to the sound, too. When Mackay weighs in on saxophone five songs in, for '1970', the aural onslaught is as thrilling as rock 'n' roll ever gets.

3. RAW POWER ★★★★★

Recorded: CBS Studios, Whitfield St, London, 10 September to 6 October 1972; **Mixed:** October 1972, Western Sound Recorders, LA; **Released:** CBS, May 1973 (US), June 1973 (UK); **Chart peak:** – (UK), 182 (US); **Personnel:** Iggy Pop (v), James Williamson (gtrs), Ron Asheton (bass), Scott Asheton (drums); **Producers:** James Williamson and Iggy Pop; **Mixed:** David Bowie; **Remix:** Iggy Pop at Sony Music Studios, NY 1996.

Raw Power was a desperate, final assault on the music industry that had proved so impervious to the Stooges' charms, a last gasp which, the lyrics told us, was irrevocably doomed. Bad-boy guitarist James Williamson brought a new Detroit aggression to the sound, his cranked-up Les Paul sounding more manic, if more conventional, than his predecessor. Ron Asheton, demoted to bass, became one of the instrument's greatest exponents, even if his comrades cared so little about the rhythm section that they didn't bother to record them properly. The album followed a strict structure suggested by MainMan supremo Tony Defries, with an up-tempo opener ('Search And Destroy', 'Raw Power') on each side, followed by a ballad ('Gimme Danger', 'I Need Somebody'). Despite Defries' efforts, the album was a mess, with guitar piled on guitar, screamed, semi-coherent lyrics and those inaudible drums. But it was a magnificent, inspiring mess, its confusion the perfect metaphor for its makers' increasingly deranged state. In 1996 Iggy remixed the album, meaning that the original Bowie-mixed version, which did so much to launch the UK punk scene, is shamefully unavailable.

4. METALLIC KO ★★★★

Recorded: Michigan Palace, 6 October 1973 and 9 February 1974; **Released:** Skydog Records, September 1976; **Chart Peak:** – (UK), – (US); **Personnel:** Iggy Pop (v), James Williamson (gtr), Ron Asheton (bass), Scott Asheton (drums), Scott Thurston (pno).

A magnificent ruin. *Metallic KO* depicts the pathetic but nonetheless grandiose spectre of the Stooges on their doomed last tour, magnificently documenting the expiration of all their energy and ambition: 'we don't hate you – we don't even care.' Features awesome, powerful renditions of 'Raw Power' and 'Search And Destroy', inspiring, desperate new songs such as 'I Got Nothing', potty-mouthed throwaways like 'Rich Bitch' and a brilliantly numbskull 'Louie Louie'. This recording spooked Iggy Pop for many years, convincing him there was a hex on the Stooges; released as punk exploded in Europe, it would signal his rehabilitation.

5. THE IDIOT ★★★★★

Recorded: Chateau d'Herouville, Paris, Musicland, Munich, Hansa 1, Kurfürstendamm, Berlin and Cherokee Studios* LA (for 'Sister Midnight'), mostly June–July 1976; **Released:** RCA, March 1977; **Chart Peak:** 30 (UK); **Personnel:** Iggy Pop (v), David Bowie (Baldwin electric pno, gtr, Arp Axe synth, Roland drum machine), Phil Palmer (gtr, most songs), Carlos Alomar (gtr, 'Sister Midnight'*), Laurent Thibault, George Murray (bass), Michel Santageli, Dennis Davis (drums); **Producer:** David Bowie; **Engineer:** Laurent Thibault; **Mixed:** Tony Visconti, Laurent Thibault*.

The Idiot seems an album that is praised rather than treasured, but it ranks as some of Iggy and Bowie's best and most under-appreciated work, its humour, courage and inventiveness rendering it easily the equal of Bowie's own *Low*, for which this album, recorded in Paris, Munich and Berlin, was a dry run. The staging is relentlessly stark and severe, with dark synthesisers and doomy, gothic guitar, but practically every song is a jewel – 'China Girl' an affecting ballad that warns away his intended, 'Dum Dum Boys' a warped tribute to the Stooges, 'Nightclubbing' all deadpan restraint, delivered impossibly slow, but robotically joyous.

6. LUST FOR LIFE ★★★★★

Recorded: Hansa Tonstudio 3, Köthenerstrasse, Berlin, June 1977; **Released:** RCA, September 1977; **Chart Peak:** 28 (UK), 120 (US); **Personnel:** Iggy Pop (v), Carlos Alomar, Ricky Gardiner (gtr), Tony Sales (bass), Hunt Sales (drums), David Bowie (pno); **Producer:** David Bowie; **Engineers:** Edu Meyer, Colin Thurston.

From its joyous opening groove, now familiar via the movie *Trainspotting* and a host of commercials, *Lust For Life* proclaims itself Iggy Pop's most effervescent, optimistic album – one that saw his collaborator David Bowie at a towering peak in his songwriting – accompanied by a stunningly inventive band. Where *The Idiot* had been a Bowie-influenced experimental affair, *Lust For Life* was determinedly an Iggy album, recorded in two weeks of schnapps and cocaine-fuelled sessions at Hansa Tonstudio 3 by the Berlin Wall. The optimism and electricity generated in the sessions is exemplified by the closing fade-out of 'Success', where Iggy ad-libs about buying Chinese rugs, while the Sales brothers, singing impromptu backing vocals live, try not to break into hysterics.

Sadly, much of the optimism dissipated as the album suffered death by cheeseburger in the US, when RCA diverted its pressing plants to churning out Elvis Presley albums after the King passed away on his toilet at Graceland.

7. KILL CITY ★★★★

Recorded: Jimmy Webb's home studio, Encino, LA, plus two tracks recorded at Scott Thurston's apt, Venice Beach, December* 1974; **Released:** Bomp, November 1977; **Chart Peak:** – (UK), – (US); **Personnel:** Iggy Pop (v), James Williamson (gtrs), Scott Thurston (gtrs, kbds, bass), Brian Glascock (drums), Hunt and Tony Sales (backing vox, plus drums and bass on 'Lucky Monkeys', 'Mastercharge'); **Producer:** James Williamson; **Engineer:** Gary Webb.

Desperately sad, yet perversely inspiring, *Kill City* was recorded for a pittance at a home studio at a time when Iggy Pop was a pariah, seemingly doomed to forever wander Los Angeles as a pathetic lost soul. Songs like 'Kill City', 'Beyond The Law' and 'I Got Nothing' unblinkingly documented this life on the edge. Although scrappy in places, thanks to its origins as a demo for Rocket Records, with a subdued mix courtesy of James Williamson – who had, says Iggy Pop, 'gone Hollywood' – it's an affecting, late-period work. According to *Creem* writer Ben Edmonds, who bankrolled the sessions, the original, lost mix 'rocked like a mother'.

8. TV EYE LIVE ★★

Recorded: Cleveland, 21–22 March, and Chicago, 28 March 1977 (I); Kansas, 26 October 1977 (II); **Released:** RCA, May 1978; **Chart peak:** – (UK), – (US); **Personnel:** Iggy Pop (v), David Bowie (pno, I), Hunt Sales (drums) Tony Sales (bass), Ricky Gardiner, Stacey Heydon (gtr, I and II respectively), Scott Thurston (pno, II); **Producer:** Iggy Pop.

An adequate live album that shamelessly flaunts its origins as a contract-filler. Recorded for a pittance, it temporarily solved its maker's financial problems, but left its purchasers feeling cheated and thus frittered away all the momentum Iggy Pop had built up over the preceding two years.

9. NEW VALUES ★★★★

Recorded: Paramount Studios, LA, 1978; **Released:** Arista, March 1979 (UK), October 1977 (US); **Chart peak:** 60 (UK), 180 (US); **Personnel:** Scott Thurston (gtr, kbds), Jackie Clark (bass), Klaus Kruger (drums), James Williamson (gtr, 'Tell Me A Story', only); **Producer:** James Williamson.

The last successful collaboration between Iggy Pop and ex-Stooge James Williamson, this stripped-down, minimal album is filled with subtle pleasures. Its atmosphere recalls *Kill City*, the pair's last collaboration, but revels in optimism and coherence rather than despair and confusion; 'Five Foot One', 'I'm Bored' and 'Endless Sea' rank among the best Pop songs of any era. Frustratingly, Williamson extracted fine performances from all concerned, yet hampered the album with an MOR mix, which means that otherwise fine material, including 'Angel' and 'Don't Look Down', occasionally sounds subdued or cloying.

10. SOLDIER ★

Recorded: Rockfield Studios, Wales, July–September 1979; **Released:** Arista, March 1980; **Chart Peak:** 125 (US), 62 (UK); **Personnel:** Iggy Pop (v), Glen Matlock (bass), Barry Andrews (kbds), Klaus Kruger (drums), Steve New (gtr), Ivan Kral (gtr, kbds); **Producer:** James Williamson (initial recordings), Pat Moran.

A mess. *Soldier* started out seemingly without any masterplan bar the vague idea of uniting Iggy with a bunch of English New-wavers. The singing is generally dreadful, the bass and drums leaden, the songs are a bunch of disparate ideas in search of a theme, while the guitar seems entirely missing in action – the result, says bassist Glen Matlock, of an act of self-sabotage by Iggy after an argument with guitarist Steve New. 'Play It Straight', directed by Bowie, was intriguing, but inspired a final bust-up between Iggy and long-term collaborator James Williamson.

11. PARTY ★

Recorded: Record Plant, NY, August* 1980; **Released:** Arista, June 1981; **Chart peak:** 166 (US), – (UK); **Personnel:** Iggy Pop (v), Ivan Kral (gtr, kbds), Rob Duprey (gtr), Michael Page (bass), Douglas Bowne (drums); **Producers:** Thom Panunzio, Tommy Boyce.

A laughably banal album, deriving from record-company pressure to deliver a crossover hit. Some fans rate the pedestrian, predictable 'Pumping For Jill', or 'Bang Bang'; those two songs certainly sound like classics compared to 'Happy Man', a risible attempt at reggae with brain-dead lyrics and an oompah Eurovision brass-band backing courtesy of the Uptown Horns; it's undoubtedly the worst song ever recorded by Iggy Pop.

12. ZOMBIE BIRDHOUSE ★★

Recorded: Blank Tapes, NY, May 1982; **Released:** Animal Records, September 1982; **Chart Peak:** – (UK), – (US); **Personnel:** Iggy Pop (v), Rob Duprey (gtr, kbds), Chris Stein (bass), Clem Burke (drums); **Producer:** Chris Stein.

Iggy's vocals are obviously slurred, his pitching is suspect, much of the material is pretentious and indulgent, bad Kurt Weill knockoffs abound and the arrangements are hit-and-miss. Yet behind the alcohol haze it's possible to discern the inventive Iggy of *The Idiot* or *Lust For Life*: 'The Horse Song' is an off-kilter romp, 'The Ballad Of Cookie McBride' a bizarre but catchy downhome cowpoke ditty, 'Platonic', despite occasionally erratic singing, is dreamy and meditative, and 'Ordinary Bummer' is an almost transcendently beautiful ballad, infused with a thrilling defiance worthy of Judy Garland.

13. BLAH BLAH BLAH ★★★

Recorded: Mountain Studios, Montreux, May 1986; **Released:** A&M, November 1986; **Chart Peak:** 43 (UK), 75 (US); **Personnel:** Iggy Pop (v), David Bowie (kbds, programming), Kevin Armstrong (gtrs), Steve Jones (gtr, 'Cry for Love'), Erdal Kizilcay (bass, kbds, programming); **Producer:** David Bowie.

'Not my favourite album,' says Pop, 'but it got me some hits, so maybe it should be.' *Blah Blah Blah* was a demonstration of almost stunning efficiency by David Bowie, who extricated his sparring partner from a mire of financial problems and lack of commercial credibility and selflessly donated some of his finest recent songwriting efforts. If you can bear the thought of a happy Iggy Pop, who's a skilful songwriter ('Cry For Love'), enjoys sunny vacations ('Hideaway') and is the doyenne of office parties ('The Wild One'), you will love this album.

14. INSTINCT ★

Recorded: Sorcerer Sound, NYC, BC Studio Brooklyn (vocals), winter 1987; **Released:** A&M, June 1988; **Chart peak:** 61 (UK), 110 (US); **Personnel:** Iggy Pop (v), Steve Jones (gtr), Seamus Beaghen (kbds), Leigh Foxx (bass), Paul Garisto (drums); **Producer:** Bill Laswell.

It was hardly a surprise that Iggy would follow up the high-tech sheen of *Blah Blah Blah* with a guitar-led album harking back to the elemental power of the Stooges. What was a surprise was that the results would be far more bland and studio-bound than its predecessor. *Instinct* is an album of dull corporate rock that today sounds like a poor imitation of AC/DC or ZZ Top. The drearily predictable guitar riffs and plodding drums are expertly recorded by producer Bill Laswell, but technical proficiency can't conceal the utter lack of inspiration in the songwriting. The most memorable song on the album, 'Cold Metal', is a workmanlike rehash of 'Raw Power', with all that song's tension and quirkiness surgically excised.

15. BRICK BY BRICK ★★★

Recorded: Ocean Way and Hollywood Sound, LA, March 1990; **Released:** Virgin, August 1990; **Chart Peak:** 50 (UK), 90 (US); **Personnel:** Iggy Pop (v, gtrs), Kate Pierson (v on 'Candy'), Slash (gtr), Duff McKagan (bass), Kenny Aronoff (drums) and others; **Producer:** Don Was.

Don Was wanted to craft an album that revealed Jim Osterberg as well as Iggy Pop, augmenting dumb aggression with wit and intelligence. The album is dominated by A-grade sessionmen, which gives it a brisk, businesslike air; the sparkly production showcases Iggy's considerable abilities as a conventional rock singer and songwriter, although, unsurprisingly, this is pleasant rather than thrilling fare. 'Candy', his love song to Betsy Mickelsen, is a conventional ballad with a quirky New Wave edge and it became Iggy's first US hit single.

16. AMERICAN CAESAR ★★★★

Recorded: Kingsway Studios, New Orleans, October–November 1992, Bearsville Studio NYC, February 1993 ('Louie Louie', 'Sickness', 'Beside You'); **Released:** Virgin, September 1993; **Chart Peak:** 43 (UK), – (US); **Personnel:** Iggy Pop (v), Eric Schermerhorn (gtr), Hal Cragin (bass), Larry Mullins (drums) plus guests including Henry Rollins and Lisa Germano; **Producer:** Malcolm Burn.

An overlooked album that failed to match the chart success of *Brick By*

Brick, *American Caesar* is a far superior work, the most vital of Iggy's tenure on Virgin Records. The title track is powered by a weighty guitar riff; it's skewed and unpredictable, far closer to the spirit of the Stooges than anything on albums like *Instinct* or *Naughty Little Doggie*; elsewhere, there's intriguing experimentation, with ethereal ballads like 'Jealousy' and the angry, self-pitying 'Fuckin' Alone'. 'Beside You', an anthemic ballad dating from *Blah Blah Blah* demos, and 'Louie Louie' were added at the behest of Virgin, and they gave a variety and historical sweep to this album, which, aside from being a couple of songs too long, is generally intriguing and vital.

17. NAUGHTY LITTLE DOGGIE ★

Recorded: Track Record, N. Hollywood, LA, 20 June to 1 July 1995; **Released:** Virgin, March 1996; **Chart Peak:** – (UK), – (US); **Personnel:** as *American Caesar*, plus Whitey Kirst (gtr); **Producer:** Thom Wilson.

The rehearsal sessions for *Naughty Little Doggie* were full of experimentation and invention, all of which was apparently abandoned on the recording proper, to make for a dull, meat-and-potatoes rock album. 'I Wanna Live' comes closest to being memorable; it's based on a similar three-chord trick on 'Real Cool Time', with none of the latter's menace or originality.

18. AVENUE B ★★★

Recorded: 262 Mott Street, The Theatre, and Hal Cragin's Studio 12A, New York, May–June 1998; **Released:** Virgin, September 1999; **Chart Peak:** – (UK), – (US); **Personnel:** Iggy Pop (v), Whitey Kirst and Pete Marshall (gtrs), Hal Cragin (bass), Larry Mullins (drums) plus guests including Martin, Medeski, Wood (on drums, Hammond organ and bass); **Producer:** Don Was.

An occasionally gripping, brave album depicting the wreckage of Iggy Pop's emotional life and rocky relationship with his then girlfriend, Alejandra, *Avenue B* was intended to evoke masterful autumnal releases like Frank Sinatra's *September Of My Years*. Sadly, the tasteful jazz backings occasionally veer into MOR blandness, and hardcore fans stayed well away.

19. BEAT 'EM UP ★★

Recorded: Hit Factory Criteria, Miami, December 2000; **Released:** Virgin, July 2001; **Chart Peak:** – (UK), – (US); **Personnel:** Iggy Pop (v), plus the

Trolls: Whitey Kirst & Pete Marshall (gtrs), Lloyd 'Mooseman' Roberts (bass), Alex Kirst (drums); **Producer:** Iggy Pop.

Rather like *Instinct*, *Beat 'Em Up* was a transparently predictable retreat to the bonehead rock that Iggy Pop now regarded as his USP. But *Beat 'Em Up* at least features high-energy performances, a sense of anger and, on the best songs – 'Mask', 'VIP' – Iggy's tirades are entertainingly tasteless, like a wino spouting conspiracy theories. Ultimately, though, the endless sub-metal clichés, with riffs recycled from Led Zep's 'Kashmir' or Iron Butterfly's 'In A Gadda Da Vida' seem mind-numbingly repetitive.

20. SKULL RING ★★

Recorded: Hit Factory Criteria, Miami, January–February 2003; **Released:** Virgin, November 2003; **Chart Peak:** – (UK), – (US); **Personnel:** Iggy Pop (v) plus guests including the Stooges (Ron and Scott Asheton), the Trolls, Blink 182, Green Day and Peaches.

Skull Ring was celebrated for Iggy's long-awaited reunion with Ron and Scott Asheton; their first four songs together in thirty years are competent but lack the tight sonic focus of their classic work (a fault corrected on 'You Better Run', their raucous contribution to the 2005 Jr Kimbrough tribute *Sunday Nights*). Six songs with the Trolls surpass their work on *Beat 'Em Up*, while 'Little Know It All', a formulaic collaboration with theme-park punks Sum 41, resulted in Iggy's first appearance in the US rock charts in a decade, peaking at number 35.

21. THE WEIRDNESS ★★★

Recorded: Electrical Audio, Chicago, October 2006; **Mastered:** Abbey Road, London, December 2006; **Released:** Virgin, March 2007; **Chart Peak:** 81 (UK), – (US); **Personnel:** Iggy Pop (v), Ron Asheton (gtr), Scott Asheton (drums), Mike Watt (bass), Steve Mackay (tenor sax); **Producer:** Steve Albini.

Occasionally workmanlike, intermittently deranged, the reunited Stooges' first full studio album sparkles with energy and commitment. It fails to capture the monumentality and brutishness of their early work – but then, what album today does? Songs like 'Trollin' and 'Free And Freaky' are bouncy but predictable, while 'Greedy Awful People' evokes, of all people, '50s rocker Eddie Cochran. Incredibly, though, on the very best songs, in particular the defiantly numbskull 'Idea Of Fun', the years simply melt away – its relentless driving powerchords and cynical misanthropy, given the Stooges' picaresque history, seem bizarrely poignant.

Recording dates or details with * are estimated. Recording dates come from *Popped* newsletter (*The Stooges*), Elektra Records (*Fun House*), MainMan itinerary (*Raw Power*), Ben Edmonds (*Kill City*), Laurent Thibault and Edu Meyer (*The Idiot*), Edu Meyer (*Lust For Life*), Julie Hooker (*Soldier*), Kris Needs/*Creem* (*Blah Blah Blah*), JO to PT (*Brick By Brick*), Larry Mullins (*American Caesar, Naughty Little Doggie, Avenue B*), Virgin Records (*Beat 'Em Up*) and *Creem* (*Skull Ring*).

FURTHER READING

All written sources used in the book are cited within the notes. The following books made for invaluable background reading and reference.

Alias David Bowie, Peter and Leni Gilman (NEL 1986)
An Unquiet Mind, Kay Redfield Jamison (Free Press 1993)
Backstage Passes, Angie Bowie with David Carr (Orion 1993)
The Brücke Museem, Magdalena Moeller (Prestel 2001)
The Dark Stuff, Nick Kent (Penguin 1994)
David Bowie: A Chronology, Kevin Cann (Vermilion 1983)
Grit, Noise and Revolution, David A. Carson (UofM 2005)
Guitar Army, John Sinclair (Douglas 1972)
In Broken Wigwag, Suchi Asano (United 1997)
I Need More, Iggy Pop and Anne Wehrer (Karz-Cohl 1982)
Johnny Thunders In Cold Blood, Nina Antonia (Jungle 1997)
The Life and Death of Andy Warhol, Victor Bockris (Bantam 1989)
Low, Hugo Wilcken (Continuum 2005)
Midnight At The Palace, Pam Tent (Alyson 2005)
Moonage Daydream, David Thompson (Plexus 1994)
Neighbourhood Threat, Alvin Gibbs (Britannia 1995)
The New York Dolls: Too Much Too Soon, Nina Antonia (Omnibus 1998)
New York Rocker, Gary Valentine (Sidgwick & Jackson 2002)
Please Kill Me, Legs McNeil and Gillian McCain (Abacus 1997)
Q Encyclopedia of Rock Stars (DK 1996)
Rebel Heart, Bebe Buell (St Martins 2001)
Strange Fascination, David Buckley (Virgin 1999)
Trash, Kris Needs (Plexus 2006)
Wheels of the World, Douglas Brinkley (Penguin 2003)
The Wild One, Per Nilsen (Music Sales 1990)
Wonderland Avenue, Danny Sugerman (Plume 1989)

The principal magazines used for background reading were *Back Door Man, Billboard, Circus, Coast FM & Fine Art, Creem, Denim Delinquent, East Village Other, End Times, Entertainment World, Evo, 5th Estate, Fusion, Gay Power, Goldmine, GQ, The Guitar Magazine, International Musician, Jazz & Pop, Long Island Free Press, Melody Maker, MOJO, Motorbooty, Motor City Rock and Roll News, NME, Pavilion, Phonograph Record Magazine, Q, Record World, Rock Scene, Rolling Stone, Sounds, Stereo Review, Strange Things, Trouser Press, Uncut, Variety, Village Voice, Vintage Guitar Magazine, Wire* and *Zig Zag.*

ACKNOWLEDGEMENTS

It seems to be a writers' convention to open acknowledgements with fulsome praise of agent and editor, and this is a convention I'm happy to adhere to. I had embarked on an Iggy biography more than ten years ago, before joining the staff of *MOJO*, and it was Julian Alexander, subsequently my agent, who singlehandedly re-fired my enthusiasm, and then, along with Celia Hayley, helped hone my ideas into a book that was far more intriguing than the project I'd abandoned a decade before. Antonia Hodgson, of Little, Brown/Sphere, and Gerry Howard, at Random House in New York, both grasped what this book was about, seemingly instantaneously; I count myself privileged to have worked with both of them. Barbara Henry, the wife of Ann Arbor High student George, unlocked a huge resource, presiding over an effort that tracked down around five hundred of Jim Osterberg's high-school contemporaries. Attending their reunion, and speaking to dozens of people who knew Jim as a boy, gave me an invaluable insight into his upbringing and also enabled me to track down other crucial contacts, notably Jim's first girlfriends. Dale Withers Peck provided great company at the reunion. Don Swickerath, one-time bassist of the Iguanas, is a delightful gentleman with whom I spent many happy evenings; he also gave me the use of a house in Ann Arbor on one of my first trips, and I will be forever in his debt. Scott Morgan was a great source, and I spent a terrific day with him touring the city's rock 'n' roll haunts, including the ten-foot bridge where Scotty trashed the Stooges' van, and the armoury where an entire generation of Ann Arbor musicians fagged out of the draft. Robert Matheu was a mine of information and great company; he took me on a rock 'n' roll tour of LA (in a convertible, natch); Tony and Gretchen Horkins were also invaluable friends to me on my stay in LA. Thanks to Carl Glover and Christine Bone for the albums and the tolerance; Keith Cameron and Andrew Perry for their thoughts on grunge; all the staff of *MOJO* magazine, especially Jenny Bulley, Danny Eccleston, Andrew Male and Phill Kalli for their constant assistance and patience; Barry Andrews and Marilyn Fitzgerald for a pleasant summer barbecue. Clare Hulton first suggested writing an Iggy book many years ago; Cliff Jones was my collaborator on that first venture and on my first *MOJO* feature on Iggy; we spent many long hours discussing Iggy and his work, all of which has helped inform this book. Nick Kent and Ben Edmonds are the two writers who've consistently shown the most insight into Iggy and the Stooges; they were unfailingly generous with their help. Historical research on James Osterberg Sr's background was carried out by Al Hahn.

Kat Johnson transcribed literally hundreds of thousands of words of interviews. Per Nilsen supplied his records of Stooges gigs and other information, which was of great help in establishing the timeline of several crucial events. Per also read through an early manuscript, making useful suggestions and correcting several errors. Loren Dobson provided invaluable suggestions and corrections. Esther Friedmann provided a wealth of information; Florian Feineis kindly let me use his apartment during my stay in Frankfurt. I should also thank my schoolfriend Nick Hunter, who brought home a cut-out copy of *The Stooges* when we were fifteen.

Although this is in no respect an official or authorised biography, I must sincerely acknowledge the assistance given by James Osterberg Jr and his manager Henry McGroggan. In several instances, where potential interviewees asked if he approved of their speaking to me, Jim Osterberg not only gave his approval, but actively encouraged them to speak; in particular, he gave me written permission to interview his psychiatrist from NPI, Dr Murray Zucker, an example of openness that is without precedent in my (interminable) experience of working with rock stars and their courtiers. At no point did he or his associates attempt to exert any influence on this book. I have enjoyed my visits to his turbulent, intriguing life and hope I've done it justice. Thanks to Iggy Pop, the Stooges and his other musicians for the pretty music. And my enduring gratitude to Curtis and Lucy for their inspirational support, tolerance and lust for life.

Other crucial sources of help were Robert Altman, Simon Bentley, Rodney Bingenheimer, Johnny Black, Joolz Bosson, Dave Brolan, Duane Brown, David Buckley, Paul Burgess, Garth Cartwright, Sharon Chevin, Rick Conrad, Richard Deakin, Loren Dobson, Clarence 'Rusty' Eldridge, David Fricke, Christophe Geudin, Pat Gilbert, Holly Givens, Robert Gordon, Marcus Gray, Julie Hooker, Barney Hoskyns, Jayne Houghton, Mick Houghton, Russell Hunter, Bill Inglot, Mike Kappus, Stuart Kirkham, Bobbie Lam, Patti Maki, Ann McArtor, Margaret Moser, Dennis Muirhead, Kris Needs, Nite Bob, Mark Paytress, Jeremy Pierce, Ira Robbins, Johnny

Rogan, Tricia Ronane, Carlton P. Sandercock, Lynn Seager, Joel Selvin, Sylvia Skelton, Dave Thompson, Don Waller, Ed Ward, Holly George Warren, Alex Wende, Lois Wilson, Bob Young and Marc Zermati.

Special thanks go to all my interviewees. Many of them submitted to repeated interviews and email queries, and most submitted to this pseudo-stalking with unfailing patience. In some cases interviewees are not directly quoted in the book, but all of them provided crucial help. They are: John 'Twink' Alder, Janie Allen, Carlos Alomar, Barry Andrews, Mike Andrews, Pete Andrews, Kevin Armstrong, Kathy Asheton, Ron Asheton, Scott Asheton, Robert Ashley, Hugh Attwooll, Evita Ardura, Jim Avery, Jay Babcock, Hiawatha Bailey, John Baird, Bob Baker, Michael Bartus, Roberta Bayley, Seamus Beaghen, Leo Beattie, Johnny Bee, Rodney Bingenheimer, Al Blixt, Richard Bosworth, Dan Bourgoise, Angie Bowie, Joel Brodsky, Freddie Brooks, Duane Brown, Bebe Buell, Clem Burke, Mary Booth Calder, John Cale, Keith Cameron, Joan Campbell, Ed Caraeff, Dan Carlisle, Bob Carow, Jim Carpenter, Patricia Carson Celusta, Bill Cheatham, Leee 'Black' Childers, Bill Coleman, Don Collier, Jayne County, Hal Cragin, Doug Currie, François De Menil, Jannie Densmore, Liz Derringer, Rick Derringer, Michael Des Barres, Pam Des Barres, Wolfgang Diebeling, Dennis Diekman, Richard Dishman, Sigrid Dobat, Richard Dorris, Johnny Drake, Dave Dunlap, Rob Duprey, Ben Edmonds, Robin Eggar, Clarence 'Rusty' Eldridge, Luke Engel, Dan Erlewine, Joan Erlewine, Michael Erlewine, Tina Fantusi, Mick Farren, Fayette (the Cockettes), Olivier Ferrand, Danny Fields, Pete Fink, Ted Fosdick, Kim Fowley, Charles 'Black' Francis, Dennis Frawley, Esther Friedmann, Rick Frystack, Don Gallucci, Ricky Gardiner, Thom Gardner, Pleasant Gehman, Russ Gibb, Skip Gildersleeve, Dana Gillespie, Brian Glascock, Jeff Gold, Lynn Goldsmith, Tarquin Gotch, Gary Grimshaw, Bob Gruen, Jason Guy, Bob Hallock, Steve Harris, Nigel Harrison, Kathy Heller, Ricky Hodges, Jeep Holland, Jac Holzman, Peter Hook, Julie Hooker, Pat Huetter, Ron Ideson, Frank Infante, Brian James, Nancy Jeffries, Sherry and Bob Johnson, Brad Jones, Lenny Kaye, Andrew Kent, Nick Kent, Dan Kett, Francie King, Bill Kirchen, Whitey Kirst, Erdal Kizilcay, Lynn Klavitter, Annie Klenman, Cub Koda, Bob Koester, Nick Kolokithas, Esther Korinsky, Ivan Kral, Barbara Kramer, Wayne Kramer, Klaus Kruger, Harvey Kubernick, Bill Kurtz, Bobbie Goddard Lam, Sally Larcom, Bill Laswell, Sam Lay, Jenny Lens, Dave Leone, Charles Levison, Lonnie, Dayna Louise, Steve Mackay, Lori Maddox, Gerard Malanga, Andrew Male, John Mann, Ray Manzarek, Dave Marsh, Pete Marshall, Carol Martin, Robert Matheu, Glen Matlock, Nancy McArtor, Maria

McCormack, Nancy McCrado, Jim McLaughlin, John McLaughlin, John Mendelssohn, Lewis Merenstein, Eduard Meyer, Arjay Miller, Connie Miller, Rumi Missabu, Philippe Mogane, Scott Morgan, Margaret Moser, Larry Mullins, Laurence Myers, Jon Newey, Kuelan Nguyen, Nite Bob, Ric Ocasek, Richard Ogden, Denny Olmsted, Jim Osterberg, Hugh Padgham, Mike Page, Phil Palmer, Mark Parenteau, Jim Parrett, Phast Phreddie Patterson, Steve Paul, Cynthia Payne, Dale Withers Peck, Randy Poole, Gary Quackenbush, Sharon Ralph Gingras, Joan Raphael, Ron Richardson, Scott Richardson, Lisa Robinson, Mick Rock, Michael Royster, Andrew Sacks, Hunt Sales, Tony Sales, Eric Schermerhorn, Natalie Schlossman, Rachel Schreiber, Roy Seeger, Joel Selvin, Robert Sheff (aka 'Blue' Gene Tyranny), Vivian Shevitz, Jimmy Silver, John Sinclair, Leni Sinclair, David Stopps, Robert Stotts, Mim Streiff, Don Swickerath, Sam Swisher, Laura Taylor, Laurent Thibault, Dennis Thompson, Scott Thurston, Michael Tipton, Jaan Uhelszki, Gary Valentine, Cherry Vanilla, Tony Visconti, Jimmie Wade, Jeff Wald, Mike Wall, Don Waller, Sandra Ward, Don Was, Anne Wehrer, Joseph Wehrer, Dana Whipple, Bill Williams, James Williamson, Irvin Wisniewski, Janet Withers, Charlotte Wolter, Ygar of Zolar X, Tony Zanetta, Marc Zermati, Glenn Ziegler and Murray Zucker.

INDEX

SCAR TISSUE

Anthony Kiedis

The *Sunday Times* Bestseller

In 1983, four self-described 'knuckleheads' burst out of the neo-punk rock scene in LA with their own unique brand of cosmic hard-core mayhem funk. Over twenty years later, the Red Hot Chili Peppers, against all the odds, have become one of the most successful bands in the world. Though the band has gone through many incarnations, Anthony Kiedis, the group's lyricist and dynamic lead singer, has been there for the whole rollercoaster ride.

Scar Tissue is Kiedis's searingly honest memoir of a life spent in the fast lane. It's a story of dedication and debauchery, of intrigue and integrity, of recklessness and redemption – a story that could only have come out of Hollywood.

'An entertaining account of being the most priapic, junkie member of California's most priapic, junkie rock band, but also implicitly a pretty solid explanation of how he came to be this way'
Guardian

'Kiedis recounts his pharmacological odyssey as lead singer with the Red Hot Chili Peppers with wide-eyed relish and a refreshing lack of rehab remorse'
Sunday Times

'Even the eye-popping edition of VH1's *Behind the Music* dedicated to this infamously hedonistic Californian quartet could not prepare us for the excesses of their lead singer's unexpurgated life story . . . everyone who reads this genuinely outrageous book will have their own favourite scene'
Independent on Sunday

'The year's most astonishing rock autobiography'
Observer

Sphere
978-0-7515-3566-2

THE LIBERTINES: BOUND TOGETHER

Anthony Thornton and Roger Sargent

The *Sunday Times* Bestseller

In the short time they existed, The Libertines accomplished the impossible: they kick-started the new British music renaissance. They erased the barrier between bands and fans; they inspired thousands; they generously encouraged other new bands and gave away entire albums of material free on the internet. Yet, on the whole, the media failed to grasp what they really stood for, preferring live-fast-die-young clichés and headlines screaming for Kate Moss to abandon 'Junkie Pete' Doherty.

Award-winning writer Anthony Thornton was the only journalist to interview the band at every critical stage, and Roger Sargent was the band's photographer of choice. They were both eyewitnesses everywhere, from a tiny gig in Peter and Carl's flat to the emotional prison reunion and beyond. *The Libertines: Bound Together* is a fascinating and honest portrait of the band and its two battling creative geniuses, Carl Barât and Peter Doherty, chronicling their astonishing highs, devastating lows, and the fallout following the break-up.

It will stand as the definitive representation of The Libertines; a unique, beautifully produced record of the most important British band of this generation.

'Dedicated and visionary . . . Roger Sargent was the perfect mirror; truthful without doubt, perceptive without ego . . . bedside manner of a minotaur!'
Carl Barât

'Anthony Thornton is a better writer than Lester Bangs'
Peter Doherty

Sphere
978-0-316-73259-8

THE LAST TRAIN TO MEMPHIS/CARELESS LOVE OMNIBUS

Peter Guralnick

Last Train To Memphis and *Careless Love* represent two volumes of arguably the first serious biography that refuses to dwell on the myth of Elvis Presley. Aiming instead to portray in vivid, dramatic terms the life and career of this outstanding artistic and cultural phenomenon, they draw together a plethora of documentary and interview material to create a superbly coherent and plausible narrative. The first volume, *Last Train To Memphis*, covers Presley's stunning rise and ends with his departure for Germany and his mother's unexpected death in 1958, while *Careless Love* covers the great years of the 60s and the difficult, decadent later part of Elvis's life, up to its untimely end in 1977.

Praise for *Last Train To Memphis*:
'Unrivalled . . . Elvis steps out of these pages, you can feel him breathe, this book cancels out all others'
Bob Dylan

'Wonderful . . . Guralnick deserves to live in Graceland'
Roddy Doyle

Praise for *Careless Love*:
'Beautifully written and refreshingly sincere, sets new high standards'
Daily Mail

'Homeric in its play of beauty and folly, this is a monumental work'
Independent on Sunday

Sphere
978-0-316-34523-1

Now you can order superb titles directly from Abacus

☐ Scar Tissue	Anthony Kiedis	£6.99
☐ The Libertines:	Anthony Thornton and	£6.99
Bound Together	Roger Sargent	
☐ Last Train to Memphis/	Peter Guralnick	£6.99
Careless Love Omnibus		

The prices shown above are correct at time of going to press. However, the publishers reserve the right to increase prices on covers from those previously advertised, without further notice.

─────────────── ⬭ ABACUS ⬭ ───────────────

Please allow for postage and packing: **Free UK delivery.**
Europe: add 25% of retail price; Rest of World: 45% of retail price.

To order any of the above or any other Abacus titles, please call our credit card orderline or fill in this coupon and send/fax it to:

Abacus, PO Box 121, Kettering, Northants NN14 4ZQ
Fax: 01832 733076   Tel: 01832 737527
Email: aspenhouse@FSBDial.co.uk

☐ I enclose a UK bank cheque made payable to Abacus for £ . . . . .
☐ Please charge £ . . . . to my Visa/Delta/Maestro

☐☐☐☐☐☐☐☐☐☐☐☐☐☐☐☐☐☐

Expiry Date ☐☐☐☐   Maestro Issue No. ☐☐

NAME (BLOCK LETTERS please) . . . .

ADDRESS . . . .

. . . .

. . . .

Postcode . . . . Telephone . . . .

Signature . . . .

Please allow 28 days for delivery within the UK. Offer subject to price and availability.
Please do not send any further mailings from companies carefully selected by Abacus ☐